Praise for *MOTHERLESS DAUGHTERS*,
the phenomenal *New York Times* bestseller

"Absorbing . . . insightful . . . a moving and valuable treatment of a neglected subject." — *The New York Times Book Review*

"A moving, comprehensive and insightful look at the lifelong ramifications of the loss of a mother."–*San Francisco Chronicle*

"Beautifully written." — *USA Today*

"Groundbreaking . . . Brutally honest, exhaustively researched . . . exploring the myriad issues that motherless daughters face in their daily lives." — *The Atlanta Journal & Constitution*

"A beautiful book, wonderfully written and gently crafted . . . Enlightening." — *The San Diego Union-Tribune*

"An important book. One that will help so many people."—*New York Newsday*

"A wealth of anecdotal evidence, supplemented with psychological research about bereavement. . . . Succeeds in opening up cathartic dialogues, personalizing a life-changing event and offering guidelines to help women of any age live with their loss."—*Publishers Weekly*

"Comforting . . . Painful but reassuring."
— *Kirkus Reviews*

Motherless
Daughters

Motherless Daughters

Second Edition

The Legacy of Loss

Hope Edelman

Da Capo Lifelong Books

Set in 11 pt. Stempel Garamond by Cynthia Young

Library of Congress Cataloging-in-Publication Data

Edelman, Hope.
Motherless daughters : the legacy of loss / Hope Edelman.—2nd ed.
     p.   cm.
"First Da Capo Press edition."
Includes bibliographical references and index.
ISBN-13: 978-0-7382-1026-1 (pbk.)
1. Deprivation (Psychology)   2. Loss (Psychology)   3. Maternal
deprivation.   4. Mothers and daughters.   5. Bereavement—Psychological
aspects. I. Title.
BF575.D35E34 2006
155.9'37--dc22

2005033840

First Da Capo Press edition 2006
ISBN-13 978-0-7382–1026–1
ISBN-10 0-7382–1026–9
Published by Da Capo Press
A Member of the Perseus Books Group
http://www.dacapopress.com

Da Capo Press books are available at special discounts for bulk purchases in the U.S. by corporations, institutions, and other organizations. For more information, please contact the Special Markets Department at the Perseus Books Group, 11 Cambridge Center, Cambridge, MA 02142, or call (800) 255–1514 or (617) 252–5298, or e-mail special.markets@perseusbooks.com.

20 19 18 17 16

For my parents

It is the image in the mind that links us to
our lost treasures; but it is the loss that shapes
the image, gathers the flowers, weaves the garland.

—Colette, *My Mother's House*

Contents

Dear Hope,

I'm sitting here alone on Mother's Day. I am twenty-three years old. My mother died almost ten years ago—I was thirteen.

There is an emptiness inside of me—a void that will never be filled. No one in your life will ever love you as your mother does. There is no love as pure, unconditional and strong as a mother's love. And I will never be loved that way again.

I feel as though my development as a woman was irreversibly damaged/altered. I've always (since then) had male friends. I feel I can only relate to males and I think I'm a very masculine woman—not my overt appearance—but I never learned how to socialize, how to engage in meaningless chit-chat, how to talk on the phone for hours. And now, as men do, I "look down" on that type of behavior.

And there are all of the selfish reasons I miss my mother: I will have no one to help me plan my wedding (I don't even know where to begin, I'll have to find a book about it), no one to stay with me after my first child is born. The list goes on and on.

There's nothing I want more in the world than to have children, but I don't know if it would be fair to her if I had a daughter. There are so many things about being a woman, a daughter, and a mother that I don't know and can't see any way for me to learn. Plus, I feel like I'll probably die when I'm thirty-nine and leave my children to suffer the pain and confusion that I have.

St. Paul, Minnesota

Dear Ms. Edelman,

Do you ever get over it? Do you ever get on with your life? Yes, you do get on with your life, but it is always a part of your life. And it does affect everything you do. Does it ever get easier to talk about her? No it does not. But what amazes me now is how other people never talked about my mother to me, even when I did not. Did they think that we forgot her? I could talk about other people I cared for who died years later, but subconsciously I suppressed any thoughts I had of my mother's death and tried to bury the pain. As you approach the age your mother was at the time of her death, you are acutely aware of your own mortality. Through the happy times and through the difficult times, I am always painfully aware of not having her to share it with; and the awful fact of never knowing her as an adult, only as a child; never able to relate to her intellectually on an equal level.

My brother was married last summer, and for the first time I felt like I had found my family again. I have a picture on my office desk of the four of us. It is bittersweet, but I realize how lucky I am to have them.

Woodside, New York

Dear Hope,

Twenty years ago my mother died when I was 14 and even now, after this ocean of time has passed, tears spring to my eyes in a moment when I remember her and the loss. So much of what you wrote rang true for me and I'm glad for that. I've felt guilty about the unhealed wound I carry, but the emptiness is real. The sense that I am alone, that death is inevitable, that I feel insecure in my mothering, that I still search for her in so many ways and faces; these tell me the loss is real.

I have reflected on the loss of my mother and tried to distance myself somewhat from the grief by trying to gauge its effect on my life as objectively as possible. This is effective when I am in my conscious self, but like most of us, a good deal of my time is spent in unconscious thought and choice, and there the grieving fourteen-year-old reigns.

Being a mother myself has been the most difficult area in which the loss has affected me. The desire to remain the child in relationships, even parent-child, is a struggle to overcome. How does a mother act, anyway? How do I give a wealth of love when I feel empty in the place where a mother's love grows? How do I help my daughters feel good about their femininity, sexuality and womanhood when my mother died before I could learn these things from her? How do I convince my three daughters that I will always be here for them, that I won't die before they're ready, or ever, as they would wish? I know it wasn't true for me . . .

Lakewood, Ohio

Dear Ms. Edelman,
I lost my mother to cancer when I was twenty-five years old. She was diagnosed in April and died in July. Nothing prepared me for the pain or the depth of the loss. Every thing you said about a lifetime of grieving is true. And everything you said about being mentally strong because there is no mother to help you, is also true.

I am 38 years old now and although the pain is no longer present every minute of every day, somewhere in the back of my mind is always a sense of missing her and needing her. Sometimes still, that sense of loss won't stay in the back of my mind and comes forward with such intense pain that I don't know that I will be able to bear it.

I truly believe that the death of my mother has made me what I am today. I am a survivor, mentally strong, determined, strong-willed, self-reliant, and independent. I also keep most of my pain, anger and feelings inside. I refuse to be vulnerable to anyone, especially my husband. The only people who see that more emotional or softer side are my children. That too is because of my mother.

Bulverde, Texas

Dear Ms. Edelman,

My mother, age forty-nine, died when I was fifteen years of age and that nameless, elusive and simply terrible feeling of hopelessness has been with me since. Even after twenty-five years of "living with my loss," there is a general, chronic melancholy that has been inexplicable to me, much less anyone else.

You clearly define what happened to me when my mother died. My father had a nervous breakdown almost immediately after her death, was institutionalized for a year, and never quite recovered. My brother grieved for a while and seemed to go on with living. It tortured me so to think that I couldn't get over it; couldn't seem to move on. I used to think there was something terribly wrong with me and this loss was visited upon me by some wretched twist of fate just to make me suffer. Photographs taken subsequent to my mother's death reflect an unsmiling sixteen-, seventeen-, eighteen-year-old girl.

Losing my mother has affected my life drastically. Yes, it molded me into a "tough" woman who could, seemingly, handle anything that was tossed her way. It also destroyed almost entirely my ability to trust. It has returned to haunt me when I sustained further losses of loved ones through death, divorce, rejection.

Thank you so very much for writing about mother loss.

San Antonio, Texas

Acknowledgments

Over the past twelve years, so many people have been instrumental in getting this book on the shelves and keeping it there: Elizabeth Kaplan, my agent; Carl Klaus and Mary Swander, my early mentors; Elizabeth Perle, my first editor; Jackie Cantor, the book's paperback editor; Marnie Cochran, its current editor; and the sales, marketing, and publicity departments at Addison-Wesley, Dell, and Da Capo. You've helped hundreds of thousands of women find a framework for their experiences.

The Motherless Daughters groups currently operating around the country have worked toward this end as well. Cami Black, Casey Enda, Laurie Lucas, MaryAnn McCourt, Vicki Waldron, Day Cummings, Ruta Grigola, Dawn Klancic, Linda Mills, Colleen Russell, and Irene Rubaum-Keller deserve special notice, as do the ninety-nine women who volunteered their time and their stories for inclusion in this book.

The work of Phyllis Silverman, J. William Worden, Maxine Harris, Laura Munts at Mommy's Light Lives On, and everyone at the Dougy Center in Portland, Oregon, continually guided and inspired my writing. Many thanks to all of you for your generosity and your research.

Ten years ago, a woman stood outside the *Today* show studio in Rockefeller Center with a handmade sign that read, "Thank you, Hope." I handed her a brochure about support groups in New York City. She turned into one of the most dedicated volunteers the children's bereavement community has ever known, a valued resource, and a trusted friend. She also did a stellar job as the research assistant for this book. Michele Cofield, stand up and take your bow.

Thirty years ago, an Archie comic book pen-pal service matched me with a girl my age in Minnesota. We wrote letters almost every week for eight years, through my mother's death from cancer and then, unpredictably, through her mother's death two years later as well. For many years, she was the only other motherless girl I spoke with about my loss. Sylvia, where ever you now are, please know how important your friendship was to me at a time when I needed it most.

My siblings were always staunch supporters of this book, even when my version of events differed from theirs. My father died before this new edition was completed; he would have been proud to know the book has such a life of its own. And my mother, whose life and death gave me the inspiration to write and my first story to tell—she is the real heroine of this book.

Finally, if not for a small and dedicated group of women in New York City in 1994, there would have been no Motherless Daughters organization; if not for the Motherless Daughters organization I never would have met my husband Uzi; if not for Uzi there would be no Maya or Eden, who each carry a portion of my mother's name. Because of them, I believe in immortality. Through them, pieces of her live on.

Introduction

Twelve years ago, the first edition of *Motherless Daughters* was published. It was the final step in a long odyssey for me, the end result of years I'd spent searching for just such a book. I was seventeen when my mother died of breast cancer, no longer a child but not yet quite a woman. I was old enough to drive, however, and one of the first trips I took after the mourners dispersed was to a local library. I was a reader, and in lieu of a support group or teen-grief therapy, neither of which existed in my town in 1981, this was my best option for support. I needed information. I wanted to know how you were supposed to feel at seventeen when your mother had just died. I wanted clues for how to think about it. How to talk about it. What to say. I wanted to know if anything, ever, would make me feel happy again.

I didn't find that book, not that year, nor the next year, nor in any of my subsequent searches in bookstores and university libraries and computer databases in any of the next four states in which I lived. In every book I skimmed about mother-daughter relationships, the assumption was that a mother's death occurred after a daughter had reached mid-life or beyond. I was seventeen, twenty, then twenty-four years old. These books weren't speaking to me. The same was true for the academic texts I found, some of which discussed the short-term effects of early parent loss on children, but none of which talked specifically about daughters who'd lost mothers and how the loss affected them over time. I knew I had a specific set of difficulties, and a point of view that departed significantly from most of my friends', but I couldn't find anything written about this. The silence that descended upon my family after my mother died seemed echoed on the bookstore shelves. I had no idea that thousands of other girls like my sister and I were out there. In my mind, we'd gone through something so strange, so rare and aberrant, that it didn't even merit inclusion on the page.

Then, when I was a senior in college, my boyfriend clipped an Anna Quindlen column from the *Chicago Tribune* for me. "My mother died when I was nineteen," Quindlen wrote. "For a long time, it was all you needed to know about me, a kind of vest-pocket description of my emotional complexion: 'Meet you in the lobby in ten minutes—I have long brown hair, am on the short side, have on a red coat, and my mother died when I was nineteen.'" I read it four times on the el train on the way to my part-time job that afternoon, and carried it around in my wallet for years. Only later, much later, would I learn how many other motherless women around the country had saved that same syndicated column, and how many, like me, had felt as if someone had discovered a secret portal into their innermost thoughts.

Losing my mother wasn't just a fact about me. It was the core of my identity, my very state of being. Before writing the first edition of this book, I had no sense of how many other women felt the same way. The answer, as I soon learned, was a lot. Within two months of its initial publication, *Motherless Daughters* landed on the *New York Times* bestseller list. I hadn't unlisted my phone number, and I'd come home at the end of the day to find long, heartfelt stories of mother loss left on my answering machine. I was living in New York City at the time, and about once a week the clerk at my local post office would hand me gray mailbags filled with envelopes—letters that readers had sent to the publisher, who had forwarded them on to me. "What kind of business are you running, woman?" she once asked me. "I want a piece of *that*."

The letters were filled with women's stories of loss and abandonment, and of the coping strategies they'd adopted to emotionally survive. Often, the women included words of gratitude, thankful that someone had validated the magnitude of their losses, relieved that they'd finally been given a framework within which to fit their experiences and a platform from which to discuss them. Hundreds of motherless women would show up at readings and seminars, eager to sit in a room with others who understood. "It's like we share a secret handshake," one woman said. Another put it even more succinctly. "I feel like the alien who just found the mother ship," she told the group.

When a mother dies, a daughter's mourning never completely ends. This is something motherless women have always intuitively known, though in 1994 it wasn't yet a widely accepted idea. Twelve years ago, the general public still held fast to the notion that grief had to follow a set, predictable series of stages or else it was progressing wrong. Mourning was (and sometimes still is) treated as something that had to be fixed or overcome, not as a lifelong process of accommodation and acceptance. The idea that mourning might be cyclical, sloppy, and erratic was still considered novel to those who weren't already part of the bereavement community itself.

When my mother died in 1981, our town offered no support services for grieving families. We didn't yet have a local hospice, just a well-meaning hospital social worker whose officious manner I found so offputting that I ducked into the nurse's lounge whenever I saw her coming down the hall. After the funeral, my father attended a Parents Without Partners meeting, our New York suburb's single nod to the single parent, only to find himself the only widower, and the only man, in a room full of women left partnerless by divorce. He never went back. As for children's bereavement programs, they were still years away from reaching our county. The Dougy Center for Grieving Children, the grandmother of children's bereavement programs in the United States, wouldn't open its doors in Portland, Oregon for another year, and it would take another six or seven years for its influence to reach the East Coast. Until then, families were essentially left to muddle along on their own.

By the time *Motherless Daughters* was released in 1994, this situation had improved a great deal. By then, The Dougy Center had been training facilitators in other states for seven years; a number of weekend camps for children who'd lost loved ones had launched; and hospice had become an international movement. We had developed a much better sense, as a culture, of what grieving children needed, and better means for providing it.

While all this was undeniably helpful for families in the midst of losing mothers, it was somewhat less useful for readers of *Motherless Daughters,* whose losses had occurred ten, twenty, and in some cases forty years in the past. These women had grown up surrounded by more rigid ideas about bereavement. Most had been discouraged from ever talking about the loss. Many years later, they were still experiencing residual effects of loss—not only as a result of the death, but also from their families' and communities' responses (or nonresponses) to their needs.

As adults who'd experienced loss as children, they didn't yet have a niche in the bereavement support field. They'd call local hospices, looking for support groups, only to be told they didn't qualify because their loss had occurred too long ago. Or they'd join bereavement groups, to discover that everyone else was in the acute phase of a recent loss. Other group members couldn't relate to, and became deeply troubled by, the idea that a daughter could still be mourning a mother a decade or more after she'd died.

Fortunately, quite a lot has changed since then, too.

Motherless Daughters groups, dedicated to bringing support and services to girls and women whose mothers have died, now exist in more than a dozen locations, including Boston, Chicago, Detroit, Los Angeles, and the San Francisco Bay Area, all run by volunteers. Two nonprofit organizations have incorporated: Motherless Daughters of Orange County, in Irvine, California, and Circle of Daughters outside Buffalo, New York. The Internet has also become a significant form of support, connecting thousands of motherless women through message boards and chat rooms worldwide. Online memorials for mothers who've died have become so pervasive that a group of psychologists even conducted a research analysis of the phenomenon. Expansion within the children's bereavement community over the past twelve years has been equally as exponential. The Dougy Center Web site now lists more than 370 children's grief centers in the United States and seven other countries. There's also a National Alliance for Grieving Children forming to help educate and provide resources for grieving children, families, and bereavement professionals throughout the United States.

The highly publicized deaths of Nicole Brown Simpson in 1996 and Princess Diana in 1997 also focused the country's attention on maternal death, and on the well-being of the children left behind. As Phyllis Silverman, Ph.D., a bereavement expert and the author of *Never Too Young to Know,* has written, the whole "death system" in the United States is changing as the culture becomes ready to hear about dying and mourning, due in large part to television and print media coverage of loss events. One need only remember the outpouring of televised, national grief after the terrorist attacks of September 11, 2001, and the newspaper memorials printed for each victim, to understand the effect the media has on the culture of grief.

The attacks of September 11, perhaps more than any event in the past thirty years, thrust grieving and parent loss into the forefront of national consciousness. At least 2,990 children and teenagers lost a parent in New York City or Washington, D.C., that day, 340 of whom lost mothers. Six years earlier, more than 200 children had lost one parent and 30 children lost both in the Alfred P. Murrah Federal Building bombing in Oklahoma City.[1] Due in large part to these two attacks, "traumatic bereavement" has become a distinct field within children's grief counseling, as the particular needs of children and teens who lose parents to sudden, violent causes have become known.

The means by which children are losing mothers has changed in both predictable and unanticipated ways over the past ten years. Accidents and cancer are still the leading causes of death among women ages eighteen to fifty-four, but the U.S. cancer rate among women has slowly, yet steadily, gone down since 1990.[2] The AIDS epidemic in the United States, which created 18,500 maternally bereaved children by 1991, never reached projected estimates of 80,000 by the year 2000, although it's taken the lives of millions of mothers worldwide. And mothers are dying as military casualties of war for

[1] Of the 168 people who died that day, 87 were adult women, although no data exists to show how many of them were mothers.
[2] This is driven by steep declines in the death rates of certain cancers, such as breast cancer. The death rate from lung cancer has actually gone up slightly, and the death rate from cancer among African American women has increased as well.

the first time in U.S. history. As of March 2005, seven American mothers had died serving in Iraq, leaving behind at least eight children, one of whom had made her mother pinkie-swear, before shipping out, that she wouldn't die.

We know a good deal more about motherless children such as these, and what they're likely to face as they grow up, than we did twelve years ago. Results from the landmark Harvard Child Bereavement Study, a two-year study of parentally bereaved children conducted in the Boston area and directed by Phyllis Silverman, Ph.D., and J. William Worden, Ph.D., were published in 1996. Among some of its findings are:

1. In general, mother loss is harder on children than father loss, mainly because it results in more daily life changes for a child. In most families, the death of a mother also means the loss of the emotional caretaker, and a child has to adapt to all that this means and implies.

2. Two years after the loss of a parent, children whose mothers have died are more likely to have emotional and behavioral problems, such as anxiety, acting out, lower self-esteem, and lower feelings of competence, than those who lost fathers.

3. Children remain more emotionally connected to mothers who have died than to fathers who have died.

4. The degree to which a surviving parent copes is the most important indicator of the child's long-term adaptation. Kids whose surviving parents are unable to function effectively in the parenting role show more anxiety and depression, as well as sleep and health problems, than those whose parents have a strong support network and solid inner resources to rely on.

5. The children who were doing best, after two years, were those in families that coped actively with the loss rather than passively, and managed to find something positive even in difficult situations.

And yet, the more we know about children's bereavement, it seems, the more the actual experience of losing a mother remains the same.

I received an e-mail from a college freshman the other day. Her mother died five years ago, and throughout high school in her small town she was known as the Girl Whose Mother Died. Now she's in college in another state, far from anyone who knows her, and she's feeling terribly isolated and lonely. Nobody there ever knew her mother, and her new friends don't understand the profundity of her loss. When someone asks about her parents, she tries to answer without using the words "mother" or "died." Putting those two words together, she has learned, is a guaranteed conversation stopper. No one wants to talk about a mother dying. No one, it seems, wants to hear about it. Some even claim not to understand. "I don't have a mother anymore," she once mumbled to a classmate. "You don't *have* one?" the classmate repeated, incredulous. "You mean, like, your parents are divorced?"

Who can blame a peer for acting on what we all wish were true? *Mothers are immortal. Mothers don't die young. Mothers never leave the children they love.* "My dad never even began to grieve my mother's death," says thirty-four-year-old Leigh, who was three when her mother died. "He was overwhelmed by it. It didn't fit in with his picture of how life should be. Mothers should not die and leave five children behind. He told himself that shouldn't happen, so it wouldn't. And then it did." The same false security protected Kristen until her sixteenth year, when her mother was diagnosed with ovarian cancer and died the following year. Kristen, now twenty-four, still sounds slightly stunned when she talks about the loss. "If you'd asked me ten years ago if I thought my mother could die, I would have said, 'Me? Never. My mother? No way,'" she says. "I'd never, ever, *never* thought about it. I knew no one in my secluded, little town whose mother had died. I thought it couldn't happen to me because my family was so happy. My mother's death completely rocked my world."

A father's death, although often equally as traumatic, usually doesn't inspire such indignation or surprise. It violates our assumptions about the world a little less. To some degree, we expect our fathers to die before our mothers. Females may be stereotyped as the weaker sex, but they have more physical longevity. In every racial group in America for the past hundred years, men have been expected to die younger than women. Today, the average twenty-year-old Caucasian male is expected to live to seventy-six, but a twenty-year-old Caucasian woman has a good chance of turning eighty-one. Among African Americans, the difference is even more dramatic: The average twenty-year-old man lives until only seventy, but his wife will probably see seventy-seven. American men of all races are almost *twice* as likely as women to die before reaching fifty-five.

Yet this hardly means that mothers don't die young. Quite the opposite. In 2003 alone, more than 110,000 American women died between the ages of twenty-five and fifty-four, one-third of them from cancer. More than 676,000 American children currently under age eighteen have lost a mother, about 330,000 of them girls. Nearly 25,000 girls have lost both parents. I calculate that there are more than 1.1 million girls and women under the age of sixty in the United States who lost mothers to death during childhood and adolescence—an extremely conservative estimate because it doesn't include daughters who were ages eighteen to twenty-five when their mothers died, or daughters who lost mothers through abandonment, divorce, alcoholism, incarceration, or long-term mental or physical illness.[3]

And yet, at some very deep level, nobody wants to believe that motherless children exist. It's a denial that originates from the place in our psyches where *mother* represents comfort and security no matter what our age, and where the mother-child bond is so primal that we equate its severing with a child's emotional demise. Everyone carries into adulthood the child's fear of being left alone and unprovided for. The motherless child thus symbolizes a darker, less fortunate self. Her plight is everyone's nightmare, at once impossible to

---

[3] More than 532,000 children are currently in the U.S. foster-care system, three-quarters of whom have been placed with nonrelatives. Approximately 126,000 children have mothers who are imprisoned; most of these kids are being raised by grandparents.

imagine and impossible to ignore. Yet to accept the magnitude of her loss, or the duration of her mourning, would mean to acknowledge the same potential for one's self. I remember a phone conversation with my best friend in high school, a few months after my mother died. I was describing some current hardship or another, and relating it directly to the fact that my mother had just died. "Hope," she said, gently yet firmly, "you've got to stop thinking like this. You can't keep blaming everything bad that happens to you on your mother's death. How much of your life is it really going to affect, anyway?"

She had a point, I knew. I was looking for relationships that didn't always exist, connecting dots that might not legitimately warrant connections, in an effort to explain and excuse any untoward behaviors. Sometimes the act felt inauthentic even as I was doing it. Yet at the same time, I knew without doubt that my mother's death had irrevocably altered who I was and who I would become. When a parent dies young, says Maxine Harris, Ph.D., in *The Loss That Is Forever*, children have a personal encounter with death that influences the way they see the world for the rest of their lives. "Some events are so big and so powerful that they cannot help but change everything they touch," she writes. How could all I thought and felt, then, not trace its path back to the event that had created such a jagged fault line through my history, dividing it into a permanent Before and After?

I was fifteen when my mother was diagnosed with cancer, barely seventeen when she died. Unlike the adult, who experiences parent loss with a relatively intact personality, a girl who loses her mother during childhood or adolescence co-opts the loss into her emerging personality, where it becomes a dominant, defining characteristic of her identity. From learning at an early age that dependent relationships can be impermanent, security ephemeral, and *family* capable of being redefined, the motherless daughter develops an adult insight while she is still a child, with only juvenile resources to help her cope.

Early loss is a maturing experience, forcing a daughter to age faster than her peers—both cognitively and behaviorally. As Maxine Harris points out, more than any other event, the death of a parent marks the end of one's childhood. A teenage daughter may have to plan a funeral, take on responsibility for younger siblings or the home, and care for an ailing grandparent—all before graduating from high school. When a mother's death also means the loss of the consistent, supportive family system that once supplied her with a secure home base, she then has to develop her self-confidence and self-esteem through alternate means. Without a mother or mother-figure to guide her, a daughter also has to piece together a female self-image on her own.

While most girls separate from their mothers during the teen years to create an individual identity and then spend the later years trying to return as an autonomous adult, the motherless daughter moves forward alone. Adulthood, marriage, and motherhood are significantly different adult experiences for the woman who travels through them with a maternal void and the memory of a dramatic loss. "You have to learn how to be a mother for yourself," says Karen, a twenty-nine-year-old woman whose alcoholic mother died nine years ago. "You have to become that person who says, 'Don't worry, you're doing fine. You're doing the best you can.' Sure, you can call friends who'll say that to you. And maybe you can call other relatives you're close to, and they'll say it, too. But hearing it from the person who taped up all your scraped knees, and consoled you through all the Cs you brought home from school, and helped you with your first lemonade stand, that person who watched you take every step and really knows you, or at least the one you perceive as really knowing you, that's the one you count on. That's the one you keep looking for."

How often is one able to revisit and revise the past? Motherhood gives me that opportunity, as the daily minutiae of life with two daughters repeatedly kicks me back in memory to moments when I was the child, and my mother stood in the place I occupy today. I see her so differently now. How resourceful, and patient, and devoted she was, I have come to realize. Yet also how inexperienced and frustrated. And how very, very young. I turned forty-one this year, the same age she was when her cancer was first found. Next year, I'll turn the age she was when she died. And the year after that, I'll pass her by. How strange that will be, to be older than my mother, and to reach that personal tipping point so young.

This issue is one, among many, that motherless women of all backgrounds talk about in great detail. No matter how many years this book remains on the shelf, no matter how many motherless women I meet in my travels, I never stop being surprised by how much we have in common, despite our obvious differences. This is true regardless of the ages we were when our mothers died; the exact causes of loss; our families' racial, ethnic, or socioeconomic makeup; and the ages we are now. Mother loss is a great equalizer among women, as if the core identity issues it creates cut straight through the superficial variables that might otherwise define us. As mother-less women, we share characteristics we don't usually find in other female friends, including a keen sense of isolation from family; a sharp awareness of our own mortality; the overall feeling of being "stuck" in our emotional development, as if never having matured beyond the age we were when our mothers died; the tendency to look for nurturing in relationships with partners who can't possibly meet our needs; the strong desire to give our children the kind of mothering we lost, or never had; an intense anxiety about losing other loved ones; a gratitude for the "small moments" in each day; and the awareness that early loss has shaped, toughened, and even freed us so that we can make changes and decisions we might not have otherwise made.

Most of the original interviews in this book remain, although I have added some new women's voices, in addition to the words of four experts whose research had not yet been published in 1994. This new edition now includes interviews with ninety-nine motherless women interviewed in person and by way of e-mail, as well as data from the original Motherless Daughters survey in 1994 (see appendix 1) and a new Internet survey of 1,322 motherless mothers conducted between October 2002 and June 2005. Although these women all volunteered to be interviewed and therefore do not represent a ran-dom sample, they come from a variety of racial, ethnic, and socioeco-nomic backgrounds. When interviewed, the youngest woman was seventeen and the oldest eighty-two, and were anywhere from infancy to their early thirties when their mothers died or left their families. All names and hometowns have been changed, and only in rare instances, and with a woman's permission, does a woman's profession appear in print.

Writing a book is a fluid, evolutionary process, one that continues even after the product appears on the shelf. I have been blessed over the years with readers who send me their stories of mother loss, sometimes as many as five or six a day, to help me keep learning about what motivates them, what challenges them, and what helps them feel whole. As a result, this new edition includes expanded sections on subjects that readers have specifically asked for: more information on very early mother loss (before age six); mother loss as an adult; the loss of both parents during childhood; chronic illnesses and ambiguous loss; and the transition to motherhood. I've also included a new appendix featuring popular motherless protagonists in contemporary memoirs, novels, and young-adult fiction, including synopses of the books in which they appear, and another appendix listing contact information for Motherless Daughters support groups worldwide.

A good deal has changed in my life, too, since the first edition of this book. Twelve years ago, I was single and living in a tiny apartment in New York, just starting my career and wondering whether I'd ever marry and have children. Today, I share a house in the Santa Monica Mountains with a husband and two young daughters who are the very epicenter of my world. I pack school lunches, braid hair, schlep around to after-school activities, listen to heartbreaking playground stories, play Tickle Monster, and bandage fingers and knees. In many ways, I have become that which I once lost.

And yet there is a great deal that has not changed at all. There is still a huge hole in my life where a mother—and now a maternal grandmother for my children—should be. I still wish I had a mother to call when something good happens, when something bad happens, or when nothing at all has happened, just to talk about the day. I'm still stubbornly self-reliant, and still find my highest levels of comfort in an orderly, predictable existence. And I'm still afraid of dying young, and of losing someone else I love. Even more so now, when the stakes are so much higher. Every day, I look at my daughters and pray that what happened to my mother won't happen to me. Or to them.

Sometimes I think of calling back that high school friend, the one who asked me how much of my life my mother's death would affect, anyway. And with the certainty of twenty-four years, I would tell her: Everything. It affects everything. When a mother dies, a daughter grieves. And then her life moves on. She does, thankfully, feel happiness again. But the missing her, the wanting her, the wishing she were still here—I will not lie to you, although you probably already know. That part never ends.

Los Angeles, California
October 2005

I
Loss

The loss of the daughter to the mother,
the mother to the daughter, is the
essential female tragedy.

—Adrienne Rich, *Of Woman Born*

Chapter One

The Seasons of Grieving
Mourning Takes Time

MY MOTHER DIED IN THE MIDDLE of summer, with everything in full bloom. It had been sixteen months since the afternoon she returned from a doctor's office with the news of a malignancy in her breast, sixteen months of chemotherapy and CAT scans and desperate attempts to hang on to the little rituals that amounted to a normal day. We still took our orange juice and vitamins together in the morning, but then she swallowed the white, oval pills that were supposed to stop the cancer's spread. After school I would drive her across town for her oncology appointments, and on the way home in the car she promised me she would live. Because I wanted so badly to believe her, I did, even as I watched her lose her hair, then her dignity, and finally her hope. The end came quickly, and we all were unprepared. On July 1 she was sunning herself in the backyard; before dawn on the twelfth, she was gone.

My mother was forty-two when she died, just past what should have been the midpoint of her life. I had just turned seventeen. My sister was fourteen, my brother nine, and our father was left with little idea about how to manage the three of us and his own grief. Before cancer reduced us to four, I'd always thought of us as the most typical suburban family in New York: a father who commuted to a job in the city, a mother who stayed home with the kids, a house in a carefully manicured subdivision, a dog, a cat, two cars, three TVs. Tragedy was supposed to pass over a home such as ours, not burst through its door.

Like most other families that lose a mother, mine coped as best it could; which meant, essentially, that we avoided all discussion of the loss and pretended to pick up exactly where we'd left off. We were not an expressive family to begin with, and we had little idea about how to mourn. We had no friends or relatives who'd been through a similar experience, no blueprint for action, no built-in support. During that first year we continued with the routines of schoolwork, vacations, and bimonthly haircuts as if a central family member were so dispensable that her absence required only a minor reshuffling of household chores. Anger, guilt, sadness, grief—we suppressed all emotions, letting them shoot out like brief bullets only when we couldn't contain them any more.

When I left home to attend college in the fall of 1982, I headed to the Midwest with a desire to become a journalist and a conviction to experience life as my mother had never done. She had graduated from college in 1960 with a degree in music and a diamond ring, and her domain had quickly become a split-level suburban ranch home. Mine, I decided, would be the world. In the years following her death, I criss-crossed the country in my car, studied Kafka and de Beauvoir, dated men of varied ethnic backgrounds, and backpacked across Europe alone. But wherever I traveled, I carried within me a sadness I couldn't leave behind, no matter how forcefully I tried. Someone dies, you cry, and then you move on: This was no mystery to me. Far less clear was how the effects of this loss were likely to appear and reappear throughout the rest of my life.

It would take seven years for me to begin to understand a central rule of grief: The more you avoid mourning, the tighter it sticks to you. The only way to release it is to grit your teeth and feel the pain.

By the time I had figured this out I was several years out of college, working for a magazine in Knoxville, Tennessee. The company had its offices in a twelve-story red brick building, a former hotel where both Hank Williams and Alice Cooper's boa constrictor were rumored to have spent their final nights. The building was on a main thoroughfare downtown, next to a high-tech, mostly vacant, mostly glass skyscraper built by the notorious Jake Butcher, who was then doing time in jail. I tell you all this because position will be important. In front of the Butcher Building was a traffic light and a crosswalk, which I used when I crossed Gay Street every day.

A perverse sort of history had settled on this block, which may or may not have had something to do with what I experienced there the autumn after I turned twenty-four. I hadn't been having a very good year. In May I abruptly ended an engagement to a man I'd deeply loved, and my world turned painfully inside out. I tried to fix it by jumping into bed with another man, who was wise enough to walk out on me by summer's end. Two weeks later I got caught in the middle of a Southern bar brawl that landed me in the emergency room with a split lip and a bump the size of a golf ball on the crest of my head. Things, you might say, were getting out of control. I was living alone on two acres in a small white house I could barely afford to maintain, and that season, escape was on my mind. I was considering graduate school in Iowa, the Peace Corps, and a vegetarian commune in central Oregon, in no particular order of preference. Worried I would scare away my friends with this litany of woe, I spent most of my time alone on my land with a noncommittal kitten I often turned to for advice. In the evenings when I felt lonely I walked across the street to pick wildflowers and play with my neighbors' goats and sheep. I'm sure that part sounds idyllic, but the truth is, I was scared. There was no one to take care of me but me, and I didn't feel up to the job.

By mid-October, I was oversleeping and getting to work late every morning, taking two-hour lunches, and crossing Gay Street several times a day. On this particular afternoon I was returning from the post office, and as I reached the middle of the crosswalk I looked up. A cloud passed just then, and I saw the midday sun bounce sharply off one of the glass panels of the Butcher Building. Or should I say I felt it? Like a size-twelve work boot kicked into my gut I felt it, and I clutched my stomach, unable to breathe. The light turned green and cars started honking; a few drove around me; someone leaned out of a truck window and shouted, "Hey, you! Are you okay?"

I was not okay. I was definitely not okay. All I could think as I stood there holding myself was, "I want my mother. I want my mother. I want my mother, *now.*"

From what depths did I dredge up that one? I hadn't allowed myself to miss my mother once in the seven years since she'd died. Instead, I'd spent that time convincing myself I conveniently didn't need the one thing I didn't have, and that my freedom and independence were an unfortunate but much-cherished outcome of my early loss. With the kind of cocky certainty usually reserved for either the very young or the very naive, I'd decided by twenty-four that I'd already sailed through the five stages of grief so neatly outlined in the pamphlet the hospital social worker pressed into my palm as my mother had lain dying in a room down the hall.

Denial, anger, bargaining, disorganization, acceptance. It had sounded simple enough to me then, a straightforward five-step ascent to normal life again. The night before my mother died I'd broken down and prayed, asking God to accept a clean trade. Although I'd never seriously thought about dying before, that night I asked to be taken as I slept, in exchange for letting my mother live. I knew the family needed her more. I'd missed out on all the intermediary steps, all the times when I might have prayed *Please God, make my mother well, or I promise I'll never talk back to her again* because I'd never known she was dying, and now, in these final hours, I believed that only an act of great selflessness could still save her. Sunrise reminded me that such miracles are rare, but I later found small comfort in knowing that the attempt placed me firmly in the bargaining stage, already at midpoint along the emotional ruler of mourning.

Seven years later, I'd reached the point where I no longer cried each time I talked about my mother, and when someone said, "I'm sorry," after learning about her death, I could finally respond with a deferential smile and a nonadversarial nod. Time had worked its healing magic, as everyone had promised it would. And I'd proven I didn't need a mother to survive. So I thought I'd done it properly; I thought I'd somehow won. Until that moment in the middle of the crosswalk, which left me wondering how it had all gone so horribly wrong.

Here's what I've learned about grief since then: It's not linear. It's not predictable. It's anything but smooth and self-contained. Someone did us all a grave injustice by first implying that mourning has a distinct beginning, middle, and end. That's the stuff of short fiction. It's not real life.

Grief goes in cycles, like the seasons, like the moon. No one is better created to understand this than a woman, whose bodily existence is marked by a monthly rhythm for more than half her life. For centuries, writers, aware of grief's organic cadence, also have used seasonal metaphors to describe a process that continually leads us from the deepest sorrow toward the peak of renewal, and back again.

Mourning works like any series of cycles: One ends and a new one begins, slightly different from its predecessor, but with the same fundamental course. A daughter who loses a mother does pass through stages of denial, anger, confusion, and reorientation, but these responses repeat and circle back on themselves as each new developmental task reawakens her need for the parent. Say a girl of thirteen loses her mother to a heart attack. In the midst of the initial shock and numbness, she grieves to the best of her ability at that time. But five years later, at her high school graduation, she may find herself painfully missing her mother and grieving all over again. Years after this episode she may be back in the mourner's role again, when she plans her wedding, or gives birth to her first child, or gets diagnosed with a serious illness, or reaches the age at which her mother died. At each milestone a daughter comes up against new challenges that make her long for a mother's support, but when she reaches out for her, the mother isn't there. The daughter's old feelings of loss and abandonment return, and the cycle begins again.

Seven years, as it turns out, wasn't such a terribly long delay. I've since received letters and e-mails from women who say their grief was put on hold for twenty years, thirty years, or more. "Some individuals become conscious of the effects of the loss on them only midway through adulthood," explains the Israeli psychologist Tamar Granot, the author of *Without You*. "At times, this belated awareness is sparked by a change in their lives, especially in the wake of a crisis during adulthood." Vacillation over a career choice, difficulties in maintaining a relationship, or problems with one's own children, she says, can suddenly make a woman aware of the connection between her present-day behavior and the trauma she experienced as a child.

We're an impatient culture, accustomed to gratifying most of our needs quickly. But mourning requires a certain resignation to the forces of time. Elisabeth Kubler-Ross's *Five Stages of Grief*, so popular as a bereavement model in the 1980s and 1990s, were originally developed for terminally ill patients receiving news of their grim diagnoses, not for the family members they would leave behind. (One grief counseling Web site now suggests renaming them "The Five

Stages of Receiving Catastrophic News" and ditching them as a bereavement model because they've done mourners more harm than good.) I prefer J. William Worden's Four Tasks of Mourning: accepting the loss (task I); dealing with the reality of the loss (task II); adjusting to the new environment (task III); and emotionally relocating the lost loved one (task IV). But truly, I've found there are really only two stages of grief that matter: the one in which you feel really, really bad, followed by the one in which you feel better. The transition from one to the other is bound to be slow, sloppy, and emotional, and neither has hard-and-fast rules.

Expecting grief to run a quick, predictable course has led us to overpathologize the process, making us think of it as something that, with proper treatment, can and should be "fixed." As a result, we begin to view normal responses as indicators of serious distress. The woman who cries every Christmas when she thinks of her mother—is she really a woman who can't let go of the past, or just a woman who continues to miss her mother's warmth and cheer at holiday time? And who can count the number of friends and co-workers who expected our mourning to be contained within the confines of those magical six-month or one-year bookends? How many of us came to expect that of ourselves? The messages that so frequently leaked through other people's words as the summer of my mother's death melted into autumn and the snow began to fall became exactly the ones I used to criticize myself: *It's been six months already. Get on with your life. Get over it.* I tried. I really tried. But it's impossible to undo fifteen or twenty years of learned behavior with a mother in only a few months' time. If it takes nine months to bring a life into this world, what makes us think we can let go of someone in less?

Ready or Not, Here It Comes

Psychologists debated for decades whether or not children and adolescents have the capacity to mourn the death of a loved one. Unlike adults, who invest emotion in several different people they can depend on—spouses, lovers, children, close friends, and themselves—kids typically direct it all toward one or both parents. When a daughter says, "My mother's early death completely pulled the rug out from under me," she's not exaggerating.

Most bereavement specialists now agree that fully adapting to the loss of a parent requires elements most young children don't have: a mature understanding of death; the language and encouragement to talk about their feelings; the awareness that intense pain doesn't last forever; and the ability to shift their emotional dependence from the lost parent back to the self before attaching to someone else. These capacities develop and accumulate as a child grows, like a train that picks up a new passenger at each stop, and she may have very few riders at the time a parent dies.

This doesn't mean children can't mourn at all; they just do it differently than adults. Their process is more protracted, extending over the course of their development as their cognitive and emotional abilities mature. A five-year-old who believes death is an extended form of sleep may, in her eleventh year, finally understand that death means her mother is never coming back. She'll then have to work through the sadness and anger that arise with this new realization, even though she's six years past the actual loss.

The best example of this process I've come across is a story from twenty-year-old Jennifer, who was four when her mother committed suicide. As a young child, Jennifer knew only the most basic facts about the death. Still, she couldn't fully understand their implication until she became cognitively able and emotionally ready to process the truth.

"My mother died in the garage, from carbon monoxide poisoning," she explains. "For a long time, I thought the gas cap had fallen off the car and that she had died from that. It was totally ridiculous, but it was the story I had in my head. Years later, when I was in junior high, I finally realized she had done it on purpose. I was telling the story to someone and right in the middle of it I thought, 'That's pretty stupid. Why would the gas cap just fall off like that?'" Nearly ten years after her mother's death, Jennifer began a new cycle of grieving, for news she says she is still trying to reconcile.

Adults usually start their griefwork immediately after a loss, but children tend to mourn in bits and pieces. They do it in the midst of the rest of life, dipping in and out of grief, with intense bouts of anger and sadness punctuating long periods of apparent disregard. "They know how much pain they can tolerate at any given moment, and when they reach their limit, they simply shut it off and do something else," explain Mary Ann and James Emswiler, the authors of *Guiding Your Child Through Grief*.

Adults often mistake this process with blocked mourning, believing that a child either doesn't understand what happened or is denying the loss, when in fact she knows quite well that her mother is gone. Children can't withstand severe emotional pain without support from an adult they trust. Instead of grieving openly, they often speak through play. A girl who lost a mother in the World Trade Center attacks on September 11, 2001, for example, may have returned from the funeral and headed straight for her toy chest, appearing oblivious to the day's events, but her play might have been telling. If she created a tall stack of blocks and knocked them down, over and over again, she probably would have been acting out her experience of parent loss.

Therapists at the Barr-Harris Children's Grief Center in Chicago have observed that a child's grief response is directly influenced by the surviving parent's behaviors. "The loss is tougher for kids when the recovery of the surviving parent is slower, when that parent is exceptionally depressed, goes on as if nothing has happened, or is so exhausted that things get disorganized," says Nan Birnbaum, M.S.S.C., who was a Barr-Harris staff member throughout the 1990s. "We noticed that kids tend to start dealing with the loss six to nine months after the actual death, when the surviving parent is beginning to cope better. They need the safety and psychological security to be able to feel that intense distress. Surviving parents have to be picking up the pieces of their lives and running things relatively comfortably before kids can let down their hair and feel safe enough to grieve. Sometimes the surviving parent takes a year before he's doing better, and then the child won't begin grieving and having intense reactions until a year and a half after the loss." It's difficult for children to move beyond a surviving parent's place of progress in the mourning process. If a parent gets stuck in a particular stage, chances are the child will, too.

Researchers have found that children who lose a parent need two conditions to continue to thrive: a stable surviving caregiver to meet their emotional and physical needs, and open and honest communication about the death and its impact on the family. Sheer physical care isn't enough. The child who can express her sadness and who feels secure in her environment is the one most likely to integrate the loss and avoid serious ongoing distress. But the child who faces continuing difficulties—a father who can't stop grieving, a stepmother who rejects her, an unstable home life—can end up a long way from the point where she once began.

Adolescents—with their attachments to peer groups and their capacity for abstract thought, which allows the leap from "My mother is gone" to "My life will never be the same"—come closer to modeling an adult mourning process, but their experience is still limited by developmental constraints. Some therapists have viewed adolescence itself as a form of mourning—for the lost childhood and for the foregone image of the omnipotent, protective parents—and believe that until we complete this type of mourning process in our late teens or early twenties, we can't adequately grieve for a loved one later on. Adolescence, inconsistent and insecure as it is, may be our built-in preparation for learning to let go.

Women who lost mothers during adolescence frequently speak of their inability to cry at the time of loss, or even for months or years afterward. This often serves as a personal black mark in their pasts, a point of self-recrimination when they look back as adults and discuss their mother's death: What was wrong with me? Why couldn't I cry? *What was my problem?*

Sandy, thirty-four, whose mother died of cancer twenty years ago, still remembers the confusion she felt at the time. "Never cried at the funeral," she says. "Didn't want to let anyone know that I had feelings at fourteen. I mean, I remember sitting in the way back of the funeral parlor with my friends, hanging out—because I didn't know how to handle it. You know, I didn't want to stand up and act like it bothered me. I didn't know how to act. But we had a lot of timberland, and I'd go down there and sit on a log and be alone. I cried a lot then, but not at the funeral."

In response to a major loss, both older children and adolescents cry less freely than adults do. Teens, in particular, often feel threatened by the potential magnitude of their emotions. While a young child may cry impulsively, without thought of whether the outburst will end, a teenager who feels she may "lose it" in front of others sees mourning as a threat.

If the loss occurs at a time when a girl is struggling to assert her independence from the family, she may associate crying and other emotional outbursts with a regression to a dependent, childish state. Because she equates crying with being "babyish" she avoids all public displays. The abandonment she feels after her mother dies is exacerbated by the alienation that comes with normal adolescence, and she's then left feeling doubly isolated with a grief she's afraid to express.

I'd like to say my family was a safe forum for expression, that we talked about both my mother's death and her life, and that each of the children found someone who provided much-needed emotional support. But none of those things was true. My father couldn't juggle the demands of his own grieving with the sudden responsibility for three children he barely knew, and he was not a man accustomed to asking for help. I don't think he discussed my mother's death with anyone at the time. He certainly didn't talk about it with us. The briefest mention of my mother's name would cause his eyes to fill, forcing him to retreat to his room while my sister, brother, and I sat staring silently at our full dinner plates. Seeing our only parent so close to total collapse was terrifying, and we were determined to prevent it however we could. He was the only parent we had left; we couldn't risk losing him, too. As we learned to dance around the words that destabilized him, silence descended on us all like dense fog. Within two months after my mother's death we had stopped talking about her at all.

Silence and suppression transformed me into an emotional mannequin, frozen and ersatz, with proportions so perfect they were never more than an ideal. The night my mother died, I entered a survival zone of counterfeit emotion: no tears, no grief, little response at all except a carefully monitored smile and an intense desire to maintain the status quo. If I couldn't control the external chaos, I could at least try to balance it with my internal reserve. And how could I give in to the intense emotion I sensed was underneath it all? My father told relatives at the funeral and in the house afterward that I was "the rock" of the family. "We'd all fall apart if it weren't for Hope," he said, and they nodded in agreement.

Their praise, of course, only served as further incentive for me to maintain a perfectly chiseled marble facade. I never did break down during those early years. My mother had always been the parent who gave the children a safe place to cry, my father more an advocate of the stiff-upper-lip school of emotional expression. I needed someone to tell me it was all right to feel anger and despair, but I received only kudos for my synthetically mature, responsible behavior. Perhaps this sounds juvenile for a girl of seventeen, this need for permission to express emotion. I might think so too, if it hadn't happened to me.

Families like mine aren't rare; many households view even the most innocuous expressions of grief as reminders of the loss, and shy away from confronting collective pain. Daughters left with fathers are at a particular disadvantage in a culture that still encourages women to express emotion and men to suppress it. Fathers may feel grief just as—or even more—intensely than other family members, but having been socialized to repress their feelings, take control, and solve problems often leaves them with little outlet or tolerance for emotional display. Twenty-eight-year-old Leslie, who was seventeen when her mother died, recalls, "My father's message, and it was clearly stated to me, was, 'Don't you start crying, because we'll all fall apart.' That was his true belief. Grieving and mourning and crying were such a hazard in my house. We just weren't allowed to do that. I wish I could have said to my father back then, 'It's not true, Dad,' and cried and cried and cried. And then looked up and said, 'See? Nothing happened. Lightning didn't strike.' He would have cried too, but so what? What was so threatening about that? I've cried a lot in therapy, and I've gotten angry at my therapist. And nothing bad has happened. I think there was this message in my home that my emotions held that much negative force. I then believed I was that all-powerful, which of course simply wasn't true."

Grief doesn't vanish just because we try to lock it up in a sealed drawer, yet that's the way many of us are encouraged to cope: Ignore the pain, and it'll go away. Anyone who's tried that approach knows what a superficial venture it can be. "Ultimately, the thing that makes you crazy isn't that your mother died," says twenty-nine-year-old Rachel, who was fourteen at the time, "but that you can't talk about it, and you can't let yourself think about it." The sounds of silence, left to echo without response, become more haunting than the actual words. To keep our mouths soldered shut only means the grief will find a way to seep out elsewhere, through our eyes and our ears, through our very pores.

To Feel or Not to Feel

An unfortunate fact we can't escape—but one we all would, if we could—is that mourning hurts. "Little things like looking at your hand and seeing hers triggers it with such intensity that you just want to run away," explains Donna, twenty-six, whose mother committed suicide three years ago. "But you don't know where you can run to, because there isn't anywhere to go. You try calling your dad to explain it to him and he says, 'We'll get you a plane ticket and you can come out here.' But what good is that going to do? You're still battling it in your own head."

Mourning involves risk: We have to relinquish control to our emotions, and let them run their course. Maintaining that control gives us the illusion of normalcy, but at what cost? And for how long? Rita, forty-three, who was sixteen when her mother died of cancer, says that deliberately avoiding her grief has given her a veneer of strength but hasn't destroyed the emotions at her core.

> My fear is that if I were to let myself feel the immense pain I know is there, I would just fall apart. I wouldn't be able to function. Intellectually, I know that's not true, but I'm not going to try it. I've been in all kinds of therapy, tons of therapy, and I always go with the intent of mourning my mother's death properly. I know I have all this pain I need to get to and through, but I could never do it. I could never make myself that vulnerable to a stranger.
>
> I hate to say that not being real and not feeling a deep, deep emotion is my strength. I mean, it sounds sort of strange. But on

some level, it's made me a survivor. I'm very good at what I do. I went from being a secretary like my mother to having a graduate degree. I'm a good worker and I deal with hundreds and hundreds of people in my job, all different kinds. I feel like I'm able to do that because I have to be very strong. I have to keep it together because the other side of it is this little girl who lost her mother, and could just fall apart from that pain.

Rita says she wants to face her sorrow, but that's only half of a mourner's journey. The other half is feeling ready to embrace the pain. Before that seven-year watershed in Tennessee, was I ready to admit that my mother's death had had a profound effect on me, or that I needed to go back and reevaluate its impact? Not a chance. I wasn't about to dive into that, not even in a shark cage. I had to wait until the equivalent of a psychic explosion occurred, until the pain of *not* mourning my mother had gotten worse than grief could ever be.

Evelyn Williams, C.S.W., a therapist who led bereavement groups for college-aged students at Duke University for thirteen years, believes we know, internally, when the moment to mourn arrives. She saw students who had lost parents during childhood or adolescence find their way into her groups in college, prepared to discuss their losses for the first time. Once they had physically separated from their families and achieved the psychological and emotional stability they needed to mourn without fear of abandonment or collapse, they could face their grief head-on. Our psyches seem to protect us until we're able to confront the pain, and then the internal alarm clock rings, telling us it's time to wake up and go to work.

Experiencing that intense emotion is what helps us, ultimately, accept that our mothers are gone. Insulating ourselves may feel better in the short run, but it's not a successful long-term coping skill. "The ability to cognitively understand and comprehend the loss of a mother only comes with numerous times of bumping up against reality—she's not here, she's not here, she's not here—as we go through life and miss her and want to see her or hold her and she's not with us," explains Therese Rando, Ph.D., a bereavement specialist in Warwick, Rhode Island, who was seventeen when her father died and eighteen when she lost her mother. "Those are the times that make you feel pain, and the person who avoids that hurt is never really going to get it. The pain, in essence, teaches you."

Some daughters, like Rita, consciously choose to avoid this pain. Others cling to it to keep the loss—and their mothers—alive. "The hurt can be a connection to the loved one for a long time," Dr. Rando says. "It may be the only thing you have that keeps you connected to the person who died. Sometimes pushing the pain away is a way of holding on, and sometimes holding it close is. I held on to my parents by staying immersed in my grief. It was the hardest thing for me to give up, but I had to do it and find other ways to stay connected."

When we allow ourselves to mourn, we make way for a virtual onslaught of emotions: fear, resentment, abandonment, guilt. And anger. Rage, rather than grief, is the most common reaction to the death of a parent during childhood or adolescence. This creates a dilemma for the motherless daughter, who's been taught from an early age that "good girls" don't show strong negative emotions, at least not for public scrutiny. Popular culture has spent decades depicting angry women as violent and crazed, hardly the tragic hero an infuriated man is allowed to be. Rambo gunned his way through the jungle to thunderous applause, but Thelma and Louise's pistol-packing road trip shocked the nation. As women, we have few adequate models for releasing rage, and we often give in to the impulse to pretend it isn't there.

Which is really an unfortunate consequence, because anger can be our ally, at least for a while. As a first-response emotion, it can protect us from feeling intense sadness until we've passed through an initial adjustment stage. But clinging to anger too long keeps us from addressing the emotions underneath, and those—resentment, desertion, confusion, guilt, love—are the ones on which true mourning is based.

For seven full years after my mother died, I carried my anger around like a righteous and heavy cross, all too willing to let it define me as a noble sufferer but secretly unsure of how to relinquish its weight. I couldn't exactly dump it in the middle of a Psych 101 lecture and nonchalantly walk home, weightless and free. I'm sure my college roommates still remember the periodic temper tantrums I threw. During the years I lived with them, I immersed myself in activity—a full class load, the college newspaper, a sorority, volunteer work, a part-time job—anything to keep me from having to spend time alone. But in the brief interludes between those commitments, I occasionally came home, slammed my bedroom door, and hurled my possessions across the room, screaming nonsensical sentences until my throat turned raw. Clothing ripped from hangers, books slammed to the floor, stuffed animals hurled against the walls. The physical release was liberating, and even necessary, but the mania of it was a terror to us all. Yet it was the only way I could think of to free the rage that kept welling up inside.

This was a diffuse anger, largely nonspecific, and one I didn't understand. Anger, I'd always thought, had to be object directed, and though I focused some of mine toward my father, I didn't know where to direct the rest. Without a discrete target, it shot out at wholly unpredictable moments: on the telephone with the electric company, over dinner with my boyfriend, at the history paper I couldn't concentrate on long enough to write. I glared at the mothers and daughters I saw trying on clothes together in department-store dressing rooms. I wanted to destroy every Hallmark Mother's Day card display I saw. Rationality was not an issue. For a long time I hated the month of October, because the leaves insisted on turning color and falling to the ground even when my mother, who'd loved the fire of autumn, wasn't there to see it anymore.

"You know this feeling," says Debby, thirty-one, whose mother died of cancer eight years ago. "You're driving in the car and you feel like your whole world has fallen apart. And people in the car beside you are laughing and carrying on. Their life is normal, and you think, 'Goddamit. What gives you the right to laugh?' Because nothing has happened to them. You don't understand how everything else can go on normally when your life will never be normal again. Ever."

This is a reactionary rage, often fueled by a sense of deprivation and a belief the world owes something to the daughter who lost her mother too young. But underneath it is usually a deep anger toward the mother herself. Even though she loved us, even though we're not supposed to be angry with someone who's dead, we resent her for leaving us behind. The mother who abandoned her child or took her own life leaves a daughter with the most direct access route to anger—she *left* me—but even the mother who falls ill and dies can be an object of blame.

"In the early sixties when my friends were getting married and having babies, I was cleaning bedpans," recalls fifty-two-year-old Rochelle, who was twenty-four when her mother died of cancer. "I was angry at my mother because she didn't have a life, and I was angry at her because *I* didn't have a life." Explains Cynthia, fifty-two, who lost her mother at nine, "In my twenties and thirties and forties, I would think back in anger at how my mother left us. It was totally irrational. She didn't voluntarily contract pneumonia and choose to die. Nevertheless, there was this gray cloud in the background of my thoughts, a cool kind of anger at what she'd done to me, personally, that ruined my life."

Like Cynthia, I know my mother didn't want to leave me. I know that she, with a desire I can't possibly comprehend, wanted to see her children grow. But the fact is that she went away and left us all to cope with the wreckage she left behind. Even now, twenty-four years later, her absence remains a terrible hole. No home to return to for a holiday celebration. No one to tell me what I was like as a child, or to reassure or comfort me as a new mother. No maternal grandmother for my children. The anger and sadness I once felt when seeing a mother and daughter shopping or lunching together has been replaced by the venom I feel when I pass three generations of women walking on the street, the grandmother and the mother pushing the daughter's stroller together, laughing at a joke I didn't hear, out for just another regular afternoon in their shared lives.

I can still get angry about this, so angry sometimes that I could stamp my feet and scream. I've substituted yoga for domestic destruction, overcome my dressing-room fits, and attacked empty chairs that represent my mother in several Gestalt-inspired episodes, but a residue of rancor persists. Am I still just trying to hold on to my mother? Or has this sense of outrage become a permanent part of me?

Like most other emotions, anger carries extra baggage, and mine tends to travel with a significant amount of guilt. From an early age I received the subtle cues that told me never to speak out against the dead. The sanctification process following a mother's death is one that surpasses the rigor of any church, elevating all subsequent mention of her to the most laudatory and idealized heights. As Virginia Woolf, who was thirteen when her mother died, wrote, "Youth and death shed a halo through which it is difficult to see a real face."

Because we loved them, because we *wanted* them to be flawless when they lived, we honor our mothers by granting them posthumous perfection, and we soothe ourselves by creating the mothers we wish we'd had. Karen, twenty-nine, whose mother died nine years ago, had a childhood so torn apart by her mother's alcoholism that she ran away from home at fourteen. Nevertheless, she has exalted her mother to nearly mythic proportion in her mind. "I know that despite her alcoholism, she's smarter and more perfect now in my head than she was when she was alive," Karen admits. "As far as I'm concerned, there was never a wrinkle in anything I ever wore from the time I was born until I left home. I know I've done this as a type of memorial, a way of remembering her in a way she would want to be remembered. She very much wanted to be perfect. Giving her that gives her the respect she always wanted."

Like anger, idealization is a normal and useful early response to loss. Focusing on a mother's good traits reaffirms the importance of her presence, and processing the happy side of a relationship is a gentle way to activate mourning. But every human relationship is affected by ambivalence, every mother an amalgam of the good and the bad. To mourn a mother fully, we have to look back and acknowledge the flip sides of perfection and love. Without this, we remember our mothers as only half of what they were, and we end up trying to mourn someone who simply didn't exist.

"Mommy was a saint," my sister once said, several years ago, to a chorus of audible nods. And I thought, *a saint?* She was charitable and compassionate, and she routinely took care of others first—all that, I maintain, is true. But she was often nervous and unhappy, and she made more than a few decisions that haven't served me all that well. I don't particularly like to remember those parts, don't necessarily want to recall the things she did that even today, from an adult perspective, seem unreasonable or unfair. I want to look over my shoulder and see my mother only as the woman who shared cigarettes and PTA gossip at our kitchen table with her neighborhood friends; who carefully and methodically combed the knots out of my long, tangled hair before school when I was six; who curled up on my bed and listened patiently to an off-key version of the haftorah I would sing at my bat mitzvah at thirteen; and who clutched a box of tampons and shouted directions at a closed bathroom door to help my best friend in the ninth grade.

But that's not all of who she was. She was also the mother who constantly coerced her children to hide information from their father so he wouldn't get upset and, when he slammed the garage door and drove off one night, sat in the kitchen and cried, "What am I going to do? I'm nothing without him"; who was so frustrated with her own constant, unsuccessful dieting that she said nothing about my rapid and deliberate weight loss in 1978 until I had dropped to 102 pounds on a five-foot, seven-inch frame; who screamed at me all the way home from my second failed driver's license road test, shouting, "If you think I'm going to continue taking time out of *my* day to drive *you* around, you can just forget it"; and who turned a sixteen-year-old daughter into a bedroom confidante, telling me all the reasons why she should leave my father as well as all the reasons why she couldn't and, in the end, turning me against him as well.

I've heard that every emotion contains within itself the impulse for its opposite, but where does one end and the other begin? When I think too long about my mother, love and anger and guilt become incestuously intertwined. I have to work actively to separate them out, to differentiate the good from the bad, and, in doing so, to allow my mother to become a composite of positive and negative traits. I couldn't mourn my mother until I was ready to allow her, after death, to be nothing less—and nothing more—than she had been in life. If I can't mourn the Bad Mother, a piece of me remains forever connected to the piece of her I refuse to see.

It's hard to understand how we can harbor negative feelings toward someone we love when the two appear to sit at such competing ends of a spectrum. But negative emotion can bind people together just as tightly as positive emotion does, which is why even daughters of abusive mothers need to mourn the loss. At first, this may sound like a cross between the impossible and the absurd: Why grieve for a mother who gave you virtually nothing but grief? Why bother mourning if you *wanted* her to leave, or if her departure freed you, giving you more than you feel you lost?

All ties, positive and negative, have to be evaluated before a daughter can reconcile her mother's death or departure and move on. When the mother was a victimizer, this process involves a more difficult, more painful, and potentially more confusing journey for the daughter left behind. She often chooses to accentuate the positive, idealizing the lost mother and minimizing the abuse, or she may focus only on the negative, unable to acknowledge that a mother who hurt her so badly could have possibly loved her, too. This bewilderment is evident when twenty-two-year-old Laura reviews her relationship with her mother, who was murdered two years ago:

> For the first few years, when I was very young, my mother was extremely nurturing, extremely loving, because I didn't talk back. As a kid, you don't really have a personality, and that's what she wanted. I was her life. She would tell me things like, "You're the reason I'm alive." "I love you kids more than your father." I actually heard more of this than my sister did, because I looked like my mother. As I got older, I started to have opinions, but she still put me in this category: "You're so cute." "You're a little thing."
>
> My parents divorced when I was nine, and I turned into her confidante. She told me everything. And at the same time, if I responded in a way she didn't want, she blew up at me, told me I was out to get her, and reminded me of twelve things I did when I was four. I fell into a deep depression. I suffered a lot of neglect, too, especially after they divorced. She just wasn't around . . .
>
> I know there was some love in there, but she was just so fucked up. She was just so fucked up. And I see some of it in me. Sometimes I'm like, Whoa. Where did that come from? It just doesn't go away, either. I have to actively work on changing myself.
>
> I'm still so angry at her. I want to get through that. I want to get right size with the anger, right size with the grief, but it all gets so distorted. Like, No, I must really hate her. No, I must really love her.

Like Laura, twenty-five-year-old Juliet first had to work through her ambivalence toward her family before she could accept the loss of her mother, who died when she was seventeen. The youngest of eight children, Juliet grew up in an alcoholic home where both parents drank. She was her mother's protector, and after the funeral, Juliet relied on alcohol to numb out her feelings for nearly seven years. At twenty-three, she found herself "just stuck." "I'd painted myself into a corner," she says. Her older sister was in Alcoholics Anonymous, and Juliet decided to join. As she sobered up, seven years of feelings slowly returned, and she began to mourn what her mother had, and hadn't, been to the family. But first she had to break through years of family training that had taught her to resist or ignore her emotions, and to sanctify her lost mother.

> Now I feel mad at my mother, and it's weird. When I got into therapy and talked about it for the first time, I whispered about it. My therapist said, "Why are you whispering?" I said, "Because I'm not supposed to be talking about this." I grew up with so many secrets and always had to keep up the facade and play the role. Now, I've had to realize that my mother was part of the family's disease. The whole family was diseased by alcoholism. And I'm so angry at her. Damn it, I needed what I needed. I needed a mother, and I needed someone to be there. But as soon as I get angry, I want to defend her. I always get caught in the conflict of, "Oh, she's so good, and she tried so hard." That's what I feel when I think of my mother now. Conflict. I don't like that.

A mother who inflicted physical, sexual, or emotional abuse on a daughter damages her child's healthy sense of self, ability to trust, belief in personal safety, and perception of the world as a meaningful place. Mourning the abusive mother is an attempt to take back as much as possible of what was robbed. It doesn't invalidate the abuse, or mean the daughter wishes the mother could return. It doesn't have to be about feeling sad. It's about letting go, and setting oneself free.

"Half of me isn't sad my mother died, because I know she's a lot happier," says Donna, whose mother committed suicide three years ago. "She felt so much pain all her life—back pains, stomach pains, and then alcoholism. She was always happy on the outside, but deep inside there was a little girl on her hands and knees, crying and just wishing somebody would take care of her. She always needed to feel loved. That was why our bond, I think, was so close. I would always hug her and tell her I loved her, and cook her meals and drag her from bed to bathroom to make her throw up.

"For a couple of months after she passed away, I have to say I couldn't think of anything good that came from her," she continues. "I couldn't think of any nice things she'd done, or anything about her person that had been pretty neat at all. But I know my mother did a lot of good. Once the haze started to clear, I was able to grab hold of the things flying in front of my face and stare at them and figure out what they were and why they made me feel a certain way. My mother's death basically released me. It gave me freedom to do things I'd never have been able to do."

When an abusive mother dies or leaves, her daughter's chance for reconciliation also disappears. As long as the mother was present, the possibility of reunion, however slim, remained. For a daughter who clung to the hope of an apology, a reversal, or a payback for all the lost years, the dashed potential is another loss that needs to be ac-knowledged and mourned. Her mother will never say, "I'm sorry." She'll never quit drinking. She'll never find the therapist who'll help her change. She'll never, in effect, become the mother she never was. But she'll also never be physically able to abuse her daughter again.

Here It Comes Again

Several mornings a year I fight the impulse to crawl back under the blankets and hide. On those days, the calendar is not my friend. July 10, my parents' anniversary, is the first, followed closely by July 12, the day my mother died. Then comes her birthday on September 19, which gives me a brief respite before the holiday season begins. One month later, while I'm trying to figure out how to revise the Roman calendar to catapult myself straight from October to January, the card stores and supermarket set up their holiday displays, reminding me we won't be flying anywhere again this year, and that whatever

Thanksgiving we have will be haphazardly fashioned with friends in California, 2,600 miles from the place that still shows up in my dreams as "home."

I used to pretend these days didn't bother me, even tried to ignore them at first, but the insidious thing about anniversaries is that the psyche always knows they're there. Our internal calendar doesn't let them just slip by. Thirty-two-year-old Eileen, whose mother died when she was three, wrote to me about the intense sadness she always felt when she saw sunsets. She physically avoided them for most of her life. Driving home one day, she finally decided to watch one and experience the accompanying emotions. In doing so, she remembered that after her mother died, she frequently ran away from her father's house at dinnertime and sat on a curb, watching the sun set and waiting for her mother to appear and bring her home. After making this connection, she went to mark the event on her calendar—and discovered her mother's birthday was the day she had finally chosen to watch the sun go down.

Certain days or times of the day, week, or year can act as cyclical triggers, resurrecting grief responses. Holidays, crises, and sensory reminders can bring up the old feelings again, too. Therese Rando calls these "STUG reactions," or subsequent temporary upsurges of grief, and points out that intermittent periods of acute longing for the lost loved one are part of the normal mourning process. When we can anticipate their arrival, as in the case of distinct calendar days, we can take steps to prepare. At a time when collective ritual has lost ground to individual concerns, we are free to create our own traditions. Thirty-one-year-old Addie, who was nineteen when her mother died of heart failure, used to dread spending Mother's Day alone. "When I was working at a gift shop, I once worked on Mother's Day for a co-worker who wanted to be with his mother," she recalls. "All day long, mothers and daughters came into the shop together. I hated it—I felt so angry and sad. Cheated. I went home that night and cried for at least an hour. Just this past year my therapist helped me to see I needed a way to still honor my mother. So I decided to garden on Mother's Day. I made a ritual of planting flowers and praying for strength, life, and light. It fits for me because I'm honoring my mother and nature, and celebrating the life-giving aspect of myself—which was truly the gift my mother gave to me."

Birthdays also activate grief responses, not only because they remind us of the phone call or card that never comes but because each one we celebrate brings us closer to the neon number: the age a mother was when she died. Because we identify so strongly with our mother's body, and because our fate was once so intertwined with hers, many of us fear that the age of her physical demise will also be our own. To reach the year is a milestone; to pass it becomes one of our most glorious achievements.

"I see this over and over again," says Naomi Lowinsky, Ph.D., a Jungian analyst in Berkeley, California, who frequently counsels motherless women. "As some women approach the age their mothers were when they died, they just start going bananas in one way or another. They have weird symptoms, they're depressed, they're suddenly having heart palpitations, or other things there's no medical explanation for. It's a very, very powerful connection." Vanderlyn Pine, Ph.D., a professor emeritus of sociology at the State University of New York at New Paltz and one of the country's leading experts on death and American society, found this grief response to be so common that he created a name for it: the "parental trigger." Dr. Pine, who was nineteen when his father died, says that reaching a same-sex parent's age at time of death suddenly catapults a child into an awareness of personal mortality and a type of mourning for the parent that he or she wasn't capable of experiencing until that point. "As I was approaching the age my father was when he died, I realized I was getting very focused on that date," he explains. "His death was triggering my reactions at the time, but it didn't trigger me back to being nineteen. Instead, I was getting ready to look at the death of a forty-eight-year-old man through the eyes of a forty-eight-year-old man. It was like, *boom.* My father had pulled a trigger inside me. When I woke up that morning, I looked in the mirror and thought, 'I'm forty-eight years old. But I look pretty good for forty-eight.' I sort of looked myself over and thought, 'How could you have been so *young*? How the fuck could you have *died*? There I was at forty-eight, judging my father's death in a way I wasn't capable of at nineteen. I was suddenly a forty-eight-year-old man looking at a 48-year-old man dying and thinking, 'How shocking!'"

And then there are the subtle triggers, the ones that sidle up to you without warning, emerging from around a corner, tapping you on the shoulder when you thought you had other things on your mind. These grief responses are often related to transitional times in a woman's life—graduation, a wedding, childbirth, a new job. As maturational steps, these transitions involve added responsibility, which calls up fears and indecision that leave us longing for protection and searching for a safe haven. "In a general sense, these responses have to do with the danger of growing up," says Benjamin Garber, M.D., the director of the Barr-Harris Children's Grief Center. "If you grow up, bad things happen to you. You die." On a more personal level, he notes, "Transitional times come with heightened expectations. More will be expected of you. Each time you move forward, there's a wish to regress. And when you regress, you watch for the parent to be there. If you look back and there's nobody there, it's really scary." Evelyn Bassoff, Ph.D., a psychotherapist in Boulder, Colorado, and the author of *Mothering Ourselves*, adds, "In those times of transition, our psychic systems are not in harmony. There's a lot of inner conflict. We cling to protective figures or memories of protective figures. There's a longing to be safe."

When we reach these milestones, a mother's absence is painfully obvious. Either consciously or subconsciously, we once imagined these occasions and expected her to be there. When she isn't, our assumptions clash with reality in the most dissonant of ways. The daughter mourns not only what was lost, but what will never be—and, if her mother didn't offer protection and support when alive, the daughter also grieves for what she once needed but never had.

I missed my mother, terribly, when I graduated from college and no one from my family was there. I missed her when I got my first job promotion and wanted to share the news with someone who'd be proud. I missed her when both my daughters were born, I miss her when I can't remember what works best on insect bites, and when nobody else cares how rude the receptionist at the obstetrician's office was to me. Whether she actually would have flown in to act as baby nurse or mailed me cotton balls and calamine lotion if she were alive isn't really the issue. It's the fact that I can't ask her for these things that makes me miss her all over again.

The Resolution Hoax

I wish I believed that mourning ends one day or that grief eventually disappears for good. The word *resolution* dangles before us like a piñata filled with promise, telling us we need only to approach it from the right angle to obtain its prize. But if grieving truly did have an attainable, ultimate goal, more of us would feel we were reaching it. Of the 154 motherless women surveyed for this book, more than 80 percent said they were still mourning their mothers, even though their losses occurred an average of twenty-four years ago.

Full resolution of mourning is a state of consciousness so difficult—if not impossible—to reach that most of our attempts will inevitably fall short and leave us feeling inept. Some losses you truly don't get over. Instead, you get around them, and past. *"Resolution?* I hate that word," Therese Rando says. "I use the term *accommodate,* because at different points in time you can have accommodated the loss, made room for it in your life, and have come to a relative peace with it, but then something else can bring it up again later on. Grief is something that continues to get reworked. Even if you lose a parent after childhood, in your teenage years or later in life, you're still going to have to rework it, and rework it. The notion of 'forever-after resolved, never going to come up again' is one I don't buy at all." Says fifty-three-year-old Caroline, who was eleven when her mother died of heart disease, "I still miss my mother. If I were someone listening to me, I'd be surprised that someone can miss somebody for forty-two years. Like, Why don't you get over it? I used to think grieving was like going through a tunnel, and after you get through it, somehow at the other end the pain and feeling of loss would be gone. When I realized that I didn't have to get over the loss, and that if I didn't get over it I was still okay, then it took the pressure off me. I could just sort of embrace it and say, 'Well, this happened, and then this happened, and then this happened.'"

Sigmund Freud believed that true mourning involved a slow and total psychic detachment from the loved object, with an ultimate goal of later reattachment to someone else. His theory served as the basis for decades of mourning research, but more recent scholars of bereavement have seriously questioned whether this is even possible, let alone beneficial. When Phyllis Silverman, Ph.D., Professor Emerita at the Massachusetts General Hospital Institute of Health Professions and the author of *Never Too Young to Know*, studied eighteen college-aged women who had lost parents during childhood, she found that instead of detaching from their parents completely, these women were trying to remain connected and find a place for the lost parent in their current lives. Especially for women, who are socialized to maintain relationships rather than break away and seek emotional autonomy, ongoing connections to a lost parent may be a more natural and comfortable response. Asking them to sever ties to the past, Silverman says, may only confound their bereavement.

Many of the 125 children interviewed in the Harvard Child Bereavement Study, all of whom had lost a mother or father, also found ways to remain connected to the deceased parent. In fact, children who could not construct an internal image of the dead parent, or maintain a relationship with him or her, seemed to have the most difficulty over time. It seems that a child's memory of the missing parent, and the ability to maintain an ongoing, evolving inner relationship with that parent, is vital to the child's healthy development. We're finally moving, Silverman explains, to "a relational view of grief," in which maintaining connections to our lost loved ones will be valued more than disengaging or cutting the ties to minimize pain and suffering.

When a daughter loses a mother, the intervals between grief responses lengthen over time, but her longing never disappears. It always hovers at the edge of her awareness, prepared to surface at any time, in any place, in the least expected ways. This isn't pathological. It's normal. It's why you find yourself, at twenty-four, or thirty-five or forty-three, unwrapping a present or walking down an aisle or crossing a busy street, doubled over and missing your mother because she died when you were seventeen.

Chapter Two

Times of Change
Developmental Stages
of a Daughter's Life

MY FATHER BOUGHT the raccoon jacket for my mother in 1973. It was mid-thigh length with a sturdy brown zipper, and she wore it through the suburban New York winters of my childhood. She didn't really need a fur coat, of course—wool would have served her just fine—but in the mid–1970s in Spring Valley, New York, a fur fell somewhere between the Cuisinart and the Cadillac. A few years after my mother started wearing the raccoon jacket, my parents put a swimming pool in the backyard. That was the order of things.

A raccoon jacket didn't make quite the same statement as a full-length mink, but it was a fur coat nonetheless, and my mother wore it during the day and to informal social events at night. She was a tall woman, with wide, square shoulders, and she carried the jacket well. Its fur was the color of a graying brunette, almost exactly the color of her short, frosted hair, and against this monochrome, her splash of red lipstick always looked like a surprise. When she drove, I liked to sit in the passenger seat and rest my hand against the soft fur on her arm. Late at night when my parents came in from the movies or their bowling league or dinner parties at the neighbors', my father drove the babysitter home and my mother came into my bedroom to say goodnight. I stood on the bed and pressed my face into her neck. The cold still clung to the fur collar, and I could smell the last traces of Chanel No. 5 on her skin. Chanel was her night perfume. She wore Charlie during the day.

A few of my classmates wore rabbit jackets to school, but all other furs were reserved for adults. Some of the women in our sub-division wore ankle-length coats of fox and mink that their husbands had given them as anniversary gifts. These were usually the women who drove four-door Mercedes sedans. My mother drove an Oldsmobile station wagon. It was big enough to transport six of my friends at once, and I thought it was just fine, until everyone started wearing designer clothes in the ninth grade. I didn't have any, and these things started to matter. My mother took me shopping one afternoon and bought me two pairs of Gloria Vanderbilt corduroys and a pair of Jordache jeans. She knew how badly I wanted to fit in, she said.

I was fourteen then and not yet embarrassed to be seen in public with my mother, but by the end of that year I had traded her company almost exclusively for that of my friends. I spent my hours in parking lots and other people's rec rooms, willing to acknowledge my parents' existence only when I needed a ride home. Yet somehow I still felt a sense of security and relief in knowing that although I had rejected my mother, she had not, in turn, abandoned me. One winter when I was in the tenth grade, I got sick in Spanish class and had to phone her to pick me up from school. I was lying on a couch in the nurse's office when she arrived, wearing the raccoon jacket. Her cheeks were pink from the cold, and a designer handbag dangled from the crook of her elbow. I thought she was the picture of vibrancy and competence, as she hurried across the room to press her palm against my forehead and quickly signed the release form before taking me home. As we walked together through the wide halls toward the parking lot, I wanted to fling open the doors to all the classrooms and shout, Look, everyone. *Look at my young, pretty mother. She's come to rescue me.*

That was before she got sick. Later that year, after she had surgery and lost her hair and gained forty pounds from the white pills she swallowed every morning, she would cry when she looked in the mirror, and she started to spend more time inside the house alone. When I drove her home from chemotherapy treatments in the late afternoon, she would grip my arm to help her fight the nausea. She only had one more winter after that, and I don't remember her wearing the raccoon jacket. In fact, I can't remember her wearing anything during those sixteen months except nightgowns and bathing suits, although I know she had a closet filled with other clothes. In my imagination, I dress her in stylish outfits as if I'm pressing two-dimensional dresses onto a paper doll. When memory slides into uncertainty, fantasy is often the result. It's been more than two decades now, and every year I remember less.

And yet there are some things I would rather forget. I suspect I was not a particularly easy adolescent to raise. Caught up in the full-time job of declaring my independence, I had little interest left in family matters by the time I turned fifteen. I was occupied in other ways. When my mother was doing lunch and a manicure with her friends, I was trying drugs with mine. When her mah jongg group traded gossip and ivory tiles across the card table downstairs, my boyfriend and I were on the floor in the next room with his hand up my shirt. Typical adolescent fare for 1980, perhaps. But then, one day, it all stopped.

"The lump is cancer," my mother said one afternoon in the middle of the March before I turned sixteen. She had just returned from the surgeon's office, and I rushed to meet her at the top of the stairs.

"What does that mean?" I asked, already stepping back.

"Oh, God," she said, gripping the banister for support. "It means the surgeon has to remove my breast."

She said more, I think, but that was all I heard. "No!" I shouted, pushing past her and down the steps, hurrying to my room. When, right behind me, she knocked on the closed door, I screamed, "Go away! Leave me alone!" I knew even then, as I lay on my bedroom floor, that this event would mark the end of my childhood more definitively than menstruation or my first kiss ever could. I called a friend from the telephone in my room—"My mother has cancer. Can I come over?"—and then ran a mile to meet her at the halfway point, where she was already waiting with two other friends. I ran toward them without restraint, leaping over the low tombstones in the cemetery I had to cross, pushing myself through space as if the sheer force of my motion could catapult me into another place and time.

After the mastectomy, when my mother sat in the kitchen squeezing rubber balls to strengthen the muscles the surgeon left behind, I learned to reshape anger into silence. The message *Do not upset your mother* was unspoken, but it was clear. So I played my music low, spoke at the dinner table only when spoken to, snuck boyfriends in and out after dark through the window of my sub-basement-level room. I vacillated between resentment and fear, suspended in developmental limbo, afraid to stay separate from my mother (because what would happen to her if I did?), yet angry at her cancerous cells for trying to hold me back (because what would happen to me if I didn't go?). Every time I felt confident enough to take another step toward autonomy, the scene at home firmly pulled me back. Oh God, it was a mess.

On July 4, two weeks after my seventeenth birthday, I came home from a concert and stuck my head into my parents' bedroom to announce my return.

I'm home.

My mother was sprawled in a reclining chair, idly flipping through TV channels, but when she saw me, she sat up straight and smiled. "How was the concert?" she asked.

Fine.

Who was it that played?

James Taylor. And someone else.

That's nice. For how long?

Two hours.

Two hours? That's a long time. Was there an intermission?

No.

Tell me—what was the audience like?

Big.

Her questions continued, and my irritation grew, until after five or six more I exploded—"What is this? The goddamned third degree?"—and stormed down the stairs to my room. My mother had been a classical pianist; she'd never cared about pop music before. Why the sudden interest in the concert? My father strode into my room without knocking a few minutes later. "Why the hell did you have to do that?" he said. "You've made your mother cry. She can't go out herself. All she's asking is for you to share a little of your day with her. Can't you do even that?"

I forced myself to look at him, my cheeks warm with shame. He was so angry he was trembling, but he didn't yell. That's when I first suspected she was dying.

After the funeral, I packed up her clothing in boxes destined for Goodwill. "I can't do it," my father had said, calling from his office one morning in late July. "Can you, please?" I did it that afternoon, with my best friend sitting silently on my parents' bed for support, and I did it deliberately and mechanically, carefully unfolding and refolding each sweater, waiting for the goodbye note she never wrote to flutter to the floor. I tried not to pause long enough to think about individual pieces of clothing. How could I? Each one had its own narrative: the green-and-white housedress she had worn while cooking dinners in the Crock-Pot, the red postmastectomy bathing suit we'd selected together, the purple velour sweater I'd worn in my tenth-grade school photo. I went through her drawers one by one, methodically from left to right, filling the large cardboard boxes that covered the bedroom floor.

When I had finished, I dragged the boxes down the hall to the coat closet, and then something happened—the phone rang, or I went to get a drink—and I never did empty that last closet. And so the raccoon jacket stayed in the back, behind my father's old sheepskin coat and my sister's ski overalls, until I left for college the following year.

Why did I take it with me? Surely, I didn't think I could sneak it away without notice, but that's what I tried to do, stuffing it into a trunk I shipped to Chicago. No one in the family ever mentioned that the jacket was gone. Maybe they didn't notice. Maybe they just didn't mind. I don't know. In the Midwest, I hung it in the back of my own closet, first in a dormitory room and then in an off-campus apartment, where I lived for the next three years. I had no clear plans to wear it, but I suspected I would, someday.

It was curious, the response I got from roommates who saw that I had my mother's fur coat. The morning she had died, I'd gone into her jewelry box before dawn and removed her wedding ring, which I wore on my right hand for years. "How beautiful," people sighed when I told them what it was. The raccoon jacket provoked a different reaction, usually of surprise or disgust. A friend tried to explain this to me once. "A wedding ring represents your future," she said. "But dead raccoons? That's like wrapping yourself in the past."

I never tried to explain that the dusty old jacket gave off a warmth that was timeless to me—who would understand? And I never told anyone that sometimes during those first few years I would lean into the closet and stick my face into the fur, trying to find the patches that retained the faint scent of Charlie perfume.

In the four years I kept the raccoon jacket at school, I wore it only once. My college friends were hardcore campus liberals, and before long I joined them as they gave up meat, signed petitions, and attended rallies for animal rights. Indignation and resistance were impulses I knew well. In an odd way, they kept me feeling close to my mother, or at least to the last days we'd shared, and I continued rebelling for far longer than I needed to, after she died. I moved through college tallying grievances the way my sorority sisters collected add-a-beads, defining my personal politics only by the dramatic contrast between black and white. It didn't even matter whether the facts I pointed to were true, as long as I could identify and side with an obvious victim—preferably myself—every time.

When I was a junior, I heard that in downtown Chicago people like me were throwing red paint at fur coats, or maybe that was just a rumor. Either way, whatever material attraction I'd once had to fur had long since faded by then. One day, I was reorganizing my closet for the winter and sprang back in horror when I saw a pile of dead animals in the back. Then I realized what it was.

I'm almost ashamed to admit I didn't get rid of the coat then. I kept it for another year. And then one day, without premeditation, I pulled it from the closet before classes and shrugged it on. It was a brutally cold morning along Lake Michigan, which somehow seemed justification for wearing fur. But after I'd walked only two blocks toward campus, I realized how incredibly foolish I felt. Standing on a street corner surrounded by L. L. Bean parkas and ankle-length down coats, I understood that I could not wear that coat again. It had nothing to do with mink farms, or the fear of red paint. A fur coat is serious business—the business of women and wives and mothers, of dinner parties in February, and opera in New York. The kind of business, I realized, that had everything to do with my mother and very little to do with me. With enough time still to make it to class, I rushed back to my apartment. I put the coat in the closet.

Two weeks later, without any fanfare, I finally packed it into a bag of clothes destined for Goodwill, and gave it away.

Sometimes I still wonder what losing my mother would have been like if I'd spent just a few more years with her, or if I'd known her for a few less. Would we have been spared the years of antipathy and argument? Would we have had time to become friends? Women who lost their mothers in early childhood often look at me with envy, seeing the years they never had; women who were in their mid-twenties tell me they never could have survived it at seventeen. Is it better to have a mother and lose her, or to never have had one at all? I can't answer that question. I do know that mother loss is difficult at any time, and at any stage. Regardless of our age, we yearn for a mother's love throughout our lives, reaching for the security and comfort we believe only she can provide at times of illness, transition, or stress.

So much has been written about the mother-daughter relationship, but comparatively so little about mother loss, that the natural impulse is to look at what exists when a mother is alive and then expect the inverse to be true if she's gone. But it's not that simple. To say that a mother helps her child develop self-esteem doesn't necessarily mean that a child without a mother has no self-esteem, but instead that she must develop it in alternate ways. That's why her age at the time of loss is important. It indicates which developmental tasks she's likely to be working on, and which emotional and cognitive tools are available to help her cope with the stress of the immediate crisis, and guide her into the next stage of her life.

Early Childhood
(Age Six and Younger)

Tricia was three when her mother died after a two-year struggle with cancer, and what she can best recall now, at twenty-five, is the general feeling of confusion and abandonment she experienced at the time:

I can remember about a month before my mother died. It was Christmas. She was able to come and sit in my dad's chair in the living room to watch us open our presents, and I remember this feeling that we had to be quiet. Just kind of an aura of calmness. And also that it was very, very unusual and special for her to be able to come and watch us. I remember she had her wig on, and not quite getting that. It's funny, because there are pictures of me wearing her wig. I like that now. But I remember thinking then, "Isn't that goofy? She's wearing a wig. Why isn't anyone laughing?"

And then I remember when my dad came in to tell us she had died. My sister, who was five, and I were in bed. I remember not even understanding what that meant, but seeing my dad cry. My sister immediately cried, but I was kind of confused. A lot of my feelings from that time are confused and really fuzzy. I also remember the funeral a month later. My sister and I wore little red velvet dresses. I remember how the velvet felt against my skin. And I remember feeling lost. My father told me once that the hardest part of those next few months for him was that I would wake up in the night screaming for her. Screaming and screaming. But I don't remember that.

Tricia spent only three years with her mother, but it was enough time for her to feel a deep connection to her and to understand that an important part of her livelihood had been taken away. She's been trying to recapture it ever since. Today, she still seeks out stories, photographs, and items that can tell her more about her mother's life and the brief time they shared.

To experience the loss of her mother, a child first must develop the ability to miss someone. This usually occurs between the ages of six months and one year. A girl who loses her mother before this time grows up with little sense of connection to her. Preverbal, sensual memories of very early care may be lodged deep within her psyche, but she retains no conscious memories of being held, talked to, or fed by any particular caregiver. Twenty-seven-year-old Lisa, who was four months old when her mother died, says with evident regret, "I don't feel anything between us. I have pictures of her and my father when they first got married, and pictures of her by herself, and I look at them and wonder, What was she like? It's like I'm looking at someone who's a stranger but not a stranger. I'm sure that just from being in her womb, I have some subconscious connection to my mother, so there has to be something there, but I don't have anything I can point to and say, 'This is my mother and this is how I knew her.'"

Daughters whose mothers died when they were infants or toddlers grow up feeling a strong sense of absence rather than loss. "Because the parent was never known, the surviving child does not have the experience of being torn away from a parent who was loved and cherished," explains Maxine Harris. These children have to contend with what's known as "the absent memory," the story of a mother whose face is neither remembered nor preserved in the family album. "Loss requires some prior relationship," Harris writes in *The Loss That Is Forever*. "One can experience emptiness, however, when one has known only absence. For the survivors of the very early death of a parent, emptiness and void are inextricably tied with the enigmatic image of a parent they never knew."

Although young children's capacity for memory and understanding is limited, as the British psychiatrist John Bowlby emphasized, it is not zero. He observed that children as young as one will look for a mother in the last place she appeared, and that this association may persist into adulthood. The daughter whose mother favored a particular wing chair, for example, may continue to look toward that chair longingly as she grows up, and associate such chairs with desire or distress as an adult.

A woman who was a toddler when she lost her mother may be able to recall specific tactile or visual images—such as hair, hands, or skin—that she associates with her mother. Amanda, thirty-three, who was separated from her mother at the age of three when her parents divorced, says she's still not sure whether some of her early memories of her mother are real or imagined. "In my twenties, I started asking my father about places and people I remembered, and he'd say, 'Well, that sounds pretty accurate,' or 'That doesn't sound right to me,'" she recalls. "Once, I remembered her taking her hair and rubbing it on her face, and he remembered that about her, too. It blew me away, because it was like this hidden, weird thing that I did. Whenever I was under stress, I would play with my hair and pull it."

Discovering this connection, small as it may be, Amanda says, helped her feel closer to the mother she never expects to see again.

The trauma of separation often illuminates a particular scene or event and fixes it in a young child's memory. Women who were three or four when their mothers died report having fairly detailed memories of particular events. Although toddlers don't yet fully understand death, and typically won't for at least another five or six years, they can sense when something has gone seriously wrong, often from interpreting the responses of those around them. If a child of this age is left alone with her confusion, certain memories may continue to trouble her for years after the actual event.

Claudia, forty-one, who was four when she lost her mother, remembers the night her mother died, the casket in the home, the funeral, and the burial. "I remember going to the interment, and standing over the grave," she says. "It seemed like it would never stop when they were lowering the casket. I wondered how deep they were going to put her. They gave us flowers to put in, and when I walked over to put mine in, the hole was so deep. I felt like I should jump in. I didn't, but really I wanted to jump in with her. That's what I felt." The moment left such an emotional imprint on Claudia that she refused to return to the cemetery for more than twenty years, until her father died. As she stepped up to the family plot again, the sadness and fear she'd felt at the age of four returned. "My aunt touched me on my back and said, 'Go ahead, baby. Go ahead. Put the flower on his casket,'" she recalls. "I didn't want to do it, because I could remember looking into that hole before. I didn't want to get near it. So I went up very quickly, put the flower in, and rushed back."

Young children are totally dependent on someone to help them through the intricate maze of early developmental skills and to offer encouragement and support. This person is usually the mother. A child's first and most profound social experience is with her mother, and that relationship influences her psychological and physical development. As Bowlby and other attachment theorists have observed, children whose mothers are responsive to their signals and interact socially with them during their first year are likely to become more socially advanced and more capable of forming secure attachments to others than infants whose mothers are preoccupied or avoidant.

When this first consistent relationship is interrupted or severed, a father, grandmother, older sister, housekeeper—any warm, involved, stable caretaker willing to invest time and patience in the child's growth—may fill this role. Among children of all ages, the critical factor that determines later distress is not mother loss per se but instead the availability of consistent, loving, and supportive care afterward. A child who can attach to another adult after losing a mother has the best chance of developing without serious ongoing difficulties. Although she often makes it clear that her substitute is second-best to the mother she lost, a daughter may find comfort in recreating with this new mother-figure some version of the relationship she had with her own mother.

Amanda believes she eventually managed to enter a stable marriage, start a family, and find happiness despite her early abandonment and later difficulties with a distant father and stepmother because she spent four years in her grandmother's care. After her parents' divorce when she was three, Amanda lived with her paternal grandparents and uncle until her father remarried. "That was a very nurturing family," she explains. "I don't know why my grandparents let me stay with them, but I always wished they'd said to my father, 'Let us keep Mandy, and you go on with your life.' I'm still very close with my grandma and grandpa. We relate to each other better than I can with my father and stepmother." Throughout her childhood and adolescence, Amanda relied on her grandmother for the love and care she never found at home. Her grandmother helped her through her first menstruation and gave her financial assistance to return to school just last year.

Amanda's ability to bond with a stable adult in early childhood and maintain that bond until the present gave her the solid foundation she needed to leave her father's home at eighteen and feel confident in her ability to create a life of her own. If Amanda hadn't found a substitute after her mother died, her early development might have detoured in a number of ways. Elizabeth Fleming's case study of Lucy, which appears in Erna Furman's book, *A Child's*

Parent Dies, illustrates the resonating effects of early mother loss when subsequent caretakers are inconsistent or indifferent.

Lucy was ten weeks old when her mother suddenly died. Maternal relatives raised Lucy for a short period until a cousin took over while her father traveled for work. When Lucy was six, her father married a woman with three children and brought Lucy to live in the new home. Throughout this time, he refused to answer her questions about her birth mother, about whom she knew virtually nothing. Lucy was eleven, overweight, and still wetting the bed when she started seeing Fleming. The therapist believed that the combination of a lack of early consistent mothering, childhood instability, and a taboo surrounding the natural mother had led Lucy to overeat, isolate herself, tune out her feelings, take on the traits of people around her, and consistently start new relationships with the hope that she would find what she had lost.

> She had never been a participant in changes in her own life. She had a tendency to let relationships with others drift off, rather than really ending them. Lucy had to fight the wish to see me because it contained the desire to get more from me than I, as her therapist, could give. [Her] sporadic attendance also put separations under her control. I was the one who waited and never knew when she would appear, just as she had earlier never known when her father would leave or return from his trips. The inability to control life and death, the comings and goings of other people, and her own bodily functions contributed to her being a very controlling girl in her relationships. . . . She warded me off as if fearing the repetition of painful disappointments if she invested in our relationship. She told me she would not form close friendships with staff because they left too often.

Lucy's resistance to later attachments was a defense against her expectation of abandonment. Many motherless women who were young children when their mothers died or left echo Lucy's experience. To love someone, they say, involves the risk of loss. Trust and security already were destroyed once. Why should they chance losing those again?

"If a child doesn't have a secure and stable relationship after a parent leaves, she keeps her feelings inside because it's not safe to put them out there," Therese Rando explains. "Later on, the child thinks, 'I'm not going to trust. I've learned it's not safe. You might be nice, but I'm not going to trust you.' Her future attachments get compromised, because she never worked through the attachments she did have. All she had to do was protect herself, and part of that protection was not to attach to anyone."

Thirty-nine-year-old Janine says she has encapsulated herself in this kind of protective cocoon for almost thirty-seven years. She was twenty-one months old when her mother died, and twelve when she lost the grandmother who became her mother substitute. The double loss, followed by an adolescence with an emotionally distant father and stepmother, forced her into a withdrawal she's just learning how to emerge from today:

> I have a dog. I love my dog. Somebody spent the night with me recently, and it was the first time anyone had slept in my bed since I got the dog. He was very mad at me, and he chewed up my glasses. It was the first time he'd ever done that. I was furious at him. It sounds stupid to learn these lessons from a dog, but I all of a sudden realized I could be furious at my dog and still love him. And I thought, "This must be what it would have been like to grow up with a mother." You know that you can mess up, do something that makes somebody really mad, and they'll still love you and won't try to take you back to the pound. I'd never felt that before. I think feeling it, letting myself risk love and letting myself be loved, is one of the biggest challenges left for me.

Late Childhood (Six to Twelve)

Some therapists believe that children who lose a parent during this next developmental stage have the hardest time coping. They're cognitively and emotionally advanced enough to feel a profound loss, but their resources for managing their emotions haven't yet reached a level of mastery. Stuck between change and adaptation, school-age children often try to ward off their sad feelings forcefully. As the psychologist Judith Mishne writes:

> [They] will skirt the mention of the lost parent, engross themselves in play and suggest "let's change the subject." The avoidance of the finality of the loss is supported by fantasies of the parent's return. While such expectation persists, there is also an acknowledgment of the fact that the parent had died. These two trends of acknowledgment and denial coexist without being mutually confronted.

Sigmund Freud called this phenomenon—allowing fact and fantasy, acceptance and denial, to exist side by side—"splitting the ego," and to some degree, we all do this when a parent dies. During late childhood, however, this inner tension intensifies when a girl receives minimal or false information about what she knows is a dramatic event. Whereas a young daughter usually is told that her mother has "gone away" or is in "a deep sleep" and often takes these euphemisms literally, an older child—who typically understands most of the implications of illness and death by age seven or eight and recognizes euphemistic language—feels left out of the action, like a bit-part player in the family's drama.

Mary Jo, who was eight when her mother died, knew her mother was gravely ill but received no concrete information against which to test her reality. She heard her mother screaming from pain—an image she says she has suppressed, even though she knows that the event occurred in her presence. But her family's reticence confused her so profoundly that she kept her fear and loss to herself for nearly thirty years.

> No one was talking to me as my mother died, but neither could I think about what was going on and what it meant. When I did try to talk about it, I would get a response like, "Who do you think you are?" or "We don't talk about that." There was both an emotional push not to discuss it because it was too painful, and also an inability and inexperience among most of my family members to deal with feelings in any way. For years, I just did

what everyone else did, which was to say don't think about it, and believe that I just had to accept and live with it. The reason my father didn't talk about it was it was just too painful, but what an eight-year-old processes is not that it's too painful, but that it's not appropriate to talk about. So that was the kind of gestalt that held over the years for me.

For years, I felt I'd come to accept that, until my midthirties, when I went into therapy for the first time. During one of my first visits we were talking about my mother, and my therapist took me on a guided fantasy. She said, "Imagine your mother is sitting next to you and saying, 'I'm here, and I want to come back and be in your life again.'" I literally folded up my body and said, "No, no, no. I can't take that pain." That was a revelation to me, because I thought I'd pretty much learned to live with it by then.

The year after her mother died, Mary Jo lost her younger brother in an accident. Her father, having suffered these two losses, as well as the death of his father the previous year, defended himself against the pain by refusing to discuss the events. "That was very difficult for me, because as a child, I sort of thought it was all my fault," Mary Jo explains. "I believed that maybe if I'd done something differently, things would have turned out otherwise."

Mothers leave because children are bad; parents die because their children want them to go away—these are examples of "magical thinking," which grows out of a child's egocentrism and cause-and-effect belief system. Magical thinking has been observed in children as young as three, and motherless women report evidence of it throughout childhood and beyond. These daughters see a mother's death or absence as the result of something they did—or didn't—do. Terrified and awestruck by her own power, this daughter then feels guilt and remorse. She may structure her behavior so that she is either so bad her mother will have to come back and rescue her, or so good that no one would ever want to leave her again.

A daughter who loses a mother during late childhood may have fairly detailed memories of their time together, and she may depend on these later for clues about femininity. The mother is a daughter's first and most influential model for female behavior. She's the one who gives the first lessons about relating to men, running a home or combining family and career, and being a mother. A daughter's early identity forms in large part from the experiences she has with her mother, the behaviors she observes and the quality of their relationship.

"A five-year-old can understand about being a little girl with a mom, and on top of that comes her seven-year-old experience of it, and then on top of that is a nine-year-old layer," explains Nan Birnbaum. "It's not that the original identifications disappear; it's like increments get added onto each other. What then happens is the girl's view of her mom slowly matures, and she sees her mother in more realistic ways, with flaws. She begins to see there are things her mom isn't able to do so well. She still values her a lot, but she just doesn't see her as God. Along with that, the girl's view of her own capacities is growing. She begins to realize, 'I'm better than Mom at this,' or 'I'll have to go to Dad or someone else for that.' It gets more and more realistic."

Losing a mother can bring this process to a premature halt, freezing a daughter's identifications at a very specific point and time. "Without live experience, no new layers of identification are being added on," Nan Birnbaum says. "Kids who've had mother loss at age eight or nine sometimes have a view of how things ought to be done, based on their earlier experience, and they see what they need to do to obtain what the mother could do in very rigid and fixed terms. They may judge themselves very harshly, be very critical of themselves, or have an overblown, idealized view of what the parent did and of what they have to do to be like Mom. That's one of the major things loss confronts kids with—their identifications don't have a chance to mature."

Caroline, fifty-three, says she still thinks every day about her mother, who died when she was eleven. But the mother she imagines is the mother of her childhood, the one who cooked big breakfasts and sang to her daughters. Even though Caroline is a mother today, she says that whenever she meets a nurturing woman, she's delighted to be cared for in these ways. When we met for our interview, she had just returned from a visit with her father and his third wife, who is offering Caroline exactly the kind of mothering that, after forty-two years, she still craves.

> Coming home today on the ferry, I was thinking about how much I love my new mom. She packed me a lunch for the ride home, because I had to scoot to get here in time. I pulled it out of the bag, and here was celery stuffed with cheese, and this wonderful sandwich with lots of mayonnaise, which I love, and spinach instead of lettuce, which I also love. She noticed. And there were two nice dinner-sized napkins and a plastic bag with a damp paper towel in it so I could wipe my hands and face in the car, because where would I find water? Instead of three wonderful sugar cookies, there were eight. It was just wonderful. I do that for other people, but nobody does that for me. And now here's my new mom, doing it. Just because you lose a birth mom doesn't mean you lose the need to be mothered. Here I am, fifty-three years old, with this seventy-five-year-old woman I've only known for two years doing a fabulous job of mothering me, and I'm letting her. I love it.

Children and Loss:
Trying to Cope, Trying to Grow

When a mother dies, a daughter—no matter what her age—faces changes and upsets. The psychological defenses a child develops to cope, however, are more primitive and vulnerable than an adult's. While an adult brings cognitive and emotional maturity to a loss situation, a child usually regresses, projects, identifies, or turns against herself to a more dramatic degree.

DISPLACEMENT. The severe emotional pain associated with losing a mother is often too much for a child to bear alone, and bereaved children may stuff their feelings underground. They may refuse to discuss the loss, pretend it never occurred, or allow themselves to feel the pain only in diffuse and displaced ways. When Anna Freud observed abandoned children during World War II, she noticed that they frequently displaced their own feelings of distress and loneliness onto their lost mothers. "I have to telephone my mummy, she will feel so lonely," was a common wish among those who longed for their mothers' return.

Other daughters allow themselves to mourn only from a distance. Hillary, thirty-two, says she didn't cry as a six-year-old when her mother died, but five months later she came close to virtual collapse when her pet hamster died. She'd kept her core feelings about the loss of her mother buried under protective layers until an external event months later pulled them to the surface. For some daughters, this release may not occur for years.

TRANSFERENCE. An adult who loses a spouse can manage without a close connection to another person for a period of time, but a child who loses a parent can't exist alone emotionally without significant cost. She'd be left in what Anna Freud called the "no-man's land of affection," isolated and withdrawn from everyone and with an impaired ability to attach to other people in the future. So instead of detaching from her lost mother, a daughter may try, quickly and directly, to transfer her feelings of dependency, her needs, and her expectations onto the nearest available adult. This may be her father, an older sibling or other close relative, a teacher, a neighbor, or a therapist. During adolescence, a boyfriend or an older female friend often serves the same purpose. Transference can be helpful when the child is too young to detach all her emotion from her caregiver, but if she doesn't return later to pull away from the image of her mother enough to mourn the loss she will continue to search for her in the people she chooses as replacements.

ARRESTED DEVELOPMENT. The loss of a mother creates a significant developmental challenge for a child. She may be forced to take on responsibility for herself very quickly, causing her to advance some areas of development. At the same time, she may continue to identify with her earlier stage of maturity as a way to maintain a relationship with her mother and deny the finality of the death. The result is an adult who retains some characteristics of an earlier developmental time, one who feels as if a piece of her were still "stuck" in childhood or adolescence. To this daughter, "growing up" feels not only like a mystery but also a practical impossibility: She's still too wedded to her childhood. "Parent loss per se doesn't lead to an arrest in development, but it can happen if circumstances don't support mourning in the interim," Nan Birnbaum explains. "All the girl's other means and interests develop, but some immature aspects are still a part of her. It's like the child of ten coexisting with the woman of twenty. As long as her mourning is incomplete, she feels there's something she can't quite recapture, and she remains in a state of yearning."

The daughter whose development arrests in some areas may later have trouble emotionally connecting with the tasks and responsibilities normally associated with her chronological age. Without the socializing influence of her mother, she has a difficult time reaching complete intellectual or emotional maturity. Twenty-five-year-old Tricia, who was three when her mother died, says she begins every adult romance with the hope that she's found someone who'll hold her and care for her like a child. As her friends marry and start families of their own, she admits, "I'm just looking for someone who'll lullaby me. It's kind of like I'm out of sync."

DELAYED REACTIONS. When researchers at the Harvard Children's Bereavement Study looked at school-age children one year after the death of a parent, they found no significant behavioral or psychological differences between these kids and those who hadn't experienced a loss. At the two-year point, however, the parent-loss kids exhibited much more aggressive and disruptive behaviors than their non-loss peers. They were also more socially withdrawn, and suffered from lower self-esteem. Other studies have found that bereaved children don't show symptoms of disturbance until as much as three years after a death—usually long after hospice or other family support programs, which typically work with families for a year, have exited the scene.

Adolescence (Teen Years)

Adolescence, a period of intense internal chaos even without mother loss, is perhaps the only time in human development when obsessive, phobic, and paranoid behaviors are actually considered normal. In the frenzy of maturation, all the rules seem to suddenly change. Parents become oppressive and embarrassing; friends, unpredictable and competitive; the boys at school, mysterious and suddenly worthwhile. The real changes, of course, are occurring internally, where a girl's swiftly changing moods, emerging sexuality, and newly advanced cognitive skills blend to create a sense of disharmony unlike any she has experienced before. "It's just a stage," our parents say, and to some degree they're right. Most of adolescence is about losing and regaining equilibrium, and about allowing a new, more mature identity to emerge slowly from the family's cocoon.

At least that's how it works according to the master plan. When a traumatic event occurs during these years, however, the whole process can get thrown off course. Any of the developmental tasks of adolescence—developing autonomy, dealing with authority figures, learning to live with ambivalence and ambiguity, developing a capacity for intimacy, solidifying a sexual identity, learning to manage emotion, developing a personal value system, and maintaining a sense of adequacy and competence—can be disrupted or halted by mother loss at this time. In addition, sleep disturbances, academic difficulties, poor concentration, withdrawn behavior, decreased appetite, depression, alcohol abuse, and delinquency are common in bereaved adolescents during the first year after a major loss. Two years after the loss these teens score higher in anxiety, depression, and social withdrawal, and perceive themselves to be less socially adept and less in control of their destinies than their non-bereaved counterparts.

Mothers and Daughters: When the Bond Breaks

As humans, we are social creatures, dependent on others for fulfillment. When we detach from one person or group, we naturally want to attach to another. During a normal adolescence, as a girl loosens her attachment to her mother she invests more energy in her peer group and possibly in a romantic partner. Although this break is significant, it's not complete: A daughter still periodically returns to her mother in times of stress. Traveling along this two-steps-forward, one-step-back trajectory, the adolescent prepares for the passage into a stage of increased autonomy, a transition that helps her ultimately detach from her family of origin and begin a family of her own.

It's normal for a girl to feel both positive *and* negative emotions toward her mother at this time, often within minutes of each other. Feelings of love and security connect her to a vital source of nurturing and support, while anger and resentment help her establish and maintain the distance she needs to begin to venture forth alone. These are the years when a daughter fully acknowledges that her mother is less than perfect and may even feel embarrassed or ashamed when comparing her to other women. The teenager takes an important step toward developing an independent identity when she realizes that she doesn't want to duplicate her mother, recognizes she has the power to differentiate, and begins to do it.

This separation is rarely clean or easy, and often is complicated by a mother's behavior. Because a mother frequently perceives her daughter as an extension of herself and thus identifies with her daughter more strongly than she does with her sons, she may try to hold on as a daughter breaks away. At the same time, because she has gone through adolescence herself and understands that her daughter must achieve autonomy, she pushes her daughter toward adulthood and independence.[1] This is not a time of mutual understanding between most mothers and daughters, and the struggle typically lasts into a daughter's late teens or early twenties. As a study of a hundred autobiographical accounts from Wellesley College students in the early 1980s revealed, more than 75 percent of the daughters at that age still had unfavorable or unflattering views of their mothers.

When a mother dies during her daughter's adolescence, what would otherwise have been a temporary separation with the hope of later reconciliation then becomes an irrevocable physical fracture. "Wait a minute!" the daughter wants to shout. "I didn't really mean it. Come back!"

A daughter at the peak of rebellion may be left with tremendous guilt and regret if her mother dies at this time. In her memory, their fifteen-year relationship may then deflate to the six awful arguments of the past year. When I think of the times I hurled hurtful phrases at my mother, using the word *love* like a knife—"You don't love me!"

---

[1] This is not always true for mothers who never separate or who separate incompletely from their own mothers, and who expect to maintain a similar bond with their daughters.

"I don't love you, I *hate* you!" and that most horrid and self-fulfilling of all, "I wish you would go away and leave me alone!"—I'm furious at the adolescent I once was. I never believed my mother died because I wished it, but for many girls a certain residue of childhood magical thinking does persist beyond childhood.

"Whenever someone we've had an ambivalent relationship with dies, especially if we've just had an argument, we often feel a lot of pain and remorse for the angry thoughts we felt toward them," explains Arlene Englander, LCSW, MBA, a psychotherapist in North Palm Beach, Florida, who specializes in bereavement and complicated grief. "When people are under stress, they tend to regress, and at those times adolescents and even adults can reactivate magical thinking at a conscious level. They then believe they were in some way responsible for the death."

Lea, now thirty-four, remembers a conversation she had with her best friend when she was thirteen. "We were talking about issues thirteen-year-old girls thought were important," she says. "I asked, 'If you had to lose a parent, which one would you want to lose?' I said my mother, because I was closer to my father, and my life would change less. A couple of months later, my mother had a stroke and died. Between the way a thirteen-year-old's mind works, and the guilt taught in my Catholic school, it took me a long time to get over the idea that God had heard me."

An adolescent daughter may also blame herself for not being a "good" daughter and may feel intensely sad about the lost opportunity for later redemption. Paula, twenty-seven, attributes most of the guilt she felt after her mother died when she was fifteen to wishing she'd fought with her less and comforted her more. "It just seems that if I'd known how sick she was, I wouldn't have said all those terrible things," she says. "Sometimes I catch myself even now, telling myself what a horrible thing I did on such and such day back then. But now I also say to myself, 'Well, you were a teenager. You were going through all that,' or 'Maybe you were suffering from PMS.' Something to make it all right. Because I don't have the chance now at twenty-seven to sit back and laugh with a mother who's fifty and say, 'Oh, remember when?'"

"You hope that your mother was able to see you were going through a bad period, and that it wasn't always going to be like that," she continues. "You hope she didn't leave with the terrible feeling that you didn't love her. That's always my fear. I try to catch myself whenever I'm feeling that way and tell myself, 'It's okay. You did what you did at the time, and that's it. She understood. You didn't have more time together, but it would have worked out all right if you did.'"

Like Paula, I try to coax myself beyond self-blame, into a place where I can find comfort believing my mother once said the same things to her mother, too. And though their relationship had complications of its own, it can stand as a loose model for me of what might have been.

"It's very important for the daughter to understand that the mother knew the antagonism was normal," says Evelyn Bassoff. "Do you remember that scene in *Terms of Endearment* when the mother is dying and the older son is so angry and rebellious? She insists, 'I know you love me' in that dying scene. That's really wonderful, that little sequence. I think it depicted a very non-narcissistic mother, a very giving and generous mother. I think when she said that to her older son in spite of his horrible behavior toward her, she gave him an incredible gift. But I think that even if there wasn't that kind of reconciliation, even if it didn't happen like it does in the movies, you can come to understand that yes, it was bad at the time your mother died, and you weren't getting along, but that your mother was mature enough to know you would have mended your relationship in time. The healing thought is, 'My mother, because she was older and wiser than I am, understood that I was going through a stage.'"

Because maturation is such an individual process, different adolescents separate from their mothers at different ages. Some never do it at all. If a mother dies or leaves when the connection with her daughter is loving and close, the girl may find herself faced with little guilt but much pain. Her reaction to the loss may be closer to that of the dependent child suddenly set adrift without a firm connection to shore. Mariana, who at sixteen was the oldest of two daughters when her mother died of kidney failure, told me how frightened she'd been to lose her mother because she was so timid as an adolescent. I must have given her a skeptical look—and it's true I had trouble believing it at first; Mariana was probably the most effusive person I'd met all week—because she nodded her head vigorously to emphasize her point.

> I was an extremely shy person when my mother died. I really kept close to home. My family used to call me "The Hermit," because sometimes you'd see me come out of my room, but generally not. I'd just peek out. My mother and I were very tight. She was my best friend in addition to being my mom, so not only did I lose my mother, but I also lost a close friend. She just did everything for me, so I was totally unprepared for what it meant to be without her there to protect me from everything.
>
> I went straight to work after high school. If Mommy had lived, I probably would have gone to a college close to home, but I was too nervous to leave Daddy. He was in and out of the hospital because of diabetes and depression. I ended up working for a year, and I decided to also volunteer for my congressman. It took time away from what I could spend with my sister and the household, but I felt if I didn't get out of the house, I'd turn into a lunatic. Working for Joe made a big difference. He was very young, only ten years older than me, and I was working with young, hip people. I had to become more outgoing to work in the political arena. It changed my personality. I stopped being so inside myself all the time.

Losing her mother propelled Mariana into an autonomy that she might not have otherwise achieved as quickly, if at all. For other daughters, particularly those who lose mothers during their most turbulent periods, some areas of personality development may get stopped short. Arrested development isn't exclusively a childhood phenomenon. It can happen during adolescence as well, occurring when a teen feels deeply ambivalent toward her mother at the time of loss and isn't able, for any number of reasons, to mourn adequately and separate from her. Gayle, thirty-two, who was eighteen and the youngest of eight children when her mother died, was so tightly (and unhappily) bound to her mother when she was alive that Gayle's separation did not occur until almost twelve years after her mother's death.

> My relationship with my mother was so many things. She was very sick, both emotionally and physically, from before the time I was born. And I was born when she was forty, pretty late in her life. She was at times my friend, but at times very domineering. She knew exactly how I needed to live my life, and she told me. I was her last child, and she held on tight. She let my other brothers and sisters go, with a fight, when they were ready to leave, but I never broke away from her during adolescence. I would make leaps to do it, but I was really tied to her, almost as if the umbilical cord was never cut. When I think of it now, it's almost as if we shared bodily fluids. I was of her, for her, with her, and as much as I would scream—and I did my screaming during adolescence, trying to fight her that way—when push came to shove I would always give in, because there was no way I could win against her.
>
> These last few years have been a period of redefining my life. I've had to take a look at my relationship with my mother and realize I never really mourned her death. I went through a good part of my adult life having shut the door on it, thinking, "Fine. We'll just go on and not think about this." Now that I'm finally doing it, I feel like I'm just starting to go through adolescence today.

Because mourning often reactivates the emotions that existed at the time of loss, a daughter who returns to that juncture in her past as an adult also may find herself working through the developmental tasks she never completed during adolescence. Daughters like Gayle who feel stuck in a prior stage can finally emerge from it as adults. Likewise, daughters who were forced into adult responsibilities too soon and feel they missed out on adolescence entirely report giving themselves license to act irresponsible or carefree ten or fifteen years beyond their teens.

With mother loss magnifying the typical strains and stresses of adolescence, is it easier for children who lost their mothers earlier to pass through these stormy years? Probably not. A 1950s study of orphaned children at the Hampstead Child-Therapy Clinic in England revealed that children deprived of a stable mother-figure for their first five years actually have more *difficult* adolescences than children whose mothers die or leave during that time. Many of the children who'd lost their mothers before the age of five experienced a preadolescent phase that was often characterized by a frantic search for a mother-figure, possibly to form an attachment that could then be loosened.

Lucy, the child who lost her mother as an infant and appeared in Elizabeth Fleming's case study earlier in this chapter, plunged into a mother-daughter void when she reached adolescence. She had never accepted her stepmother as an adequate mother substitute, and knew little about her own mother. At fifteen, she experienced a depression, according to Fleming:

> It was marked by feeling dejected and hopeless and being unable to wake up in the morning, losing interest in social activities, and not attending school and analytic sessions. She seemed immobilized bodily and mentally—a characteristic she had never shown before. In addition, old difficulties were exacerbated; she gained weight, experienced increased physical symptoms and, on one occasion, scratched her wrist. Consciously, Lucy linked her difficulties to her disappointment at her first boyfriend's withdrawal. . . . Her greatest despair stemmed from not having an image of her dead mother from which she could divorce herself as a child and with whom she could choose to identify, or not identify, as an adult woman. During the following two years Lucy searched out independently enough detailed knowledge of her mother to form the coherent picture she had always lacked. Then, on her own and for the first time, she visited her mother's grave. These achievements marked the end of her depressive symptoms.

Separating from a mother or mother-figure during adolescence, it seems, is an essential part of the process that turns a girl into a self-confident, autonomous woman.

Adolescents and Loss:
Matters of Appearance

In college, I pledged a sorority. Like most sorority houses on campus, mine had its annual traditions, and one evening during the pledges' Hell Week, all sixty-four sisters assembled on the living room floor. We sat in a haphazard circle on the powder-blue rug as the pledge trainer explained the rules: Everyone had to tell a story that began with, "Something my mother doesn't know . . ." One woman told about a drunken midnight roadtrip to Milwaukee; another shared a vignette about sexual advances in a neighbor's suburban hot tub. The stories crept around the circle, punctuated with small bursts of laughter and an occasional "You didn't!" and "No way!" And then sixty-three eager faces turned to me.

I'd been siting there quietly, examining my fingernails and considering my options—Should I go along with it? Tell the truth? Excuse myself from the room?—when the woman to my left prodded me with her elbow. "Your turn," she said.

I looked up. "I think I'd like to pass."

"No way!" "Come on." "Tell us, tell us, tell us."

"No, I mean it. I'd like to pass."

More laughter. "Come *on!*" "What, are you trying to hide something good?" "No, no, no. Everyone has to say."

I panicked and I stammered, until words formed purely by impulse appeared. "I don't have a mother," I said, "but I do have a father. So I can tell you something he doesn't know. The room fell silent, widely and uncomfortably silent, as I spit out some convoluted story about a man I'd met that winter in New Orleans. I don't remember the details now, and I doubt I paid much attention to them then. My goal was to finish quickly and remove myself from the spotlight I'd been trying to avoid all year.

I managed to sit through a few more stories, until the pledge trainer noticed my wobbling chin and led me to her room. "I'm so sorry," she said, feeding me Kleenex as we sat on her bed and I cried. "I'm so sorry. I didn't know."

No one knew. I hadn't told them. These friends were my refuge from the tragedy I'd left behind, the sorority house, a place where I could reinvent myself as a carefree party girl unencumbered by baggage from my past. In the house's tastefully decorated living room, I could pretend to be a girl no different from the others, 800 miles from the high school where I'd been known as the girl whose mother died.

The peer group, that all-powerful teenage tribunal in the life of an adolescent girl, plays a critical role in the aftermath of a mother's death. Most adolescents transfer much of the energy they once invested in their parents to their peers or a "best friend" so common at this time. In fact, a teen is more likely to turn to a friend for help during her bereavement than to any other source of support. But because most adolescents have little experience with profound loss, a girl's peers often are unable to validate her feelings, or to understand the magnitude of her loss.

Robin, twenty-seven, who was sixteen when her mother died, remembers how difficult her peer relations were at that time. She still remembers and appreciates the classmate who helped her through the following year:

> I couldn't deal with most of my friends at the time. They would complain about how much homework they had to do, and I would think, "Big deal. How can you be upset about that when my mother has died?" I also felt there was a competition between them about who I would depend on the most. That drove me crazy. I felt I couldn't say anything to one of them without the others feeling they'd been slighted and getting upset. I had one friend who would always look at me like I was a lost puppy dog and constantly say, "Oh, I feel so *sorry* for you." I felt like *I* had to make *her* feel better, to help her feel that I was okay so she didn't have to feel bad. I could barely maintain myself. How could I possibly make anyone else feel better?
>
> But when my mom was sick, I did some volunteer work at a refugee center for Vietnamese people. I had another friend who was working there with me, who I hadn't been very close with before. She was a very analytical person and she had that ability to remain objective, to not get emotionally involved. She really talked with me about my mom's illness and death. She

never said, "I feel so sorry for you, you poor little thing." Instead, she would ask, "What is this like for you?" She allowed me a place to talk about how I felt without having to feel that I was being pitied. I think a lot of my other friends were so freaked out and scared of the implications for them, and for their mothers, that they couldn't really talk about it with me. This particular friend didn't know my mom, which made a difference, too. All my other friends knew her, so it was even more real to them than it was to this friend. I ended up spending a lot of time with her and talking, which was a big help.

Few adolescent anxieties are greater than that of the girl who fears rejection or an upset within her clique, especially when family members coping with the loss have less time to devote to her. Adolescents, as they undergo symbolic separation from their families, actually have much in common with orphans: Characterizing both groups are feelings of alienation, isolation, and low self-esteem; turbulent home conditions; and a fear of being left out. Adolescents without mothers are often deeply ashamed of having lost the parent other girls view as so central to a daughter's well-being. The teenaged girl who thinks her mother's absence will make her appear different or abnormal—and therefore subject to rejection from her peers—often will avoid talking about the loss or revealing any anger, depression, guilt, anxiety, or confusion to her friends, to her friends, adopting a stoic and unemotional coping style instead. This is in part to conform to "acceptable" group behavior, but may also be a self-protective act to shield her from overwhelming feelings of anxiety and grief. The more composed a teen appears, however, the greater her risk is of experiencing long-term, unresolved grief, and researchers now know that unresolved grief in turn places individuals at risk for depression, physical illness, and drug and alcohol abuse.

At the same time the teenager pushes the mourner's emotions aside, she may also be expending a great deal of energy to appear as normal as she can to the outside world. It's almost as if she's saying, "Look—I'm captain of the soccer team, class treasurer, an honors student, and the lead in the school play. Nothing's wrong with me!" Her self-definition began forming in a family with a mother, only to be changed by the force of an event she didn't anticipate and couldn't reverse. To let her identity continue developing along this new pathway would mean having to define herself as a teen without a mother—not exactly the description she would have chosen for herself, and not one she wants to advertise. So she tries to manufacture a new identity, one that exists independent of her past.

In this quest to reinvent herself, she frequently aims for a persona of competence and control. It's no coincidence that motherless women who report having eating disorders and drug or alcohol addictions say these compulsions began during their teen years. Adolescence is a time of anxiety and exploration anyway, but for the motherless daughter who needs to feel in command of her body or environment, addictive or self-destructive behavior is a common manifestation of suppressed grief. Bereaved children often internalize their feelings, but adolescents have more resources for acting out. Juliet, twenty-five, started smoking and drinking the year her mother was diagnosed with cancer, and every time her mother's condition worsened, she acted out. "The day before she started chemotherapy I was caught shoplifting with $30 in my pocket," she recalls. "I went and stole a $1.69 bottle of fingernail polish and got arrested. Then she went into remission, but the day she had her thyroid removed because of a precancerous growth, I got drunk at a dance, threw up on everybody, and almost got into a fight. I was acting out with pot and alcohol when she died, and it just progressed until I was about twenty-three, and finally sobered up." When change is occurring both around her and within her, the adolescent motherless daughter looks for comfort in what she can—or thinks she can—control.

The New Woman of the House

Almost immediately after my family completed the eight-day mourning period designated by Jewish law, I began driving my brother for haircuts, taking my sister to the dentist, and carrying the household's incidental cash in my wallet. I even inherited my mother's car. I'd somehow stepped on a fast-forward button that transported me from seventeen to forty-two, and though I never questioned taking over my mother's role like this, I secretly counted the minutes until I could flee. When the time to begin college arrived the following autumn, I was out of town so quickly that I left skid marks. And then my sister, at fifteen, had to take over where I'd left off.

Adolescent daughters often become involuntary minimothers to fathers and siblings when the biological mother falls ill, leaves, or dies. An unfortunate byproduct of a culture that still views child care and domestic duties as "women's work" is that the eldest or next-to-eldest daughter—even when an older brother lives at home—is the one expected to step into the mother's role. When the daughter is an adolescent, her very identity is at risk. After Mariana's mother died, Mariana had to take over the household chores at sixteen, including responsibility for her younger sister. "When you're sixteen and your mother always did those things before, you respond like, 'What do you *mean* I have to do the laundry? What do you *mean* I have to do all the dishes?'" she says. "Those first few months were very difficult. My aunt, who I called Mrs. Clean, would come in and inspect the house. It would drive me crazy. To this day, I hate doing dishes. I was also cooking dinner every night, and trying to take care of my sister, who was always a wild kid. In other words, I was doing all the normal things a teenager is supposed to do during the day at school, and then I'd come home and cook and clean, like a mother or a wife."

Faced with this kind of responsibility, a girl has three options: She can try to meet the demands fully, meet them partially, or not meet them at all. Sometimes, if she's old enough or autonomous enough to resist actively, she refuses to take on her mother's role—but then feels guilty for abandoning her family. Sometimes she realizes that she alone cannot meet the family's needs only after trying and failing for several years. "Girls who have to take over their mother's roles can run into all kinds of problems," says Phyllis Klaus, MFT, LCSW, a psychotherapist in Berkeley and Santa Rosa, California, who frequently counsels motherless women. "Either they become overachievers and exhaust themselves trying to meet their own expectations, or they get out of the responsibility in some way that's unhealthy, such as getting into a bad relationship or running away."

The adolescent who must become the nurse for an ailing mother, a parent for younger siblings, or a caretaker for a grieving father may develop characteristics, such as compassion and empathy, that serve her well in the future. Many of the admirable qualities society associates with caregivers—and especially with women—surface in the teenage girl who must care for others. And some research suggests that children who take responsibility for others after the death of a loved one gain a sense of competence and are more likely to accommodate the loss successfully. But the caretaking role is a premature one for an adolescent girl in Western cultures, and it hurtles her into the responsibilities of a later developmental stage before she can complete the one she was already in. It also forces her into maturity at exactly the time she needs to regress and be taken care of.

There's nothing like the death of a parent to make an adolescent grow up fast. Her thoughts, responsibilities, and realizations mature tenfold overnight, but her body and environment constantly remind her that she's not fully grown. It's hard to be a real adult when you're still taking a bus to school every day. "I felt so much older than people my age," says Francine, thirty-two, who was thirteen when her mother suffered a massive heart attack that caused a permanent vegetative state, and seventeen when she moved out on her own. "Most of my friends now are still ten years older than me. I always wanted to hang out with people who were independent and on their own, like me. Yet at times I feel like a baby. My husband says sometimes I'm so mature and capable and other times I seem like I'm barely an adult. I had to grow up so fast, I wasn't able to be a kid. One of the reasons I recently decided to work off hours and have three-day work weeks was to have time to be a kid. I'm glad that I finally feel safe enough to do that now."

So much of the last twenty-four years of my life has been about trying to figure out what feels right for my chronological age. I've often felt that when my mother died, I split into even thirds. A part of me immediately aged to forty-two and took over some of her concerns; another part of me got stuck at seventeen, hanging on to the image of my mother and the relationship we had then; and a third part, the one I've often felt I know the least about, developed along normal lines. For many years I wanted nothing more than the ability to spread my arms and grasp forty-two with one hand and seventeen with the other, and then to pull both ends in tight, until they met somewhere in between.

Young Adults (The Twenties)

If adolescence is all about forming an identity, the twenties are about taking that identity and putting it to use in the larger world. That's why a woman who loses her mother at this time may well be the most overlooked and misunderstood daughter of all. She's the one most likely to be living outside the home, already caring for herself or for a family of her own—which also makes her the most likely to feel frustrated and confused when the loss of a mother reduces her to an emotional puddle. And she's the one who most often hears, "When you were twenty-three? Well, you really didn't need a mother anymore," as if a mother's importance somehow diminishes to zero the moment her daughter emerges from adolescence.

A departure for college, marriage, or a move out on one's own all serve as developmental milestones, but the act of establishing a new home base doesn't sever our emotional ties to the one left behind. Paradoxically, a successful launch depends on the young adult's continuing to have a secure base—usually the nuclear family—to return to at times of stress. She's in a revolving-door period of her life, trying things out and coming back home for encouragement or respite.

"If a woman loses her mother during early adulthood, from nineteen to maybe twenty-three, the loss presents a conflict because it touches every base," says Phyllis Klaus. "She's at the point of really beginning to develop her own career and move out, and that's when she needs encouragement. But instead, she may need to go back to the family house and be helpful. Also, because the level of intellectual understanding is so much greater, all the thoughts of 'How will I manage all of the events coming up in my life without my mother?' come up. So she loses not only her mother but also the encouragement and revalidation of the self she needs as well as the real sharing she would want to do with her mother at that time."

It's not much different from the toddler who ventures forth in stages and repeatedly returns to the mother for security and reassurance, except that now the child is a woman, her journeys span several weeks or months, and her reconnections may be by e-mail or by telephone.

"There's an enormous yearning to be in relation to a home ground in your twenties and thirties," says Naomi Lowinsky. "And mother is a reference point. You might be mad at her and not want to be like her, but your mother is the source. She's the origin. You're always kind of looking back at her to see where you are. If you're twenty-five and you know your mother is full of bullshit, you know where *you* are. It's very defining. But if you're twenty-five and you've lost your mother, how do you know where you are? It's really, really difficult to not know where you are at that age. You need to be in relation to something. Dad may be really important and helpful, but he's not a woman. His is a different kind of help, a kind of attention that's contrasexual."

For daughters of the post–World War II generations, the twenties are the period when a daughter's experience begins to differ from her mother's the most. A mother who married at twenty-three and gave birth to a daughter by twenty-five may watch that daughter postpone marriage and motherhood until her thirties. Today, a woman whose job opportunities were limited to teaching and sales may well have raised daughters who run companies or obtain advanced degrees. Many of us have had access to education, employment, health care (including cohabitation, birth control, and legal abortions) and marital options (including uncontested divorce) that women of previous generations could only imagine. Civil rights, the sexual revolution, the women's movement—all have contributed to differentiating our experiences from our mothers' and have allowed us to define our own identities by the distance between us and them.

As cultural and social beings, mothers and daughters are rarely produced by the same mold. But because of their powerful early bond and their shared femaleness, differences between the generations can make both sides uneasy. Mothers and adult daughters can be paralyzed by assumptions, unable to communicate much beyond nitpicking and complaint. A mother wants a daughter to become what she once was—or what she never got to be—and expects her daughter to want the same. A daughter is defensive about the choices she's made, believing that her mother can't possibly understand them, or her.

As a daughter matures, and especially as she becomes a mother herself, her vision of her mother typically evolves. Like the child who first realizes her mother can't solve all her problems, the young adult begins to see her mother more clearly as a multidimensional woman with human limitations, one with both strengths and weaknesses. And though the daughter retains some of her earlier desires for the perfect mother, she also becomes more willing to loosen her expectations. The mother, in turn, begins to accept her daughter as an autonomous individual, one with the ability to make and implement decisions for herself. Both sides give and take, push and pull, ideally arriving at an ideological compromise based, if not on understanding, then at least on mutual respect.

From the moment a girl first leaves her mother's side, she is always trying to get back to the mother of her earliest memories. The attention and affection that her mother once provided become the ideal for which a daughter continues to search; departure was a necessity, but reunion is perpetually the goal. Although the mother's place in her adult daughter's life is hardly the site she occupied two decades before, an adult reconciliation can lead to a second bonding for a mother and daughter. After the adolescent girl completes her individuation from the family, she often comes full circle to reunite with her mother as a tentative partner in a woman-to-woman camaraderie.

The twenties are the years most women pinpoint as the time they first realized their mothers had qualities—empathy, wisdom, experience—they would value in a friend. To lose a mother at this time, just at the point when one seems to have found her again, feels like a cruel trick. Thirty-five-year-old Christine, who had a particularly tumultuous adolescence, had just begun to enjoy a close relationship with her mother when death broke their bond.

I was eighteen when my mother was diagnosed with breast cancer and twenty-three when she died. I was living out of state at the time. We had a fairly good relationship because I wasn't around her all the time. She missed me, I missed her, and we wrote a lot. She did come to visit me once, and that was a lot of fun. When she died, it was harder for me than for my sisters, I think, because I'd been so far away. I felt very guilty about that, and my sisters also laid a bunch of guilt on me as well. That was hard, too. My mom did say to me, "Go out there and have a good time. Do whatever you feel you need to do." My sisters didn't understand that. They were always upset that I moved away and didn't come back for eight years. I think my mom was surprised, too, but I think she actually was glad that I was out traveling and doing things.

I was very fortunate that we had established a relationship before she died. But I thought, "Gee, that's not fair. We just became friends, really." When I was a little kid, my father was a waiter, and we used to go into the bar and drink kiddy cocktails. When I got older, I could go in and have a real drink with my dad. It was the same thing with my mother. I was able to actually be an adult with her and talk about adult things. We didn't carry all the other crap from the past to that point. I had my life, she had her life, and we had some fun.

The desire to reunite with one's mother is a developmental impulse that arises whether the mother is alive or not. A daughter who, during childhood or adolescence, lost her mother, reaches her twenties and feels ready to reconnect—but with whom? With what? In my early and midtwenties, I felt the need for a strong female figure in my life for the first time. Those years were characterized by what felt like a desperate search for someone to guide me, but the person I wanted to connect with most was missing, and my efforts to replace her always seemed to fall short. Twenty-nine-year-old Karen, who lost her mother nine years ago, expressed my sentiments exactly when she said, "It's almost a rite of passage in a woman's life to be able to come back to her mother and be friends, to meet on an equal ground. But when she's not there, you can't do that. I felt kind of like I was in limbo, waiting for something to fill that void, some way I could have that coming back. And I can't. But it's kind of haunting, because the need doesn't go away." When a mother dies too young, something inside her daughter always feels incomplete. There's a missing piece she continues to look for, an emptiness she keeps trying to fill.

The loss of the mother as an adult friend is what therapists call a "secondary loss," which may not be apparent at the moment of actual separation but reveals itself to us over time. Twentysomething daughters often leap ahead to imagine the secondary losses—no one to help plan a wedding, no one to consult about child rearing, no grandmother for the kids—they envision as long-term effects of mother loss. This is a scenario ripe for idealization. The mother who bandaged an eight-year-old's knee probably would not, if she had lived, have been able to fix an eighteen-year-old daughter's heartbreak, or stop the pain of a twenty-six-year-old daughter's labor, yet at such moments that is the mother we long for, the only one we can remember, and the one we desperately want.

Would my mother, who quit her job in 1964 at the age of twenty-five to raise me, have given me the advice I sought in 1988 to solve a problem at the corporate level? Would she, a virgin at her wedding, have been a supportive listener when I had a pregnancy scare at eighteen? Or would she have been horrified by my standards of sexual morality, which seem to differ so dramatically from hers? When I try to piece together a more mature version of the mother I knew, the one who taught me to use tampons and spoke freely of her own methods of birth control, I come up with a question mark every time. My mother, as a woman in her sixties, is mostly a mystery to me. In my mind, she's an eternal forty-two, and as her daughter, I never get past seventeen.

There's a sad beauty to this, that my mother will remain forever young. I'll never have to watch her grow old or have to worry about her care during old age. But this also means I will pass my mother and grow beyond her very soon. Back in my twenties, I'd already felt this starting to begin. Although we came of age in different eras, my adolescence and hers were fundamentally the same: we loved our parents but disagreed with them, took final exams in public high schools, went off to college, and fell in love. But she married at twenty-one, and the choices I made then—to support myself, to go

on for a graduate degree, and to delay marriage and motherhood until my thirties—are the ones that firmly separated my adult experience from hers.

Well, this is nothing unusual: Most of my friends whose mothers
are still alive can say exactly the same thing. Daughters frequently
surpass their mothers. That's just fact. But many of my achievements
have been tinged with bittersweet, because they are things my mother
once hoped to accomplish but never got the time to do. I've visited a
dozen foreign countries. I went to my brother's wedding. I saw the
first day of a new century. In two more years, I'll turn forty-three.

The Later Years

I've been consistently surprised by the number of women who have
contacted me over the years to be interviewed about mother loss,
even though they had been in their thirties, forties, or beyond when
their mothers died. Because I was so much younger when I lost my
mother, I naively assumed a woman past the age of twenty-five or
thirty would accept the death of a mother in her sixties or seventies
as part of the natural course of events. She wouldn't feel as if something vital had been ripped from her prematurely.

I couldn't have been more wrong. I remember an afternoon not
long after I'd moved to New York to write the first edition of this
book. I was shopping for a couch in a furniture store on Broadway,
and as the final purchase was being rung up, the saleswoman, Sonia,
and I began to talk. One conversation led to another, and then I was
telling her about my work. When I explained I was writing about
young women who had lost their mothers, she pushed aside the pa-
perwork and grasped my arm above the elbow. Blinking back tears,
she asked, "Do you want to interview me? My mother died just a
few years ago. I wasn't a child—I'm forty-two now. But let me tell
you, it isn't easy at any age." And one of my friends in her mid-
forties is now shuttling back and forth between Los Angeles and
Phoenix every other week to help her ailing mother, who is in the
midst of chemotherapy, get her final affairs in order. Her experience
is just as frightening and heartwrenching as any young woman's I've
ever seen. Even harder, in some ways, because not only must this

friend come to terms with full knowledge of her mother's illness and its likely outcome, but the tremendous amount of caretaking responsibility she's taken on as an only child greatly complicates the emotional and practical tasks she has to juggle back in Los Angeles as a grieving daughter, a mother, and a wife.

Elizabeth Nager and Brian DeVries, two researchers at San Francisco State University studying the relatively new phenomenon of online memorials created by adult daughters for their deceased mothers, acknowledge that the death of a parent during one's middle age is a common and expected event. Between the ages of forty and sixty, more than 50 percent of American women will experience the death of one or both parents. Still, Nager and De Vries say, mother loss during adulthood "represents myriad emotions and psychological experiences. A parent's death represents the loss of the history and memories that shaped and remain part of that relationship. A parent's death signals a different sense of time and self as the buffer between life and death dissipates. The death severs, or forever alters, the attachment bond that was established in childhood."

Middle-aged daughters continue to miss and long for their mothers long after a loss, even when the death was expected and accepted. Several studies on adults who have recently lost mothers reveal that:

- Three months after the loss, 80 percent say they still miss their mothers very much.
- 74 percent said losing a mother was one of the hardest things they had ever dealt with.
- 67 percent continued to experience emotional reactions, including sadness and crying, for one to five years after the death.
- 86 percent reported a shift in their priorities after a mother's death. Sixty-six percent reported making changes in their professional lives one to five years after the loss.
- 40 percent reported they grew closer to their siblings. Twenty-five percent said they were experiencing more sibling conflict than before. This was usually in families when siblings were perceived to be unhelpful as a parent was dying, or where sibling relationships had been strained from the start.

- 36 percent developed a closer relationship with their fathers after their mothers died. But 18 percent say their father-daughter relationships became more conflicted or distant.
- 75 percent saw it as a blessing that their mothers died when they did.
- 72 percent did not feel it was unfair that their mothers had died.
- 80 percent believe they will be with their mothers again some day.

Women who were younger—closer to forty rather than sixty—had a harder time accepting the loss, as did those who'd had positive mother-daughter relationships. Daughters who were still very emotionally dependent on their mothers also had difficulty adjusting. I have also met numerous women at seminars and lectures who devoted years of their lives to caring for ill mothers, sometimes to the exclusion of marrying or having children of their own. To these daughters, the eventual death of the mother requires a reorganization not just of daily living habits and responsibilities, but also a relinquishing of one's identity as caregiver.

The tensions an older adult daughter experiences when her mother dies are no less or no more important that those of theyoung adult, but they are different. Because an adult daughter is likely to occupy more roles—lover, wife, mother, grandmother, co-worker—her relationship with her mother is usually less central to her identity and also less central to her mental health. Yet her mother may occupy more roles in *her* life, too: maternal grandmother to her children, mother-in-law to her husband, and adult confidante. These are also valid losses in a daughter's life, and ones that must be grieved.

Research from the Wellesley College Center for Research on Women reminds us that because of men's shorter life expectancy, the relationship a daughter has with her mother is likely to be one of the longest-lasting relationships of her life. When this is cut short, the death is perplexing and profound, no matter what the daughter's age. She is still her mother's child, and the loss leaves her feeling abandoned, angry, and sad.

The adult daughter does, however, confront the loss with a relatively intact personality and more mature coping skills than an adolescent or a child. Instead of having her personality emerge from a grieving period, she brings an already-formed personality to it. Although intense crying, denial, or withdrawal may occupy her initial mourning cycle, she understands at some level that adjusting to the death of a parent is a developmental task of middle age. Losing a parent at this time violates fewer assumptions she has about her future. In the healthiest scenario, she internalizes the positive aspects of her mother that she wants to carry on, rejects the negative ones that troubled her, and continues on—motherless, but intact.

"Although the primal bond between mother and daughter may become warped, twisted, and violated, it never can be severed," writes Martha A. Robbins in *Midlife Women and Death of Mother*. A motherless woman continues to renegotiate her relationship with her mother throughout her life, changing her perceptions and trying to find a place for each new image as it develops.

A woman who lost her mother during childhood, adolescence, or young adulthood often finds herself mourning the secondary losses as she reaches certain maturational checkpoints of middle age and beyond, and longs for the guidance of a more mature, experienced woman. Says Caroline, fifty-three, who was eleven when her mother died, "I've really grieved for her a lot as an adult. I could have used the passing down of woman-knowledge, to know what it's like to be an adult woman and to go through menopause. And what it's like to look back at your life, and think about dying. Of course, Mother never got to do that. She was forty-seven when she died. She probably never went through menopause. I don't know. But all the wise-woman ways that she *could* have had—I'm grieving for the loss of those." Even though Caroline has had two stepmothers she's loved and many close female friends, her mother's knowledge is what she's wanted all these years.

Our mothers are our most direct connection to our history and our gender. Regardless of how well we think they did their job, the void their absence creates in our lives is never completely filled again. Says thirty-three-year-old Suzanne, whose mother died three years ago, "When my mother died, a lot of people tried to comfort me by saying, 'Well, you still have your father. You still have a brother and sister. You have a wonderful husband and beautiful children.' And you know what? That's all true. That's all completely true. But I still don't have my mother."

Chapter Three

Cause and Effect
No Way Is the Best Way

MY MOTHER DIED the kind of death no one ever likes to discuss. It was sudden. It was dramatic. It was a panicky, dissonant scene. Her body weakened by a ubiquitous cancer, her spirit squashed by false hopes, she crawled onto the ambulance stretcher and sobbed on her back between the drawn curtains in the hospital emergency room. She no longer had the strength to sit up. I held her hand until the doctor arrived and my father sent me into the hall. Leaning against a row of silver pay phones, I stared at the tile floor in disbelief. I had never seen my mother that helpless before or watched a body fail to such a degree. I had never known such defeat.

But this is all emotion I recall here, because that's what I always remember first. The visuals are more difficult to share. The final stage of cancer, when a person struggles to maintain control over a body that is failing her so completely, is a heartwrenching sight. "That's your mother, that's your mother, that's your mother," I had to force myself to remember each time I looked down at the hospital bed. Sixteen months of chemotherapy had transformed her into a woman of indeterminate age, had ballooned her body and stolen nearly all her dark, curly hair. When the cancer reached her liver, her abdomen swelled so large that at the moment of death she looked ready to give birth. There was a sick irony about it all. A few hours before she lost consciousness, she lost the capacity for audible speech, and though we tried to decipher the desperate, honking noises she made, we never found out what she was trying to say.

My father later told me that her last words were "Take care of my children," which she whispered to him just as she slid into a coma. I'd like to believe she somehow managed to force that dying request through. You hear about people who've been unconscious for weeks suddenly opening their eyes or making the sign of the cross or even sitting bolt upright and barking out a coherent sentence moments before they die, so I suppose anything can be true. Anything, in those last moments, if you want it to be badly enough.

But those final words are my father's story, not mine. By now, we each have our own version, our own mythology, our own fragile grasp of the truth. My sister remembers a moment one way, I remember it another, and a friend of mine from high school reminds me of parts I could swear never happened at all. Fact or fiction, I'll never know. The only story I can believe in is my own, and in my version, my mother doesn't have a deathbed request because she never knows she's going to die.

What she told me, what I heard, what I created to fill in the crevasses: It's all pieced together like an awkward mosaic, forming a jerky path that somehow leads to a semiprivate hospital room. I know it began when an allergist found a lump in her left armpit in 1979. She had her gynecologist check it. "It's nothing," he said. "And besides, you're only forty. Come back in six months and I'll check it again." Six months later, he said the lump was exactly the same size. "If it hasn't grown, it can't be cancer," he told her. "There's nothing wrong with you. It's just a cyst. You're fine." One afternoon two months later, as we sat together at the kitchen table, eating peanuts and dumping the shells into a green Tupperware bowl, she said she should probably get it removed, just to be safe, but that operations were expensive and money was tight that year. And after another six months, or maybe it was more, she finally went to a different gynecologist, who immediately sent her to a radiologist for a mammogram. Who sent her to a surgeon for a biopsy. Who shook his head and recommended she get a second opinion, just to be sure.

As I sat on the hospital bed after her mastectomy, she told me the cancer had spread to some of her lymph nodes but not to others, which meant, she said, that the doctors had been able to remove it all. Preventive chemotherapy began the following week. She responded to the first six months of treatment, and a CAT scan in November was negative. The following April, she came home from the next scan smiling. "All clear," she said. "Good news." In May, when the oncologist started a new regimen of drugs, she told me it was just a precaution because her white blood count was a bit low.

In my story, we all saw cancer and chemotherapy as temporary inconveniences, as though my mother's illness were a minor malfunction that any trained handyman could fix. When I found her crying in the bathroom, holding the first handful of hair, I reminded her it would all grow back within the year. We turned the purchase of her first wig into a comedy sketch, parading me through the store in Farrah Fawcett curls and agreeing I was never meant to be a blond. In May, she started knitting me a ski sweater she would finish before her treatment ended that fall. Only as she grew noticeably weaker and her stomach began to swell did it occur to me that something might be going seriously wrong.

I wonder: What level of precision determines when a body crosses the line between functional and dying? Is there a distinct moment, a millisecond or a nanosecond, when the number of healthy cells suddenly drops too low to permit the recovery of life? Or is there a single cell whose abnormal division creates a threshold where previously there was none, just one outlaw cell to blame? My mother seemed to speed across that line so fast. As I remember it, she was sitting in a reclining chair in front of the television one evening, bouncing her foot and impatiently waiting for her abdomen to recede, and the next morning she just didn't get out of bed.

When my father, whose religious affiliation had formerly consisted of writing an annual check to cover synagogue dues, took an hour one afternoon to go speak to a rabbi, I stayed with my mother alone. She was lying downstairs by then, at sub-basement level, where the air was cooler against her flushed skin. When I carried her to the bathroom, she sat on the toilet and handed me a wad of tissue without looking me in the eye, too ashamed to admit she wasn't strong enough to use it herself. "I'm so sorry you have to do this," she said over and over again. As I was trying to help her back into bed, she stumbled, fell onto her side, and cried out, "I just want to die already. If I have to live like this, I just want to die."

"Don't *say* that," I ordered, as I tried to slip a pillow under her head. "You don't mean it. Don't ever say that again."

I'm sure I didn't think it then, but now I know that hour was the closest I've ever come to hell, sitting in a dark basement with a dying mother, the air-conditioning turned up high in the middle of a heat wave in July. Everything around me had been reduced to sets of extremes: life and death, heat and ice, crazy hope and utter despair. Somewhere in that hour I lost all relation to a middle ground, and I didn't regain it for what ultimately became a very long time.

In the morning, my mother woke up vomiting black bile, and my father called an ambulance. We'd done all we could for her at home. As she rocked from side to side in an agitated sleep downstairs, he sat me down in the living room and told me she was going to die. "Your mother has to go to the hospital, and I don't think she's going to come back"—that's what he said.

I stared hard at the upholstery on his chair, blue and green paisley paramecia floating in a beige sea. When the muscles in my neck constricted, I could almost see their cilia beat. "How did it get this bad?" I asked, still eyeing the chair.

"I've known it for a long time," he said. "Since the operation last spring."

"You *what*?"

"The surgeon came out of the OR and told me he couldn't remove it all," he said. "He just closed her back up. He said, 'At most, I give her a year.' But how could I tell her, or you kids?"

You *what*? I thought, and he saw the accusation in my eyes.

"We've been lucky," he said, rising from his chair with his palm pressed against his forehead as he heard the attendants on the front path outside. "We had her four months longer than she was expected to live."

Lucky? I thought, as I stood behind an emergency room curtain an hour later, holding my mother's hand and trying to press ice chips between her cracked and blood-stained lips. *Could someone identify the lucky people here?*

When my father left to take care of the insurance forms, my mother and I were alone again. She lay on the stretcher and cried with her eyes closed, the tears oozing through the corners. "I'm so afraid," she whispered. "I'm so afraid I'm going to die." She tugged on my forearm. "Tell me," she pleaded. "Hope, tell me I'm not dying."

What does a daughter owe her mother in this last moment together? To do as she asked would mean to lie to her. To tell the truth would mean to dishonor her request. I had no easy answer, and allegiances were tricky: Was I to side with the parent I trusted most, who had borne me, or the one with whom I'd be left? My fingernails cut painful half moons in my palms as I whispered, "I'll stay right here with you. I won't leave you alone." Even as I said it, I knew I was avoiding the point, and I've never quite overcome the feeling that in that most critical moment, I somehow failed.

As the family members arrived one by one that afternoon, my aunt and I sat together on the black vinyl couch in the hospital waiting room. "This is a nightmare, a total nightmare, and I'm surrounded by clowns," I said. We were mixing our metaphors, talking in non sequiturs, but nobody seemed to notice or to care. There was too much to process, too fast. My mother had just telephoned her oncologist from the hospital bed. "What's happening to me?" she asked him as I held the phone against her ear, and I could tell whatever he said still wasn't the truth. That's when I realized the extent of this, how many people had been hiding information from her all along.

The next evening she slipped into a coma, and the attending physician gathered the family in the hall. He warned us she might stay that way for days or weeks, even as long as a month. He told us we should try to prepare. *"A month?"* I thought, covering my mouth to push the protest back in. "How can we go on like this for a *month*?" Maybe my mother sensed the same. She died with my father holding her hand at 2:43 the next morning, as my sister and I slept on the couch in the waiting room down the hall.

The night before my mother died, I had dipped behind the curtain divider and showed the woman in the next bed a photograph of the family taken the previous spring. "I wanted you to see her as she really was," I said. "And not to remember her as she is now." But even as I said it, I knew the words were meant for me. It took years before I could remember my mother as she was before she learned she had breast cancer, years before I could bypass the terrible image of her lying jaundiced and comatose in a hospital bed, even though the first image lasted for almost two decades and the second for only two days.

When people ask how my mother died, I say, "She had breast cancer." What this tells them is the cause of death. What it tells me is that I can still see the inside of the shop where we bought her first prosthesis, and can hear her voice singing out false CAT scan results, and can feel her hand gripping mine from the hospital bed. I may be able to tell you what my mother died from in only four words, but their subtext fills the page.

My mother died from cancer. My mother committed suicide. One day, my mother disappeared. These may be grammatically simple sentences, but they aren't simple statements. To sit up all night with a mother in pain, to find her suicide note on the kitchen counter, or to hear the graphic details of her accidental death are all images that, unless we block them out completely, remain with us forever. Psychologists agree that the cause of a parent's death—along with the child's developmental stage and the surviving caretaker's ability to cope—is a leading factor in determining a child's long-term adaption. As Nan Birnbaum explains, the cause of death influences how the family reacts, what type of support system is available, and what kind of stresses the child has experienced before the actual loss. "Let's say an eight-year-old girl's mom has been sick with cancer for three years, off and on," she says. "That means from the time she was five, her mom has undergone various treatments, has been under various anxieties, and has had to cope with keeping up her relationship with the kids. All that has had some impact on the child already, before the mother actually dies. So that's a different story than an eight-year-old whose mom is killed in a car accident. One is not necessarily more traumatic than another, but the child's growth is affected in different ways."

Of 149 motherless women who knew their mothers' causes of death, 44 percent reported cancer; 10 percent, heart failure; 10 percent, accidents; and 7 percent, suicide. Three percent each cited pneumonia; infectious diseases; complications of childbirth, abortion, or miscarriage; kidney failure; and cerebral hemorrhage. The remainder named alcoholism, overdoses, aneurysms, strokes, and complications from surgery. Five women said they didn't know.

In the Motherless Daughters support groups I've led, part of the first session is always devoted to talking about a mother's cause of death. Women who've lost mothers to long-term illnesses always believe that losing her quickly and not witnessing her suffering would have been easier. Women whose mothers died as the result of accidents or other sudden deaths disagree: they would have done anything, they say, to have had time to say goodbye. Only after they hear each others' stories do they concede there's no good way to lose a loved one—just, in the words of one twenty-six-year-old woman, "different kinds of hell." Every cause is painful, and every loss leaves us wondering how we could have acted otherwise to prevent the death. But because different causes of death provoke sufficiently different responses—anger toward suicide victims; blame for homicide, terrorism, and war; helplessness and fear with natural disasters; and hopelessness with terminal disease—the specific way a mother dies or leaves determines how her daughter will respond.

Long-term Illness

When Kelly contracted a urinary tract infection a few years ago, she was blunt with the gynecologist who diagnosed it. "I don't like doctors," she told her. "I don't trust modern medicine, and I won't take pills." What she didn't tell her doctor was the reason why. Ever since her mother's death from metastatic breast cancer fifteen years ago, Kelly, now thirty, has associated the medical profession with chemotherapy and failure.

> My mother was sick for three years. She received massive doses of radiation the summer before she died, and I was the only child still living at home. I remember going with her to the hospital and watching them prep her for radiation treatment and just thinking, "This is insane." I have no doubt that my feelings about doctors and medicine go back to those years, seeing her pumped up with IVs and basically being used as a pincushion. She looked like a junkie, with bruises all over her arms. It got to the point where she didn't have any place left for them to take a blood sample from. I just thought, "This is not for me."
>
> A few days before she died, I heard my father talking with the doctor in the hospital. He said, "No way. We just can't put

her through another surgery." I finally broke down that night, because I realized at that point that everything had run out, that nothing more could be done, and it was just a matter of how long her body would hold out. That experience shaped my belief in the humaneness of euthanasia and my resistance toward heroic last-minute efforts of medicine or technology. I keep Dr. Kevorkian's name in the back of my mind, thinking that if anything happened to me, he's the first person I'd call.

I won't even go to doctors now unless I'm really sick, and I don't like taking any kind of medicine. When I got the UTI, my doctor was very understanding. She explained that because of the bacteria, she couldn't recommend any natural or homeopathic treatment that would work. I had to take the antibiotics, and I had to take the whole dose. I took two days' worth and stopped. I just hate anything that has to do with medicine.

Like Kelly, daughters of terminally ill mothers usually face several conflicts at once: watching the physical deterioration of someone they love, feeling helpless and angry, trying to maintain as normal a life as possible, and having to readjust each time a new crisis develops. That's a lot to cope with at once. After fifteen years, Kelly has overcome the guilt she once felt for subjecting an ill mother to her adolescent strife, but she still mistrusts doctors and is terrified of developing cancer herself.

Though the actual death is the most profound loss, a child whose mother dies from a long-term illness usually experiences other losses throughout its duration. The family's previous way of life may vanish as the group reorganizes to accommodate a sick member; the active attention of one or both parents may diminish, leaving some of the child's needs unmet; financial resources may dwindle; and a daughter's perception of her mother might change several times. A younger daughter may, as an adult, remember her mother only as a patient, never having had a relationship with a mother who's healthy. An older daughter may resent having to give up the interests and concerns of her peer group to spend more time at home. As the illness progresses, a daughter may have to become a caretaker for her mother—a distinct and premature role reversal that can make both sides angry and resentful.

A daughter also finds that her assumptions about parental power are shattered. No longer is her mother an all-powerful icon in the family, the one with an awesome ability to shelter her children from distress or harm. "When a child witnesses the slow deterioration of a parent, he or she sees not only impending death but the collapse and destruction of a powerful protector as well," Maxine Harris explains.

Daughters of all ages might find that they have no one in the family to talk with about their fears, because their parents and siblings are preoccupied with the same stresses. A mother is a daughter's natural refuge at times of distress, but a mother often can't fulfill this role when she's overwhelmed by worries of her own.

This was particularly troubling for Stacey, who grew up as an only child in a single-parent home. Her father died when she was nine, and her mother was diagnosed with the virus that causes AIDS when Stacey was fifteen. For the next four years, Stacey took care of her mother, attended school, and tried to cope with the stigma and shame surrounding AIDS—all without the emotional support of the mother who'd been her closest confidante. "I was losing her as she was alive," Stacey recalls. "I remember a few times when I was sick and I wanted to go and be with her, just to lie next to her and feel that comfort. But I couldn't, because my germs were dangerous to her. I couldn't go to her to be taken care of, and that hurt a lot. My father died suddenly, and I remember thinking, 'I wish that I'd known, so I could be by his side.' And there was my mother and it was the slow process, and I think that was even harder."

Most therapists agree that sudden death is more difficult in the short term, because all major family adjustments have to take place while shock and disbelief still fill the house. A death that's anticipated—provided the facts are out in the open and discussed, which they often are not—permits families to prepare gradually for the loss. Thirty-two-year-old Samantha, who was fourteen when her mother died after a two-year illness, remembers how her mother tried to prepare her five children for coping without her. "She knew she was going to die, so she did certain things she thought were important from her frame of reference," Samantha recalls. "Like, 'How is this household going to function when I'm not here? Who's going to clean the house? Who's going to cook?' She used that period of time to pull us all together and teach us how to do those things. She never said, 'I'm going to teach all of you how to cook,' but she was doing it from her bed. We all took turns making dinner, and each day she would explain how to cook that night's meal. We would run back and forth between the kitchen and her bedroom to write down the recipe and get verification. So we were being taught without even knowing it." After her mother died, Samantha and her four siblings ran the house without much turmoil, which she says helped them feel competent and self-assured, both as children and, later, as adults.

Long-term illness also allows a family time for anticipatory grieving, in which mourning begins before the mother dies. When a daughter knows what the outcome of her mother's illness will be, she has time to adjust to the idea piece by piece, relinquishing one hope and expectation at a time.

As twenty-eight-year-old Beth discovered, anticipatory mourning is possible to an extent, but it's rarely a complete process. She was twenty-four when her mother was diagnosed with cancer, and had almost two years to adjust to the idea that her mother would die. "My father says he mourned while she was sick," Beth says. "But for me it was different. Yeah, we all cried and grieved while our mother was dying, but when it was over and she was never coming back, I really fell apart." This kind of response is normal, says Benjamin Garber, who believes that even with time to prepare for a loss, you can't really experience a death until it happens. "You can anticipate it, and sure, it's easier if you're not immediately overwhelmed, as is the case with a violent death," he explains. "But in the long run, preparation for the loss doesn't carry that much weight. As long as the person is right there talking and laughing and crying with you, then they're alive. That's all there is to it."

This is true when the mother is still vital and functional, but in the advanced stages of many illnesses, a patient often is in severe pain, if she is conscious at all. In such a situation, long periods of anticipatory grieving are often complicated by a daughter's resentment that her life is on hold and—even more troubling to her—her unexpressed wish for her mother to finally die.

"Particularly when the patient is extremely ill, and especially with teenagers, who want to be out individuating and spending social time with their friends, at some level daughters will just wish for it all to be over," Arlene Englander says. "Which means they wish their mothers would die, because they want their lives to get back to normal, and then they experience tremendous guilt for even thinking that."

"Women need to recognize that in times of great stress, such extreme thoughts are normal," she says. "It's a very human impulse to want to live your life in a happy, healthy, productive way, and it's a terribly stressful experience to watch someone you love in pain and know she's not enjoying life herself. When we wish a loved one would die not only so that she's out of her pain but also because we want our lives to continue as normally as possible, it's neither good nor bad. It's simply human."

Beth and her sister, Cecile, remember grieving throughout the twenty-one months their mother was ill. Sort of. In their family, the word *cancer* was viewed as a synonym for *death*. No one ever spoke the word after the diagnosis or discussed the poor prognosis. Even as the sisters watched their mother's health decline and knew what the inevitable outcome would be, they tried to hide their fear from their parents, who insisted on modeling optimism and hope. So the sisters would cry in the car on the way to their parents' house, smile and pretend to be happy during their visit, and then cry again in the car on their way home. To share their grief openly, they believed, would have been more disruptive to the family system.

Today, Cecile understands how harmful those twenty-one months were to her. She leans forward, her chin-length hair swinging against her face. "It took a long time for me to get used to not living like that anymore," she says softly. "I was so used to putting on that kind of show, and living at a heightened state of urgency, and panicking every time the phone rang. I couldn't grieve until about six months ago, way after the first year, and it wasn't until things felt somewhat normal again. And then I realized that I was really angry at my mother for never talking about it, and for making me go through such a show. That one realization just made all the difference to me. It happened like this"—she snaps her fingers—"but to get to that point took me more than a year."

Witnessing a mother's slow physical decline can be the equivalent of experiencing a long-term trauma . The daughter's feelings of helplessness, anger, and fear persist. And persist. And persist. She may alternate between wanting to protect her mother and resenting her, an advance-and-retreat dance of identification and rejection that can span years.

Holly, twenty-six, was twelve and the youngest of three children when her mother was diagnosed with ovarian cancer and fifteen when she died. The only time during our two-and-a-half-hour interview when she came close to crying was when she talked about an incident she says represents her mother's struggle with a disease that refused to go into remission, and her own frustration and anger as an adolescent who couldn't do anything to change it.

I remember one time when my mother came home from chemotherapy. Tough, tough woman that she was, she drove herself home from the appointment. I was fourteen or fifteen and didn't have a license, so she drove herself to and from this thing. She kept herself together physically from the chemo long enough to drive home successfully, but then she got home, sat down at the kitchen table with her coat still on, and threw up all over herself. I was sitting there and it was such a horrifying moment. So scary. So painful. It was such a symbol of her illness, that she threw up all over her winter coat, such a symbol of everything that was out of control. I felt traumatized, helpless, very afraid for her. I had an extreme surge of love for her at that moment, combined with fear and helplessness. I wanted to take care of her like she'd taken care of me when I was sick, but I couldn't do it.

I once wrote in my journal that if my mother had gotten better there might have been a rift between us, because it was such a trauma to have her be ill for so long. How could I have forgiven her for putting us through such fear and tremendous unhappiness, for backing out on me and for going away? Now I realize that if she had recovered, we would have been eventually joyful and come to a point of great happiness about that. But her illness was such a trauma that for a long time I thought it would have been impossible to get back to a normal life with her again.

The mother who returned home from chemotherapy treatments was not the same mother Holly had emulated for her first twelve years. To an adolescent, this new mother appeared helpless and weak. The side effects of chemotherapy—nausea, vomiting, hair loss, and weight loss or gain—as well as the final stages of AIDS and other degenerative diseases can turn a mother who was once vibrant into a figure a daughter finds frightening or repulsive. In a culture that places a premium on a woman's physical beauty, the ill mother is seen as an aesthetic deviant. The daughter, by association, feels inadequate and ashamed.

A mother's ability to cope with these physical changes gives her daughter clear messages about illness, stress, femininity, and body image. A mother who adjusts well to losing her hair, for example, passes along the message that appearance doesn't define a woman, but a mother who falls into a depression and refuses to leave the house transmits messages of shame. Twenty-five-year-old Ronnie, who was sixteen when her mother died after four years of chemotherapy, says, "I always looked up to my mother's vanity. I grew up playing with her makeup and wanting to look as good as she did. But when she got to the point in her treatment where she was, to her, ghastly, she'd look in the mirror and say, 'It's horrible. I can't even look at myself. Don't you hate me?' She wouldn't let her friends come over and visit because she didn't want them to see her less than perfect." Ronnie, who describes herself as "the kind of woman who brings makeup on a camping trip," admits that on days when she feels ugly and depressed, she, too, isolates herself at home.

The daughter who absorbs her mother's anxiety about physical transformation may, after the loss, become determined to win the war against body image that her mother lost. In seeking to gain the control over her body that her mother never had, she sets rigid standards of physical perfectionism for herself. Every hair must be in place, every calorie counted. To slip, she believes, means to move one step closer to death. Eating disorders such as anorexia and bulimia are extreme examples of this need for control, but many women describe other physical preoccupations they rely on as crude barometers of their health. I know that I still wear my hair long because I remember the horror of seeing my mother crying in the bathroom the day her hair began to fall out in clumps. It's not rational, I know— drugs, not cancer, made her lose her hair—but at some level I'm convinced that the more hair I have, the farther I am from death.

Andrea Campbell, Ph.D., a therapist in Santa Fe, New Mexico, who frequently counsels motherless daughters, was ten when her mother died of breast cancer. She says weight became her source of security. "My mother was heavy and always concerned about her weight," she explains. "When she was dying, she was only about ninety pounds. So when I lose weight, I get terrified I'm going to die. For eight years, I carried at least an extra ten pounds on me. Until then, I'd lose some and then gain it right back. I know I was trying to make myself feel safe."

A daughter's individual identity depends on her ability to adopt some of her mother's characteristics and reject others, a process that's complicated when the most recent and striking memories she has of her mother are of a woman who was seriously ill. "The daughter doesn't want to be like the mother, because that means these awful things are going to happen to her," Naomi Lowinsky explains. "She's going to be in a terrible state, she's going to lose her hair. The memories of the mother are not of somebody she'd ever want to be like."

To separate her body from her mother's—and therefore ensure her own survival—a daughter's impulse is to create emotional distance between herself and her mother. Yet to attempt such a complete rejection also cuts a daughter off from the Well Mother, the one who was once young, healthy, and unencumbered by hospitals, drugs, and worry, and a woman the daughter might want to be like. "Most of the women I see, whether their mothers are alive or not, are working with their internal relationship with their mother and their capacity to mother themselves," Dr. Lowinsky says. "The woman who lost her mother at an early age may not have access to that, because all she sees is her sick mother. Part of her work is then to bring the image of the well mother back to life, so she can have an alive relationship to apply to her own capacity to mother herself." To do this, a daughter has to focus on the days preceding her mother's illness. Looking at photographs of mothers taken when they were healthy and learning the stories of their lives helps us see them as they were before we were born, and in our earliest years together.

Chronic Illness and Ambiguous Loss

A small but notable group of motherless daughters grew up in families where mothers were living with chronic, degenerative illnesses such as multiple sclerosis or early-onset Alzheimer's, or were kept alive in hospital settings or nursing homes for extended periods. Under such circumstances, the mothers were unable to function in the maternal role, and the daughters struggled with losses that felt ill-defined. The mother was alive, yet incapacitated; she was still considered a member of the family, yet she was unable to be involved in a meaningful way. When a mother's condition was brought on or accelerated by childbirth, a daughter often carried guilt for her perceived role in her mother's decline.

Fifty-one-year-old Josephine was raised by her grandmother and her father after her mother, who suffered from multiple sclerosis, became physically unable to care for her. She was twenty when her mother died, but she considers herself motherless from a much earlier age.

> I really didn't have a mother. She got MS when she was pregnant with me. I'm an only child. She had brain surgery while she was pregnant. They didn't find anything. They thought it was water on the brain and finally figured out it was MS. She started to become paralyzed by the time I was born, so my father had his mother move in to take care of me. My mother was in and out of hospitals until I was about nine, and then she went into a permanent facility. And she was there until she died, when I was twenty.
>
> We used to visit her every weekend, but the only thing I knew of her was of this woman who was in the hospital. Because I was too young, I don't have any memories of her as a

mother at all. She could talk, but she was bedridden. I recall very little of her mothering.

Mothers who are institutionalized or kept alive in a permanent vegetative state for extended periods exist, to a daughter, in a no-man's-land between life and death, neither a functional mother nor a lost one. When death does come, its course and timing are usually unpredictable. As one daughter, whose mother was in a long-term, stroke-induced coma for much of her adolescence, recalls, "Even though we knew she was going to die eventually, when it happened it was still a terrible, rude shock. I thought I was prepared, but when it happened I fell apart. That's when I realized I'd been hanging onto the hope, however slim, that as long as she was alive she might some-how get better."

Sudden Deaths

Death always feels sudden, even when it's anticipated, Phyllis Silverman says. "But when a parent simply 'drops dead' the assault on a family cannot be overestimated," she emphasizes. Heart attacks, aneurysms, accidents, suicide, homicide, complications during preg-nancy and childbirth, acts of terrorism, natural disasters, war, and other forms of sudden death[1] throw a family into an immediate and unexpected crisis. To survive such a loss is truly a test of the human spirit. "It is one of the mysteries of our nature that a man, all unpre-pared, can receive a thunderstroke like that and live," wrote Mark Twain, who lost his favorite daughter, Susy, in 1896. Life changes with the news of a moment, too quickly for anyone to adjust with grace or ease.

The immediate shock, disbelief, and disorganization that follow the sudden death of a loved one often force mourning into a holding pattern until family members can process the circumstances sur-rounding the loss. When a daughter's assumptions about the world as

---

[1]When a daughter is not aware of a mother's long-term illness, or when the death is unexpected—such as when a mother whose cancer is in remission dies of sudden heart failure—she often responds to the loss as a daughter who has experienced a sudden death.

a safe, nurturing place are shattered in an instant, she has to restructure her beliefs and rebuild some of her faith before she can devote much energy to accepting her mother's absence. We mourn only when we feel stable and secure enough to relinquish some control—not when we're anticipating another blow from behind.

Donna, twenty-six, remembers the seventy-mile-an-hour car ride she made through San Francisco to reach the hospital after she heard her mother had committed suicide. "I ran into the emergency room," she recalls. "I was running on adrenaline. I couldn't cry. I couldn't speak beyond saying, 'I'm Donna Barry. Where's my father?' The nurse walked me back into the room, and I saw my mother lying there with the tube in her mouth and the tape on her face. My dad was sitting next to her, holding her hand and crying. I turned around and started punching the nurse. I was a basket case. Reality had not hit, and it didn't hit until months afterward. I knew my mother was gone, but there was still this idea that maybe she'd come back. I kept having dreams that I'd see her again. People kept saying, 'How *are* you?' after she died. I'd say, 'I don't want to talk about it,' and they'd say, 'Donna, you have to.'"

To outsiders, Donna's initial coping behaviors may have resembled denial, but as Therese Rando explains, this immediate response to sudden death is more a sense of disbelief. "When somebody dies suddenly, you don't have time to gradually shift your expectations, to tell yourself, 'Well, next Christmas she's not going to be here,' or 'She won't be here when I walk down the aisle,'" she says. "Instead, everything is gone all at once, and you cannot bend your mind around the idea that fast. There's been such an assault on the way you've conceptualized your world, which includes that person. And especially with your mother. Your mother is your *mother.* How can she not be here?"

Sudden deaths, more than any other form of loss, teach children that relationships are impermanent and liable to end at any time, an awareness that can dramatically shape their emerging personalities. Carla, forty-four, says she delayed marriage and childbirth until her forties because she spent her twenties and thirties afraid to form lasting attachments. The deep rejection and abandonment she felt at the age of twelve when her mother committed suicide, and again three years later when her father did the same, made her terrified of losing another loved one without warning. "Since my parents' deaths, I've lived a life in which I always felt calamity might be lurking around every corner, and that some terrible loss might come at any moment for which there is no preparation and no defense," she explains. Today, Carla is a successful professional, a wife, and the mother of two. But her childhood experiences made it hard for her as an adult to understand that others intend to stay.

Losing a parent to suicide is one of the most difficult types of death a child can experience. It's sudden and usually unexpected, it often involves violence, and even daughters who understand the part mental illness and depression often play still experience suicide as a clearcut and real rejection. "To a child, parental suicide is a 'fuck you,'" Andrea Campbell explains. "It's an 'I can't live for you. I can't stay alive for you. You may hurt, but I hurt more.'"

A mother's suicide leaves a daughter to contend with a complex array of emotions, including heightened anger, guilt, and shame; lowered self-esteem; shattered self-worth; feelings of inadequacy, deficiency, and failure; fear of intimacy; and an eroded capacity to trust that this type of rejection won't happen again. Therapists have observed that among young children, poor school performance and eating and sleeping disorders are typical symptoms, whereas older children are more likely to act out with drug and alcohol abuse, truancy, social withdrawal, or aggression. Child survivors also may exhibit posttraumatic behaviors such as distortions of memory when asked to recall the death; the belief they will die young; a collapse of earlier developmental skills; and a tendency to repeat the trauma through dreams, nightmares, and play. And all this takes place in a cultural milieu that typically projects shame and guilt onto the family members left behind, no matter how young.

"After I figured out that my mother had killed herself, whenever I heard the word *suicide,* I felt embarrassed," remembers twenty-year-old Jennifer, who was four when her mother died. "I don't even think I knew exactly what the word meant, but anytime anyone mentioned it, I could just feel my face get warm from my collar up. I was always afraid somebody was going to turn around and say, 'You! You're the one whose mom killed herself!'"

When the psychologists Albert Cain and Irene Fast, two early researchers of parent suicides, studied forty-five children between the ages of four and fourteen who were being treated for psychological disturbances after having lost parents to suicide, they found that guilt was a predominant response and that questions such as "Why couldn't I save her?" and "Did I cause her despair?" were common. They also discovered that few surviving parents had discussed the suicide with their children, and some overtly refused to talk about it. In one-fourth of Cain and Fast's case studies the child had witnessed some aspect of the suicide yet was told that the parent had died some other way — an additional reason why parental suicide often destroys a child's basic sense of trust.

Cain and Fast also found that child survivors occasionally, in adolescence or adulthood, identified with the parent to such an extent that they repeated the mother or father's suicidal act. In some instances the parallels were striking, such as the eighteen-year-old girl who drowned herself alone at night at the same beach and in almost the same way as her mother had drowned herself many years before. Jennifer solemnly reports that in her family, which never openly discussed her mother's death, that she and an older sister attempted suicide in their teens. When she was feeling depressed and isolated as a college freshman, Jennifer explains, suicide seemed a simple solution to her pain.

Other daughters develop isolated symptoms that relate to a mother's suicide in some way. Margie, twenty-five, describes the chaotic scene that took place when she, as a seven-year-old, awoke in the middle of the night to her grandmother's screams and learned that her mother's body had just been found in the garage. "A main thing I remember from the rest of my childhood is this rigid fear at night, just lying in bed stiff and terrified out of my wits," she recalls. "I think the fear came at night because I was so obviously alone then, and also because my mother died at night. I've been an insomniac for most of my life, which I've just recently connected with that."

The violence or mutilation often involved in sudden deaths such as suicides, homicides, and accidents may consume a daughter's thoughts, even invading her dreams, and often takes on elements more horrific in imagination than they were in reality. Children who witnessed or were physically involved in the death have another layer of distress added to their loss. Janine, thirty-nine, has no conscious memories of the automobile crash that killed her mother when she was twenty-one months old, even though she was sitting in the back seat. "But after I went off to college, I started to dream about the accident," she says. "I still don't know whether or not my images were real or just my imagination. I know some of it was fabrication, but I think I was having those dreams to try to live it, remember it, and put it to rest. I would dream I was in the front seat, and I would have feelings of suffocation and see red. I would imagine that my mother covered me with her body to protect me, and that's why I felt suffocated. Of course, that's not what happened, but I wanted her to have protected me. Then, in waking hours, when I would hear sirens or hear flashing lights, I would start to shake and get scared. I think it was sort of my way of saying, 'You deserve some attention around this stuff.'"

Janine's response may also have been a delayed form of posttraumatic stress disorder, a syndrome that often afflicts accident survivors. Lenore Terr, M.D., a specialist on childhood trauma who studied the twenty-six children involved in the 1976 Chowchilla, California, school-bus kidnapping, found that terror, rage, denial, shame, guilt, misperceptions of the event both as it occurred and in memory; a sense of futurelessness; and recurring dreams were evidence of posttraumatic behavior. She found that many of the children's posttraumatic fears remained literal, specific, and related to the kidnapping, such as the fear of vans (like the ones used by their kidnappers) and school buses (like the one that was hijacked). They also feared actions they associated with the initial trauma, such as slowing down on a road. Some of these fears, she discovered, lingered well into the children's adulthood. The psychologist Lula Redmond observed similar characteristics in hundreds of family members who'd lost loved ones to homicide. Even when they hadn't witnessed the death, children and adults nevertheless experienced nightmares, flashbacks, eating and sleeping disturbances, fear of strangers, irritability, and angry outbursts immediately following the murder, with some symptoms persisting for as long as five years.

In the aftermath of a homicide, blame, anger, fear, and fantasies of revenge often surge to the surface of a survivor's psyche. The intensity of her responses may frighten a child, making her question her own stability and sanity. These emotions are further complicated when the child witnesses the murder or knows the aggressor. In 43 percent of all homicides in 2003, the victims knew their assailants, and more than 30 percent of all female victims were slain by husbands or boyfriends. Children of those women often lost two parents: one to death, the other to arrest or incarceration. One need look no farther than the night of Nicole Brown Simpson's death in 1994, when her children sat in a police station for five hours, refusing candy, wondering why neither of their parents came for them, to imagine how terrifying such a scenario must be.

Because homicides are sometimes random and always violent, they leave survivors feeling particularly vulnerable and helpless. Children whose parents die this way may later need to collect as much information about the murder as possible, as horrific as some of those facts may be. Trying to find meaning and assigning blame act as important attempts to restore control, predictability, and justice in a daughter's world.

Twenty-two-year-old Laura was nineteen when her mother was stalked, shot, and killed by an ex-boyfriend. When the case came to trial the following year, Laura decided to attend.

> I tried to get through the whole trial, but I only made it through three days. The lawyers told me I could leave when they showed the pictures and evidence, but I said, "No, I want to see it." I didn't believe she was dead. I needed to see it. . .
>
> Mark, the guy who killed her, got the maximum sentence, twenty-five years to life. I sat there and thought, "I'm looking at you, you son of a bitch." When I said that, it wasn't just me looking at him. It was me and my mom. While I was there, it was like my mom seemed to come through me. Or I pretended I was her, and her energy got in me. I didn't have my own anger yet, but I had hers, so I pretended I was her. I sat in the back of the courtroom and twisted my hands like she did when she was angry.

By identifying with her mother this way, Laura could experience some of the intense emotion she's just starting to work through in counseling today. Such delayed or protracted grief responses are often found among children who lose mothers to homicide. Counselors at the Dougy Center for Grieving Children in Portland, Oregon, have found that children who have lost a loved one to murder often say their feelings were "put on hold" until an investigation or trial ended, until the shock started to wear off, or because of confusion surrounding the facts. When police officers, journalists, lawyers, and judges typically become involved after a homicide, pertinent information about the death may be withheld pending trial. Many times, even when details are out in the open, kids aren't told what has happened and are left to piece the story together on their own.

Furthermore, homicides, along with acts of terrorism and natural disasters, bring a family's intensely private grief into the public eye, an experience that can both help and hinder a child's recovery. Perhaps nowhere has this been more evident than among the nearly 3,000 children under the age of eighteen who lost parents in the attacks of September 11, 2001, about 340 of whom lost mothers, and the more than 200 children who lost a parent in the Oklahoma City Federal building bombing in 1995. News coverage and a period of national mourning can initially offer a sense of community and validation, but when the cameras stop rolling and the country moves on, the grief can be brutally isolating and intense.

Annual memorials, meant to commemorate the deceased, often serve to reactivate survivors' grief. For the "9/11 kids," as they're called, every September now brings a flood of reminders—television specials, classroom discussions, magazine photos—of the horrific circumstances of their parents' deaths. The annual publicity can interfere with a child's ability to separate good memories of the parent from the tragic scene of his or her death, which is an important goal of mourning.

Children who lost parents in Oklahoma City and on September 11 have the difficult task of recovering from what's known as "traumatic bereavement," the devastating intersection of trauma and loss. Traumatic bereavement is likely to result when a death is sudden and unanticipated; when it involves violence, mutilation, or destruction; when it has an element of preventability and/or randomness; and when it involves massive or shocking multiple deaths. Survivors must contend with the dual demands of posttraumatic stress and grieving—an experience, Therese Rando explains, that's much larger than the sum of its parts.

Conversely, the national attention focused on traumatic bereavement after the September 11 attacks gave some motherless daughters a public forum for discussing their losses for the first time. Thirty-seven-year-old Beatrice, who was eleven when her mother died in a commercial airline crash, always felt marginalized as a griever because of the dramatic and unusual circumstances of her mother's death. Shortly after September 11, she was standing with a group of commuters at a train station discussing the horror of the attacks. "I said to someone, 'I remember what it felt like when someone drove my mother's car home from the airport, and how that was when I realized she was never coming back,'" she recalls. "I was never able to say something like that before in the course of conversation. September 11 normalized my experience somewhat. It made it seem less bizarre."

Daughters who lose mothers to forms of sudden death often believe they could have prevented the tragedy *if only they had been there, delayed her, apologized in time.* Daughters may imagine themselves as key cause-and-effect players in events otherwise too arbitrary to comprehend. "Why hadn't I heard her walk down the stairs?" wonders Alice, the 15-year-old narrator of Leslie Pietrzyk's 2004 novel *A Year and a Day,* who loses a mother to suicide. "Why hadn't I kissed her when I went to bed? I didn't even have a bad dream that night; I didn't get up for a glass of water. I went to bed and slept through the night like everything would be exactly the same in the morning. Why didn't Mama come into my room and wake me up? I would have said something. One word might have been enough."

This phenomenon is prevalent enough to be called the "if only" syndrome: "If only I'd asked my mother one more question before she walked out the door, she wouldn't have been crossing the intersection at that precise moment" is the type of statement that allows a daughter to blame herself and impose a sense of order and control on an otherwise unpredictable world.

Sheila, who was fourteen when she found her mother dead from a heart attack one morning, says it took her more than ten years and several maturational phases to stop blaming herself for the death.

What haunted me for a long time was that I got there too late. My feeling that I could have saved her was focused on the moment that I found her lying in bed, and that if I'd gotten there earlier, she'd still be alive.

For months at a time in high school, I wouldn't allow myself to think about it. Then in college I was reading my abnormal psychology textbook and I saw a list of stress-related symptoms that could result in cardiac problems. I saw my mother had had many of them, and I decided I should have been able to see those things at fourteen and save her. And then I started fixating on the moment *before* her death. My brother was the last one to see her alive, and I thought maybe if it had been me, I would have known something was wrong, and we could have gotten her to a doctor in time.

Now, I still have a lot of anger and feelings of rejection and loss, but I don't have as much blame. I accept things happen as they do, and people do the best they can, even though it's not enough. That realization came when I began to understand that my father and stepmother, even though they weren't the greatest parents to me, did the best they could. I really believe that on a level I didn't before, and that makes a big difference for me. Emanating from that comes the realization that as a kid, I did the best I could do, and when I accepted that, I was able to step back further and say I couldn't stop my mother from dying. I didn't cause her to die, and I couldn't have caused her not to die. I always knew I didn't kill her, but I'd thought I should have stopped her. And finally, in my midtwenties, I realized that act wasn't within what I had the power to do.

Many daughters who lost a mother to sudden death say the experience guided them into a new state of awareness. Having learned that life can end at any moment, they become determined to appreciate each moment for its beauty. They make sure they say "I love you" to their husbands and children before saying goodbye, just in case they never see them again. And in their attempt to attach a meaning to the loss, some of these women choose to view it as a necessary step in their personal journey. As twenty-five-year-old Heather, who was fourteen when her mother was murdered, explains:

> I don't know how I had this kind of knowledge at fourteen, but I remember saying to some friends, "I don't want to become bitter. I don't want to become angry. I want to become a stronger person as a result of this." That hope stayed with me throughout high school and college. I tried to rise above the tragedy, and I think that was ultimately a good thing. I've found out in recent years that there was a lot of anger and blaming that I didn't go through because I was trying to be the strong one. There were some stages of grieving I missed and had to go through later. But I'm proud that I survived it, and I think I was able to become a better person because of it all.

Abandonment

The mother who abandons her daughter leaves a pile of questions behind: Who was she? Who is she? Where is she? Why did she leave? Like the child whose mother dies, the abandoned daughter lives with a loss, but she also struggles with the knowledge that her mother is alive yet inaccessible and out of touch. Death has a finality to it that abandonment simply does not.

A daughter whose mother chose to leave her or was incapable of mothering may feel like a member of the emotional underclass, like a dispensable part of society whose needs the government has ignored. As a result, she often develops a sense of devaluation and unworthiness even more profound than that of the daughter whose mother has died.

"Loss by death, as hard as that is, doesn't imply a rejection," explains Gina Mireault, Ph.D., an associate professor of psychology at Johnson State University in Johnson, Vermont, who was three when her own mother died. "Daughters whose mothers walk away are at much greater risk, psychologically, than women whose mothers die.

Because at some point, if your mother died, you can say, 'I know she didn't want to leave. She didn't choose to die. This was an illness or an event she couldn't control.' But kids whose parents do choose to leave are left with this baggage of, 'What could I have done? I must not have been good enough as a kid. I wasn't loveable enough. I must have made her so miserable that she wanted to leave.' And that's a harder pill to swallow."

Whether a mother leaves physically or emotionally, the result is invariably a blow to her daughter's self-esteem. Judith Mishne, in her article "Parental Abandonment: A Unique Form of Loss and Narcissistic Injury," explains that abandoned children may suffer from lack of empathy, depression, feelings of emptiness, delinquency, addictions, uncontrolled rage, pathological lying, hypochondriacal preoccupations, and grandiose fantasies of the self. These children often have trouble mourning a lost parent, she says, because they have difficulty letting go of the image of an idealized mother they hope will one day return—either in person or in spirit.

An abandoned daughter is left feeling angry, resentful, and sad. She also has the emotional injury of having been given up, put aside, left, or lost. The question "Why did she leave?" always includes the appendix "me."

Physical Separation

Amanda, thirty-three, remembers how she used to sit at the curb, pulling on her hair and wondering where her mother was, and if she would return. She was three when her mother lost custody of her and then disappeared, and Amanda recalls a childhood filled with longing. "I wanted a mommy so bad," she says. "My favorite book was *Are You My Mother?* by P. D. Eastman. My grandmother would read it to me. The baby bird gets separated from its mother and goes up to all the different animals and objects and asks, 'Are you my mother?' I would fixate on that book. I don't even think I paid attention to the end, when the bird finds its mother. I was more interested in the search. The feelings of loss were so real to me."

Fantasies of a mother-daughter reunion and the desire to compensate for lost years may consume an abandoned daughter's thoughts. At the same time, the fear of a second rejection or an absence of information may prevent her from taking steps to find her lost mother as an adolescent or adult. "She would want me now" is complicated by the thought "But she didn't want me then," and the daughter grows up in a motherless limbo, left to piece together a feminine identity based on scraps of memory, idealized images, and whatever nuggets of information she can uncover from family members and friends.

When a mother deserts her child, or when a mother is incarcerated, family bitterness or shame may discourage a daughter from uncovering the details of the past. If the marriage went sour, Evelyn Bassoff points out, the loss may not be as severe for the father as it is for the daughter, and her fact-finding efforts that require his help may dead-end. Amanda's father occasionally validated her early memories, but he was reluctant to share new information with her. "Whenever I felt bold enough to ask him, he would tell me stories like, 'Well, Amanda, she joined the Hell's Angels, and the reason I know that is because she had a leather Hell's Angels jacket. Do you know how you get one of those?' I said, 'No, Dad,' and he told me you get one by having sex with thirteen of them on a pool table, which just made a lasting, sick impression on me. That time when I asked, it was like he was tired of my questions. He just wanted to bury this so deep. But there was always some dialogue going on with her in my head. I would hear a song, and I would know that my mom liked that song. You know? I don't know how to describe it, but I know the cord was never fully cut."

An abandoned daughter's illusion of the mythic mother hardly meshes with the reality of a biological mother who chose to leave her child, or who consciously jeopardized their chances of staying together. Without the ongoing presence of the real mother, against whom the daughter can test her images of her fantasy mother and modify her expectations accordingly, the hyperidealized version often takes over. A daughter then clings to her image of the Good Mother because she fears the anger and pain that will result if she acknowledges the Bad Mother. But until she can accept both mothers, and relinquish the extremes, she can never truly mourn or accommodate her loss.

Linda, now forty-three, says she finally let go of her idealized images of her mother when she realized in her early twenties that the mother-daughter reunion she'd hoped for was never going to occur. Unlike Amanda, Linda had occasional contact with her mother throughout most of her childhood. She was one when her parents divorced, and she went to live with her grandparents, seeing her mother and father on alternate weekends. When she was five, her mother remarried and moved seven hundred miles away. Instead of bringing Linda to live with her, she bought her a plane ticket once a year so that she could visit. "As far as I know, my mother always had legal custody of me," Linda says. "But my mother and my grandmother never got along. My mother claims she wanted to take me, but my grandmother threatened to take her to court if she tried. My mother said she didn't want to put me through a custody battle, but as far as I'm concerned, that's ridiculous. You don't leave your child behind because you're afraid your mother will fight you. Even if it were true, it's not a reasonable explanation, as far as I'm concerned."

After her grandmother's death when she was eleven, Linda went to live with her father and stepmother. Her mother, who'd given birth to three more children during her second marriage, never made an attempt to claim her. Nine years later, as an autonomous adult who was angry about the repeated abandonments of her childhood, Linda wrote to her mother and explained her distress. She never received a response. After her surprise had turned to indignation, she swore she'd never contact her mother again. Hard as it was for her to accept this ultimate rejection, Linda says, she hasn't regretted her decision. Today, she's a working artist, has a happy second marriage, and is the mother of a six-year-old son. "I think it all turned out for the best, in terms of what happened with my life," she says, without evident resentment. But she also says she has to work hard every day to overcome a deep fear of abandonment in her adult life, the enduring reminder of her early loss.

Emotional Unavailability

Alcoholism, drug addiction, mental illness, childhood abuse—all can render a mother incapable of responding to her child emotionally.

Victoria Secunda, the author of *When You and Your Mother Can't Be Friends*, describes this type of mothering as a "sort of muteness." The mother is physically present but offers no emotional substance; she is like the body of a car with nothing under the hood. But the daughter keeps turning the key in the ignition, hoping that if she does it just right, the motor might start up this time.

"These kind of abandonment issues are much more confusing," says Andrea Campbell. "When a mother leaves mentally, that child feels, even more strongly than the child whose mother dies, 'I didn't deserve to have her with me. I must have done something bad. I'm not worthy of having Mother stay. If I were lovable, she would have stayed.'"

Thirty-seven-year-old Jocelyn remembers being five years old and believing her mother's mental illness was her fault. Between the ages of five and eight, Jocelyn lived with her grandmother while her mother was institutionalized; her repeated requests to see her mother and to be taken home were ignored. "Eventually, I reasoned that my mom must not love me or she would come and get me, and I also felt that way about my dad, because he wouldn't take me home either," she recalls. "So from a very young age, I really felt that I was on my own." That conviction, she says, has been a determining factor of her adult life. Though she speaks in a calm, thoughtful voice, her anger is obvious. "Yes, my mother was physically there," she says. "But I couldn't depend on her. That's what it came down to. I had a real bitterness about that. Because I never had anyone to depend on, I knew I had to take care of myself all the time. Now, I have this attitude that I don't need anybody, and that I can do everything on my own."

Jocelyn says she's had to relinquish the hope that her mother will one day become the mother she always needed. As Evelyn Bassoff explains in her book *Mothers and Daughters: Loving and Letting Go,* a major step in the abandoned daughter's healing process is to acknowledge that her mother did not love her properly, or did not love her at all.

Because acknowledging that one was not loved by Mother hurts so much, many deprived women fight against this fact. Even when their mothers continue to undermine them, they do not turn their backs on them. Rather, they remain devoted and un-separated daughters, eternally waiting for the maternal validation and approval that never comes. Or, even if they distance themselves from their unloving mothers, they recreate in their present lives situations that simulate the early relationship with her.

For example, some may quite unconsciously select lovers or husbands who respond to them the way their mothers did. By trying to soften the hearts of these men and win their love, they are indirectly appealing for mother love.

Twenty-nine-year-old Karen says she has done just this. At fourteen, Karen willingly left home to escape her mother's alcoholism, and despite her mother's emotional coldness during and after her departure, Karen nevertheless spent the next six years expecting her mother to welcome her back.

When I turned thirteen, I didn't know the words for it then, but I think that's when my mother really lost what was left of her mind. Overnight, she pushed me out of her life completely. She didn't want to have anything to do with me, and just set up as many emotional wedges as she could. I was devastated to the point where I tried to kill myself about a year after it first happened. It was on the advice of my psychiatrist that I left home. But I'd always hoped, from the time I left until she died nearly six years later, that some way, somehow, we'd come to a sort of reconciliation. I spent those years waiting for her to say, "Karen, I'm sorry." It never happened. That's why I feel I lost her twice. The day she died, I thought, "That's it. I'll never, ever get that validation from her now."

Ever since her mother's death, Karen has been searching for the validation she never received. Among lovers, friends, and colleagues, she has developed a reputation for being "adoptable," she says. This is her method for winning the attention and praise as an adult that she never received as a daughter. When an unavailable mother dies, a daughter often finds herself grieving not just for what she has lost but for what might have been, what she didn't get but might—one day, maybe, under different circumstances—have gotten from her.

Many women have found ways to compensate for the lack of mother love, Dr. Bassoff says. "Feeling and talking through the pain—the humiliation of being an unloved child, the anger toward the cold mother, the anxiety of turning into her, the fear of maternal retribution for hating her—became the healing salve," she writes. "Where therapy was successful, these women came to understand that their mothers, who were unfortunate, inadequate, insecure people, *did not have the power* to hurt them anymore. If their mothers continued to act destructively, they could walk away from them."

The presence of a nurturing and involved father also can help soften the daughter's feelings of rejection, and many of the women who describe their mothers as emotionally detached credit their fathers with giving them the love and security they believe helped them develop self-esteem and go on to have fulfilling relationships as adults.

Thirty-five-year-old Shari grew up with a mother who was manic-depressive and erratic in her parenting behaviors. Her father, however, was a warm and stable parent, and she believes he made her childhood more bearable than it otherwise would have been.

Living with my mother was very difficult. I loved her, and I hated her. As kids, my sisters and I used to think, "God, I wish she would die. How can we kill her?" Which was a horrible thing. And then she died when I was twenty-three, and I thought, "I can't believe it. She died? This cancer actually killed her?" When you're around someone who's mentally ill, and they're crazy and scream and hit you, you think, "These people are going to live until they're two hundred." So then I had to deal with all the guilty feelings about, "I didn't really mean to wish her dead at the time." But I did, and there's really nothing I can do about it now, so I just move forward.

My father was really the one who told me I could be whatever I wanted to be and should do whatever it was I wanted to do. He was the cheerleader, the person who was the source of encouragement. Although when my mom was okay, she was very supportive and very encouraging, when she was not okay—and that could flip-flop at any time—that was all taken away. It was very confusing for me as a young child. My mother was very loving at times, and I know that she loved us and loved me. But it was really my father who helped us to move forward.

Two years after her mother died, Shari moved back to her hometown to care for her father, who had been diagnosed with cancer. She wanted to provide him with the secure base that he had given her during times of stress. As she prepares to marry, Shari says, her father remains her model for how she would like to parent one day. Her mother, she says, has provided her mostly with an example of what she doesn't want to be.

The fear of identifying with one's mother as a mother is particularly profound in daughters such as Shari, Phyllis Klaus says. "Women who've had bad mothering often get very frightened," she says. "They wonder, 'Will I hurt like my mother? Will I get angry like my mother?' They'll often do many things to be the opposite of their mother, but if they're not conscious of it in a clear, reflective way, they will in fact re-create those activities and ways of being." The pattern repeats when women who had to care for their mothers become mothers, she says, and expect their daughters to nurture them.

Like a woman who loses a mother to death or to physical separation, a daughter who is emotionally abandoned must move beyond the image of the Bad Mother and also push the mythic to the side. Her task is to look at her mother as objectively as she can, choose the memories and traits she wants to adopt, and carry them with her as she moves forward. Ultimately, the abandoned daughter is never completely abandoned unless she, too, leaves herself, her needs, and her desires behind.

Chapter Four

Later Loss
Learning How to Let Go

WE MET AT A PARTY in college, where I heard him discussing Thomas Hardy's poetry on the back porch. I'd read only one of the poems, and even that was back in high school, but I joined the conversation anyway. He was someone I wanted to know. Before the night was over, we found other topics to talk about . . . and talk about and talk about, and by the end of the week I knew this was a man I could marry. Three and a half years later for Christmas he gave me a teddy bear and a diamond ring.

By then he was finishing graduate school, I was ready to leave Tennessee, and we were planning a move to California, where he had already accepted a job. On the surface, our future together looked as limitless as the tableau the West once was. But underneath, there had been problems all along. The first one was my mother, whose absence I was trying my best to ignore. And the second was his mother, whose presence was harder to overlook. I was of the "wrong" ethnicity, not from a "good" family, and breaking up their tight-knit group: These were the complaints. She was vocal in her disapproval, I was terrified by her rejection, and my meek attempts to improve the situation were inhibited by my conviction that one mother had left me and another wanted me to disappear. By the time we began to reach a small sort of truce, her son and I had been arguing about it for too long. I'd felt abandoned and wanted him to take a stronger stand; he felt pressured and kept insisting there was nothing he could do. Around and around we went, until the only exit I could see was mine. One month before our move to California, I placed the diamond ring on his coffee table and walked out the front door.

Death, I knew how to manage. Separation, I could not bear. So I turned the end of the engagement into a mini-death. I refused to answer his letters. I got involved with someone else. I packed everything he'd given me, including the teddy bear and all the photos of us together, into a box I pushed to the back of a basement shelf. I'm not proud of how I handled this, but it was the only way I could think of to cope. I knew how to end relationships, not how to fix them. When an unmourned death is your paradigm for loss, later separations have an evil way of echoing back to that earlier one.

This time, though, the pain refused to stay underground. As the initial shock of separation slowly wore off, I began to grieve with a ferocity that, quite literally, one night brought me to my knees. It didn't matter that I was the one who'd walked away; I still felt an overpowering sense of loss. Five months later, I was still mourning with an intensity that even a four-year relationship didn't seem to warrant, and I realized that my feelings had to be coming from a place deeper, much deeper, than a space once occupied by a man I loved.

Eva, forty-five, nods her head vigorously when I share this story with her. She was eight when her mother died, and her experience with later separation closely parallels my own. "My husband left two and a half years ago, and the divorce was final a year after that," she says. "At the time, I couldn't understand why I was so inordinately taken by it. I've seen a lot of people go through divorces, and most of them didn't suffer as I think I did. I really suffered. At first, I thought, 'Well, maybe I feel things more intensely than other people,' which may in part be true. But that experience made it clear to me that a lot of my suffering wasn't about my husband. It was about my mother. So I'm trying to understand more about that first loss, and what it's done to me."

For thirty-seven-year-old Yvonne, however, loss has become progressively easier. She says her divorce three years ago and her teenage son's decision to live with his father provoked minimal emotional pain compared with what she, as a twelve-year-old, felt when her mother died. "I view separation and loss as inevitable," she says. "I'm ready for it. I never want to be lulled into thinking that something can't change at any moment. I know this sounds cruel, but I believe I come by it honestly. I have loving relationships with many people. If anything, I want to make sure that I'm remembered when I die."

Why do some women who've experienced early loss adjust easily to later separations, whether in the personal or professional world, while others live in perpetual fear of abandonment? Nobody knows for sure. Most therapists agree that a child's specific experience with an early, major loss shapes her emerging personality, which then determines how she views and handles later separations. Exactly how her personality is affected—if at all—depends on the factors below.

Individual Constitution

We're all born with different temperaments, and some children appear to possess a natural resilience that protects them from long-term distress. "There is a certain hardiness of personality that allows some people to do better than others," Therese Rando says. "That doesn't mean these people are unmoved by death, but when they are moved by it, they're going to deal with it in a way that's better than someone who had a weaker personality to begin with." Other children seem to have an innate, deep sensitivity to loss that leaves them nearly crippled by it every time. The psychologist and author Clarissa Pinkola Estés, Ph.D., calls these people "sensitives." In her audiotape, "Warming the Stone Child: Myths and Stories About Abandonment and the Unmothered Child," she explains, "It is true hell for a sensitive to be unmothered and abandoned, because they're the people who, if you just scratch them, bleed. They're the people who are like the skinless man. They walk around with exposed nerves." No matter how well supported these daughters are as mourners, they're constitutionally incapable of bouncing back quickly from loss.

Early Attachment Patterns

The British psychiatrist John Bowlby believed a child's earliest pattern of attachment determines her resilience or vulnerability to later stressful life events. Although he studied children only until the age of six, his hypothesis suggests that the kind of bond a girl forms with her mother predicts how well she'd cope with losing her. A young daughter with an anxious attachment, such as one who panics each time her mother leaves her sight, may lack the emotional skills to accept the loss of her mother or a later attachment figure without intense protest and distress. Paradoxically, kids who securely attach to a primary caregiver may be the ones most able to let later relationships come and go.

Perception and Response

A daughter who perceives herself as capable and takes responsibility for herself after a mother's death often gains a level of mastery over her environment. When she believes she has acted, rather than reacted, to the loss, she can develop a certain self-esteem and self-confidence that helps to insulate her against later stresses. She knows she can rely on her own resources.

The daughter who perceives herself as helpless and powerless against adversity, however, is more likely to grow up fearing future loss. These are often individuals who have what psychologists call an "external locus of control," the belief that things happen *to* them, rather than as the result of their own efforts. Instead of trusting her own ability to cope, this daughter lives with an ongoing fear that another major loss will occur and that she will collapse.

Forty-three-year-old Mary Jo, for example, who was eight when she lost her mother and nine when her younger brother died, was raised as an observant Catholic and concluded that God must be punishing her for bad behavior. Believing she was powerless against divine will, as a child she lay in bed and practiced lying in her coffin, convinced she would be the next family member to die. She was also terrified of losing her father, and as an adult, she extended her fear to include losing her husband, her job, and her home. "I've always had a sense of alarm, worrying who or what I'm going to lose next," she explains. A divorce in her twenties left Mary Jo even more convinced that she lacked power over her life.

Ability to Mourn

A motherless daughter who has the personal maturity and the environmental support to express her feelings, attach meaning to the loss, and form other secure attachments is most likely to accommodate the death of her mother and approach future separations without excessive trauma or pain. But a daughter who was prohibited from feeling angry or sad, who became bogged down in denial or guilt, or who grew up with a further threat of abandonment may never mourn that first loss. Erna Furman, who studied parent loss with a group of Cleveland child analysts in the 1960s and 1970s, found that when childhood mourning is incomplete—as it often is—the death of another loved one in adulthood frequently reactivates elements of the early loss, including the same coping mechanisms the child relied on then. As a psychologist I know explains it, "The stone drops straight to the bottom of the well." The problem, as many women discover, is that what helped a child through a loss at twelve doesn't necessarily work for a woman of thirty-five.

When a subsequent loss sends a mourner spiraling back to her mother's death, it encourages her to continue working on grieving the initial loss. Experiencing subsequent losses, then, may be an important part of a daughter's long-term mourning task.

This is true when a later loss cycles back to an earlier one, but that sequence isn't inevitable. Later loss reactivates early loss selectively, depending on who dies or leaves the second time, the cause of that loss, the timing in a daughter's life, and the proximity in time to another major loss. Eva, for example, lost her father twenty-five years after her mother died. The circumstances of this second death were sufficiently different for her, as an adult, to perceive it as an isolated event and keep it separate from her mother's. But when her husband, on whom she'd depended for most of her emotional needs, walked out eight years later, the abandonment and despair she felt were so similar to her experience after her mother's death that this loss was the one that sent her back to do the mourning she hadn't done as a young child.

This is all complicated even further when the death or departure of a mother isn't the first major loss of a daughter's life. The death of a father or a sibling, a parental divorce, family dysfunction, or a traumatic move may have already occurred before a mother dies. Six percent of the 154 motherless women surveyed for this book lost their fathers first, and 13 percent said their biological parents separated or divorced before their mothers died. For these women, a mother's death often re-triggered elements of an even earlier loss, and reactivated coping mechanisms developed and relied on at that time.

As unusual as it may sound, family dysfunction such as alcoholism or abuse may help daughters cope with the loss of a mother, at least in the short term. "Loss isn't a new event for these kids," Therese Rando explains. "They've had practice feeling helpless and dealing with it. But I'd much rather be a daughter who's had what I call 'too good a childhood,' without any loss, because over time that person will be able to cope better." The child with a troubled past who learned to "numb out" at an early age may depend on this skill to get through the initial shock after a mother dies or leaves, but she probably lacks the solid foundation she'll need to handle the changes that follow and the subsequent losses she'll inevitably face.

Predicting the Future:
Negative Projection

Not long after my first daughter was born, I was sitting in a Mommy & Me group and listening to other exhausted new mothers share the stressors that now filled their days. One mother couldn't get her newborn to nap for stretches of more than forty-five minutes at a time; another was concerned that the minerals in her bottled water were disturbing her son through her breast milk. The woman next to me expressed the irritation she felt when her mother-in-law criticized her daughter's use of a pacifier.

Surrounded by such tame concerns of new motherhood, I was reluctant to share my own new fears. I could just imagine the way heads would turn and eyebrows would arch if I were to say, "Ever since my daughter was born, I've been afraid that I'm going to die and leave her motherless, or that she's going to get sick with an untreatable disease, spend weeks in the hospital ICU, die in my arms, and leave me and my husband incapable of living without her."

I knew that I was projecting an innocuous new-mother moment into a full-blown annihilation scene, but it didn't seem all that far-fetched to me. Early loss has a way of making adults turn even the most mundane, everyday events into a catastrophe. Children never miss dinner because they forgot to check the time; they've been kidnapped by ex-cons. The headache is never a migraine; it's a brain tumor, and you've waited too long. There's no such thing as turbulence; the plane is going down. It's part of what Maxine Harris, Ph.D., calls the "terrifying insecurity" that marks life after the full-scale disaster of an early death occurs. "For these individuals, the world seems changeable and unpredictable, and they fear that even that which seems most secure could be taken away on a moment's notice," she writes.

As thirty-two year old Jess, who was thirteen when her mother died, admits, "I insist that my husband call if he's going to be home later than expected. If he doesn't, I panic. I don't fear that he's out having an affair. I'm convinced he's dead on a highway somewhere."

Someone we love has left us before. Who's to say it can't happen again?

These visions of gloom usually have little to do with reality. Instead, they're outgrowths of a woman's perceived vulnerability, which is linked to her expectation for future loss rather than to incomplete grief in her past. People don't usually think of themselves as vulnerable to threatening events unless they've experienced a loss or disaster—such as the early death of a parent—in the past. When a daughter loses a mother, she learns early that human relationships are temporary, that terminations are beyond her control, and her feelings of basic trust and security are shattered. The result? A sense of inner fragility and overriding vulnerability. She discovers she's not immune to unfortunate events, and the fear of subsequent, similar losses may become a defining characteristic of her personality. "I know my mother's death led to this huge cynicism I have," says twenty-five-year-old Margie, who was seven when her mother committed suicide. "I often feel like, well, why wouldn't my boyfriend get hit by a bus? It's not *that* strange. What's going to prevent it from happening? What tremendous luck is going to prevent all the people I love from dying?"

Anyone who's experienced a traumatic loss will react more dramatically to the risk of future loss, perceived or actual, says Tamar Granot. "Often, adults do not understand why a child may exhibit such intense anxiety when faced with seemingly simple situations," she writes. "The child's overreacting has to do with the traumatic memories that immediately surface whenever he gets close to a situation that contains elements of a potential loss and separation. For children who have already experienced a traumatic loss, even the beginning of a situation that involves a risk of loss will stir up the deepest fears and anxieties." And this isn't a state that evaporates after childhood: We often retain these characteristics well into our adult years. Says Carla, forty-four, who lost both parents by the age of fifteen, "When we go off in the car, I often think, 'What if a car comes careening across the median and one of my sons is killed?' I know other mothers think of that, but I think it occurs perhaps more often to me. And yet I recognize it for what it is and I tell myself, 'Okay. You've thought the thought. Now put it aside. You have the beautiful gifts of your sons and a life that is full and for the moment very satisfying.' I don't think people would refer to me as a gloomy person, but there is a sense in which I'm racking in, I don't know, in a kind of darkness. It's a curious way to live."

Motherless daughters frequently feel this intense and disproportionate fear of losing a loved one and, because of their psychological identifications with their mothers' bodies, they also develop an excessive concern for their own safety or health. "The same person might not have any aversion to risk in her career or in other areas of her life," Phyllis Klaus explains. "Her fears are very specific, linked to illness, or accidents, or whatever. There's a residue of delayed post-traumatic stress from the first loss that gets triggered by the potential for certain events."

Potential: That's the critical word here. It's not certainty we're frightened of. It's what might happen. When the loss of a mother results in family chaos or feelings of abandonment, even the risk of subsequent loss can cause anxiety in a child and inspire behaviors designed to preserve the status quo. As the child matures, this anxiety may extend to concerns beyond and unrelated to the original loss, turning her into an adult who has difficulty making decisions out of fear of catastrophic results. Taking chances may feel too risky to her, and instead she seeks safety through controlling whatever aspects of her life she can.

Candace, thirty-two, describes her romantic past as a patchwork of compromise and denial, a series of attempts to hold onto relationships she knew were destined to fail. "Many times, I put up with deterioration rather than risk the possibility of separation," she admits. "I'm also a people-pleaser, in part, I think, because I don't want to risk *anyone's* rejection. At some level, I've equated my mother's death when I was fourteen with her rejection of life, and of us—her family." When potential change evokes the memory of disaster, sameness represents security. That's one reason why so many motherless women will cling to outmoded relationships, jobs, or homes, long after they know they should have moved on.

Someone recently asked me what the biggest challenge of my adult life has been. I didn't need to think about it for long: It's been learning to cope with separation and loss. Some days I can make the critical decision to walk away from a friendship or an obligation, trusting that my reasoning is valid. But there are also days when I'm so hypersensitive to abandonment that I start crying as I leave my cheerful three-year-old at preschool, afraid that she'll miss me during the day and I won't be there. "Is everything okay?" the school receptionist asks, and I know she's asking about me, not my daughter.

"It's just so hard to leave her sometimes," I explain.

"She'll be fine," the receptionist assures me, with the wisdom of someone who's seen hundreds of children pass by her desk over the years.

Okay. So she's probably right. My daughter isn't going to curl up unresponsively in a corner because I've driven off to work. (In fact, through the window on my way to the car I can see that she's already doing Play-Doh with the other kids.) And my husband isn't going to disappear without warning or explanation at any moment. And my sore throat is probably just a sore throat, and not an esophageal tumor. I know the odds are in my favor. But until I see concrete proof these things won't happen, until I know for certain, a part of me is always watching. Always waiting. Always making elaborate, unnecessary plans.

Loss of the Second Parent

When I was twenty, I demanded that my father tell me the terms of his life insurance policy. He wasn't in particularly poor health, but I needed the assurance that my brother, sister, and I would be provided for. Anything could happen to him, at any moment; that was all I knew for sure. Late at night, I would pause outside his closed bedroom door as I walked down the hall, listening for the steady breathing on the other side. If I didn't hear it, I'd open the door a crack, just to see his chest rise and fall.

Just checking, I told myself. Just making sure we're still safe.

He lived for another twenty years. As sad and tragic as his dying was, it contained a small element of relief, the knowledge that the worst had finally come to pass. Like my mother, he died of liver failure; but his death took place while he was under hospice care at home, in a setting of full disclosure, surrounded by family until the end. His was an entirely different departure from that of my mother in 1981, and it was healing for that reason. Yet at the same time, I hadn't fully anticipated what a large hole his death would leave behind, how much I would miss him as a father and grandfather.

I'd lost a parent before, yes, but this was something else. "You've been through this," friends reminded me, trying to help me find perspective. Well, yes. And no. My role as daughter, had narrowed when my mother died. Now it had been taken away completely. With my father's death, there was no longer any space in the world for me to be a child. For weeks, I sleepwalked through my daily activities, stunned that I was no longer anyone's daughter.

Losing one parent teaches us about just that—how to lose one parent. It doesn't prepare us for the loss of the second. "The death of the last parent is a whole other dimension," says Therese Rando, who lost both of her parents by the age of eighteen. "When one parent dies, the world is dramatically altered, absolutely, but you still have another one left. When that second parent dies, it's the loss of all ties, and where does that leave you? You lose your history, your sense of connection to the past. You also lose the final buffer between you and death. Even if you're an adult, it's weird to be orphaned."

A daughter's identity changes dramatically when both her parents die. The roof above her is stripped away. When she's a young adult, capable of making her own decisions, this second loss pushes her into a phase of individuality where she's accountable only to herself. "I lost both of my parents by the time I was twenty-six," says Christine, now thirty-five. "And suddenly I didn't have anybody telling me what to do. I could do whatever I wanted. That's a scary feeling, when you're suddenly let loose and realize there's nobody to check in with. Nobody to ask, 'What are you doing?' or say, 'Maybe you should think about this.' All of a sudden you have all this responsibility for yourself, and you think, *What do I do?*"

Losing both parents so young, Christine says, helped turn her into a more mature, independent woman than she believes she would have been otherwise. As Clarissa Pinkola Estés says, orphans both lose and gain. "They're highly intuitive, because they've suffered so much," she says. "They learned to develop radar to know where the next kick or hit was coming from. So as adults, they're very, very alert, and often uncannily so. They not only can tell bad things but also good things about people. The only problem is, they often override their intuition, especially if they think they'll get love. It's almost like a currency exchange that they do."

For the daughter who loses one parent young, the death of the second parent may trigger a new mourning cycle for the first. Thirty-two-year-old Mariana was sixteen when her mother died, and after an initial two-month period of shock and denial, she began to mourn intensely.

It took me five years to get over the grief. Every year around her birthday, around my parents' anniversary, around the time she died, I was totally miserable. And then, after about five years, it just went away. It wasn't that I stopped missing her, but the hurt wasn't always there anymore. But when Daddy died, I really lost it. He died last November, fifteen years after Mommy. And then it was like, there's nobody. I felt like I was losing two instead of one. So his death brought back all the memories of her, as well as the grief for him.

Though her second loss reactivated additional mourning for her mother and introduced the new pain of being left parentless, Mariana approached her father's death as a thirty-one-year-old adult, more self-reliant and emotionally mature than she'd been at sixteen. Her acute grief phase for him began immediately and lasted for less than a year. As she prepares for the first anniversary of his death, Mariana says she feels stronger and more prepared to face the day than she did as an adolescent after her mother died.

Eva, who lost her mother when she was eight and her father when she was thirty-five, attached a different meaning to parent loss as an adult. Her peers were beginning to experience the same, and she perceived the death as a traumatic but timely event. As a result, she could mourn and accommodate the loss without long-term, ongoing distress. "A child really has a different perception of death than an adult does," she says. "I just didn't have a clue when I was eight. As tragic and as sad as my dad's death was, it wasn't confusing. It made sense to me. I hadn't known how confusing my mother's death was until my father died twenty-five years later."

The loss of one parent during childhood or adolescence is traumatic enough, but for some unfortunate young daughters the death of a mother either follows or is closely followed by the loss of a father. Every month I receive several e-mails from women who've lost both parents young, detailing the uniqueness of their situations.

Although *orphan* is defined as a child under the age of eighteen who has had at least one parent die, most of us associate the term with a Dickensian image of a child alone, without either biological parent alive. In 2003, 29,140 U.S. children under eighteen fit this description—"double orphans," they're called—and about another 32,000 were between the ages of nineteen and thirty-six.

For such a child, Tamar Granot says, "the sense of calamity and loss is absolute. The child's entire world is instantaneously shattered, and he feels he is left alone in the world. Suddenly, he goes from being an ordinary child with parents and a family to one who has nothing." To a child in need of a legal guardian, the loss of the last surviving parent usually means a change of residence and new caretakers. Outsiders intrude on the family system in the form of relatives, neighbors, social workers, and other professionals compelled by altruism or law to intervene. The child may go live with relatives or move into a foster home. If she has siblings, they become her only living connection to her nuclear family, and their importance to her may increase.

Darlene, forty-three, says her younger sister became the only constant figure in her childhood after she lost both her parents in separate accidents by the age of ten. "My sister and I were always very, very close," Darlene recalls. "If anyone had tried to separate us, that would have been the last straw. I don't think I would have been able to accept that at all. If I were an only child, I would have had to handle things differently, I think. But because I had my sister, we depended on each other a lot for support and acceptance and approval. As adults, we still do."

Multiple losses within short periods can seriously stress a child's coping skills. Instead of mourning for the lost parents, an early orphan often has to pour all her emotional energy into just getting from day to day. The enormity of such a trauma is too overwhelming for someone who is still a child to touch. Only years later, as an adult who's found stability within herself and through external relationships, can she revisit the losses, take in the significance of the pain, and begin to process it.

Along the way, the early orphan may endure long and lonely stretches in her quest to find a replacement for the parental love she lost. After both her parents died in a car accident when she was thirteen, Diane, now thirty-nine, lived in nine places over the next three years, searching for one where she felt she belonged. "I was such a lost soul," she says. "I tried drugs. I was pretty loose and easy with the sexual things in my early years. I was looking for love, looking for anything that would dull the pain and make me feel like I fit in." Jokes, she discovered, decreased tension and earned her positive feedback, and humor became the coping skill she relied on to alleviate her feelings of dislocation and isolation.

Today, Diane is a successful stand-up comedian. Her early experience as an orphan instilled in her a strong will to survive, which she believes members of her audience can recognize and appreciate. "The life force is very strong in me, and people are drawn to it," she says. "You wouldn't believe the stories I get after my shows, just incredible stories of pain and anguish. A lot of women come over and tell me they're on the road to healing themselves. They say, 'You know, you've given me a lot of strength.' I'm not sure why. I don't particularly talk about my past on stage. It's just something they get out of me."

The very term *orphan* reflects the uniqueness of a solitary, insightful state. The alchemists originally used the word to name a unique gem once found in an emperor's crown, similar to what we call a solitaire today. They compared the orphan stone to the lapis philosophorum, or the philosophers' stone, considered worthless and priceless at the same time, despised by fools but loved by the wise. Even then, it was believed that orphans held special knowledge and had acquired an insight that others had not attained.

Some early orphans find solace in this archetypal association, using it to attach meaning to and justify their double loss. Twenty-five-year-old Margie, who was seven when her mother died and then went to live with an indifferent father and antagonistic stepmother, neither of whom she speaks to today, says, "I've felt emotionally alone since my mother died, and that kind of heightens my feelings of difference and uniqueness. I've felt that I've had to raise and take care of myself. Sometimes I wonder if my feeling of uniqueness is all bad. I wonder if I'm getting something out of that, thinking that I'm extraordinarily different." Reminding herself that she was "special" became the defense that helped Margie through a difficult and lonely adolescence. It became her compensation for losing her mother physically and her father emotionally at such a young age. As an adult, however, she's now aware of how risky this self-definition can be. She's secretly pleased about being different from most other women she knows, but she's cautious about letting her self-perception slide into delusions of grandeur.

As Margie's example illustrates, a woman need not lose both parents to death to identify with the orphan archetype. Many unmothered women who still have one or both parents nevertheless describe themselves as spiritual or emotional orphans. "Functionally orphaned" is a term they understand well. Their mothers, though physically present, may have offered them little emotional support; their fathers, though still alive, may have played minimal roles in their lives. As children, their most crucial emotional needs were never met.

As early orphans search for a reason why such tragedy would befall them, they reach for religion, metaphysics, rationalizations, even platitudes—anything that will help them believe the cosmos is not so random that disaster can strike anyone at any moment, and that they are not doomed or marked in any dark way. A girl uses whatever cognitive and emotional resources are available to her at her time of loss, and in adolescence and then adulthood she continually reworks the images, seeking renewed comfort at each developmental stage.

Darlene, who lost her father and then her mother to separate accidents by the age of ten, says her search for meaning has continued well into her adult life:

Between thirty and forty, I really felt like I needed an answer. My husband and I both came from a pretty religious background, but after we married, we didn't go to church very much. After my son was born, we wanted him to have an upbringing similar to ours, and we started going back to church. I prayed a lot then, for help and guidance. My husband is really good about talking about things like this. I've talked with him for hours and hours. It's just something I'll never know, why it happened, or why it happened to me. I want to believe there was a reason why my mother had to die, too. I like to think maybe it's because she missed my father an awful lot, and now they're happy together. That's helped me a lot, to think about it that way.

Loss is a part of life as involuntary as a heartbeat, as inevitable as nightfall. This is even more poignantly true for women, whose gendered experiences are so closely linked to natural separation and loss. In her essay "The Normal Losses of Being Female," Lila J. Kalinich explains that although a man experiences potential and real losses throughout his life, a woman encounters a significant loss about once every decade: the first individuation from the mother during her toddler years; the end of childhood when menstruation begins; the second individuation during adolescence; the loss of virginity during adolescence or young adulthood; the possible loss of her original surname when she marries; the sacrifice of certain elements of motherhood or career if she decides against combining both; her children's departure from home; the loss of her childbearing capacity at the onset of menopause; and, because women are likely to outlive their husbands, the possibility of widowhood. Biologically and socially, women are surrounded by loss. Within this larger landscape, the loss of a mother is an inevitable, though tragic, female experience.

Eva, Mary Jo, and Margie, as adults, each found a compassionate counselor to help them mourn their mothers' deaths. Other women interviewed for this book mentioned strong religious beliefs, dependable lovers and spouses, and close friendships as supports that have helped them cope with subsequent separation and loss and approach it with less trepidation.

"After the first death, there is no other," Dylan Thomas wrote. He understood how influential that first loss can be. It continues to sit on our shoulders, guiding our response to future separations, until we can put it to rest. When you lose a parent early, you develop an increased sensitivity to later loss. The challenge isn't to bury that early experience, but to understand it, to accept it, and to keep it from interfering with your ability to enjoy and fully experience the rest of your life.

II

Loss

Sophie stared at the pans lying upside down on the counter. "Doesn't it seem kind of pathetic—just us?"

"What do you mean?" said Caitlin. "We're a family."

"Yah, but it doesn't feel like we're all here."

"We're not," Chicky said.

"Joanie Nathan said the first year needs to go by before you get used to it," Caitlin said.

"We have a month, then," Chicky said. It had been eleven months since the accident.

"I'm not expecting to *get* used to it," said Delilah with disgust.

"Well, it feels like more than just Mum," Sophie said.

Everyone nodded. It wasn't just one thing; a thousand things were missing. The house was filled with missing things, despite the Christmas decorations being up. . . The girls put the decorations where they always got put—the creche on the Chinese table in the hall, the laurel looping down the banister, the wooden fruit poked into wreaths. They taped Christmas cards to the stair railing the way Mum had and lit the pine candle. Nothing was the same.

—Susan Minot, *Monkeys*

Chapter Five

Daddy's Little Girl
The Father-Daughter Dyad

MY FATHER WAS NEVER much of a talker. Even when my mother was alive he preferred to stay at home listening to the radio and working crossword puzzles while she went out at night. She scheduled the social events, organized the dinner parties, made all the new friends. After she died, it wasn't much of a surprise that he spoke even less. Over the years, his occasional phone calls consisted mainly of questions about the weather and the performance of my car. Later, he'd ask about my daughters. He wanted to hear only the good news. If I mentioned my mother or said I was having a hard day, silence was typically his response. If I brought up his drinking or his weight, I'd hear a quick goodbye and a click. Maybe he'd call back in a few days or weeks. Long portions of my adult life were spent wondering which one of us would break down first and pick up the phone.

The easy explanation for my pervasive fear of abandonment is that my mother died when I was seventeen, but that's never been a reason that's made much sense to me. Although it taught me a quick lesson about the impermanence of relationships, I know, and have always known, that my mother did not want to leave. But my father, well, that was a different story. The threat of his departure, which was both symbolic and real, began with the moments in my childhood when he stormed out of the house after an argument and reached a terrifying peak one evening when I was a sophomore in college and my sister called me, crying, pleading with me to do something, because my father, momentarily overcome by the demands of single fatherhood, was packing his bags to leave.

In the end he didn't go anywhere that night, but my siblings and I quickly learned how to tiptoe through the minefield in this new landscape we all shared, careful not to tread too hard on any topic that might make our father explode. A friend of mine who at age eight lost her mother describes this kind of tentative choreography as a dance between the threat of rejection and a denial of the self. To confront any painful issue with her father, especially concerning her mother, meant risking that he, too, would leave her, but to pretend such topics did not exist was the most blatant denial of her reality. Because the children in my family were too young—and too afraid—to risk total abandonment, we chose silence. The times our father did show emotion and let us see his pain, we deliberately forced him back into the safety of suppression. When he broke into jagged tears at my brother's bar mitzvah, I elbowed him hard and hissed at him to stop. To me, his crying signified the first stage of what I was afraid would lead to complete collapse, undermining the only security I had left. While my father never gave me a safe place to air my feelings, neither did I, until much later, give him the chance to express his.

My father died at the age of seventy-four. His children and grandchildren were around him at the end, but he didn't have a partner or even any close friends. He never remarried. As far as I know, he never even dated. He lived alone in a small, tidy apartment with dozens of photos of his children and grandchildren clustered on the walls. Twenty-four years after my mother's death the mention of her name still brought him to tears. Until the very end of his life, he refused to talk about her final days or the role he'd played in them. And so, as fate would have it, he had to live them instead. Her primary cause of death was liver failure, and liver cancer was what finally did him in. The last seventy-two hours of his life, as his liver shut down, mirrored the last three days of hers with eerie precision. If I hadn't believed in karma before that experience, I surely would have started believing in it then.

Bereavement experts talk about the importance of maintaining a relationship with the deceased, and about how the inner dialogue continues long after a loved one has gone. When I reach for my father now, I find only silence, but it's neither uncomfortable nor unfamiliar. Long pauses and audible ellipses always demarcated our conversations when he was alive. I try to speak to him sometimes, silently; but, even now, I don't know what to say. For the last twenty years of his life, we rarely managed to communicate at a level more significant than the meteorological report. And it makes me wonder: Did we ever communicate any other way?

I have to go backwards, to look at where it all began.

I know little about my father's life before I was born, only disconnected snapshots meted out from time to time. He grew up, with both parents and his older brother, in New York City during the Depression. His grandparents ran a corner newsstand. On Saturday afternoons, he saw double features for a quarter and bought three candy bars for a dime.

The stories he told of his childhood were brief and intermittent, deliberate parables linked to lessons he meant for me to learn. When I asked for a raise in my allowance, he told me how once he had asked his mother for a nickel to buy an ice cream cone and she couldn't come up with enough change. When the school system wanted me to bypass kindergarten and go straight into the first grade, he insisted that I stay back with the children my age. He'd skipped two grades in elementary school, he said, and was miserable as a result, always too young to make real friends.

I can tell you a great deal about my mother's family, about her grandparents' immigration from Russia and Poland, and about her eight aunts and uncles, her two younger sisters, and her parents, all of whom I knew. But my father's family was always a mystery to me. It's small—only his brother and his brother's children survive. And he's always kept his past firmly locked away. In the cufflink box on his dresser I once found a picture of his father, a small black-and-white mug shot of a dark, serious man who looked remarkably like him. I used to stand on tiptoe and sneak looks at it during the day, trying to figure out where my father had come from and what he might become. My mother once told me that my paternal grandfather, who died just after my parents met, had a heart attack at fifty-two. "That's why I'm always nagging your father to stop drinking and smoking, and to keep his weight down," she explained. When I mentioned this to my father a few years ago, he looked genuinely puzzled. "But my father died of cancer when he was fifty-seven," he told me, and he didn't say much more.

When the author Victoria Secunda says, "Mothers represent the day, fathers the night—and the weekend, the holiday, the special dinner out," she succinctly describes the family I knew for my first seventeen years. My mother was the continuous presence in my life. My father was the parent who waxed and waned, leaving for work each morning before I woke and returning in time for dinner and prime-time TV. The quick and the physical—that was my father's domain. He taught me to throw a softball and mow the lawn. He corrected my math and chemistry equations. He showed me how to pitch a tent. He was the disciplinarian of my childhood, the distant yet larger-than-life figure who set the house rules. He handed out allowances and he reprimanded us. When we traveled as a family, he always drove the car.

My mother was the parent who woke me each morning, made sure I drank a full glass of orange juice with breakfast, and always called, "Have a nice day!" as I bolted for the bus. She was there when I came home. She chose my clothing, accompanied my grade-school classes on field trips, and read me stories before I went to bed. My mother taught me how to play the piano, cook a three-course meal, and knit a simple scarf. The lessons that required patience and repetition came under her tutelage, and as a result, it was in her company that I spent most of my time.

The morning my mother died, my father assembled his three children around the kitchen table at dawn. He looked at us and blinked quizzically, as if to ask, "Have we met?" and I understood fully for the first time that I had only one parent left, and that he was one I barely knew and didn't particularly like. So much prose has been devoted to the Good Mother/Bad Mother complex, but far less to the corresponding split in our fathers. "One man, two fathers. Daddy and the Other Father," is how Letty Cottin Pogrebin describes her father in the memoir *Deborah, Golda, and Me*. When memory fails, the old home movies from the sixties show me that I had a daddy who carried me on his shoulders and let me blow out the candles on his birthday cake. This daddy is the man who, during the first years after his wife died, tried to compensate as best he could. He rearranged his work schedule to be home by 5:00 p.m. He gave us money to buy our own clothes. One day he came home with a microwave and taught himself how to cook. I used to set the table and watch him as he prepared the meals, a big man in a chef's apron thumbing through his new cookbooks as his Scotch and soda sweated droplets on the counter by his side. In the warmer months he barbecued, and two nights a week we ordered in.

I loved him for these efforts, only vaguely understanding how difficult his transition from husband and part-time father to full-time single parent must have been. I remember how his face pinched up the first time we took a car trip after my mother died, when nobody wanted to sit in the passenger seat. But most of the time, all I could see was the Other Father. I'd been my mother's protector, the one who always defended her when they argued, and our afternoons of bedroom "girl talk" had given me information about their marriage that no sixteen-year-old daughter should have to know. I've heard that when a mother shares with her daughter bitter feelings toward her husband, the mother keeps that daughter allied with and bound to her even after she dies, and prevents the daughter from forming her own relationship with her father. I know some of my anger toward my father developed this way. And I know some more of it came from knowing he had withheld information from my mother about the severity of her illness, denying her the opportunity to turn to the religion she believed in so deeply, or to fashion any sort of goodbye. And beyond all that, I was angry with him for being just a father. When my mother transformed into a saint after her death, I turned my father into the ultimate sinner. As hard as he tried, nothing he did could possibly please me. His most grievous fault was that he wasn't her.

I always knew that my father fiercely loved his children. He showed this love as best he could: with his brief telephone calls; with the ten-dollar bills he stuffed in my pocket each time I walked out his door; with the Priority Mail packages that arrived, like clockwork, the day before someone's birthday, with a preprinted card inside signed "Love, Grandpa" or "Love, Dad." My adult friends and boyfriends who met him in his later years knew him only as a gentle, quiet, sober, lonely man. Yet I once knew him to be hard drinking and emotionally unpredictable, a man who behaved so much like a child that his children felt as if they needed to parent him. It was one thing to accept the good/bad duality in my mother, the parent who was dead. It was much harder to reconcile feelings of love and resentment toward the one who was still alive.

I used to think the distance between my father and me was peculiar, even shameful in some way, but when I asked ninety-three other motherless women to describe their current relationships with their fathers, I discovered that I was by no means unique. Only 13 percent of these women described their father-daughter relationship as "excellent." Thirty-one percent said it was "poor," and the remainder categorized it somewhere in between. Some of these daughters had once been close to their fathers, only to lose the connection after their mothers died. Others said the relationship soured when a stepmother entered the family. And still others said their father-daughter bonds had never been strong, although they hadn't really noticed that when their mothers were still alive.

Whatever the circumstances, these figures are disheartening at best, and troubling at worst. A good deal of research in the past ten years has focused on the importance of the surviving parent to a bereaved child's long-term adaptation, and in every study conducted the verdict has been clear: A good relationship between a bereaved child and her surviving parent helps buffer the ill effects of the loss. A strained relationship, or one characterized by neglect or abuse, puts the child at risk for numerous long-term adverse effects, including depression, high blood pressure, diminished feelings of self-worth, and vulnerability to stress.

Researchers once looked for a direct cause-and-effect relationship between early parent loss and depression. Now, it's widely believed that the surviving parent provides a crucial intermediary link. Depression is much more likely to surface among bereaved children who receive little or no emotional care from a surviving parent than among those who receive compassionate, reliable care from that parent after the loss. "Without a doubt, the most important external influence on the emotional state of the child and on how he copes with his loss is the parent or adult who raises him," Tamar Granot says.

The work of Phyllis Silverman and William Worden has provided us with far more knowledge about motherless children raised in father-headed households than we had only a decade ago. When they compared a group of children who'd lost a mother to a group who'd lost a father, they found that the motherless kids were more likely to experience changes in daily living routines, and less likely to have their emotional needs met. They were also quicker to get a stepparent and more likely to be living with a depressed parent—which in turn increased their own chances of becoming depressed.

In 2002, approximately 840,000 American girls under the age of eighteen were living with their single fathers.[1] Of all children raised in single-parent homes, these girls may have the most personal difficulties, especially during the teen years. The Harvard Children's Bereavement Study revealed that adolescent motherless girls being raised by their fathers were more likely to act out or engage in delinquent behavior than girls who'd lost their fathers. "A lot of times they were the oldest child in the family and were given responsibility for childcare and meals," William Worden explains. "That was part of the resentment. And the dads would often bring a new honey into the house, and that was part of it, too. There wasn't one particular reason. But the significant acting out on the part of teen girls who lost mothers was way, way beyond that of teen girls whose dads had died."

According to Richard A. Warshak, Ph.D., a clinical associate professor at the University of Texas Southwestern Medical Center and an expert on father custody, girls raised by fathers show lower self-esteem and higher anxiety than father-raised boys and mother-raised children of either sex. This is partly because of a father's doubts and insecurities about raising daughters, he says, and partly because of a girl's anxiety about becoming a stand-in spouse.

---

[1]According to U.S. Census data, about 63,000 of these girls were living with widowed fathers. The rest lost mothers to abandonment or divorce. The 840,000 figure, however, doesn't include girls whose widowed fathers remarried. Approximately 400,000 girls in the United States are currently living with a biological father and a stepmother, although no bureau statistic exists to tell us how many of these girls lost their mothers to death.

"When a father has to raise a child of the opposite sex, it's complicated," Nan Birnbaum explains. "He's in part influenced by his own identifications with his parents. A dad's identifications with his own mother help him understand his daughter, and his memories of how his father treated his mother and sisters, if he had any, are embedded in his ideas of how to treat women. If a man feels relatively comfortable with the aspects of his mother he felt in tune with and shared, then he has something to draw from. But if he had an uncomfortable relationship with his mother, he doesn't necessarily have a firm bedrock for relating to his daughter."

When a mother dies or leaves the home, fathers and daughters find themselves in an unexpected and awkward position. They are strangers and intimates, allies and foes. Explains thirty-two-year-old Maureen, who was nineteen and the youngest of three children when her mother died, "My relationship with my father was nonexistent when my mother was alive. She'd really alienated me from him. I had to totally start from scratch with him. When he started dating six weeks after the funeral, there was so much tension in the house. I had a lot of anger toward him I just didn't know how to cope with. My stepmother has been instrumental in getting my father and me to talk as adults, and my own maturity has allowed me to patch some things up. We're getting better at relating to each other today."

Many motherless daughters trace their current struggles—particularly in intimate relationships—not just back to the loss of their mothers but also to their relationships with their fathers. Twenty-five-year-old Margie, who was seven when her divorced mother committed suicide, went to live with her father and stepmother, neither of whom helped her mourn as a child or feel emotionally secure.

> My father was very angry, very . . . I don't know what the opposite of nurturing is—indifferent? I was always afraid of my father. He could always say something mean to make me cry. My stepmother was just really terrible. She and I never got along. Recently, I began to conceptualize that not allowing me to grieve for my mother as a seven-year-old was abusive. If my father couldn't take care of me emotionally, he should have found me someone who could.

I had to develop coping skills as a child to survive in his house, and I'm realizing what worked for me then might not work so well for me now. One of my basic ideas is that I don't trust anyone. I could never trust my father or my stepmother, and now I feel like no one's worthy of trust, and in fact trust is kind of stupid. It's like setting yourself up. And I feel like I always have to be hypercompetent, and never have any vulnerabilities or express any needs. There was a time when I couldn't have any needs. I had to shut them down. But now I'm in a good relationship with a man, and I have good friendships. I'm starting to feel more emotionally secure, and I think I might be able to open up a bit more now and maybe express some needs.

In a 1993 University of Detroit–Mercy study of eighty-three adults who lost parents between the ages of three and sixteen, the psychologist Bette D. Glickfield found that the subjects who remembered their surviving parents as warm and nonrejecting were most likely to believe that they could depend on others as adults. "Being able to talk freely with the surviving parent about the circumstances surrounding the death, to express sorrow to the surviving parent about the death, or to ask questions about the deceased parent, as well as having a parent who encourages independence and trust in others, predicts one's ability to feel emotionally supported," she says. The idea is that daughters who feel secure after a mother's death are able to go on to form secure attachments with others.

Twenty-six-year-old Holly doubts that she'd avoid adult romance the way she does if she trusted that she could depend on others. For her, such trust was shattered when her father abruptly withdrew from her soon after her mother died. Holly says she never felt emotionally attached to her father when she was a child, and after her mother died when she was sixteen, she did not expect their relationship to improve dramatically. But she also did not expect her father to move in with a girlfriend six months later and leave her in the care of an elderly great-aunt until she left for college the following year. Feeling angry and abandoned, Holly swore she'd never make the mistake of depending on anyone else again:

My father continually lectured me during my childhood about the value of family togetherness. So the way he ditched me was a shock, and it left deep scars. Now, I often feel as though I can't let myself get married or even head toward marriage. I haven't yet figured out how to take consistently good care of myself, and because of my father's behavior, I'm deathly afraid of accepting from someone else what I want or need but can't give myself. I'm afraid of the dependence that kind of acceptance would imply. This is especially true with me and men. I'd rather go without what I need than get it through relying on someone else.

A father is a daughter's first heterosexual interest, and her relationship with him becomes the most influential blueprint for her later attachments to men. Throughout a daughter's childhood and adolescence, she picks up clues from her father about how to relate to males. Though it may sound implausible at first, given what we know about same-sex role modeling, some of a girl's *feminine* identifications come from having a father who exhibits the traditionally *masculine* traits of instrumentalism and assertion. Fathers also tend to reinforce sex-typed behavior in their daughters, subtly urging them to conform to behaviors and play that emphasize caretaking and cooperation. But when a mother dies or leaves, a father's traditionally masculine behaviors can't meet all of a daughter's needs. His ability—or inability—to take on the expressive parenting role is suddenly magnified, and his strengths and weaknesses in this area become more apparent and more important than they were when his wife was present.

On top of this, another layer—the father's ability to cope with mourning—is added to the post-loss father-daughter relationship. "Even today, fathers still tend to be people who will not talk at length or reveal their feelings to their children, and in some cases do not want their children to reveal their feelings to others," says Russell Hurd, Ph.D., an assistant professor of educational psychology at Kent State University in Canton, Ohio. And we must not forget that surviving parents are themselves trying to cope with a devastating loss. Husbands don't expect to outlive their wives, and they're often emotionally and practically unprepared for the demands of daily family life. Right when children are the most needy, widowed fathers, understandably, have the least to give.

Four Types of Fathers

Interviews with more than ninety motherless women revealed four common coping strategies that fathers adopt after the loss of a spouse. These categories are not mutually exclusive; a father may show evidence of more than one response, or switch from one to another over time. Like the mourning process in general, a father's adjustment to single-parenthood is fluid and evolutionary, and a daughter has different needs at different ages. A good indicator of where the father-daughter relationship will ultimately end up is the point at which it began. Still, a mother's absence can change the way a father relates to his daughter during the interim. The events of those months or years are the ones that can deeply affect a daughter's feelings of security and self-worth, and her ability to form satisfying relationships as an adult.

The I'm Okay, You're Okay Father

Tricia, twenty-five, has just started grieving for the mother who died when she was three. Until recently, she wasn't aware that she could. Her father hadn't mourned, and neither had her four older brothers and sisters, as far as she could see.

After Tricia's mother died, her father's response was a quick, three-part sequence of silence, avoidance, and remarriage. He encouraged the family to continue on as if the death had never occurred, as if the empty place at the dinner table had been there all along. I call this "the Bonanza syndrome," in honor of Ben Cartwright (played by Lorne Greene), the family patriarch of the television series *Bonanza,* who fathered three sons from three different wives, all of whom died young—one in childbirth, one at the hands of Indians, and one in a fall from a horse—none of whom were spoken of in any meaningful way. One notable exception takes place in the episode where the middle son, Hoss, falls in love with a dying woman. Ben takes him aside and solemnly shares with him, "Son, I've buried three wives, and my advice to you is that you've gotta take it like a man."

Growing up surrounded by such silence, Tricia passed through childhood and adolescence disassociated from her loss, yet she was still deeply traumatized by it.

"Up until the last couple of years, I never thought of my mother's death as something that really happened to me," she says. "In my head, I would think, 'What a terrible thing to have happened to a three-year-old girl—to a child out there, but not to me.' I couldn't relate to it at all. But what an awful thing, for someone else. At the same time, I couldn't even talk about my mother until I was nine or ten, because I'd get so choked up with emotion. I think that confusion came from never having permission to deal with any of my feelings."

As Tricia learned at an early age, the "I'm okay, you're okay father" uses a relentless forward motion as a defense against his own emotional pain and a means of avoiding his children's grief. He rarely speaks about his deceased wife out of a reluctance that may stem from his commitment to be the protector of his family, a job he believes involves shielding his children from emotional pain. He often remarries quickly, immersing himself in a new relationship. (Fifty-two percent of all widowers remarry in the first eighteen months after a wife dies, although it's estimated that more than half of these quick marriages end in separation or divorce.)

Tricia's father remarried within two years after her mother's death, presenting his new wife as a replacement—rather than as a substitute—for a mother all five children remembered and still missed. "When he married Marian, it was like, 'Here's your new mom,'" Tricia recalls. "It was very confusing to me, growing up and having to call my stepmother 'Mom,' because I knew I'd had a different mom, whom no one would talk about. It was like everybody was role playing; everybody was not dealing. I ended up really resenting my stepmother. I picked her because she was the mother figure, the person I wanted most that I didn't have, and I blamed her for everything that went wrong in the family afterward."

Because children often mimic the loss response of the family's most significant surviving member, children of this kind of father often try to convince themselves that their grief should be as minimal as their father's appears to be. The siblings in Tricia's family ranged in age from three to sixteen when their mother died, and this coping strategy began to backfire visibly as they acted out their confusion and grief. The oldest daughter became pregnant and gave birth to a child at sixteen; the oldest son, who'd been particularly close to his mother, entered a period of intense rebellion and virtually disappeared from the home. The family evolved into a loose group of isolated individuals that reunited for a strained and awkward Christmas at the family home each year.

Without a firm sense of family support, and unable to communicate on any meaningful level with either her father or stepmother throughout her childhood and adolescence, Tricia became a global nomad, living in England, China, and Japan before finally settling back in the United States. "I've always felt defensive, just like nobody's there, nobody's supporting me at all," she explains. "And I often feel that I'm more needy than the average person. Just recently, I've realized why. I *am* needy. And it doesn't make for very good relationships right now, especially with the men I date, because I'm looking for a strong parent. I always wind up feeling resentful when I don't find one."

For more than twenty years, Tricia modeled her father's coping approach, trying to push her loss firmly into the past and denying that it had long-lasting effects. But when her boyfriend died in a car accident two years ago, she found she couldn't keep the grief for her mother contained any longer. Part of mourning her mother's death now, she says, has involved calling her stepmother 'Marian' instead of 'Mom,' and confronting her father with her feelings. "When I was grieving my boyfriend's death, I went back to my father's house. I took him outside one night and said, 'I'm here, and the reason I'm here is because I'm grieving, and I'm going to sit here and do it until I'm done,'" she recalls. "And I said, 'You know, a lot of it really comes from my mom's death. It's had a major impact on me, and regardless of what anyone else in this family does, I'm very upset about it.'" The moment was a turning point in her relationship with her father. "It's ironic, because now I'm the only child who ever sees his tears," she says. "I'm the only one he feels safe enough to cry with." She and her father, she says, are now tentatively trying to make up for their years of silence.

The Helpless Father

When Oedipus discovered that he'd killed his father and married his mother, he stabbed himself in the eyes and set off on a self-imposed exile. As the two of them wandered, hungry and barefoot, through the Theban countryside, his daughter, Antigone, became his sight and his guide. Devoted, compliant, and motherless—her mother, Jocasta, had killed herself when she had learned her husband was really her son—Antigone was the quintessential daughter of a "helpless father." Had she lived to adulthood, she no doubt would have felt the effects of such single-minded subservience.

Tragedy takes on slightly less epic proportions today. Prolonged grief, addiction, and an inability to manage without a woman's care are the typical reasons for a father's helpless state after the death of his wife. Holding a job, raising children alone, and maintaining a home can overwhelm these fathers to the point of paralysis. "I'm working with a man right now whose wife just died in a car accident," says Therese Rando. "This woman had done what a lot of women do: She paid all the bills, made all the decisions. This man knew nothing about the grocery shopping, nothing about where the IRS forms were. He was really very dependent upon her. In many cases, if the man dies, the woman still knows enough about operating the home because she's had more experience in those roles. Even though a father's death may mean a loss of income, it's easier for kids to adapt if the surviving parent is the one most familiar with the ongoing daily routine. And many times, that's the mother."

When chronic bereavement causes a father's helpless state, when his grieving seems to have no limits, he often succumbs to a mixture of intense despair, apathy, and depression. He may lose interest in his appearance and let his home deteriorate, and his children may suffer emotional or physical neglect. Only one parent has died in this family, but a daughter feels that both have disappeared. "This can be mitigated somewhat by a grandmother, an aunt, or siblings," Russell Hurd says. "But to these children, it's like a double blow. It's really the loss of two parents—the death of one and the emotional withdrawal of the other."

Who, then, steps in to keep the family together and run the house? Usually a daughter. This was the family situation for Denise and Jane, who met for the first time last year, during an informal focus group for this book. Over wine and cheese in my living room, they discovered that both of their fathers had had great difficulty adjusting to the loss and had expected their daughters to become the family caretakers.

Denise, now thirty-five, describes her father as a "tender, lovable, boyish, but highly avoidant man" who suffered a virtual emotional collapse after her mother's death. Although she was just twelve at the time, Denise quickly realized that she was the only family member who could run the house and care for her two younger sisters, one of whom became dangerously anorexic shortly after their mother's death. Propping up her father became Denise's first and most significant relationship with a man, and this deeply influenced her criteria for romantic relationships today.

When my father answered the call from the hospital, he dropped the receiver and burst into tears. I just stood there, ice cold, and thought, *Someone has to talk to the doctor.* So I picked up the phone. From that time, I took on the role of the one who doesn't have any feelings, who exists for the physical care of people who are important. I'd been trained ahead of time by my mother to pride myself on how little I felt I deserved. She'd sort of begun raising me to be the martyr, so it was a natural role for me to adopt after she died. I became the little housewife. I defined myself as the person who was special because she could do with so much less than all those grieve-heads out there who demanded so much more attention and love. And I developed, over the years, an enormous rage underneath all this.

My father was never going to deal with the fact that I was playing the role of his wife and my sisters' mother, so I never had an adolescence at all. I was never around boys. No sexual experimentation. I never wore makeup, never put on a dress. But I would have wonderful, larger-than-life romantic dreams. I would imagine a hero carrying me off on the back of a horse.

The kind of relationship I dream of now is with a man who's always bigger than me, stronger than me, protecting me. Because I know I can't be diminished. My father was a jellyfish. I can't imagine ever being cowed by a man, or being put in my place by a man, and I'm not intrinsically impressed by men. I found out at a very early age that the Daddy God has feet of clay. I now have a relationship with my father, but I still think of him as the one in the family who would whine and cry. Every time I hear about the new, sensitive man who can cry, I think, "Oh, I grew up with one of those. You can keep him."

Pushed into premature adulthood and expected to attend to everyone else's needs in addition to her own, Denise grew into a hypercompetent, fiercely independent woman who says learning to depend on others is one of her biggest challenges as an adult. "I'm still trying to learn that I can delegate tasks at work," she says. "And I'm very close with my rabbi, who supports me in a way I'm not used to. I'm not used to having a strong figure who won't topple over if I direct some energy toward it." She's still searching for a romantic partner who can meet the standards she set after living for seven years in a helpless father's home.

Leaning forward attentively as Denise tells her story, Jane, thirty-eight, grasps the first opportunity to speak. Jane was thirteen when her mother, who was an alcoholic, died of ovarian cancer, and she became her father's only source of emotional support until his death four years ago. Today, Jane says she fears relying on a partner, yet longs for a relationship with someone who will care for her. "I attract every wimp and his brother," she says. "But I was never mothered, and I never had children. I feel like saying to some men, 'You want to be mothered? Fuck you. I don't want to be anybody's mother.' I find all these men who want mommies, but I want them to be my *father*. I want somebody now who'll come home and take care of *me*." Instead of looking for lovers or husbands they can care for—though that does happen—women who played the parental role too young may look to their adult partners or their own children to take care of *them*.

The Distant Father

Ronnie, twenty-five, describes herself as "ultra-independent, and much more hard-nosed than most women I know." These are qualities she had to develop at the age of fifteen when her mother died, leaving her with a seventeen-year-old sister she constantly fought with and a father she felt she barely knew. Her mother had been her primary parent, and after she died, Ronnie's father maintained the emotional gulf that already existed between him and his daughters.

"My father was always the pseudo-boss of our family," Ronnie says. "My mother let him think he was the boss, but everybody knew that she was. So after she died, my father just had no clue. I think he was afraid of us, because we were two women and he had no idea how to raise two girls. My mother had done all the raising, and my father had been the breadwinner. So after she died, he would just say, 'Okay. Here's my checkbook. If you need anything, write yourself a check.'"

Ronnie is the daughter of a "distant father," one who had little involvement in his daughter's life to begin with and withdrew even further after her mother's death. Whereas mothers tend to think of their children as extensions of themselves, fathers are more likely— even when they're well-versed in childcare—to create boundaries between themselves and their children. After a mother dies or leaves, a father's distance can be either psychological, the result of addiction or emotional withdrawal, or physical, as with divorce or departure. Oftentimes, this distance intensifies during a daughter's adolescence, when fathers feel particularly inept and fearful about raising daughters. At the same time, daughters recognize their fathers as sexual beings and retreat in a panic. Adolescence is such a tricky time for fathers and daughters that even fathers with young girls become preoccupied with thoughts of how they'll handle those years.

Several women—all of whom were adolescents when their mothers died—told me that shortly after the loss, their fathers moved out of the family house, leaving teenage children to fend for themselves with minimal supervision at home. That's what happened in Ronnie's family. Less than two years after her mother died, her father accepted a job promotion that required a move to the Midwest. The sisters remained in their East Coast home with a full-time housekeeper while their father bought another house in Michigan. At first he commuted back on weekends, then twice a month, and then just for holidays. "At the time, I was very understanding," Ronnie says. "I wanted everyone to think I was mature and had total control. But subconsciously, I was very resentful about him leaving us. About five years later, after I graduated from college and wasn't dependent on him anymore, all that anger came pouring out. I couldn't even talk to him for eight months. I was that furious."

Left alone in the house during their teen years, Ronnie and her sister hosted all-night parties and spent huge sums of their father's money. Financial support was the only consistent connection they had to him. "That was his love—the checkbook," Ronnie explains. "It was the only way he knew how to show his affection, and my sister and I totally took advantage of him. We would buy two hundred dollars' worth of food for one week, and even then, he wouldn't complain." Those years scrambled Ronnie's ideas about money and love, and she says some confusion persists today. When she's feeling sad or upset, her first impulse is to buy herself a gift—the same tactic her father relied on to keep her happy as a teen.

When Ronnie and her sister woke the neighbors with their parties and spent money designated for household expenses on makeup and clothes, they were really trying to evoke a response—any response—from the father who was quickly receding toward the horizon of their lives. I've heard similar stories from women who say they smoked marijuana in the kitchen and had sex with their boyfriends in the den while their fathers watched TV in the next room, all desperate attempts to force their fathers to pay attention to them and exercise parental control.

The daughter of a distant father views any attention—even anger—as evidence that he cares. She may alternate between being so good he'll have to notice her, and so bad he can't ignore her. But as a daughter often learns, her efforts to be good typically receive little more than a quick smile and a pat on the head. Trouble is more likely to push a father into action, if for no other reason than to force him to reinstate family peace. So the motherless daughter provokes her distant father, trying to elicit a response. Her catch–22 is that the attention she really hopes to receive—affection and warmth—invariably doesn't come from disruptive behavior. Instead, she gets anger and conflict. After her initial rush of success, disappointment leads to a feeling of worthlessness, and from there it's a quick slide into resentment and shattered self-esteem.

"I swore I was going to get my father to recognize me," says thirty-three-year-old Jackie, who was thirteen when her mother died. "But after about two years of getting notes sent home from school and staying out past my curfew, I realized he was never going to say anything about it to me. What was he thinking? That if he ignored it, it would just go away? Well, my need for attention didn't disappear. What happened was, I eventually gave up on my father and tried to get it from other men. I went through a very promiscuous period in college, and I lost my first job because I was trying to please my male department supervisor instead of my female boss. That's been a major theme of my life: trying to get men to notice me."

A 1983 study of seventy-two female college students, the first to look at the significance of father control (the degree to which a father sets and enforces appropriate regulations), found that daughters whose fathers exercised high levels of support, affection and—as the researchers had suspected—structure, were the girls most likely to become secure, content women who had developed age-appropriately. In a home run by a distant father, however, such rules and restrictions are often ambiguous, and sometimes altogether absent. Ronnie feels fortunate that the anarchy of her home was offset by the strict rules of her parochial high school. "I think I really would have gotten into a lot of trouble if I didn't have authority figures around me most of the day at an all-girls' school," she explains. "They became my only models for self-control."

Like many other daughters of distant fathers, Ronnie developed a strong sense of independence. While the daughter of a helpless father develops a hypercompetent *physical* self-reliance that encourages her to take responsibility for those around her, the daughter of a distant father becomes more *emotionally* independent. As an adult, she's wary of depending on others; feeling physically abandoned by one parent and emotionally abandoned by the other, she selects only a handful of people to whom she'll get close. "Very removed, very cold: That's how people sometimes describe me," Ronnie admits, with a hint of sadness—or is it resignation?—in her voice. "I really need to be with the right person before I feel that I can open up. I'm so afraid of abandonment."

A distant father's incapacity to give his daughter emotional support after her mother dies arises not from his inability to care about her, but his inability to show his concern. We're often told that our fathers did the best they could and that by understanding their limits and lowering our expectations we can heal some of our past father-daughter wounds. And this is all true. But such advice doesn't erase the memory of inadequate emotional support; it doesn't magically turn "the best they could do" into "good enough." Daughters of distant fathers either must learn to parent themselves or find nurturing from other sources. "When my father got into therapy a few years ago," Ronnie says, "he decided he wanted to redo all those years I spent alone, and be the father to me that he never was. I had to tell him, 'It's too late. I'm already grown up.'" Like many other daughters of distant fathers, Ronnie has become so highly proficient at taking care of herself that she's reluctant to let anyone else—especially someone who let her down before—try.

The Heroic Father

Samantha's father held a full-time job, headed a household, and attended to his five children's emotional and physical needs. He was a "heroic father," and his daughter credits him with the security and emotional strength she feels today.

Her family had always been close, says Samantha, now thirty-two. After her mother's death when Samantha was fourteen, her father continued and even deepened his relationship with his four daughters and one son when he became their only parent.

> When my mother was alive, my father was always very available, from the moment he walked in the door after work. We greeted him with the day's events, and then after he changed his clothes, we would sit down for dinner. We talked and talked and

talked, and then he'd help us with homework or go outside with us and play ball. So when my mother died, he was working with a solid foundation to begin with, and then he did the even harder job of keeping that going. He saw it as a lifelong commitment to her. It wasn't the case in my family that we lost both parents. We still had one, and he doubled his energy to make the family work and keep us all happy.

Throughout my adolescence, I always felt secure, because that's how my father always made us feel. Like, "Everything will be okay, this is a loving environment, a trusting environment, and this is what you're functioning from." He never said that outright, but that was the underlying feeling I had, and that's how I've always gone through life. I think that's why I now feel so secure within myself. It's not that I don't have things to learn, or ways in which to grow, but I feel very healthy in terms of psychologically dealing with each day.

The heroic father typically shared child-rearing and household tasks when his wife was present and had warm, loving relationships with his children before their mother died. After her death, he mourns appropriately, providing his children with a safe forum for expressing their feelings, and reallocates roles fairly, taking on what he can and delegating the rest. Most daughters who describe their fathers as heroic come from families with several children, where siblings could offer additional support when a father felt overburdened or overwhelmed. This is an important characteristic of the heroic-father family. When a daughter can split her needs between her father and other reliable family members, when she doesn't have to place unrealistically high expectations on him, his chances of disappointing her decrease.

The heroic father isn't perfect and is still prone to bouts of depression or doubt, but he's clearly a parent in control. Despite his own grief, he manages to maintain a safe, supportive environment that absorbs some of the shock of a daughter's loss and helps her continue developing confidence and self-esteem. For these reasons, his death is likely to be a major blow to her. Unlike daughters of helpless or distant fathers, who must either withdraw some of their dependency needs or face disappointment, the daughter of a heroic father has a dad she can depend on. Even as an adult, she typically continues to rely on him for emotional support. Although her response to his death is free of the intense resentment and guilt that often plague other daughters, the loss leaves her feeling truly alone for the first time—a state that daughters of other fathers say they felt soon after their mothers died.

The only time that thirty-two-year-old Kim begins to cry during our two-hour interview is when she speaks of her father's death from cancer seven years ago. After her mother died when she was two, Kim lived with her older sister and brother, and a father she describes as "awesome, generous, great." Even though her father remarried three times, Kim says she never felt displaced or overlooked.

> My dad. We were very close. See? The tears only come when I talk about my dad. He was great. I mean, I was the last kid, and he had basically been through everything by then. He was quiet and patient, a good role model. I was into some crazy stuff when I was a teenager, experimenting with drugs, sex, you know what I'm saying? But I never did anything that I knew would seriously harm me. Like I got myself on the [birth control] pill immediately, and there were certain drugs I definitely wouldn't take. I was a pretty sensible kid, and I thank my father for that. It was nothing he even said to me, like, "Don't you come home pregnant," or anything like that. He was just a model person. A good citizen. Like he would never cheat on his taxes. He trusted me, and I trusted him. Everybody loved him. When he died, we all said, "It shouldn't have been him."

Kim credits her heroic father, who was the only consistent parent of her childhood, with helping her achieve the emotional stability she says is central to her happy marriage today.

Like Kim, Kristen, twenty-two, praises her heroic father and her heroic stepfather, who both helped her mourn her mother's death five years ago and gave her an emotional foundation she knows she can rely on today. Even so, she acknowledges that the heroic father has his limits. When she recently developed a gynecological condition that required immediate attention and she needed financial and emotional support, she appealed to both fathers for help. "As soon as I found a physician, they both were like, 'So it's taken care of? Good!' They didn't want to talk about it anymore. They just wanted to make sure I was okay." Her voice and her eyes drop slightly as she says, "As wonderful as the two of them are, they never 100 percent understand."

Despite all his assets, the heroic father can't fully replace an attentive, nurturing mother. In his quest to try, he runs the risk of devoting too *much* time and energy to his children, which can cause parent-child conflict when he begins dating or pursuing interests beyond the home.

Daddy's Other Girl

Let's imagine a best-case father-daughter scenario after a mother's death: Parent and child mourn together, and the family slowly adjusts to its new configuration. The daughter still misses her mother but feels secure enough to trust her father to fill most of her needs. She's his little girl, and he's her perfect dad. The seasons change once, maybe twice. And then one night the doorbell rings, and the father walks into the den and says, "Kids? I'd like you to meet Marjorie (or Angie, or Sandy, or Sue)."

Corinne, thirty-five, still remembers every detail of that moment twenty-four years ago. She refused to acknowledge her father's girlfriend when they started dating eight months after her mother's death, when Corinne was eleven.

She walked into the house, and I turned around and walked the other way. My father had sat my older brother and me down one night and asked us for permission to date, and I thought, "He's got to be kidding. Date? My father?" I guess because I didn't say anything, he figured I was fine with it. The minute that woman walked through the door, I didn't want a thing to do with her. He was furious at me, and we fought about it all the time. He only dated her for about six months, until she broke it off. I was so cruel to her, I think I might have been part of the reason why she left him. I know my father understood why I acted like such an obnoxious brat, but I also know it took him a long time to forgive me for it.

A father's entry into the dating sphere requires a significant reordering of a daughter's psyche. No longer does she have Dad to herself; he's now a commodity to be shared. When a daughter has to make room for a new adult woman before she's ready, the father-daughter relationship suffers. Among the women surveyed for this book, those whose fathers remarried quickly were most likely to have long-term father-daughter problems. Seventy-six percent of the women who described their current father-daughter relationships as "poor" had fathers who'd remarried within one year of a mother's death, compared to only 9 percent of those who said their relationship is now "excellent."

Twenty-six-year-old Audrey remembers the shock she felt at fourteen, when her father announced his upcoming marriage only six months after her mother had committed suicide. An only child, Audrey had been accustomed to receiving both of her parents' undivided attention, and after her mother's death she secretly expected her father to devote twice as much time to her.

"I went through an enormous rebellion against him at fifteen," she says. "It was like, Father with *another woman*? And she had two kids. I thought, 'Who is this person in my father's life with all her tagalongs, and what makes her think she can become a part of my life, too?' I gave her a really hard time until after I left for college. Now, I think of her as my father's wife, and as long as she doesn't try to be my mother, we can get along fine. She's the one who tries to keep the family together, which I kind of appreciate. But my relationship with my father is still a mess. I needed him to help me through those first months after my mother died, and he was off wining and dining all the divorced women in our town. I'm still trying to work through my anger about that. In the meantime, it's hard for me to even have lunch with him."

Audrey says that much of her resentment comes from her father's resistance toward speaking about her mother after the suicide. As an only child, Audrey had taken care of her mother through her bouts of depression, and felt betrayed and abandoned after her death. She needed validation for those feelings, but her father refused to talk about the loss. His solution to his grief was to date and remarry quickly. Like many other motherless daughters, Audrey perceived her father's behavior as a betrayal of her mother and felt as if she were the only one left honoring the original connection to her.

Naomi Lowinsky refers to the Cinderella story as an illustration of this conflict. In the version by the seventeenth-century French writer Charles Perrault, Cinderella asks her father to bring her a tree branch from town, which she then plants at her mother's grave. When the tree grows, it speaks to Cinderella in her mother's voice. "So the daughter is maintaining the connection with her true mother, even though her father has abandoned it by marrying a total witch," Dr. Lowinsky explains. "That's a very, very heavy burden for a little girl to be carrying. You can see how she'd get very mad at her dad about it, and maybe project the archetypal Bad Father onto him, because it feels like by remarrying he's abandoning not only her, but also her mother."

Older daughters usually have greater compassion for a widowed father. Less egocentric than younger children, they can understand his need for companionship beyond the family. Even so, a union with another woman usually is difficult for them to accept at first, especially when it occurs before they've had time to mourn their mothers.

Cecile and Beth, who were twenty-nine and twenty-six respectively when their mother died after a two-year illness, displaced the frustration and rage they felt after the loss onto their father when, five weeks after the funeral, he told them he'd met another woman. "I immediately went from grief to anger and hate," Beth, now twenty-eight, recalls. "I was mean and miserable. I was almost possessed."

"She was," Cecile agrees, nodding her head. "But I think she had a right to be. My dad really didn't deal with the death. He started going out every single night, and then he got together with this woman. She's great today, but he just shoved her down our throats, and we resented it. We said, 'We just lost our mother. Granted, you say you grieved for two years as she was dying, but now it's time to grieve after, and you're not giving us that opportunity.'"

The sisters felt abandoned by their father at a time when they needed to rely on the close-knit family they'd always known. They both recognized their dilemma: They wanted their father to be happy, but they felt their mother deserved more respect. And they decided to side with her.

"It wasn't so much that he was dating," Cecile explains, "but that he was forcing us to accept it before we were ready to. Three months after my mother died, he said he loved this woman and planned to marry her. I mean, *three months.*"

Beth rolls her eyes when she recalls the turmoil of the next few months, as the sisters acted out of anger and fear that their father would abandon them in favor of his new wife-to-be. "We were just *mean*," she says. "I said things to my dad that I would never think I'd say to anyone, like, 'Let me out of this car. I never want to see you again. I hate you.' And he'd cry, but in his own way, he had to go on with his life, and he did."

When their father restated his plan to remarry, the sisters suggested a compromise: They asked him to wait for at least one calendar year after their mother's death. He agreed, and their relationship slowly started to improve. When the sisters realized that their father was willing to prioritize in favor of his original family, they began to regain their trust and respect for him. The year gave them time to adjust to their mother's absence, and to the idea of another woman living in their father's house. They also saw that he didn't intend to abandon his daughters.

"His priorities were very well defined," Cecile says. "He put Beth and me before everyone else. To this day, he still does it. He has distinctly separated his life with us from his life with his wife. She's turned out to be a great friend to us, and her two kids are really nice. Once we stopped feeling threatened, we warmed up to the idea like you'd normally expect. It's just when it was being pushed down our throats that we objected."

Beth laughs a little as she says, "I don't even remember when I started liking my father again. Today, I wish the circumstances of his remarriage had been different, but he's really happy. He treats his new wife as well as he treated my mother, but only to an extent. I can see the difference." And that, the sisters agree, shows the respect for their mother and their original family that they believe is deserved.

The Incest Taboo

There was a period of a month or so after my mother died when my father started drinking. That was not the norm in my house at all, and it was very scary to me. I remember feeling sexually afraid of him. I don't know that there was reason to be, other than he was a drunk man in the house. But I remember blocking the door to my bedroom one night when he was drunk. When I was five years old, I'd been molested by a drunk man in the hallway to our building, so maybe I was making that connection. I don't know if there's anything else. I'm waiting, like Oprah Winfrey and her guests, for the memories to come.

—Rita, forty-three, who was fifteen and
the only daughter in her family when
her mother died.

In a two-parent family, a mother's presence and a father's conscience ideally suppress a father's sexual impulses toward his daughter. Although some degree of father-daughter attraction is normal, as Victoria Secunda explains in *Women and Their Fathers,* the incest taboo is so deeply ingrained in most men that they can barely imagine an attraction for their daughters, let alone talk about it. These sexual feelings are unconscious in most men, yet they nevertheless cause fathers to withdraw slightly from preadolescent daughters. Daughters typically experience this withdrawal as a rejection, which adds to their overall adolescent sense of awkwardness and isolation.

A mother is both a sexual partner and a source of maternal protection in the home, and in most families she represents a symbolic barrier between father and daughter. When she is absent from the family, father and daughter lose that natural buffer. As a daughter's sexuality emerges, she becomes increasingly aware of her father as a man with needs, and, if a stepmother or girlfriend is not present, acknowledges him as an adult sleeping alone. Believing that her father's conscience may be all that keeps him away from her bedroom door, a daughter may fear the potential for sexual abuse. Especially when parent-child boundaries relax to a degree where a daughter takes over most of her mother's roles, confusion on either side of the father-daughter pair often leads to active avoidance or rejection.

"I often hear from women about how unsafe they felt with their fathers, without their mothers present," says Colleen Russell, MFT, a therapist in Mill Valley, California, who for ten years has been leading support groups for motherless-daughters. "Even if there wasn't any sexual behavior, there was a sexualized environment that felt scary and unpredictable. The daughter reminded the father of his wife, and a lot of the time his anger toward his wife was displaced onto the daughter."

As Denise, who was twelve when her mother died, moved further into adolescence, she began to fear a violation of the incest taboo. "My father was so irresponsible," she recalls. "The rule in my family was 'He's a kid, he can't help himself. He's not responsible for anything.' So I felt like I was responsible for protecting my father from sexual impulses toward me and my sisters. In my case, I was projecting, because I was the one who was an adolescent and felt the impulses, and here I was in this house. I was the mother. I was making the dinner. I was doing all the housework. I think on some level, I *wanted* my father, and I hated the fact he wouldn't sleep with me. Of course, I would have sooner died. It upsets me very much now to even say it out loud. If that thought had become conscious at the time, I probably would have slit my wrists."

These thoughts often consciously develop in response to the "seductive father" who surrounds his daughter with sexual innuendos or treats her as what the author Signe Hammer calls a "surrogate goddess," the replacement image for a sanctified dead wife. Even when sexual abuse doesn't occur, these fears are real and damaging.

"On some level, the little girl feels she's supposed to be the father's wife, either emotionally or physically," Naomi Lowinsky explains, "or the father feels the little girl is supposed to be his wife, and the burden of carrying the whole feminine side of the family gets put on a child who's not ready to carry it." If incest does occur, the trauma can confuse a girl's sexual identity, thwart her normal developmental process, and complicate her later relationships with men.

She's forced into a highly adult role too soon, becoming the equivalent of a woman in a child's body.

Ginny Smith, the narrator of Jane Smiley's Pulitzer Prize–winning novel *A Thousand Acres*, reveals what can happen to a motherless daughter who becomes a victim of incest. The middle daughter in an Iowa farm family, Ginny, who was an adolescent when her mother died, grows up with deeply ambivalent feelings about sex and marriage. As the novel progresses, she begins to recover memories of her father in her bed at night, and her recollection of incest during her teen years sends her into an emotional tailspin that ultimately ends with her decision to leave her marriage, her family, and her hometown in a quest to reclaim her life.

Beyond Resentment and Past Blame

WANTED: Female housemate . . . must love children. Enjoy the comfort of a large modern home with swimming pool etc. with a family who has lost a mother. Two daughters and a father live there now and the two girls would love to have a new "Mom," especially the twelve-year-old. Other child is sixteen.
— A father's advertisement in *The Valley Advocate*, a weekly newspaper serving western Massachusetts and southern Vermont.

My wife recently was diagnosed with aggressive metasticized breast cancer. My biggest concern of this impending devastating loss is my energetic, hopeful, naive seventeen-year-old girl. How can I get some help in helping her accept this loss?
— Personal letter from a father in the Midwest

It would be unfair and simply untrue to assume that fathers aren't concerned about their motherless daughters. They know that love requires more expression than a check sent through the mail. Yet they're also aware of the emotional limits American society forces on males. Grief does not come easily for them. As Therese

Rando explains, males in mourning tend to retreat into themselves, while females reach out. Neither party can be satisfied when a daughter needs to be comforted and a father needs to withdraw.

"*He* was the parent; he should have been taking care of *me*," motherless women insist. This is the lament of the orphan, frustrated by the father who couldn't meet her needs. We all have prescribed ideas, born at the point where society and family intersect, of what "parent" means, and we have even stricter ideas of which tasks belong to Mom and which to Dad. When a mother dies, a child typically transfers all of her expectations for care onto her surviving parent, although it's the rare father who can take them all on himself.

Surviving parents assume a larger-than-life stature in a developing child's life, Maxine Harris explains. "As the only parent, he or she bears the weight of all the child's expectations and fantasies," she writes. "No longer free to be just a parent, the survivor must be the 'perfect' parent," which, to motherless daughters, means being father, mother, protector, nurturer, champion, safety net, role model, and provider, all rolled into one.

For many years, with my father, I just expected too much. I remember a phone conversation with my sister in which I was detailing some or another current grievance against him. "You know what the problem is?" she said. "You want him to be a mother. And he's not ever going to be one."

She had a point—a valid, accurate, straight-to-the-point point. In that moment, I understood that my frustration came as much from what I wanted and never had as it did from what I did have. I knew my father had human limitations. I'd just been reluctant to accept them.

By constantly expecting my father to be more than he could be, I could hang on to the belief that the nurturing parental element of my family didn't die with my mother when, in truth, it pretty much did. And so as I worked to let go of my illusion, I also had to let go of the dream of ever having the strong, decisive, emotionally available protector I always wished for, the one who would solve every problem for me.

I know that not so deep inside my psyche still resides a place where I feel worthless and unloved, because one parent died and the other withdrew into his room. When I meet another motherless woman who feels the same way, we have that electric moment of connection, the instantaneous joy of finding someone with whom we feel no impulse to explain. We already know each other's secrets; we share each other's fears. But we always speak of our fathers tentatively, our voices low, as if a difficult relationship with the first man in our lives so damages our confidence that we then deny ourselves the right to speak about it later with conviction, or with strength.

My father and I did not have an easy time together. We were not bound by similar bodies or mutual impulses or comparable dreams. For many years, it seemed as if all we shared was a surname and the memory of a woman who died decades ago. Then my children came along and, through his interest in and love for them, we found a common ground. Sometimes it was hard to watch them enjoy the playful, curious, happy part of him, a part I hadn't known since childhood, if ever. But most of the time I would sit on my hands, press my lips shut, and let them get to know each other without intrusions from the past. The problems I had with him were my problems, not theirs.

Until the very end, my father and I both tried to have a relationship, as best as we knew how. A few weeks before he died, I flew from my home in California to his in suburban New York. My siblings and I needed to know what kind of burial arrangements he wanted, but none of us particularly wanted to ask. It was my turn to visit, so I volunteered for the task.

It was early December and my father had been bedridden for a week or two by then, attended to by a revolving staff of hospice volunteers and a devoted full-time aide. The day after I arrived, I pulled a chair up to the side of his bed. I took his hand, still pudgy despite a precipitous weight loss, and held it between mine.

"We still have some time left," I told him, "but there's something I really need to ask you now. If you don't want to talk about it we don't have to, but it would be good if you could try." I'd been prepped for this conversation by my friend Susan, a social worker, and so far I thought it was going well.

"Okay," he said. "Shoot."

"Is there anything you want me to take care of? Any arrangements you'd like me to make?"

He shook his head quizzically, as if he were surprised I'd ask. "All the finances are in order, and I have a will," he said. "No, everything's done."

"And the burial? Do you want to be buried with Mom?"

"Of course," he said.

The conversation *was* going well, *too* well, actually. Too clinical. Too different. I'd gotten the answer I needed, but I wanted something more. Something substantial, damn it. There would be no more chances to get this right. And with that thought, emotion came charging through.

"I'm going to miss you," I told him. "A lot." Tears and mucus started pouring down my face but I didn't have a Kleenex nearby. "Is there anything you want to tell me while there's still time?" I asked. "Anything you want me to know?"

He scrunched his lips and rolled his eyes up in thought, then shook his head. No.

We sat together quietly for a moment. "Are you scared?" I asked him. I couldn't help wondering.

"No," he said, more matter-of-factly than I would have expected. He angled his chin toward the photographs of his grandchildren taped to the mirror on the wall. "That's the only part that hurts," he said.

He died two weeks later, a peaceful passing just before dawn, with my sister by his side. It was the kind of death I'd always wished my mother had had. In her final days she had been blindsided by the severity of her illness, refusing to believe her life was coming to an end. In his dying, my father faced his mortality head on with a courage, a dignity, and a kind of inner strength I'd never seen him model in life. It made me wonder what other secrets he'd held, what other capacities could have been revealed. There had been, I realized, still so much to learn from him. This wasn't the answer I was looking for in his bedroom that day, but I think, over time, it will turn out to be exactly the answer I need.

Chapter Six

Sister and Brother,
Sister and Sister
Sibling Connections (and Disconnections)

MY SISTER MOVED TO LOS ANGELES in 1992, two months after I returned to New York. This hadn't been part of the plan. For months we'd been discussing how I would finally end a decade of circuitous wanderings in Manhattan, where we would then live twenty city blocks apart in mutual sibling bliss. But six weeks after I unpacked my boxes, Michele called and said an interview in Los Angeles had come up, so she flew west to check it out, and of course they wanted her immediately, and, well, it was too good a deal for her to pass up. Within three weeks she was gone.

I was, mildly speaking, devastated—that old Abandonment sign flashing its neon warning again—but I can't say I was all that surprised. Michele had moved to Manhattan the year our brother, Glenn, left for college, a silent exchange that kept at least one child in close proximity to our father (in case of emergency, as if mere presence could prevent one). Like so many agreements in our family, this one has always been unspoken, so when Michele started filling my empty boxes I didn't object. We both knew what was happening. It was my turn to be the anchor and her turn to sail.

Five years later, after Glenn had returned to New York, I left for Los Angeles. I moved there to join my fiancé, but found solace in the knowledge that my sister was nearby. She helped plan my wedding, pulling together a planner, a caterer, and a photographer in three days flat. She was my only bridesmaid, and during the reception she brought guests to tears of laughter and warmth with her toast.

Compassion and support came late to us two. Until we reached adulthood, we didn't get along. Like most sisters separated by three years—too few for us to play parent and child, too many for us to be peers—we grew up on a shared diet of rivalry and rancor as we competed for our brother's adoration and our parents' limited time. It makes sense to me now that when our mother died, Michele and I found little comfort in each other. Instead, we intensified the division we knew so well. Familiarity offers false security when change permeates the house, and competition was our established code.

We'd been raised to protect and care for our younger brother, which we continued to do the best we could. But we exhibited no such empathy for each other. Tension between siblings is often a barely restrained, misdirected rage, and after our mother died, Michele became the target of mine. She, in turn, remained perpetually on the defensive. And as we argued and glared and ignored each other, a new, bizarre competition developed between us: who'd suffered more hardship when Mommy died, who could do the most for Glenn, and who could persuade Daddy to give her more.

All this was taking place in a confusing milieu of enforced normalcy and unexpressed grief, with our father periodically delivering short speeches about how the individual is more important than the unit, and how we should all learn to fend for ourselves. This sounded, at first, like a fine idea to me. At seventeen, I didn't want the responsibility I felt for my younger siblings, and I chose to attend a college nine hundred miles from New York. Escape was my original plan. But underneath all the resentment I felt toward Michele must have been a protective instinct and a bond even rivalry and distance couldn't kill. The night my father called me at college, threatening to desert the family, I tried to negotiate with him by phone, finally resorting to threat—"If you leave those kids, so help me God, I'll bring them here to live with me"—and I understood at that moment how committed I was to those words. Despite all our previous troubles, Michele knew it, too. When we talk about that night now, she says she, too, was packing her bags, ready to come live with me.

I'm not sure I can identify a discrete turning point between us— perhaps maturity took care of most of the repair—but I know that night marked the beginning of a new understanding between Michele and me. In our shared adversity we found a common ground. Losing a mother ultimately meant we each gained a sister. I'm not sure that otherwise we'd have become friends.

Lest this story sound too pat and tidy, I'll admit we're hardly adequate mother substitutes for each other. Michele is still the younger sister, and she's often frustrated when I'm not a good role model; I'm still the older one, and I'm often surprised and annoyed when she acts more capable than I. And even when we work to overcome them, the tiny crimes of the past don't necessarily evaporate by will.

That night in 1992 before Michele moved to L.A., I finally broke down and cried.

"Don't do this," she pleaded. "I need you to be strong for me."

"I can't always be the strong one," I said. "Goddamit. You're the only security I feel I have in this family. I don't want you to leave."

And then, very quickly, as if waiting for her cue, she shot back with, "Well, what about when you left for college when I was fifteen?" and I understood how deep these memories of betrayal lie, that no matter how far Michele and I travel, we always come back to this.

Older daughter of two, middle daughter of five, younger sister of older brothers—the combinations are varied, and motherless women represent them all. Eighty-five percent of the women interviewed for this book have siblings, who are always central characters in the family histories they tell.

In an earlier chapter, I said a daughter's relationship with her mother is likely to be one of the longest-lasting of her life. But those of us who have siblings, and especially those of us with sisters, can expect these relationships to persist even longer than the ones we have with our parents. The quality and intensity of these sibling relationships fluctuate over our lifetimes, filled with as many storms and sunny days as the twenty-four-hour Weather Channel.

Sibling ties start developing the moment a second child is born. When a mother dies or leaves, their strength and quality quickly become apparent. Sibling relationships rarely do a 180 when a family undergoes a trauma such as mother loss. Instead, as in my family, previous patterns tend to exaggerate. Brothers and sisters who were close and supportive beforehand typically draw together more tightly after the death. Likewise, siblings with loose connections usually split even further apart—especially when the mother was the force that held disparate family members together. While outer influences such as counseling or support from an extended family member can prevent extreme reactions, the intensification of previous patterns usually persists until the trauma phase subsides, and often continues into adulthood.

Margie, twenty-five, remembers sitting quietly with her younger brother on their grandmother's couch the morning after their mother committed suicide. Her parents were divorced, and though Margie was barely seven, she transformed her panic and confusion into a quick and fierce desire to align with her five-year-old brother, whom she'd been raised to protect. "It seemed clear to me that all the adults around me were falling apart, and that nobody had the capacity or the desire to take care of me," she says. "So I immediately started thinking about taking care of my brother. I started thinking that *he* was my family, and that we were in this together, like a team." Today, the two siblings are "incredibly close," Margie says, and she continues to offer nurturing and support to him in the town where they both live.

Margie's immediate impulse to protect her brother may have been in part a defense against her own grief, providing her with a distraction from the confusion and anger she felt about her mother's suicide. It also corroborates studies that suggest siblings can draw security from each other when a mother or mother-figure is gone. Children as young as three have shown evidence that they can calm their younger brother's or sister's fears. About half of all preschool-age children will offer comfort to a younger sibling who's distressed.

Thirty-one-year-old Connie, who was seven when her mother died, remembers climbing into bed with her twelve-year-old sister the night they heard the news. "I was scared, and she hugged me while I cried," Connie recalls. "Ever since then, she's been the only one I feel safe enough to go to when I want to talk about our mom."

In a 2002 study of two quartets of sisters, the psychologist Russell Hurd, Ph.D., found that sibling relationships can act as a protective factor in families that experience early parent loss. In both families he studied, the girls had been between the ages of three and ten when their fathers died. Both their mothers had been preoccupied with grief, and the girls had no opportunity to discuss the loss and its impact on them. They banded together for emotional support, however, and as adults they were less likely than other daughters who had effectively lost both parents to suffer from depression later in life. "It appears that children working together and supporting each other, even being rivals with one another and learning how to resolve their conflicts together, can develop skills that carry them on to healthy mourning and non-depressed adulthoods," Hurd explains.

Forty-six-year-old Claudia learned the value of close sibling relationships during an unpredictable childhood. "We moved eight times before I finished high school," she explains. "The houses changed, the neighbors changed, the friends changed, my father was pretty absent because his affairs changed, and my mother did the best she could until she killed herself when I was fourteen." The only constant in her childhood were her two sisters, one older and one younger, and her younger brother. After their mother's death, the four children became de facto parents to each other, the older two raising the younger ones. They remain close as adults. Even though they now live in separate parts of the country, they come together for a family reunion with their children at least once a year.

Today, Claudia tries to encourage close ties between her son and daughter through discussion and modeling. "I want my kids to know in their hearts that they need to always be there for each other," she explains. "My siblings are what saved my life. I recently flew to the Midwest to take care of my younger sister's kids, and last April I left home for a while to help my older sister as they dealt with her husband's stage three cancer. Each time, I told my kids how important it is to me to be there for my siblings."

But far more common, I've found, are families in which siblings split apart after a mother's death. Daughters in these families frequently describe their mothers as "the glue that held the family together," or "the sun around which the separate planets revolved," implying that the loss of this central figure caused the whole system to collapse. And although this may be true, these families were probably never tightly bound from the beginning.

Twenty-seven-year-old Leslie, who was sixteen when her mother died of cancer, remembers interacting very little with her two older brothers when she was a child, and she has limited contact with them today. "Maybe we were already more distant than we knew because my mom was there to rally us, but it became very evident after she died that we really weren't a family," she explains in a tone of muted but obvious regret. "We basically flung ourselves to separate ends of the earth."

Thirty-one-year-old Victoria, who was eight and the youngest of three children when her mother died, is even more succinct: "My family is like the Bahamas," she says. "Same name, but not connected."

In her bestselling memoir *Blackbird*, Jennifer Lauck recreates a scene with her older brother, B.J., that took place the day of their mother's death. When B.J. heard the news he ran out of the house. Jennifer found him in a neighborhood park a few hours later, but the siblings, who had a history of bickering and rivalry, found little comfort in each other that day. Their encounter in the park illustrates how a difficult sibling relationship can further isolate children after a mother dies:

"Just go away," B.J. says.

"Daddy wants you home," I say.

B.J. drops his head, chin to his chest, and his eyes are darker with the shadows of his eyebrows. I don't know if he's mad or sad or what, but I walk so B.J. and me are toe to toe. I don't know what to do, what to say, and I reach out to touch his arm.

B.J. holds his head up and back, eyes down on me.

"She's not your mother," B.J. whispers.

I drop my arm, hand on my leg, and his words sting down my neck.

"She is too," I say.

"Just go away," B.J. says.

B.J. drops his skateboard on the sidewalk and rides away. I stand there, my arms at my sides, and my head hurts between my eyes.

I walk to the middle of the park and stand at the edge of the pond. . . . The wind blows around my legs, around my head, and pieces of hair get into my mouth and my eyes.

Without Momma there is no purpose and it's like being lost, like being on the edge of the world and you don't have anywhere else to go.

Yet even siblings who fight bitterly occasionally can come together in a moment of crisis to offer each other support. The actress Roma Downey, who was ten when her mother died of heart failure in her native Ireland, remembers the ride she and her older brother took home from the hospital that day.

We were with my mother's best friend and had to take a taxi. She got in the front with the driver and my brother and I were in the back, each looking out of an opposite window. We were of an age where a certain sibling rivalry would have been tight. We couldn't look at each other without being mean and childish toward each other. In our immediate grief we were isolated from each other, and my mother's friend said to the taxi driver . . . she was crying and he said, "Are you okay?" and she said, "No, I just lost my best friend" and he said, "Who is it?" He said, "Oh, I knew her. She was very funny." And she said, "Yeah, that's her two children in the back." And he said, "Oh, I'm really sorry kids, so sorry to hear of it." And it sort of hung in the air. And I remember feeling—not looking, but feeling—on the seat of the car and there, sure enough, to meet me was my brother's little hand. And we just held hands together.

Sibling fragmentation often finds its origin in the dynamics of a mother's family of birth, which may serve as her subconscious guide for the family she creates. A mother who was chronically jealous of her older sister, for example, may have inadvertently inspired a similar resentment between her two daughters by favoring the younger one. Or she may identify with the child who has characteristics—height, weight, personality, birth order—similar to her own. Because a manipulative mother is often the source of frustration between siblings, her death may provide them with their first opportunity to assess each other as equals and repair their childhood breaks. Such a rosy resolution is difficult to achieve after decades of accumulated grievances, however, and in some families the chance may arrive too late. The mother may have departed, but her influence continues to live on in her children's angry phone calls and disputes.

Siblings will often direct their anger or confusion toward each other after a mother's death, especially when older children in a family feel overwhelmed by new responsibilities and younger ones feel overlooked or lost. Thirty-one-year-old Joy displaced her anger onto her older sister as their mother slowly died of cancer. "I was going to the hospital every day," she says, "It was really difficult dealing with my father, and driving back and forth to the hospital every day for three weeks. My sister visited the hospital only twice during that whole time, and once she came in with a friend who barely knew my mother. I was furious. That's how I coped with the pain of losing my mother—by becoming angry with my sister."

Joy had always been the responsible daughter, the one who stayed at home and out of trouble while her sister battled a drug problem and had two children outside of marriage. Nevertheless, Joy had always believed that her mother loved her sister more. During her mother's hospital stay, she was determined to become the perfect daughter and earn the praise she'd always hoped for. After her mother died, she comforted herself with the knowledge that she— and not her sister—had eased her mother's final days.

Siblings often flaunt their good deeds, engaging each other in frustrating, circular disputes comparing one sister's sacrifice to another's. *I lost more than you did! I'm hurting more than you are! I was the better daughter at the end!*

Therese Rando calls this kind of infighting "competition among mourners." As rivalrous as these siblings may seem, they're really more interested in earning attention and recognition for their pain than they are in staging a victory. "It's a way a person tries to make herself feel special at a time when she's feeling so deprived," Dr. Rando explains. "She's trying to give herself something she can hang on to when she feels overcome by what she's lost. A different kind of competition develops when adult siblings want to be less involved in the family. That's when you hear, 'I don't want to take care of Dad. *You* take care of Dad,' or 'I took Dad last Christmas. *You* take him this Christmas.'"

Victoria says her older sister Meg, who returned home at twenty-six to care for the family after their mother died, still insists on viewing herself as the family martyr more than twenty years after the loss. Meg's preoccupation with her sacrifice damaged the sisters' relationship during Victoria's childhood and makes it difficult for them to be friends today. Victoria makes no attempt to hide her bitterness when she speaks about Meg's attitude after their mother died.

"I ruined her entire life," Victoria says. "She told me that all the time. 'I had to stay home and take care of you, you know. You ruined my life.'" Angry and resentful about her new responsibility after their mother's death, Meg had unleashed her frustration on eight-year-old Victoria, who grew up with enormous guilt for being such a burden on the older sister she'd previously adored. She still feels the need to compensate for the inconvenience she caused, and she spends long hours on the telephone listening to Meg's problems. "When my shrink said, 'You know, you don't have to listen to your sister's complaints if you don't want to,' I told her, 'You don't understand. I have to take care of my sister, because I ruined her life,'" Victoria recalls. "And my shrink said, 'Just stop it.'" Today, Victoria is trying to separate herself from Meg, who now expects her younger sister to care for her.

Victoria and Meg: sisters who might have avoided the powerful resentment they feel toward each other in the present if one had not been expected to raise the other in the past. Their story raises a much larger question: What happens when one sibling becomes an ersatz mother to another?

Minimothers and Their Instant Kids

After a death in the family, the heaviest expectations usually fall on the oldest or most parentified child. Sons are usually expected to head the family and take over financial and structural matters. Daughters typically are expected to care for the younger siblings, surviving parent, and aging grandparents.

Although taking on the role of mother usually forces a daughter to assume an identity that's inconsistent with her developmental stage, several studies suggest that caring for younger siblings can help a daughter gain self-confidence, develop a resilience toward later stress, and work through feelings of loss. When the psychologist Mary Ainsworth and her colleagues interviewed thirty young mothers who'd experienced the loss of an attachment figure during childhood, they found that those who had been most successful in resolving the loss shared two characteristics: They enjoyed a strong sense of family solidarity, with mutual comforting, expression of feelings, and sharing of grief; and they had the opportunity to take responsibility for other family members during the mourning period.

Twenty-seven-year-old Robin says that caring for her younger sister and brother helped her feel responsible and competent, but also gave her responsibilities too excessive for a sixteen-year-old to manage with ease. When her mother died, Robin became a full-time mother substitute for her thirteen-year-old sister and eight-year-old brother for the next two years, until their father remarried.

I felt the most responsibility for my brother, but I didn't know how to manage him. He was a very difficult kid. He would put up power struggles. He'd want me to take him to the toy store, and if I said I couldn't he'd throw a holy fit. I'd feel so guilty I'd give in to him. When my father was about to remarry, I remember thinking, 'Thank God this woman is moving in.' She latched on to my brother just as much as he latched on to her. That really helped me a lot. At that point, I was able to let go of him and say, 'Okay. He's my brother now. I abdicate responsibility for him.' The only reason I didn't feel guilty for attending a college across the country was because my stepmother moved in a month after I left.

Certainly, there were enormous problems and battles after my father remarried, especially between my stepmother and sister. My sister would call me all the time at college, in tears. My roommates would say, 'It's your sister on the phone again. She's crying again.' I was a big support to her, and still am. I'm always the first one she calls. She definitely relies very heavily on me.

Caring for her younger siblings helped Robin identify with her mother, and indirectly mother herself after the loss. Today, she is well aware of how to care for herself, and often gives herself the same advice she still freely offers to her siblings when they ask her for help.

Thirty-two-year-old Kathleen also coped with her loss by voluntarily "becoming" her mother. The second of four children, Kathleen was the only daughter in her family. Raised to be a nurturer for her three brothers, she took this role to heart when, at eighteen, she gained custody of her thirteen-year-old brother and then raised him by herself.

Tall, gentle, and thoughtful, Kathleen looks and acts mature beyond her years. She was sixteen when her mother died of cancer. Her father died of alcoholism the following year. When her youngest brother, Paul, lonely and miserable in a foster home, called her at college one night, she became determined to bring him to her university town. As soon as she reached legal age, Kathleen went to family court and became his guardian. "A lot of people said, 'You're so young. How can you take on a teenage brother?' but I realized helping him was doing something for me," she recalls. "I didn't have a place to go home to except a dorm room. I was just kind of out there. So by having Paul come live with me, I created a home for myself, too." Kathleen and Paul found a sympathetic dean at her school who arranged for them to live in housing for married students, and they remained together until he began college four years later and joined their oldest brother on the West Coast. But when Kathleen divorced two years ago, both brothers moved back to the small New England town where she owns a house. "I don't know if it's me they're drawn to, or if it's what I represent," she says. "I think, somehow, I'm home to them." She and Paul are roommates again, their oldest brother lives down the road, and the third brother occasionally visits from California.

Approximately 140,000 children in the United States are currently being raised by siblings, a number that's been rising steadily over the past twenty years as foster-care homes have become scarcer. The phenomenon has also been brought to public attention by the 1990s Fox television drama "Party of Five," about five siblings who lose both parents in an auto accident, and Dave Eggers's bestselling book *A Heartbreaking Work of Staggering Genius,* in which he writes of raising his younger brother after both their parents die.

When an older sibling becomes full- or part-time caretaker for a younger one, her natural family position is altered. She's more than a sister but not quite a mother. Motherless mothers who cared for younger siblings say they frequently felt inadequate in one or both roles. Who am I? they wondered. Mother? Sister? Neither? Both? "After I left for college, my sister really felt that she had to become my brother's mother," Robin says. "But she never felt that she succeeded. And how could she? She admitted this to him not long ago, and I think he gave her a great gift when he said, 'Melinda, you're my *sister.* I never expected you to be my mother.'"

Although sisters can fill some of the gap after a mother dies or leaves, I've found little evidence that a sister can become an adequate surrogate mother. As Russell Hurd has pointed out, a sibling can't reproduce the richness or complexity of adult caregiving and support. Of all the women who said they found mother substitutes after their mothers died, only 13 percent cited a sister—roughly the same percentage who named "teacher" or "friend." Most often, a sister will assume physical care for another sibling. Emotionally, however, she's rarely mature enough to meet the demands of a dependent child when she's still one herself. Leading by example can be tricky when you are only a few years ahead of your charge.

"There are real problems when a sister has to become her siblings' mother," Evelyn Bassoff says. "She can't do it very well. But she tries, and it sets her up for failure, which leads to guilt. Oftentimes, in cases where she can't control the children, she resorts to corporal punishment, which also sets her up for guilt. It's not like Wendy and the Lost Boys."

Siblings are generational peers, sharing the same lateral plane in the family hierarchy. They grow up prepared to care for each other reciprocally, not in the type of one-sided and intensely emotionally invested relationship that a parent-child dyad represents. Because a mother-child relationship is one of unequal power, when a sister takes on the mother's role and assumes more power than sibling relationships normally allow, the whole system gets thrown out of sync.

Sisters and brothers are no longer traveling on staggered but parallel paths; one has veered off in another direction entirely. Years later, this sister may find it impossible to rejoin the siblings she left behind.

Thirty-five-year-old Denise, who became a minimother to her two younger sisters after her mother died when she was twelve, explains that her feelings toward them took on a substantially maternal hue. "To this day, I don't have a sisterly relationship with my sisters," she says. "I have a motherly relationship with them. I would lay down on railroad tracks for them. I feel great love for them, but they would never tell me their innermost secrets. And I'd never tell them mine." When Denise's mother died and she took over the maternal role, her sisters began to view her as their protector and superior, instead of as their ally. In adulthood, when a six- or seven-year age difference between siblings normally shrinks in significance, these three sisters are still relating to each other according to the role reassignments that developed twenty-three years ago.

At the age of twelve, Denise saw stepping into the mother's role as a necessity, not as a choice. Someone needed to care for her sisters, and she felt she was the most qualified candidate. Her involvement in their upbringing may have been age inappropriate for her, but the knowledge that they had one person they could depend on at home—inadequate as she may have been at times—helped them develop a sense of security that Denise says they have and she lacks today.

Younger siblings often benefit from strong relationships with their older brothers and sisters after a loss, a bond that's often gratefully acknowledged during adulthood even if it wasn't always appreciated during childhood. A 1983 study of seven adolescents who'd lost a parent to death between the ages of seven and ten and a half found that the four children who coped best were all deeply involved with an older sibling. Thirty-two-year-old Kim says her brother, now forty-two, helped her develop self-esteem and feelings of worthiness after her mother died when she was two. "I always tell people I'd be a pile of mush without my big brother," she says, with a laugh. "Even when I was a little kid, he took me everywhere with him. When he was sixteen and playing in bands, going through a real wild stage, he still brought me with him. Think about it: Who would want a six-year-old sister tagging along? But he let me, and that always helped me feel like there was someplace I belonged."

There are, however, some serious risks involved when one sibling views another as a replacement, rather than a substitute, for the lost parent. An older sister or brother may become the object of a younger sibling's displaced anger toward the mother, and those feelings, if not reconciled, can turn into resentment and deep hatred. The younger sibling may feel angry and resentful when the older one leaves to pursue a life beyond the family. An older sibling may develop an exaggerated illusion of power over a younger one and refuse to let her separate. Or a younger sister may shift her expectations for total support from her mother to a sibling who just as forcefully rejects that role.

"When I was in high school, I turned to my sister, who was five years older than me," remembers thirty-two-year-old Roberta, who was fifteen when her mother died. "And she told me, 'No, I'm not going to take on your problems.' She made it very clear to me that no matter how much pain I was in, she was not willing to take it on. And I was amazed. I was totally insulted. Just stunned that she would be what I thought was that selfish. I'd always thought she had so many answers. To this day, she tells me, 'No. Go to a shrink. I don't have any answers.' Which basically isn't bad advice, but it was hurtful to hear that first time." Roberta does admit, however, that her sister's resistance to taking on the mother role allowed her to remain a sister. Although the two are not particularly close today, Roberta says she has a clear idea of what their sibling relationship does and does not entail.

When an older sister tries to become a mother replacement for a younger sister, the two may become enmeshed in the developmental struggles—including adolescent separation and rebellion—that typically occur in mother-daughter relationships. But an older sister usually is ill-equipped to handle these changes, and the younger sister may suffer developmental confusion if she begins the process and then discovers it can't progress very far.

Mary Jo, forty-three, was eight years old and the youngest of three sisters when her mother died. She was virtually raised by her older sister Patty, who was thirteen when she took over the family's cooking and cleaning, and became Mary Jo's primary day-to-day caretaker. "I went to Patty when I started menstruating, and for those type of things," Mary Jo recalls. "She really became a mother to me, which had advantages to me at the time but serious drawbacks to her. She'd been severely depressed all her life, and that, combined with her sense of 'I'm the oldest female in the house now, and I have to take on the responsibility,' was not a good mix."

Mary Jo grew up identifying with Patty, who in turn overidentified with their mother. Six years ago, when she reached the same age their mother had been when she was diagnosed with cancer, Patty attempted suicide. Mary Jo visited her in the hospital and pleaded with her to get help. A few months later, Patty overdosed again. She died that day.

Mary Jo is now in therapy working through this loss and sorting through her Good Mother/Bad Mother issues—which she has with her *sister.* "Patty really tried to make my life better when I was a kid, but she was all fucked up herself, and some of those things came out in negative and controlling ways," she explains. "We were close in such a love-hate kind of way. I'm working hard to remember and integrate those times when she was wonderful to me, but I can also see how a lot of my negative patterns come from her, and from the way she controlled my emotional life because of the power I felt she had over me."

In an ideal situation, a motherless daughter with older siblings places most of her dependency needs on an available father and draws added—but not total—security from one or more siblings, if she has them. Middle children who can take on small, additional amounts of responsibility, yet still have other family members they can rely on when they need to regress during times of stress, may fare the best. They can gain a sense of competence but also have the family foundation they need to feel emotionally secure. Thirty-two-year-old Samantha, who at age twelve was the second of five children when her mother died, had a father she could rely on, a younger sister who relied on her, and an older sister to whom she brought her questions and concerns about her body, her friends, and boys. The three oldest girls in her family were close before their mother died, and today they live in neighboring towns and talk several times a week.

My sisters and I used to wake up on the weekends, make breakfast for the family, and then climb back into bed and talk for
two or three hours, about anything. We'd do it sometimes at
night, too. So I've always gone to my sisters with my problems.
Sometimes to my friends, but my sisters are usually first. If one
of us doesn't know the answer to a question, we try to figure it
out together, or we ask around. The oldest one has an incredible
amount of knowledge about the human body, and she's our resource. She's married and has three children, and is very matter-
of-fact about pregnancy and childbirth. She'll be sort of an authority figure to me, if I get married and have children.

Samantha says that she'd like to become a mother one day but is
in no hurry. After mothering her youngest sister for almost twenty
years, she wants a rest before she starts again. Many motherless
women who've cared for younger siblings express the same opinion.
"I already raised three children," they say. "Now I want to devote
some time to myself."

Of course, it's a different experience to raise a child whose birth
you've planned and prepared for, and to do it as an adult.
Nonetheless, women who raised younger siblings and later had children of their own often find that their previous experience helped
prepare them for some of motherhood's demands. Thirty-six-year-
old Bridget, who took care of her two younger brothers from the
time she was twelve until she left home for college, says that being a
mother to her son felt like a natural role for her to assume. She never
worried that she'd be a bad mother. "The nurturing part isn't difficult at all," she explains. "But I didn't raise my brothers when they
were very young, so in some areas my experience is evident, while in
others I'm pretty clueless."

Bridget has no contact with her father or stepmother, and all of her
grandparents have died. But her brothers, she says, have stepped in to
give her son the kind of unconditional yet distanced love that she once
received from her grandparents. "My brothers don't know how to deal
with babies, so at first they were like, 'Oh, he's very cute and sweet, and
we love him,'" she says. "But now Alex is four, and he'll get on the
phone and talk with them about someone at school who's being a bully,

and he'll ask what he should do. My brothers really have to put their thinking caps on. I'm always thrilled to see them all interacting like that. That's when I have a sense that even though my mother is gone and I had to raise my brothers, the three of us are definitely a family."

Birth Order

We're not usually aware of the influence that birth order has on us, but our sibling position spawns a set of internalized roles and ideas that affect how we see the world. According to the psychologists Margaret M. Hoopes, Ph.D., and James M. Harper, Ph.D., the death of a parent changes the signals about sibling role assignments that a child received at birth. A middle child accustomed to relying on others may suddenly have to become the caretaker if an older sibling is unavailable or defects from the family. A younger child used to being babied may need to take on more responsibility for herself than she ever had to before.

Sibling roles can go haywire when a father remarries and stepsiblings enter the constellation. If, for example, a stepfamily joins two oldest children under the same roof, they often go head-to-head in competition for the slot of leader of the new sibling group. When sibling positions duplicate, confusion and conflict are typical states until a new pecking order emerges.

The following characteristics, drawn from personal interviews, survey data,[1] and published psychological research, are common birth-order responses for daughters in families that lose a mother.

AN OLDEST CHILD

• May gain quick maturity and responsibility if she takes control of the family, but exercising power at an early age can make her overly controlling as an adult.
• May develop patterns of service to others and become a highly empathetic and compassionate woman.

---

[1]Of the 154 motherless women surveyed for this book, 28 percent were oldest daughters, 25 percent were middle children, 31 percent were the youngest, 15 percent were only children, and 1 percent were twins.

• Often leaves home quickly to escape responsibility and then feels guilty, or stays home for longer than otherwise planned and sacrifices an identity of her own.

• Feels disconnected from her early childhood if she has no one to tell her about those years, but serves as a family historian who can tell younger siblings about theirs.

• May have more trouble separating from her absent mother than her brothers or sisters do. In a 1989 Amherst College study of students of both sexes and all birth orders, first-born daughters reported the highest level of involvement with their mothers and the least separate sense of self.

• Is least afraid to lose her father. Only one out of ten oldest daughters with a father still alive says she fears his death "a lot," compared to one out of four youngest daughters. This may be because oldest daughters were often closer to autonomy and less dependent on their parents when their mothers died.

A MIDDLE CHILD

• Is both an older and younger sister, and may feel confused about which role offers her more security in the family. In her normal need to regress after the loss of a parent, she may identify more strongly with the role of younger sister and turn to an older sibling to care for her. Or, if an older brother or sister is unavailable as a family caretaker, she may have to adopt that role for younger siblings and resent it as "not her job."

• May feel overlooked or excluded, and leave home earlier than the other siblings to differentiate and develop an identity of her own.

• Is least likely to find a mother substitute—44 percent of the middle children surveyed said they'd never had one.

A YOUNGEST CHILD

• Is often perceived as the "baby" of the family and shielded from the facts of a mother's illness or death, leading to confusion or resentment toward other family members. She may grow up distrusting those who told her less than the truth, or expecting authority figures to withhold information from her again.

• May find that her loss is either overdramatized or minimized as family members try to cope with their own grief. "Poor little Jenny had it the worst" shifts their focus off themselves and onto her; "Jenny had it easiest because she remembers Mom the least" allows them to avoid confronting a child's pain.

• May feel angry about having had the least time in an intact family, and have a particularly difficult time with holidays and family celebrations.

• Finds that her models for development are suddenly unhealthy or absent when older siblings zoom through adolescence or young adulthood to take on extra responsibility, act out, or vanish from the family.

• Is the most likely to be "Daddy's little girl" and has the hardest time when he falls ill or dies. Of all the women surveyed who said they feared the death of their fathers "a lot," the largest group—50 percent—were youngest children.

• May perceive herself as most profoundly affected in the long term. Forty-eight percent of the youngest children surveyed for this book said the loss of their mothers was "the single most determining event" of their lives, compared with only 27 percent, 22 percent, and 23 percent of oldest, middle, and only children, respectively. In addition, half of the adult women who said they couldn't identify any positive result of their early loss were youngest children.

AN ONLY CHILD

• Usually has received more attention from her mother than other children. Therefore, in effect, she loses more.

• Is typically more adept at dealing with adults, which can aid her in a search for mother substitutes.

• Learns about heterosexual relationships only through observing her parents, and loses that primary model when her mother dies. If she doesn't have a stepmother, or if her parents' marriage was conflicted, she may feel uncertain about how adult women relate to men.

• Has a difficult time accepting a stepmother, because she's used to having her father to herself.

• Is more egocentric than other children. Her primary concern after a loss is herself—"What's to become of *me*?"—which can lead to a nearly obsessive fear of losing her father, too.

• Feels the impulse to become "perfect" so that her father will not abandon her as her mother did.

• Learns how to behave toward a parent by observing the other parent, rather than by observing a brother or sister. Therefore, after her mother dies or leaves she behaves toward her father as her mother did, which can cause role confusion.

A DAUGHTER IN A LARGE FAMILY
(FIVE OR MORE CHILDREN)

• May have been cared for by older siblings long before the loss, because a mother's attention was divided between so many children. If a daughter's emotions are already partially invested in an alternate mother-figure, she could have less difficulty adjusting to the change in family routine when her mother dies.

• May see a natural leader/teacher emerge from her siblings, who can become a surrogate mother for younger ones. This is usually, though not always, the oldest or second-oldest daughter living at home.

• If she's that older daughter, may feel exploited and angry for having to care for several younger siblings.

• May depend on a sibling cluster for support. For example, a family of seven children often naturally divides into two separate groups based on age. Siblings then turn to their subsystem, rather than the family as a whole, after a mother dies. Because a sibling usually has the hardest time accepting the next younger one, affinities often form between a first and third child, say, or a third and a fifth.

• Must compete with her other siblings for parental affection more than ever in a single-parent home. Each child may not receive enough attention to compensate adequately for what was lost.

• Might, if she's a younger child, get sent to live with an older sibling or other relative after a mother dies, and then feels insignificant, isolated from the rest of the family, or guilty for being a burden.

• Can draw her sense of emotional security from the group, because of its size (which increases the chance of finding an ally) and varied makeup (allowing for the presence of both peers and parent-figures). On the other hand, large families often face challenges such as economic hardship that make members feel continually insecure. When a parent dies, an insecure system—no matter what its size—has trouble unifying.

• Is often raised differently than her much-older or much-younger siblings, because parents' outlook and techniques change over time. A first child's mother, though the same woman, might have parented quite differently the ninth time around. Likewise, an older daughter may have had her mother present at her wedding and the birth of her first child, while the youngest may not yet have graduated from grade school. These two sisters have different secondary losses, which means they have different mourning patterns and needs.

Your Reality or Mine?

My mother and I were pretty close. At the time she died, we'd gotten past most of the nastiness of my adolescence. I think we were getting to a point where we could have grown into something more like friends.

—A thirty-six-year-old woman who was
nineteen when her mother died

I think I was a comfort to my mother. What she was for me, I'm not really sure. We had a lot of things in common, like classical music and religion. I don't remember talking with her about things that I would think are important for girls to talk about with their mother. We had a pretty superficial, pretty thing-oriented relationship. I think she found a steadiness and dependability in me that made her life easier, and for the most part I was happy just to go along with that role.

—A thirty-three-year-old woman who was
sixteen when her mother died

I don't remember my relationship with my mother ever being close. Certainly, we did stuff, like she took me to get my ears pierced, and she got me a kitten while my dad was away on a business trip. I don't know how much of our distance was our relationship per se and how much was my age. I was a pretty snotty teenager. I was going through that phase where everything she did was embarrassing. Mom wasn't the person I talked to. I talked with my sister, mostly.

—A thirty-one-year-old woman who was
fourteen when her mother died

Three daughters speaking about three different mothers? Not quite. Those are the Lawrence sisters—Caitlin, Brenda, and Kelly—describing the same mother who died of cancer seventeen years ago.

As this example illustrates, sibling perceptions of mothers—and of mother loss—usually stop at a point short of mutual agreement. The death of a mother won't affect her children uniformly for several reasons, including their different developmental stages; birth orders; previous encounters with illness, death, or loss; individual circumstances surrounding this death; and personal relationships with both parents. Even when children are raised side by side, as often happens with those close in age, their experiences of mother loss may appear similar in some respects yet differ wildly in others, at times sounding like a tabloid story of twins raised by different mothers.

Sometimes, this isn't far from the truth. Siblings who are in late adolescence or early adulthood when a mother dies grew up mostly under her influence, and usually with two parents, while their younger brothers or sisters may spend most of their formative years with a single father or in a stepfamily. Eva, forty-five, says that until her most recent visit with her family, she always thought her thirty-eight-year-old brother's personality had been shaped by forces out-side the family. "I've always seen Andrew as an organized, conserva-tive kid," she explains. "I know I have that potential, and I've seen it in my middle brother, too, though we're much more relaxed. Andrew is the youngest, but he's the most successful of us three. He works hard and plays hard. He's very pragmatic. Last time I saw him with our stepmother, I realized it wasn't the Vietnam War that made Andrew conservative. It was the difference in our mothers. My step-mother is extraordinarily pragmatic. She's more obviously a result of the Depression, and less relaxed than my mother was." This realiza-tion helped Eva pinpoint the source of a major difference between Andrew and herself, and relieved the pressure she felt each time she compared herself to him and felt guilty for choosing a more alterna-tive lifestyle.

Even when siblings grow up with the same parents, their experi-ences of mother loss can vary dramatically. Caitlin, Brenda, and Kelly, for example, were all living at home when their mother was first diagnosed with cancer. But within two years, Caitlin had begun college, Brenda was in a boarding school eight hundred miles from home, and Kelly was the only child living with her parents. That was the year their mother began a rigorous radiation treatment program, and thirteen-year-old Kelly was the only daughter home to witness its effects. She vividly recalls making trips to the supermarket with her mother, who was so sick from the treatments that she would vomit first in the bread aisle, and again in the parking lot outside. Because Kelly was the only sister who experienced the fear and help-lessness of those moments, it's no surprise that she's the daughter who speaks of breast cancer and illness with the most fear today.

Caitlin, Brenda, and Kelly say they can depend on each other's memories to fill the blank spots in their own. But in other families, especially when siblings are distant to begin with, divergent memo-ries and differing perceptions may only widen the rifts. Because a daughter often views early loss as the central, organizing event of her life and interprets the rest of her experiences in relation to it, her memories of her mother and her loss become fundamental building blocks of her identity. She'll perceive a sibling who challenges her perception of the past as a threat to herself. A sibling with such a strong emotional interest in preserving her memories will defend her version of past events long after it no longer coincides with verifiable fact.

"My brother, sister, and I have very different opinions about the two years when our parents died," Therese Rando says. "Certainly, people are very divergent in the way they perceive things, and there's no greater divergence than when the three of us look back on that period of time. My sister remembers things that I'd stake my life she's totally wrong on. She'll say, 'Don't you remember when Uncle Bob and Aunt Rhea came up every weekend for so long?' My brother and I both know, no way did they come up every weekend. They came up like once—twice at the most. I have external validation for that. But my sister is absolutely sure they came up every weekend. You'd think the three of us weren't in the same place, but we were."

When sibling recollections diverge this dramatically, the salient issue is not whose memory is right and whose is wrong, but who remembers what, and why. Dr. Rando believes that her sister may need to believe her aunt and uncle visited because it offers her a memory of protection at a time when the three early orphans were feeling vulnerable and abandoned. To relinquish the memory would mean having to acknowledge the pain of being left parentless and alone so young.

Caroline, fifty-three, says her long-time resistance to her sister's contrary memories of their childhood stemmed both from her arrogance as an older sibling and from her own difficulties with mourning. Caroline, who was eleven and the second of four children when her mother died, describes herself as "the sister with the airtight memory, the one who can still tell you what food each neighbor brought to the funeral." So when she and her younger sister Linda started collaborating on a book about their childhood, Caroline insisted that her sister's memories weren't correct each time they didn't coincide with hers. But Caroline had begun the book as part of her mourning process, and as her healing progressed, she found herself more willing to accept and integrate her sister's memories with her own.

It's helped me to let go of the belief that I know everything. Now I realize I know what *I've* experienced, but I don't know about anyone else, even someone as close as my sister, because her life was entirely different than mine. We were together for much of our young life, but she experienced a totally different time with our mother. I was usually out playing with my brother, doing stuff, having adventures, and Linda was at home with Mother, learning to cook and speak Norwegian. I understand now that no matter how much alike we are today, she has different memories and different grieving needs, because she lost something different than I.

As Caroline became more willing to see her sister as a separate person, she realized she could mourn with Linda without arguing or disagreeing. Two months before I met with Caroline, the two sisters had taken a day trip into the mountains to grieve together for their mother and their first stepmother, who died three years ago.

The Olympic Peninsula is the farthest point northwest in the contiguous United States, and Hurricane Ridge is one of the tallest areas there. It has a spectacular view. Linda and I drove through some clouds and saw the view, and just burst into tears and laughter at the same time. It was so body thrilling. We couldn't contain all the feelings. We had planned to go up there and grieve for our mothers, and we did. We sang the songs from both of their funerals, and we called out their names. In our world, we mostly see men's names written everywhere. We don't always get to honor our mothers, whether they birthed us or not, and Linda and I were able to honor ours together.

Chapter Seven

Looking for Love
Intimate Relationships

Surely whoever speaks to me in the right
voice, him or her I shall follow, As the water
follows the moon, silently, with fluid steps
anywhere around the globe.

—Walt Whitman, "Vocalism"

MY FRIEND HEIDI SENT ME those lines on a postcard more than
ten years ago. I still remember how each word was measured out in
her neat calligraphy. Heidi and I met in the eighth grade, which gave
us ample time to watch adult patterns develop and repeat. She counseled me through the dissolution of my first adult romance, and my
second, and my third. By then, she knew my weaknesses. So on the
back of the postcard, mailed from Boston the day after we'd discussed my most recent love affair, she gently warned me about following a false prophet who lured me with words I wanted to hear,
and she signed the card, "Be careful with your heart, sweet you."

This was not mere cautionary verse. Heidi had seen me, many
times, give my heart away blindly, and too soon.

I won't recount and relive every romance I had before the one
that ultimately turned into a marriage. The details are messy, and
they start to repeat themselves before long. I had several good relationships and a few long-term ones that started slowly, plateaued for
a while, and ultimately ended when two people grew apart or found
they couldn't withstand change. But in between I had plenty of romances that ended before they really began. This is how I've always
seen it: Once is an event, twice is a coincidence, and three times is a
behavior. Everyone has her patterns. This was mine.

We would meet at a party or at a softball game or on a train. He would take my phone number, and call the next day. Then he started bringing presents, cooking dinners, asking to see me every night. I reveled in the attention, thinking, *I am adored. I am loved.* He wanted to know about every detail of my day. He told all his friends about me. "You're are everything I've ever dreamed of," he said. "I will make your life complete." He would start planning for the future. That was week one.

Week two, I would start feeling the first shiver of unease. Should relationships begin so fast? I would muse to a close girlfriend, and ignore her wise response. If he felt this way, I would tell myself, it must be real; it must be true. We would spend our first night together, and he'd call in sick to work the next day. We would make crazy promises to each other on street corners, make love at midnight and again at dawn. I would know, even as I lay beneath him, that I was letting sex masquerade as love, but inside the parentheses of the moment I could make them one and the same. In the half-light of early morning with adorations whispered in my ear, I could convince myself that when two bodies merge together in an act designed to produce a third, if only his could sink far enough into mine, we could create a perfect whole: me.

The momentum would continue for a month, maybe a little more. And then the abrupt revelation—there was another woman, or some such obstacle or preoccupation, but couldn't we still be friends? I was stunned, every time. Loss, again. Another week of crying, another month of swearing off men, and another series of hours spent sitting on a therapist's couch, reviewing the warning signs that had been there all along.

Oh, I knew about the dangers of such high-speed romance. I'd heard the advice, read some of the books, and seen a half-dozen of the talk shows on TV. I'd learned that a man who steamrolls a woman so quickly has some other agenda in mind, and that genuine intimacy takes time, and so on. But when the need for affection is so great, desire always eclipses fact. As Clarissa Pinkola Estés points out, the unmothered woman will almost consistently override her intuition when she thinks she can find love. When someone offered me instant intimacy, my impulse was always to grab it, no questions asked, pushing aside all I'd read or learned, afraid that such attention might not arrive again.

It wasn't exactly an optimal way to conduct relationships. For one thing, it was exhausting, and for another, I'd wind up naming children with someone before I'd seen him interact with anyone under four feet tall. I'm not ruling out the possibility of love at first sight; I'm just acknowledging that the operative emotion here was more a form of narcissistic need. When a motherless woman attaches to a romantic partner so quickly and completely, her attraction often derives not from mutual affection but from the one-sided hope of what he can give to her.

To some extent, the motherless woman is anywoman; looking for wholeness through relationships is a search we all—motherless or not—pursue. When I ask Andrea Campbell whether such a quest isn't hopelessly misguided, she laughs and says, "To call this kind of search misguided is to say the whole human race is misguided. Even if our parents did live, they didn't fulfill us in the ways we needed to be fulfilled. The most wonderful, perfect mother can't do it. And so we're all wounded in a way, all looking for someone out there to heal us." But the motherless daughter, she explains, feels a deprivation deeper than that of most other daughters.

In an ideal situation, a daughter's emotional foundation begins with her family and then, as she matures, expands to include her partner, friends, and self. The motherless daughter—especially one without an available and supportive surviving parent—begins from a point one step back. She first has to establish or reestablish a secure emotional base. As John Bowlby observed when he analyzed data from a 1987 British study of women who lost mothers before their eleventh birthday, a girl without a secure emotional base "may become desperate to find a boyfriend who will care for her and that, combined with her negative self-image, makes her all too likely to settle for some totally unsuitable young man. . . . Having married him, the effects of her previous adverse experiences are apt to lead her either to make unduly heavy demands on him and/or to treat him badly."

Although Bowlby's analysis describes the plight of some motherless daughters, theirs isn't the only possible outcome. Attachment theorists generally divide individuals into three groups: those who form secure attachments with others as adults; those who are anxious or ambivalent about their social and romantic relationships; and those who avoid becoming close to others. Secure adults typically divide their emotional needs between several sources, including themselves; they can comfortably give and receive care. Anxious-ambivalent adults usually look to a partner to meet most of their needs; they give care in a self-sacrificing, compulsive manner and often attempt to find security and love through sexual contact. Avoidant adults rely almost exclusively on themselves; they're unable or unwilling to give or receive care and are most likely to maintain emotional distance from others or become promiscuous.

Attachment patterns are believed to start forming in infancy, with their roots in a mother's level of responsiveness to her infant's signals. Mothers who warmly and quickly attend to an infant's cries of distress, for example, are more likely to raise securely attached children than mothers who go through the motions mechanically, or without an emotional connection, and mothers who respond late, incompletely, or not at all. Most psychologists now agree that the kind of relationship an infant develops with his mother serves as a blueprint for the quality of relationships he'll later have as an adult.

Even when an infant is raised by a loving mother and develops a secure bond with her, however, specific life events can disrupt his sense of security. These include a chronic, severe illness in the child or one of the parents; experience in foster care; mental illness in a parent; the dissolution of the family after parental death, separation, or divorce; and physical or sexual abuse of the child. A 1999 study of eighty-six children from birth to eighteen years found that those who'd experienced one or more adverse events during childhood, even if they'd received sensitive care as infants, were far more likely than other young adults to be insecure in their attachments and preoccupied with past relationships. The eighteen-year-olds who were securely attached to others had experienced few or no adverse events during childhood—a finding that points to the deleterious effect a parent's mental illness, a parent's death, and stress in the family subsequent can have on a child.

Studies that compare motherless daughters with other adults are even more illuminating. In a population of nonbereaved persons, roughly 55 percent of individuals will show evidence of secure adult attachment, 25 percent will be avoidant, and about 20 percent are anxious-ambivalent. When the psychologist Bette Glickfield conducted a study with eighty-three adults who had lost parents during childhood and adolescence, however, she found that 46 percent of her subjects placed into the secure category, with 17 percent judged as avoidant and 37 percent anxious-ambivalent. The significantly higher percentage of anxious-ambivalent adults in her study, she says, suggests that early parent loss makes a child more vulnerable to feelings of abandonment and worthlessness, which makes her fear and desire relationships as an adult.

A 2001 study at Johnson State College in Vermont had similar findings: When thirty married motherless women were compared to a control group, the motherless women reported significantly more anxiety and avoidance in their relationships with husbands than the other women did, even though two-thirds of them described their relationships with their deceased mothers in positive terms. Taken together, these findings suggest that motherless women may be afraid of losing their spouses, and may be preparing themselves for what they perceive to be another inevitable loss by emotionally distancing themselves from their partners. At the same time, they feel highly anxious about the possibility that such a loss could occur.

The Anxious-Ambivalent Daughter

Carol, thirty-six, describes her past six years as a series of rapid-fire romances that all began with the promise of immediate affection but never lasted more than two or three months each. Virtually all of the men she dated became unwitting participants in her attempt to find the emotional security she had lost at the age of seventeen, when her mother died.

Carol says she was never particularly close with her mother, whose Scandinavian stoicism discouraged any emotional displays, but she did draw security from her close-knit family. After her mother died, however, this system began to disintegrate. Within two years, both of Carol's surviving grandparents also died, reducing an extended family of six that had once spent all holidays and vacations together to only three: her father, herself, and an older sister who lived in another state. Since then, Carol has approached all of her romantic relationships, including a seven-year marriage in her twenties, with expectations too large for one person to fill.

> My relationships always begin with a strong sense of attraction and a feeling of hope—like, This is it; I'm not alone anymore. I'm looking for some kind of connection, a family feeling. I'll be out on a first date and I'll start wondering if I can be with him in the long term instead of getting to know him as a person. I put very high expectations on anyone I date.
>
> On one level, I'm really terrified of trusting someone, because I'm afraid he'll leave. I have an inner belief that whoever I love will leave, or die. So I usually choose men who won't get *too* close, but who then can't give me appropriate affection and genuine caring because they're all absorbed in their own stuff. I'll try to get something from them they can't possibly give me, and when they can't meet my demands, I get angry and withdraw.
>
> Because I've been repeating this pattern so much, I've been getting much faster at seeing who can genuinely give to me and who can't. I'm trying to learn the process of getting to know someone slowly and seeing if he's appropriate for me or not. For quite a while I thought I should take what I could get. Like, "Love is here, I've got to take it," instead of asking, "Is this the right one for me?"

Carol's deep need for nurturing extends back beyond her mother's actual death to the years spent with a mother who showed little affection or emotion. Her repeated attempts to pull affection from men too distant to satisfy her desire closely resemble a daughter's efforts to extract attention from an unavailable mother. Motherless daughters who grew up with emotionally distant fathers after their mothers died are likely to respond the same way. A 1990 study of 118 undergraduates ages seventeen to twenty-four at the University of Southern California found that those who recalled their parents as cold or inconsistent caregivers were more likely to worry about being abandoned or unloved, exhibit an obsessive and overly dependent love style, and suffer from low self-worth and social confidence than those who perceived their mothers and fathers as warm and responsive during their childhoods. During adulthood, the daughters of distant parents often formed relationships characterized by jealousy, fear of abandonment, and an obsessive preoccupation with finding and maintaining intimate bonds. As Maxine Harris also found in her interviews, many men and women who received little or no affection or emotional warmth after the death of a parent embarked on an almost desperate search for an all-powerful love they believed would save them.

The continual repetition of loss that Carol has tolerated in her adult relationships also indicates that her mother's death has influenced her attachment patterns. Rather than retreating into self-protection like an avoidant daughter, she has remained willing to travel the same route over and over again, hoping each time that she can rewrite the past with a happy ending. *This time he will give me everything I need. This time he won't leave.* In spite of her hypersensitivity to abandonment, an anxious-ambivalent lover often refuses to acknowledge a departure when it begins. As the psychologist Martha Wolfenstein pointed out in the 1969 article "Loss, Rage, and Repetition," a motherless daughter frequently denies or ignores the warning signs of a troubled relationship, insisting that this time she can be special and worthwhile enough to prevent a loved one from leaving. Clinging to a dead relationship or pleading for a last-minute change of heart is less an adult's attempt at reconciliation than a child's cry for the parent to remain. But because the daughter's behaviors do not change, neither does their outcome. What usually happens is just what she set out to prevent—she reactivates a cycle of loss.

"If the initial loss is never grieved, if there isn't a working through and a reconciliation, then you're going to have that repetition compulsion," Evelyn Bassoff explains. "Going through an active grief process, mourning the loss of the mother, and finding peace with it makes the repetition of that kind of relationship less compelling." In other words, when a daughter lets go of her lost mother, she also relinquishes the need to prevent other loved ones from separating from her.

When a woman looks to a partner to mother her, she sees the relationship through the eyes of a child. She instantaneously regresses, expecting to get what she wants, when she wants it, and she'll stamp her feet and cry or silently sulk when she doesn't win. And what she usually wants is constant affection and praise.

An inordinate "attachment hunger" typically develops in a daughter who feels she was ignored or overlooked during childhood. A daughter who can't evoke an emotional response in a parent or parent figure begins to feel unreal and to doubt her own existence. As an adult, she then needs constant expressions of affection from a partner to assure her that she's worthwhile and significant to others. But when her self-esteem and self-worth are completely dependent on this attention, she is unable to tolerate even the smallest deviation or complication in a romance. "She gets angrier quicker," Nan Birnbaum explains. "More frustrated. Insulted. And so it's harder for her as an adult to remain resilient and to maintain the tie. A narcissistic injury occurs with parent loss that makes her feel less important or not good enough. She carries that vulnerability right into adult relationships, and it makes for a difficult habit to break." She perceives every sideways glance as an indication of her deficiency; only round-the-clock affection makes her feel totally secure. "Exactly," says a twenty-three-year-old woman whose mother committed suicide when she was five. "And then the minute he stops paying total attention to me because he has to be normal—like, God forbid, go to work—I think, 'God, he hates me. He's not ever coming back.'" This daughter sees romance as a two-petaled daisy: Either he loves me or he loves me not.

Anxious lovers, who often bond with partners quickly and approach adult relationships with a child's expectations, have enormous difficulty withdrawing emotionally when a romance comes to an end. Letting go of a lover is an especially heartbreaking process for the woman who experiences the event as the loss of her mother again and perceives even temporary separations as deep, personal rejections. Blinded by an early experience that keeps her emotionally tied to her childhood, she believes—as a child believes—that she has the power to control others, and therefore interprets all failures and losses as her fault.

Once a relationship has begun, survivors of early loss tend to remain overwhelmingly faithful to it. Maxine Harris's interviewees had very low rates of divorce, reflecting the notion that relationships are too precious to relinquish willingly. But this kind of loyalty can go either way, explain Mary Ann and James Emswiler, founders and directors of the New England Center for Loss & Transition and the authors of *Guiding Your Child Through Grief*. "To the extent that it encourages someone to work hard on the knots in a relationship, it helps," they write. "To the extent that it persuades someone to stay in an unhealthy or abusive relationship, it hurts."

Even though Amanda, thirty-three, has been in a stable marriage for ten years, she still lives with the intermittent fear that she's "not good enough" for someone to stay with in the long term. She was three when her mother abandoned her, and six when her father married a chronically depressed woman who had little interest in another woman's child. During high school, Amanda looked for comfort and affection through sex, moving from one boy to the next until she fell in love for the first time at seventeen. "When that boy broke up with me, you would have thought my world had ended," she explains. "Nobody could believe how hard or how long I cried. I just couldn't get a grip. I had a really strong feeling that 'this person doesn't like me,' and that would get me somewhere deep inside. I suffered for a long time from a lack of self-esteem, and I still get bouts of it every once in a while. My husband is an entertainer, so sometimes he'll be working with a very attractive, have-it-together woman, and I get the big, green monster worse than anyone else I've ever known."

Amanda has begun to explore her feelings about mother loss in an attempt to overcome the childhood fears she has carried into adulthood. She is acknowledging that her anxieties have little to do with her husband's behaviors, which indicate only his devotion to her. For Amanda, these are important steps toward righting the wrongs of her childhood. As she is learning, a daughter who keeps her mourning at a distance stunts her emotional growth. As an adult, she responds to situations she perceives as threats to the self the same way she responded to her mother's departure when she was a child. If a young daughter, for example, withdrew into silence because she had no outlet for her rage and grief, she may sit home alone seething silently twenty years later when her husband spends a Saturday night out with his male friends. "Nothing," she says, when he asks her what's wrong, because "nothing" was all she allowed herself to feel the last time someone she loved walked out the door.

The Avoidant Daughter

Twenty-five-year-old Juliet and twenty-four-year-old Irene were strangers when they first met. But as they began to share their stories of loss with a group of motherless women, they discovered that they understood each other well. After the deaths of their mothers, Juliet and Irene developed coping skills that insulated them from further loss, but have also isolated them from romantic love.

Juliet, who grew up in an alcoholic family, lost her mother when she was seventeen. As an adolescent, she withdrew into self-reliance, insisting she could manage alone, and she grew into a relentlessly self-protective adult. "My thing was always, 'I'm good, I'm okay, and I don't need anything,'" she explains. "I had to depend on myself to survive. Now I find myself a person who's unable to trust anyone else. I've never been in a relationship with a man. I've had a string of one-night stands. It's like I say, 'I'm so fine. I'm so taken care of. I don't need you. Please keep your distance, because I'm in control.' But it's such a sad place to sit, because when I'm really upset and lonely, I want to be the kind of person who can ask for help if she needs it. And yet I feel totally incapable of intimacy. I've always needed to be so completely capable. I feel like I'm just starting to chip my way out of this block."

Irene, who lost her mother five years ago, turns to Juliet and says, "I'm so glad you just said that, because I've had the exact same problem. My mother was so dear to me that I'm afraid of losing someone else. I don't ever want to go through that again. I don't want to depend on anyone anymore, because I feel that if I don't depend and I don't love, then I won't have to go through the pain of loss again. I just keep my distance from people so I won't get hurt."

Intimacy doesn't come easy for women who see it as an inevitable path to loss. Imagine the paralysis that results when you desperately want someone to love you, yet even more passionately fear the consequences of loving back. Daughters are often raised to define themselves through their relationships, but the avoidant daughter defines herself through independence alone. Taking care of herself has been her method of survival, especially when her surviving parent is unreliable or emotionally withdrawn. "Self-reliance is perhaps the strongest of the barriers that individuals erect to keep themselves at a distance from others," Maxine Harris explains. "As long as the individual remains supremely confident, she does not need the help or assistance of anyone." Maintaining this self-reliance in adult relationships then acts as a surefire method for insulating oneself from future loss.

When a daughter fears loss so much that she believes it inevitable, she avoids forming relationships that might lead to the deep intimacy she craves. This daughter either dodges romance, chooses aloof partners, or extracts herself each time a relationship shows the first sign of long-term commitment. She refuses to make promises or respond to demands, afraid that such actions will lead to an intimacy that'll be snatched from her again. She may become proficient at abruptly ending relationships before she has to make an emotional investment, an act that also allows her to exercise the control she didn't have when her mother died. As a serial deserter, careful to leave lovers before they can leave her, she is not only sidestepping intimacy but also is looking for vindication for being left without warning once before. It's as if she's telling her mother, "See? I can leave you, too."

The psychiatrist Benjamin Garber recalls a client—let's call her Virginia—whose fear of loss and distrust of close relationships destroyed every chance she had to find acceptance and love. Fourteen when her mother died, Virginia started dating a few years later, but with an attitude so cavalier and cynical that she consistently sabotaged every relationship she began. "Every time she got involved with a boy, she'd say to me outright, 'It's not going to last,'" Dr. Garber remembers. "She always felt she had to be involved in a kind of cautious way. There was a constant uneasiness to her approach, a looking over her shoulder. She worried about it, she talked about it, and, of course, sometimes she did things to make the loss happen. The way she kept her distance automatically gave boys the impression she couldn't care less, and she went through a series of boyfriends. This was a very attractive, bright girl, but she couldn't sustain a relationship."

Virginia's behavior was a smokescreen for her fear of abandonment, an anxiety so pervasive it extended to her relationship with Dr. Garber. As a psychiatrist, he hoped his client would begin to view their relationship as a secure base from which she could venture forth and return, eventually developing the self-confidence and self-esteem to form other relationships without expecting them to end. "We'd had a good rapport, and the treatment was quite successful in other ways," Dr. Garber recalls. "It allowed her to go on to college and do well in school. But each time she came home from college, she would ask if I was willing to see her. I'd told her before she left for school that my door was always open to her, but she called on several different occasions and each time needed reassurance over the phone that I indeed wanted to see her. She just couldn't believe that I'd want her to come back." Dr. Garber believes that Virginia saw the act of leaving for school as an abandonment she had inflicted on him, and she felt guilty about hurting him as her mother's death had hurt her. She also feared depending on him to any real degree, afraid that if she did, he, too, would leave her emotionally bereft. Shortly after the phone calls he mentioned, Virginia stopped calling Dr. Garber at all.

The avoidant daughter will feel safe enough to accept love from others only when she is certain she has created a secure base for herself. Ivy, forty-one, says she deliberately avoided marriage and motherhood until her midthirties for this reason. She was eight when her mother died of kidney failure, and despite the presence of a twenty-four-year-old sister who became her surrogate mother, Ivy felt she was a burden to her family. She became determined to achieve self-reliance as quickly as she could. Although she had several relationships with men during college and throughout her twenties, refusing to depend on others—or let others depend on her—became her compulsion during early adulthood. "I felt an *obligation* to take care of myself," she explains. "As I grew older, being able to support myself emotionally and take care of myself financially became primary. Only when I felt I'd achieved that did I give myself permission to find a stable love, almost as if I had to make sure my life would have stability or foundation before I took a chance on allowing myself to be dependent on someone else again." She was willing to risk loss only after she felt certain that the departure of another loved one wouldn't destroy her emotional equilibrium again.

The Secure Daughter

Many motherless daughters can and do go on to have stable, committed relationships. Forty-six percent of the adults who lost parents during childhood in Bette Glickfield's study showed evidence of secure attachments, and the majority of women interviewed for this book report that they're currently involved in committed relationships. Of the 154 motherless women surveyed, 49 percent are married, compared to 32 percent who are single (including those with live-in lovers) and 16 percent who are currently separated or divorced.[1]

When loss—along with its accompanying fears—is such a determining event of a woman's life, what helps her form warm, loving relationships as an adult? Bette Glickfield found the presence of a consistent, supportive, and emotionally attentive caregiver after a parent's death to be the only reliable predictor of a daughter's later attachment style. Those who had a surviving parent they felt they could depend on became adults who felt they could depend on others, and did. Other research indicates that good experiences at school, such as social relationships, athletic success, or scholastic achievement, lead to an increased feeling of self-efficacy, which bolsters a daughter's self-esteem and makes her less likely to choose a marriage partner exclusively based on her overwhelming, subconscious need.

Choosing an emotionally stable partner also appears to increase a daughter's feelings of security in her relationships. When she believes she can depend on her mate, she can release some of her anxiety about abandonment. Carolyn Pape Cowan, Ph.D., a psychologist

[1]Because the survey asked the open-ended question, "What is your marital status?" the number of women currently married may include some second and third marriages, and the number currently single may include some women who have been divorced. An additional 3 percent of the women surveyed were widowed.

and lecturer at the University of California at Berkeley and the coauthor of *When Partners Become Parents,* found in her ten-year study of ninety-six couples from 1979 to 1989 that women from high-conflict families of origin (ones involving, for example, alcoholism, abuse, or loss) who married men from low-conflict families were much more likely to have secure partnerships and ease with child rearing than those who married men from troubled backgrounds.

"There's something about a man being from a more nurturing, less conflicted family that brings him to a marriage and a new family with more tools at his disposal to be a nurturant partner, and parent as well," Dr. Cowan explains. "Even when a woman comes from a family where she didn't have very good models of how to be nurturing, her partner's ability to nurture can make a difference to her. It seems to provide a relationship in which she can feel cared for without the conflict from her childhood that's so scary, or rejecting it would keep her from getting connected to him. In other words, something about the nature of the relationship with her husband makes up for or buffers some of what we expect would be the negative effects of having grown up in a difficult family. And when we look at her with her children when they're small, she appears as warm and responsive to the kids as women who come from more secure backgrounds." These women may have achieved what psychologists call an "earned-secure" attachment status, meaning that with outside influence, and over time, their pattern changed from an insecure state to one more stable and trusting.

Twenty-five-year-old Margie says that after five years in a relationship with an emotionally stable partner she's finally learning how to rebuild the trust and security she lost when her mother committed suicide eighteen years ago and she went to live with an emotionally detached father and stepmother for the next eleven years.

This man I'm involved with comes from a happy nuclear family. His parents are still in love, and the siblings are all close. Of course, they have their own family problems, like every family does, but generally they're pretty content. So he has a really different thing going for him. His givens are not necessarily my givens. It's a given for him that I love him and he loves me and we want to be together. He has this idea that I'll always be there—I'm not going to die, I'm not going to stop loving him, I'm not going to reject him. I don't have that feeling yet, but I am getting to a point where I'm ready to open up a little bit and express some needs.

I'm thinking now that I can be interdependent with others, that there are more options than pure independence and dependence, with dependence as bad, bad, bad, and that maybe I can begin to trust and express vulnerability in a way that's not destructive to myself. I'm slowly redefining myself as someone who can want and need people in her life. Yes, I can survive without them. I've proven that to myself. I can survive without nurturing and love, but it's a pretty destructive and painful way to live.

Like Margie, women who enter secure, long-term relationships with partners they feel they can trust often find that these unions act as stabilizing influences for their most intense fears of loss. Gary Jacobson, M.D., and Robert G. Ryder, Ph.D., of the National Institute of Mental Health, found that the formal act of marriage also allayed some of these concerns. As they prepared to study 120 married couples—90 with a history of parental death before marriage and 30 with no prior parent loss—they expected subjects who'd lost parents during childhood or adolescence to have the most problems during their first few years of marriage. Instead, they found that more than a third of the couples they rated "exceptionally close" had experienced parental death prior to marriage, twice the number they'd anticipated. These couples exhibited a strong degree of intimacy, were able to communicate openly, felt grateful for the spouse, and enjoyed a feeling of family reconstitution.

Forty-three-year-old Mary Jo, who was eight when her mother died, says she achieved this security in her second marriage, as she applied the lessons she'd learned from the breakup of her first. When her first husband left her, the abandonment she felt was so severe that she recognized a need for professional help. With the aid of an empathetic therapist, she began to mourn her mother's death. As she worked through those feelings of loss, Mary Jo saw how she had been approaching her romantic relationships looking for the mother love she felt lacking in her life. And she started to learn how to choose an emotionally available partner whom she hoped could meet some—but not all—of her needs. Today, she describes her second marriage as much healthier and more stable than her previous one. "My husband is really a rock of reliability and strength and love," she says. "Fortunately, he's very unlike me in terms of catastrophic thinking. He'll tell me, 'That fear has no basis in reality, Mary Jo,' but he's also wonderful about letting me cry when I need to cry. There are some times when I think about all the deaths in my life and need to cry for what looks like no reason, and he holds me or just sits with me. I think the combination of him, and my own resilience, and having good friends and a good therapist has been instrumental in getting me from a very dangerous place to here." Mary Jo says that as she learned how to diffuse her dependency needs among several different people, each of her relationships, including her marriage, began to feel more secure.

Women with Women

Motherless daughters who choose women as lovers look for the same emotional security as those who choose men, and also find solace in those who offer stability and consistent care. Their desire for mother love, however, often involves a direct search for the same-sex connection they lost. Karen, twenty-nine, who came out at age fifteen, says she specifically looks for girlfriends who can offer the nurturing she kept trying to elicit from an alcoholic mother who died nine years ago. "After my mother died, I kept trying to find the validation she never gave me through my lovers," she explains. "Being lovers with women has certainly made that one step more complex. I mean, I don't look for Mommy and Daddy; I look for Mommy and Mommy. I tend to be attracted to older women, and that gives me no end of thought. I ask myself, 'What exactly is going on here?' and 'Is there something suspect?' My former lover was ten years older than me, and in a sense she adopted me. When my mother was sick, we went to see her together, and it was clear that my lover—and not my mother—was the one mothering me." Today, Karen is living with her lover of the past three years. During our interview, she waved her arm to indicate the comfortable furnishings of their apartment and explained that all the items that surrounded us belong to her partner, who literally and figuratively provides her with the sense of home she never had as a child.

In her oft-quoted essay "Compulsory Heterosexuality and Lesbian Existence," Adrienne Rich suggests that woman-woman partnerships are far more natural than a predominantly heterosexual society likes to admit. A child's first intimate bond is typically with a female. A boy who's encouraged to choose a member of the opposite sex as a mate thus experiences a continuity of attachment. Girls, however, are expected to shift their emotional allegiance to men. "If women are the earliest sources of emotional caring and physical nurture for both female and male children," Rich writes, "it would seem logical ... to pose the following questions: whether the search for love and tenderness in both sexes does not originally lead toward women [and] why in fact women would ever redirect that search." The motherless woman searching for maternal love in a mate may find that the most natural place for her to find it is in another woman's arms.

After dating men for ten years, Sabrina, twenty-seven, is about to begin her first lesbian relationship. She's always been attracted to women, she says, but has avoided dating them because she's hyperconscious of trying to reunite with her mother, who committed suicide thirteen years ago. "When I'm with a woman, there's always a transference going on," she explains. "Sometimes I want to say, 'Oh, I'm sorry. I was just thinking you were my mother. I hope you don't mind.' But for the past seven months I've been working with a woman who's bisexual, and we've begun a sort of relationship. I haven't slept with her yet, but she offers a lot of the nurturing I'm looking for. Her mother was an absentee mother, who left her when she was a child. We're like two lost people holding each other."

About half the lesbians interviewed for this book knew they were gay before their mothers died, and several of them said their mothers' deaths freed them to come out without fear of family conflict. One lesbian, living happily with her partner of eight years, said she's so certain her mother's reaction to her sexuality would have been hysteria and withdrawal that she'd probably be living with a man if her mother hadn't died. Other bisexual and lesbian motherless daughters say they chose women as emotional and sexual partners after relationships with men failed to provide the nurturing and comfort they sought, or that they channeled their sexual impulses toward women because they feared having such impulses toward men while living alone with their fathers. Although some of these daughters may have been attracted to other women all along, they also point to specific trigger events—and not just the deaths of their mothers—that guided them into the bisexual or homosexual relationships they're involved in today.

Love Substitutes

Motherless daughters talk about empty spaces. They talk about missing pieces. They talk about the void that exists where a family once was, and the gaping hole that sits permanently between their stomach and their ribs.

This emptiness turns the unmothered into emotional hoarders. Accustomed to receiving less than they want or need, they try to take in as much as they can, as quickly as possible, as if excess today guarantees a stockpile for tomorrow. "The unmothered child often wants to grasp things because she's so afraid that they'll go away, that they won't be there when she needs them," Clarissa Pinkola Estés explains. Back-to-back relationships, overeating, overspending, alcoholism, drug abuse, shoplifting, overachieving—all are her attempts to fill that empty space, to mother herself, to suppress feelings of grief or loneliness, and to get the nurturing she feels she lost or never had.

These behaviors typically emerge during adolescence, when a newly acquired autonomy gives a girl more options for soothing herself. But without a mother-figure or caretaker to identify with, she loses some of the capacity for self-mothering, and she does not yet have the emotional maturity to obtain it in a constructive way. Trying to mother herself and drown out her pain, she then turns to sex, food, alcohol, drugs, shoplifting, or other compulsive behaviors as substitutes for love.

Instead of working from the inside out, a motherless daughter uses addictions to heal herself from the outside in. She may try to medicate with alcohol or drugs, satiate with food or material goods, and master her environment with achievement and success. The same panic that makes her spin around in a crowd to look for that single stranger who'll deliver her from a lifetime of loneliness and pain sends her bolting to the grocery store or shopping mall to let acquisition and consumption push her genuine feelings aside, even if only for a while.

"Compulsion is despair on the emotional level," writes Geneen Roth in *When Food Is Love: Exploring the Relationship Between Eating and Intimacy.* "The substances, people, or activities that we become compulsive about are those that we believe capable of taking our despair away." These behaviors develop and persist because they aid us in some way. A woman deliberately gains fifty pounds to make herself unattractive and thereby avoids confronting her fear of intimacy. A girl becomes an overachiever to elicit the praise and respect from strangers that she can't get from her family, or to force her surviving parent to acknowledge her success. An adolescent turns to drugs and alcohol to numb her unbearable feelings of loneliness and loss.

Since her mother's fatal heart attack nineteen years ago, Francine, thirty-two, has used food as her source of comfort. Of the ten children in her family, Francine was the only one who shared her mother's overeating habits, and food became her substitute for maternal love. "I would bring in anything that would sort of push everything else away," she explains. "I've had to work with this all my life. Everything is oral for me. I could easily be an alcoholic if I let myself be. I started smoking right after my mother went into the hospital and just recently quit. That was a major difficulty for me. One thing I've noticed over the years since my mother has been gone is that I'm really, really weak around dairy products. Whenever I'm hurting, that's what I turn to. I've read books about how mother's milk represents nurturance, and dairy is a good substitute for that."

After unsuccessful attempts with several weight-loss programs, Francine is now working with a therapist to address the underlying cause of her compulsions: the emptiness and loneliness she's felt since her mother's departure and her family's subsequent demise. Instead of reaching for the quick fix of cigarettes or food, she's now trying to achieve longer-lasting results by identifying exactly what she needs and obtaining it through less self-destructive routes.

"I'll still turn to booze, and sometimes I need a candy bar or I'm going to kill, but I give in to these weaknesses a lot less frequently than I used to," she says. "I'm getting stronger. I have a lot of good friends I can turn to who care about me. I also care about myself more, and I'm learning to get love from me. I write in my journal a lot, and I sing. I make crafts. I've become an activist. If something makes me mad, I'll write a letter or do something about it. That's a big difference, because I was never able to express anger before. Being a girl, I learned to hold it in and cry.

"I was doing really well a couple of years ago, until I started trying to get pregnant and couldn't. It started bringing up feelings of loss, and I started eating a lot. The past year and a half has been very emotionally trying. The difference now is that I see it as temporary, and I feel I can get through it. Before, this kind of stress would just plummet me back."

In most families, a mother's absence contributes to a daughter's compulsive behaviors, though rarely causes them The loss more often exacerbates an existing problem or forces a budding addiction into early maturity. In Francine's family, the seeds for addiction already had been planted before her mother died. Francine was overeating as a child, and her mother's heart attack and the resulting family chaos gave her even more reason to use food to suppress her feelings.

As Arlene Englander explains, women who feel helpless against their addictions often use mother loss as a convenient excuse for their behaviors. "If you insist that B follows A, that the reason you're an alcoholic is because your mother died, then your addiction becomes irreversible," she says. "The logic then is that since your mother remains dead, you have to remain an alcoholic. The daughter who can realize that her mother's death may be only one of the contributing factors, and who can understand that she re-creates herself every day of her life, becomes less of a victim. We all have to be aware that as adults, we can be responsible for re-creating our own psychological health."

That's what Carol, who spoke earlier about her difficulties with relationships, learned a few years ago, when she finally sought help for her bulimia and compulsive shoplifting. Carol traces the origin of these compulsions back to her early childhood with a distant mother, and their intensification to the period that followed her mother's death. "I was just going along until age seventeen, and then it was like somebody pulled the rug out from under me," she explains. "To compensate, I moved into a mode like my mother's—efficient, detached, we-can-handle-it-all. She rarely expressed emotion, so I didn't know how to do that. And that's when my eating got worse."

Compulsions substitute action for emotion, and eating and stealing became Carol's escapes from a grief she didn't know how to manage. "I was trying to cope with the pain by eating, and then to regain control, I'd purge or exercise like mad to try to rid myself of it," she admits. "It became almost a ritual. I always felt a slight sense of relief afterward, like 'It's okay now. I don't have it inside me anymore.' I also compulsively shoplifted and stole. I know a lot of anger was behind that. I felt like I was trying to get back at somebody even though there was nobody, really, to get back at. And it was a way to get what I never got. Stealing stayed with me until just a few years ago. I wasn't stealing from stores anymore, but in the workplace I'd take things or come up with sneaky little ways that I could try to somehow get taken care of by someone other than myself. It was like I was playing out my family issues. I wasn't getting what I really wanted through work, so I acted out by taking things."

When she was caught stealing from the workplace and lost her job, Carol joined Debtor's Anonymous, which she describes as a support group for people with financial debts to others and emotional debts to themselves. Today, she's trying to redirect the energy she once put into her addictions toward coping with her feelings of loss. She hopes she'll then be free to have a fulfilling relationship with someone else.

That's the real irony of compulsive behaviors: A woman turns to them as substitutes for love, but they then prevent her—and protect her—from finding the reciprocated human warmth she really seeks. To break addictive patterns, she has to be willing to face the emotions that initially made the behaviors attractive to her: anger, guilt, grief.

It's the same cure for the anxious lover's search, and the avoidant daughter's withdrawal. Only when we let go of the lost mother do we stop looking for her in every potential partner we meet and stop expecting her to leave us again. The strength we gain from confronting these fears is ultimately what gives us the self-worth, the self-respect, and the courage to love and be loved in return.

I met my husband in the spring of 1995, when he rented office space to the fledgling Motherless Daughters organization that was forming in New York. It took a year for us to start dating, and another year before we married. He pursued me, which was a novel and unexpected twist. For the first time, I was the one afraid to step into a relationship. This one, I knew from the beginning, was one that was going to last. I didn't want to mess it up.

There are two common relationship strategies among survivors of early parent loss, Maxine Harris explains: deliberately keeping relationships brief but intense and always being the one to leave a relationship first. Both are methods for minimizing anxiety about intimate relationships, which are often synonymous, in a motherless daughter's mind, with potential loss. I'd always thought the men I'd chosen were ambivalent and evasive. Only after meeting the man who would become my husband did I realize the truly erratic one, most of the time, had been me.

I am surprised, every day, to wake up with this man whose loyalty I have no reason to question. Yet, consistently, I do. Even after eight years of marriage, I am perenially prepared for the worst. Repetitively, predictably, every few months I need verbal reassurance that no, he is not going to leave without warning. That yes, he can be trusted. That he is in this for the long haul, to raise our children with me, to grow old by my side. These conversations exhaust me, frankly, but if he ever tires of them, he doesn't let it show.

Every day, this man who shares my king-sized bed starts the day with an upbeat attitude, always says "Love you" before hanging up the phone, and curls his body around mine each night. He doesn't hold grudges. He insists upon open communication. Month after month, year after year, he does not leave. And no matter how much time passes, to me this always remains a new and remarkable idea.

Chapter Eight

When a Woman Needs a Woman

Gender Matters

SOMETIMES IT HAPPENS LIKE THIS: I have a 10:00 a.m. business meeting, and I'm trying to decide what to wear. On one side of my closet is a stack of jeans and a row of long-sleeved T-shirts; on the other is a line of monochromatic sweaters and dark wool suits. I start trying on skirts and sweaters, but in the mirror every combination appears straightforward and drab. I look like two crayons melted together, nothing sparkling, no pizzazz. Then I remember I have a basket filled with my mother's scarves and beads. I spread the items across my bed. But I'm not sure what to do with them; I can't remember what goes with what. Surrounded by the pieces, I don't know how to make them fit.

And sometimes it happens like this: I'm standing in the backyard of my daughter's preschool, watching the kids run on the play area carpeted with soft bark chips. The other moms and I are commiserating about what we call the "Montessori socks," the white socks stained dark brown by bark. "I have to buy her new socks every two months," I admit. The other mothers look at me a little strangely. "You can't get the brown out?" one of them asks. Another says, trying to be helpful, "I can get almost anything clean with the right combination of water and bleach." *Bleach,* I think. *Why didn't I think of bleach*? I don't have any bleach, but I could have bought some. I feel incredibly inept. And, immediately, I'm ashamed. The mothers move on to another part of the playground, and I have an impulse to rush after them. I'm not like you, I would explain. I don't know about these things. And though it feels like a pathetic excuse, and a dramatic response to such a small oversight, I want to tell them. You see, I never learned about this. My mother died when I was seventeen.

And, more often, it happens like this: It's our turn to host a dinner party, and everything goes wrong. The house is a mess, despite my best efforts to tidy it. Because I've haven't timed the food properly, I'm still rushing everything into the oven when the first guests arrive. Also, there's not much I can do to hide the embarrassing fact that I don't know how to cook. I've put off the party for months already, knowing this would happen, but we couldn't continue to accept invitations for much longer without reciprocating. So here we are, flinging open our doors for another set of acquaintances and colleagues to see me flounder through the night. At some point in the evening, one of the preteen guests wanders into the kitchen, where I'm sneaking a half a glass of wine and an extra slice of cake. She likes my skirt, she tells me, or maybe it's my earrings—the object doesn't really matter. She just wants to talk. So we do. I suspect that in my awkwardness she senses a kindred spirit, and she's looking to me for clues. About what might come later for her, perhaps. I see a question in her eyes, even a little admiration. *Me?* I think. *You're looking for answers from me?* I stare at the eleven-year-old staring at me, and I feel a brief surge of empathy and responsibility, but I also feel slightly absurd, like an imposter who didn't mean to fool the town. Because really, even after all these years, I'm still not sure I know what it means to be a woman, at all.

I don't mean to reduce my mother to a set of domestic cliches, to recall her only as a clothes hanger or a hostess or a detailed recipe. There was much more to her than this: time and maturity and certainly motherhood have made her appear more complex each year. But like most other women, I began learning at an early age that physical attractiveness and social niceties are the expected accoutrements of womanhood in a culture where a female's success is so often still gauged by her involvement with partner, children, and home. My mother devoted herself to these pursuits, proudly writing "homemaker" in the space designated for "occupation" on every *McCall's* survey she mailed in. This was one way she chose to define herself, and how I defined her, too, for most of my first seventeen years.

I was too young then, or maybe just too uninterested, to pay much attention to how she filled her day. My quest was to separate from her, not to connect. Now when I'm reminded that I lack the bits of knowledge other women seem to have absorbed in their mothers' homes, I feel somehow incomplete. Deficient. Wrong.

My female friends say this is nonsense. "You just have your own style," they insist. (Thank God "Hippie Chic" is fashionable, now, I say.) But I'm not really talking about the facade here. I'm talking about interior design. I once was willing to attribute the difference I've always felt to a prolonged adolescence, or to fifteen years of patchwork geography, or even to a subtle renegade streak. Theories, I had them all; answers, none—until I sat down in a room full of motherless women and found others who felt the same way.

Jane, thirty-eight, inspired an hour-long outpouring of agreement and relief among five motherless women in my living room one evening when she described how being motherless since the age of thirteen has made the word *woman* a loaded term for her. "There are so many little nuances and subtleties in life that have just passed me by," she explained. "Because a man raised me through adolescence, and because he was a farmer for most of my life, I feel like I should wear overalls and be in cow shit up to my knees. If a company made bras that looked like what a man would wear, that's what I'd want to buy. Sometimes I just don't feel feminine, or like a woman. That's one of my biggest struggles. Am I a woman? And if so, what is a woman?"

The French author Simone de Beauvoir asked the same question fifty years ago in her introduction to *The Second Sex,* and her answer filled the next seven hundred pages. There are no shortcuts here. A serious problem arises when a motherless daughter assesses what she feels she's missing and then quickly defines "woman" by what she lacks. My mother could cook fifteen or twenty different dinners; I'm lucky if I know the recipes for five. In my memory, she knew exactly how to shop for clothing; I can't even fathom what kind of lingerie to wear underneath a cocktail dress. I'm aware that cooking and clothing and personal hygiene hardly amount to a feminine totality, and that many women with mothers don't know the difference between a clog and a mule and don't particularly care, but when you've lost your primary model for womanhood it's easy to fall into this perceptive trap. Without the presence of a woman who can show us how to be feminine in a man's world, and who can serve as a point of reference for us to either accept or reject, we default into using gender stereotypes and cultural myths as definitions. "When I first got into therapy," says Denise, thirty-five, who lost her mother at age twelve, "I realized I not only didn't know how to be a woman, because I associated all those bullshit things like knowing how to make a cake and put on a garter belt with being a woman, but that I had started to believe those *were* the things that defined you as a woman."

Like the child who mistakenly equates *to do* with *to be*, motherless daughters frequently confuse feminine behavior with feminine identity. Though one may reflect the other, they're not the same thing. Behavior is derived from conscious observation and mimicry. Identity develops through an internalized alignment with a female model. When a daughter watches her mother step out of the shower and wrap her hair in a towel, that daughter may copy the same behavior one day. But she also begins to create an image and an expectation for how her own body will mature. Likewise, a daughter learns the rudiments of infant feeding when she watches her mother nurse a younger sibling. And she also recognizes that she, too, will have the ability to nurture and sustain a life one day.

A girl who loses her mother or mother-figure has little readily available, concrete evidence of the adult feminine to draw from. She has neither a direct guide for sex-typed behavior nor an immediate connection to her own gender. Left to piece together her own feminine identity, she looks to other females for signs that she's developing along an appropriate gendered path, measuring her own adequacy by a quick and superficial comparison and contrast: Have I brought the right kind of present to the party? Does my haircut match those of the girls in my teen magazine?

All girls do this to some degree, but the daughter without a mother already carries a sense of deep inferiority and shame for having lost the figure she sees as so central to her well-being. Her need to conform extends beyond the need for acceptance by her peer group. She's looking for clues that will tell her how to be a girl and trying to create a feminine identity through observation and mimicry after her natural window to adult female experience has been closed.

"The development of femininity is complicated," Nan Birnbaum explains. "Girls usually have some identifications already built in from their early experience with their mothers—it's not like there's nothing there. But those identifications don't have a chance to mature. Sometimes an adolescent will depend on her childhood memories for guidance. What would Mom say about this? What would she advise? But memory isn't as good as the real thing, and it's not as alive as a current relationship with any other female."

One of the most poignant stories I've heard over the years comes from forty-three-year-old Mary Jo, who was eight when she lost her mother. Although she had an older sister who took over her physical care as she entered adolescence, Mary Jo longed for the guidance of a mature, experienced woman who would teach her, in her own words, "how to be."

> My father would occasionally try to guide me, but I didn't want *him* to do it. I would brush him off, saying, "I know. You don't have to tell me." But I was so desperate to feel like a regular human being. I would go down to the library in our little town and take out the *Seventeen* magazine book of etiquette and entertaining. It had little vignettes about how you were supposed to act in certain situations. I would think, "Oh, is *this* how people are supposed to be?" because I wasn't getting any role modeling anywhere. I'd literally steal those books from the library, take them home, and practically memorize them until I sort of understood, and then sneak them back. I didn't want anybody to see me taking them out, because I didn't want anyone to know I was struggling with those things. I thought if people knew they'd sort of pounce on me, feeling sorry for me. I wanted information, not pity.

Even as a child, Mary Jo equated being human with being female, aware of her gender identity but unable to feel connected to it.

She recognized that her father lacked the knowledge and her sister the adult experience she craved. Mary Jo believed that if only she could master the prescribed behaviors, she could overcome her feelings of deficiency. As she paged through books trying to learn the rules of social etiquette, she was really trying to connect with what Naomi Lowinsky calls the "deep feminine"—that subtle, often unconscious source of feminine authority and power we mistakenly believe is expressed in scarf knots and thank-you notes but instead originates from a more abstract, gendered core.

All daughters—and motherless ones are no exception—expect mothers to pass down the generational knowledge that transforms a girl into a woman. "When I was a kid, I used to wonder if your mother comes into your room at night when you're asleep and whispers something in your ear," says thirty-seven-year-old Jocelyn, whose mentally ill mother was institutionalized for most of her childhood. "Something that you don't remember consciously, but that still goes in, and that if because I didn't have a mom around, I never heard what I needed to know."

Jocelyn's metaphor aptly illustrates the silent, fluid exchange that links most mothers and daughters in an intimate duet. Adrienne Rich has described its content as "beyond the verbally transmitted lore of female survival—a knowledge that is subliminal, subversive, preverbal: the knowledge flowing between two alike bodies, one of which has spent nine months inside the other." And as Mary Jo learned, its essence can't be gleaned from a book.

As discussed in an earlier chapter, certain aspects of a girl's femininity and aptitude for relating to men are linked to the quality of her relationship with her father, but that's not the kind of femininity motherless women necessarily feel they lack. The sociologist Miriam Johnson, in a review of the research on fathers and femininity in daughters, divides a girl's femininity into "heterosexual" and "maternal" components, which makes the distinction clear. Fathers, she says, influence the heterosexual element of a daughter's femininity, which involves romantic intimacy; sexual object choice; and, insofar as marriages are perceived as male dominated, expectations of male authority. Mothers provide the maternal aspect, which relates to gender identity, the procreative capacity, the mother-daughter bond, and expectations of maternal authority in the mother-child relationship. A motherless daughter may feel perfectly comfortable in the company of men, and many do. But how much does that teach her about being female?

When the maternal element is missing from her feminine development, the daughter grows up without an internalized, gendered sense of power and authority—not only as the political and social entity the term *woman* represents, but also as a female self. The power of the feminine, already diminished in a society run predominantly by men, is even harder for a motherless woman to claim. She has difficulty understanding, appreciating, and accepting herself as a gendered being when she has no constant model for adult femininity, or when the model she has convinces her that being female is wrong. So if gender, as she's learned, is strictly either/or, where does she belong? Says Denise, "I've always felt like a creature in between a man and a woman. Like a mutant, neutered thing." In a culture fueled by binary opposition, where *woman* is inevitably defined as "not man," a motherless daughter searching for language to describe herself then wonders in frustration, *What am I?*

"I'm a survivor," many motherless women claim. What they're saying is that early adversity gave them a toughness, a resilience, a power of will that came from facing a profound loss and nevertheless finding the desire and the hope to press on. They're saying, in effect, that they've acquired the kind of personal strength and indomitability our culture normally ascribes to men.

This isn't necessarily detrimental—autonomy of spirit, after all, is what's kept the motherless Nancy Drew in business for the past seventy-six years. One out of three motherless women who could identify a positive effect of their early losses named "independence" and "self-reliance," often citing these as their passports to professional success. You don't have to lose a mother to become an independent woman, but there's often a strong relationship between the two. When a motherless daughter finds herself left with caretakers who are initially overcome by grief or who are unable to meet the demands of child rearing, she needs to develop assertion and self-sufficiency to survive childhood and adolescence as a female alone. She has to learn how to fend for herself. "When you lose a mother, there's no longer a fantasy of being able to go home to Mommy," Dr. Lowinsky explains. "You get thrown head first into the water, and you have to learn how to swim."

There can, however, be grave personal repercussions for the child thrust into self-reliance too young, which often produces adult frustration and anger in women who had to take on too much, far too soon. The girl who at sixteen or twelve or ten has to assume almost total responsibility and care for herself, her father, and even her younger siblings often develops a rigidity of pursuit and a false sense of personal power. Her vehement independence and self-assertion can become self-protective and exclusionary, setting her apart from her peers and frequently alienating her from other women. Because she was abandoned by the one woman she expected she could rely on, she may approach female friendships with a certain caution as an adult. Says twenty-eight-year-old Leslie, "When I think of friendships with women, the first thought that comes to mind is being wary. I have close women friends, but few. There always have been just a handful. I think I distrust women, somehow. I really experienced my mother's death as a betrayal, as if she had done it to me somehow and could have avoided it. And there was so much silence and deception involved. I think I'm more afraid of women. There's something very powerful about them." When four or five motherless women sit together in a room, however, the camaraderie is nearly instantaneous. *Finally,* they say. *Others who understand.* Like veterans of the same war, the unmothered are drawn to each other. They can detect the subtlest inflection in each other's behaviors, the tiniest insinuation in a gaze, the inaudible frequency of spirit that reveals: You are one of me. As a woman at a Motherless Daughters Support Group once said, "It's like a secret handshake that we share."

To other women, especially those who perceive self-reliance as threatening, the motherless woman is often seen as "too aggressive." She is "intimidating." She is—and I've actually heard this from female colleagues—"too much like a man."

A month after I started my first job, a co-worker took me out for drinks and confided that she'd found me unapproachable and intimidating at first because I "looked like I had it all together." "You come across as so confident," she said. This was the first time I'd heard such an assessment of my personality, and though I, too, would list "independence" and "self-reliance" as positive outcomes of my early loss, I remember staring into my glass of beer that evening and thinking, "Is this woman serious? If this were a glass of water, I'd doubt my own reflection."

So there I was: I looked like a woman, I acted like a man, and underneath it all I still felt like an adolescent, constantly looking for assurance that I was competent enough, attractive enough, good enough as I was.

A motherless woman is a walking paradox. At the same time that she emits qualities of personal strength, the loss of a mother frequently has damaged her self-esteem, eroded her self-confidence, and evaporated her secure base. *This* is the fundamental insecurity that makes her scan a room of women and conclude she doesn't fit in. Other women have mothers, she thinks, but I have only myself. Never mind that she has a father or siblings or close friends or a spouse. In a crowd of other women, as a female, she feels alone. Fierce independence and self-sufficiency are her shield, thrust forward as her public display of competence-despite-loss and drawn close as her private protection against the crushing loneliness she'd otherwise feel.

To depend too much on someone else, she believes, would mean to risk the pain of further loss. "No thanks. I can handle it myself," she'll say, when what she's really feeling is, "I *want* your help, but I'm afraid if I depend on you, you'll leave." When the person she relied on most has left her, the only companion she can unquestionably count on is herself. For the motherless daughter, depending on independence isn't nearly as contradictory as it sounds.

Laundry bleach and four-course meals and how to wear a string of beads—it's not that I don't know any of these things or couldn't learn about them if I tried. I have my daughters write thank-you notes for every gift they receive, and I'm always after my husband to store leftovers in Tupperware instead of sticking the used pot on a refrigerator shelf. But I resist seeking out domestic information for myself. For me to pursue such bits of knowledge actively would mean accepting at the deep, emotional level that my mother isn't coming back. And how do I know this for sure? In my dreams she returns still, her death a horrible, confusing mistake; but she's mute and distant, a shadow presence, ignorant of all that's happened in the years since she left. In this realm of subconscious double-think, where my mother is dead but not-really-dead, I am still the daughter waiting for her mother to be the guide. I can't replace her. Not even with myself.

Perhaps this is my way of honoring her, by insisting that my small domestic quandaries can be solved by her alone. Maybe that's why I was always unsuccessful at finding a singular mother substitute. Although I've longed for the presence of a more mature, experienced woman in my life, when I meet one, I'm never sure how much is appropriate to ask for, or exactly what I hope she could give. The mother of a former boyfriend once complained that I didn't respect her, and I ask myself now if that was true. I know I intended no disrespect, but my emotional distance and insistent self-reliance must have been interpreted as such. I had absolutely no idea how to . . . well, how to *be* in the presence of an older woman. It's been so long since I've known one well. How much insight does sixty years give you? What kind of authority is reasonable for either of us to command? To treat an older woman as my equal seems to devalue her experience and insight; to step into submission is to ignore mine. Unless the other woman acts first, establishing our relative positions from the start, I'm uncertain, awkward, and self-conscious, fearful of her judgment. I insist that my children behave perfectly in her presence. I never know what to do with my hands.

To allow a woman to mother me—really and truly care for me—is a proposition I've always found simultaneously appealing and terrifying. As much as I've want to feel the soft, strong pressure of a woman's arms around me when I'm sick or lonely or scared, I'm afraid an ongoing presence would feel like to much of an intrusion to me now. Still, I wonder if all the years spent alone, hoping a mother substitute would magically appear on her own, have made me too self-reliant and self-protective to ever accept one. I wonder if for me it's just too late.

Jocelyn, who spent twenty-one years searching for a woman to emulate, says that for her it was not. She was five when her mother was institutionalized, the first of a series of hospitalizations that persisted for the next twelve years. When Jocelyn's mother was home, she drank so heavily that she added even further conflict to the family. Without a stable mother figure to observe and identify with during her childhood, Jocelyn says she never felt secure or worthwhile as a female. Then, in her midtwenties, she met a woman at her church:

> Kaye was thirteen years older than me, divorced with two kids, and we became close friends. I think she was looking for someone to give her life some meaning, and I was looking for a mom, is what it came down to. I don't think she understood at the time how much she meant to me. It was just a friendship—I am heterosexual and so is she—but it was like I would study her continuously. I remember even following her into the bathroom and watching her put on her makeup. She'd get really nervous and say, "Would you get out of here? Why are you watching me?" At the time I didn't understand why I had this need to watch her, but now I realize it's like the little girl who was watching Mom. I never got to do that. After I'd known Kaye for a few years, I felt as if I'd been in a room with building blocks scattered all over the floor, and when she walked in someone said to me for the first time, "Okay, put the blue block on top of the yellow block, and then put the red block next to it." Friends would say to me, "What's happening to you? You're so different." I had such a hunger that was finally being met. Kaye and I have been friends for about ten years, and even though I live in a different city now, I really feel like it's a solid friendship. If I need a woman's advice, I know I can go to her.

I am heterosexual and so is she, Jocelyn said, inserting this statement quickly, for added clarification. After all, what other explanation besides lesbianism do we have for a woman who so deeply craves the companionship of another female the way motherless daughters do? Many women I've interviewed released sighs of relief when I mentioned this topic, admitting that the gender confusion they often feel has led them to question their sexuality. If I sometimes feel more like a man than a woman, they wonder, and if I'm looking for a woman who can enter my life, does that mean I'm gay?

"I was always very comfortable around men and boys," explains thirty-six-year-old Jane, "but I went through a stage where I thought I might be a lesbian, because I just craved that female touch. I would react like, 'Oh my God, a woman touched me' every time I got a hug. Sometimes I wished I could just rent a mommy and have her snuggle me on a couch. I get around some women who are motherly, and I'm completely mesmerized. It's like an out-of-body experience. I just want to age-regress and be snuggled, and never come out of this fantasy."

Jane's fantasies about women had more to do with the emotional and physical comfort she associated with an older, female protector than they did with her sexual preference. Amanda, thirty-two, says she came to the same realization during college, when she started dating a woman to see if her emotional impulses were somehow linked to sexual desires. She discovered that she preferred the social and emotional company of women, but that her sexual interest was still limited to men. Today, she splits her companionship needs between her husband and a close group of female friends. "I really treasure my girlfriends," she says. "I just have more fun with a girl. I remember pursuing guys as friends, and boy was that a go-nowhere thing. I've recently gotten involved with a group of women who make jewelry out of clay. I relate better to the older women, and I've made some good friends in the group who are older than me." From these friends, Amanda draws the feminine energy and emotional support she says she rarely can get from men. When she needs one mature, experienced woman she can depend on, she goes to the grandmother who helped raise her and who still represents her home base.

A mother surrogate unquestionably can help steer a girl through childhood, adolescence, and early adulthood. The most important factor that helps children who grow up under adverse family or social conditions to become emotionally adjusted, competent adults is the active involvement of at least one stable adult who cares. A feminine mentor who's emotionally invested in a motherless girl's well-being can help her develop self-esteem and confidence as both a female and as an individual. "What that child gets from that mentor is a sense that she matters," Phyllis Klaus explains. "That she's important. That she counts in the world. From that, she builds her sense of self. She hears that she's competent, and she can build competency. That then helps her feel independent and good about herself, instead of her ending up anxious, dependent, and depressed." Healthy development depends on a girl's firm belief that she's worthwhile, lovable, and acceptable as she is, and she needs that same security to develop a comfortable gender identity. "A child's natural tendency is to identify with her same-sex parent, and to have that hidden but available gendered sense of self gives her a lot of security in development," Klaus says. "So I look for what ways a motherless daughter has been able to find that in her life. Very often, there's an aunt or a friend's mother who's had some impact on a girl's sense of being a girl."

Where do daughters find female support and comfort after their mothers die? Of the ninety-seven women who said they found one or more mother substitutes, 33 percent named an aunt; 30 percent, a grandmother; 13 percent, a sister; 13 percent, a teacher; 12 percent, friends; 10 percent, a co-worker; and the rest cited, in descending order, neighbors, friends' mothers, mothers-in-law, stepmothers, husbands, lovers, and cousins.[1] The largest group—37 percent—said they hadn't found anyone and had learned to rely on their own resources instead. Some created a collage of guidance, pasting together bits of influence drawn from religion, books, television, film, and the memory of a mother that fades more with each passing year.

The logical first place for a daughter to seek a mother substitute is within her extended family. The psychologist Walter Toman says the best replacement for a loved one is someone who's as similar to the lost person as possible, which probably explains why maternal aunts and grandmothers are among the most oft-cited mother substitutes.

Such "most similar" persons, however, are as a rule hard to find. If such a person who is similar in every respect or practically identical with the person who was lost, say a parent, could be

---

[1] Some women named more than one mother substitute.

recruited. . . then the substitute person could be psychologically acceptable to the bereaved soon after the loss has occurred, perhaps even immediately after it. In most instances, however, the loss of a person requires an extensive period of mourning and waiting. This period is usually more extensive the longer one has lived with the lost person, and the less the person coming up as an eventual substitute resembles the person who has been lost.

For these reasons—as well as those outlined in chapter 6—a stepmother is rarely an immediate or readily accepted replacement figure. Her arrival in the family may occur before the daughter has had time to begin mourning and separating from her lost mother or while the daughter is in a developmental phase that involves either a strong attachment to her father or a rejection of all parental figures. In more than half of the eighty-three stepfamilies included in the Motherless Daughters survey, a stepmother arrived within two years. The daughter's feelings of anger and betrayal often prevented her from accepting her stepmother as a viable, feminine model.

When a daughter grows up perceiving an adult woman as a threat, she may unconsciously carry the competitiveness she once felt or still feels toward her stepmother into her adult relationships with other women. A female co-worker, for example, who gets the job a daughter wanted may stir up the old feelings of replacement and rejection she experienced each time she believed her father chose her stepmother over her. The adult daughter then directs her anger toward her co-worker, when it's really the stepmother she's been competing with all along.

But even this anger toward the stepmother usually comes from an even deeper source: the death of the mother. When a daughter displaces her unreconciled anger toward the mother who abandoned her onto her father's new wife, she projects all the Bad Mother images onto her stepmother—thus, the Evil Stepmother archetype—and reserves all the Good Mother images for her lost mother. As Rose-Emily Rothenberg explains in her article "The Orphan Archetype":

Because the actual mother is absent, the orphan frequently has the fantasy that the true mother must have been the perfect, ideal, all-giving mother. This leaves the living "mother" to carry its opposite, the dark and demonic side. Since the stepmother is not the "real thing," nor the stepchild her "real child," both she and the child are left to endure the "second-best" psychology in this dual mother-child constellation.

A daughter's angry and resentful charge of "You're not my *real* mother!" often provokes a stepmother's silent, yet just as resentful, response, "Well, you're not my real child, either." How many motherless women tell stories that support the Evil Stepmother archetype? Far more than those who refute it, reflecting the difficulties that develop between stepmother and stepdaughters when the birth mother is lost through death or desertion. Idealization of the lost mother, unrealistic expectations for the stepmother, and the arrival of step- or half-siblings can all create disharmony between a motherless daughter and the new woman of the house.

Amanda spent twelve years with a stepmother she once hoped would become her surrogate mom. She was three when her father gained custody of her in a divorce settlement that prevented her mother from seeing her again, and for the next four years, Amanda lived with her father and grandmother and prayed each night for a new mother. She eventually got her wish, but this new mother wasn't quite what she'd hoped for.

I wanted a mom so bad. When my dad said he was going to marry Ellen, I was really happy. I thought she was the most beautiful woman in the world. This was the mid-60s, and she was part of the Gidget scene, and a former beauty queen. Her clothes were perfect. Everything was perfect. But I would learn, even within that first year, that this was a weird person. I called her the Ice Maiden. Within ten months she had a baby, my half-sister, and she went into a depression from the time Callie was one until I left the house when I was eighteen. I more or less became Callie's mother, because my stepmother was just on the couch with the remote or shopping or getting her nails done or reading Harlequin novels. Over the course of the years, I felt totally abandoned by anybody real. And I was so disappointed.

Nobody acknowledged it, or ever asked how I was feeling. I grew up feeling like . . . just so self-absorbed and really sad and sorry for myself.

It's true that the Evil Stepmother stories I've heard are one-sided, but if even their most basic facts are accurate, many motherless women were raised by stepmothers who were, if not downright abusive, then at least coolly detached, ranging from those who gave preferential treatment to their biological children and turned stepdaughters into domestic servants to those who restricted a daughter's contact with her father and appropriated the lost mother's possessions after his death. Jealous of a stepdaughter's closeness with her father, unwilling to accept a child of the "other woman" in her new family, or simply inexperienced at mothering, stepmothers may falter, give up, or turn on a motherless child. Entering a family where the previous mother has died puts a stepmother in the hot seat. A sanctified lost mother can pique her insecurities even more than a divorced mother's presence will: a live woman, she can compete with; a saint, she knows she can't be. Her frustration and anger may get displaced onto the stepdaughter, who represents the closest approximation of the dead mother in the home.

Among older children with limited dependence on the nuclear family, a difficult stepmother may be more an annoyance than a daily trauma, but for children who still live in the home, the consequences of poor replacement mothering can be longlasting and profound. The British psychiatrist John Birtchnell, in a study of 160 female psychiatric patients who lost their mothers before age eleven, found that 82 percent of those who had poor relationships with their mother replacements suffered from depression later in life. It seems that inadequate mothering *after* a mother dies or leaves, rather than the mother's absence per se, is an important link between mother loss and a daughter's later depression.

More than a dozen women have told me that they believe their lack of confidence, their low self-esteem, and their pervasive loneliness come not from losing their mothers but from growing up with a critical and demanding stepmother they felt they could never please. When explaining the hurt she still feels when thinking of her childhood, a thirty-four-year-old woman explains, "Some of my worries and needs are because of my loss of a bond that a child is not meant to lose, but some of them are because of the sickness that followed in the form of a twisted 'stepmonster.' I'm not sure I'll ever be able to separate the pain of losing one from the pain of acquiring the other."

Yet all stepmother-stepdaughter relationships are not doomed to failure. Caroline, for example, says she deeply misses her stepmother, who died three years ago. This woman, whom Caroline refers to as her "second mother," joined the family six months after Caroline's birth mother died, when Caroline was eleven. "Mother Jean was thrilled to take over our family. She took on one teenager and three budding teenagers, and then a few years later had her own child, my half-sister," says Caroline. "My second mother appreciated us, and left us alone to be ourselves. She didn't mess with our selfhood, but we knew she was there for us when we needed her. We all loved her dearly and feel very fortunate to have had her. Losing her was no easier, maybe even harder, than losing my first mom."

Caroline, who's now fifty-three, had good replacement mothering as an adolescent and adult. Nevertheless, she has still longed for her birth mother's support and encouragement as she has reached the feminine milestones of menstruation, childbirth, and menopause. Caroline, like other motherless daughters, found that even when a stepmother provides the essential triad of physical care, nurturing, and consistent emotional support, a daughter invariably still feels that one, final missed connection. "There's a sense the birth mother holds secrets, that she's the source of certain knowledge that no one else has access to," Evelyn Bassoff explains. "Even if the motherless daughter gets all the information about menstruation, birth control, and childbirth, I'd imagine she'd still feels something missing, something her mother could have given her that other people can't. It's that sense of continuity from mother to daughter." Finding a woman isn't always enough when it's *the* woman you feel you need.

What is it we're looking for? What can't another woman provide? Time and again in my interviews, I've heard motherless women describe what they miss most. Their mothers' cooking, they say; when they bake a lemon-meringue pie, it just doesn't taste the same. Or their mothers' companionship when shopping. They say they can't bear to buy clothing alone.

Food, clothing, and the security that comes from the certainty of having both: these are basic survival needs, which a mother typically fills for a young child and gradually relinquishes full responsibility for as that child grows. Take food, for example. Over the years, the breast or bottle is replaced with spoonfuls of baby food, then with home-cooked dinners, heated leftovers, and money for school lunches with adolescent friends. At the most basic level, someone is paying attention to whether or not the daughter is eating three meals a day. When a daughter says she misses her mother's cooking, she's not just saying she longs for a slice of her pie. She's saying she misses nurturing. Sustenance. Consistent and meticulous care.

These deep losses often surge to the forefront during a motherless adolescence, as a daughter begins experiencing dramatic physical and emotional changes. Even though an adolescent daughter may reject her mother as a caretaker and insist that she can manage alone, the mother still represents feminine wisdom and a female haven for her daughter's bodily concerns. As a daughter experiences such female rites of passage as menstruation and loss of virginity and later, pregnancy, childbirth, and menopause, she's aware that her mother has experienced them first. She needs the support of someone who understands the intricacies of the female body when she feels alone inside of hers.

Roberta, thirty-two, says her mother's death seventeen years ago left her without a sounding board for her female concerns. She'd previously gone to her mother with questions about masturbation and menstruation, but when she needed advice about physical development at sixteen, she felt she had nowhere to turn. Horrified by the thought of approaching her father and emotionally distanced from her older sister, she sat alone with fears that quickly turned into full-blown anxieties. "I was obsessed with being flat-chested, and I couldn't physically use a tampon," she says. "I was really scared I wasn't feminine. I thought, 'I don't have any breasts, and I don't have a big enough vagina to use a tampon. Where am I a woman?' It's not a superficial thing like cooking that makes you a woman, but ultimately your body that makes you one gender or the other. And I was horrified by what was going on with mine. Without my mother there, these seemed like insurmountable issues. I spent at least five years freaking out."

As Roberta sensed, a father is rarely a refuge for stress during a daughter's adolescence—especially with her sudden realization that he's a sexual being. Although fathers do pass on sexual attitudes and values to their daughters through commentary and example, they aren't the preferred source for female information. A Widener University study of twenty-four intact families with adolescent girls revealed that half of the girls had gone to their mothers for sex information and none had gone to their fathers. In this study, conducted among upper- and upper-middle-class families, father-daughter discussions about sex and sexuality were most often impersonal and noninformational in nature, if they occurred at all.

Without a mother in the home, a daughter's first menstruation often represents little more than an anticlimactic and disappointing day. Naomi Lowinsky refers to menstruation—along with birthing and nursing—as one of the feminine mysteries, the deep, essentially female experiences that bind mother and daughter. For two thousand years, until A.D. 396, the Greeks celebrated this mother-daughter connection in an annual sacred religious ceremony at Eleusis. The Eleusinian Mysteries, as they were called, were based on the myth of the goddess Demeter and her daughter Persephone, who are separated when Pluto, the god of death, takes Persephone to the underworld as his bride. A grieving Demeter mourns inconsolably and halts the growth of grain on earth in revenge, until Pluto agrees to return Persephone to her mother for nine months of every year. The Mysteries, a rite so venerated that all participants had to undergo an elaborate purification process beforehand, commemorated Persephone's return to her mother as a reunion of two lost selves, as well as celebrating the natural cycle of birth, death, and rebirth. "In our culture today, it's hard enough for a woman to feel a connection to the mysteries," Dr. Lowinsky says. "Without a mother, a first menstruation is just a big sanitary event, or it's ignored. At least if the mother is there, she represents some sort of feminine energy to lean back on, to help a girl feel the largeness of it and to be moved by it, to be able to celebrate it in a female way.

"Most mothers and daughters share a secret kind of understanding about these things," she continues. "It may not be verbalized very much, but it's just that they share the knowledge of what it is to be a woman. We know we bleed monthly, and that we have other shared experiences that just aren't spoken about in a man's world. And we have our little secret ways about doing things, even if it's cooking dinner or getting dressed. If there's no one to share this with, a girl carries the whole weight of the unacknowledged and unknown mysteries, which can feel scary if she doesn't have anyone to guide her. A lot of that guidance in our culture is shared and unconscious, but still, at some level, the mother is thinking about the fact she has a daughter who's menstruating and can have children. Somebody's paying attention to the significance of the event, even if it's not verbalized. If nobody's paying attention to it, the girl falls into emotional neglect."

My first period with my mother was no grand fête—when I told her, she slapped me across the face and then hugged me, just as her mother had once done to her, an Eastern European tradition that, she later explained, signified driving away the child and welcoming the arrival of the woman—but I'm grateful she was there. Even if she wasn't bleeding on that day, menstruation was a female rite we both now shared, and the slap and the hug tied me to the generations of women in her family who'd bled before.

Helen, forty-nine, remembers her first menstruation as an attempt to reach out and connect with another woman. She was ten, with an older brother but no sisters, when her mother died. Three years later she was home alone when her period began. "I felt scared and excited, but so lonely," she recalls. I went outside and saw a neighbor walking up the street. I felt a strong need to stop her and tell her what was happening to me, even though I really didn't know her well, and this was too intimate a revelation for the level of our relationship. But at least I got to tell another woman about this milestone in my life. I felt a bittersweet mixture of loneliness, failure, and triumph."

Her own mother, Helen imagines, would have turned the event into cause for mutual celebration. In much the same way, I imagine my mother would have alleviated all my marriage and childbearing concerns. Of course we idealize. Of course. And we romanticize, too. It's more comforting to focus on scant memories of a mother explaining reproduction or tampon use and dream of her lost potential than to doubt that she could have provided the support we feel we need. Giving mothers this kind of posthumous power allows us to remain their daughters. It gives us, in some small way, the kind of mother-daughter relationship we long for.

We soothe ourselves with these "would have's," when, in fact, many living mothers offer their daughters only minimal feminine support. An adult woman dissatisfied with her own gender identity can damage her daughter's, encouraging feelings of inferiority, forcing the daughter into the same subordinate status she feels helpless to escape. Menstruation is hardly a festive event for the mother who equates a daughter's fresh red blood with the aging of her own, and a daughter's wedding is hardly a celebration for the mother who feels abandoned and bitter because her own marriage has failed.

But my mother? Oh, no. My mother would have grown in parallel fashion to me, never feeling envy, never feeling rage. She would have been the essential source for all things feminine, a font of information and support about marriage, childbirth, and aging. She would have stepped in to reaffirm my gender identity at every critical point. In my imagination, she is everything I needed and still need. And when I insist on thinking like this, it's so easy to blame her absence for making me feel deficient at the level of behavior, and at the level of feminine identity, cheated and deprived.

Explains twenty-five-year-old Ronnie, whose mother died eight years ago, "I really feel like I'm crippled without a mother. Like I can never be quite as good as a woman who has one. Like I can never know the things that she knows, or feel confident about myself." And although I understand these feelings because I have them, too, I look at Ronnie—a beautiful, successful woman who seems so confident, so in control—and think that if I saw her on the street or across a room, she'd be one of those women I'd admire, one I'd be certain holds the very knowledge I so often feel I lack.

We are so good at concealing our blind spots. And at compensating as best we can. Conventional femininity cannot be our guide. We are reinventing the feminine. And most of us have barely begun to appreciate the value, or the enormity, of this task.

III

Growth

They remember what she gave. What she made. What she did. *What we were to each other.* What she taught me. What I learned at her breast. That she made things. That she made words. That she fed me. Suckled me. Clothed me. Cradled me. Washed me. *We remember her labor.* She told us how she almost died. How she was weary. How her skin ached. What soreness she felt. What her mother's name was. How her mother made things. What her mother told her. How she was pushed away. How she was hated. How her milk was sour. What she wore at her wedding. Where she had dreamed of going. *What our first words were.* How she had quarreled with her sister. How they fought over a doll. How the other was prettier. How she pushed me away. How she hated me. How her milk was sour. *How we hated her. Her body. We remember our fear of becoming her. What we were to each other. What we learned.*

—Susan Griffin, *Woman and Nature*

Chapter Nine

Who She Was, Who I Am
Developing an Independent Identity

I TOOK A TRIP to southern Florida about ten years ago to visit my mother's best friend. There were some things I needed to know. Minor facts, mostly, and episodic detail, such as what my mother talked about at dinner parties and what made her laugh when her children were out of the room. But I had some larger questions, too, such as why she had chosen my father, and why the women's movement seemed to have passed her by. Behind the mother had been a woman, and she was someone I never knew. Sandy had been there, throughout those years. I was hoping she could give me some clues.

We sat at her round breakfast table in Boca Raton one September afternoon, my tape recorder equidistant between us. The kitchen: an appropriate site for a talk with my mother's childhood friend. Like my mother and her mother and her grandmother from Poland, I grew up in homes where the kitchen doubled as a social center, where daughters leaned against counters while mothers reproduced the recipes of their mothers, and where neighborhood women gathered for languorous gossip sessions while dinner slowly matured on the stove. I learned the family legends in my grandmother's kitchen with its blue vinyl wraparound booth and bulbous white stove, and in my mother's 1970s counterpart, with its avocado appliances and yellow wallpaper flowers the size of my hand, rooms where ancestral history hung suspended above the tables like after-dinner cigarette smoke. The smell of potato pancakes sputtering in golden oil or beef stew simmering in elbow-deep steel pots still signals the beginning of a story to me.

I live in a nine-room house now, with plenty of space to entertain. There's a living room, a TV room, and an outdoor deck that offers a panoramic ocean view. Still, every time we throw a party, everyone swaps stories around the dining room table until late into the night. Story is the elixir of the roundtable, not the sofa or the chair. Maybe this is why in Sandy's kitchen anecdotes about my mother spilled forth onto the vinyl placemats and why I, like a starving person, devoured every small detail.

Most of us know the facts about our mothers' deaths. But how much do we know about their lives? Of the 154 motherless women surveyed, 30 percent said, "a great deal"; 44 percent, "some"; and 26 percent, "very little."[1]

Grandmothers, aunts, sisters, fathers, and friends act as the conduits who convey information about the lost mother to the daughter as she ages. The mother herself, however, was usually a daughter's most valuable source. Daughters who spent the most time with their mothers are thus the ones who feel they know the most about them. More than half of the women who were twenty or older when their mothers died said they knew a lot about their lives, compared to only 2 percent of those who were younger than twelve at the time. Likewise, only 13 percent of the daughters left motherless at twenty or older said they knew very little about their mothers, while 53 percent of those who were twelve or younger said the same. Daughters who were adolescents fit right in between, with half of those who'd been ages twelve to nineteen reporting they had some information about their mothers' lives. This may be because younger daughters ask fewer questions about their mothers' pasts, or because mothers tend to share their stories slowly, meting them out as they deem appropriate for a daughter's current developmental stage.

When a mother dies, she takes her stories with her, leaving a daughter to reconstruct them in whatever way she can. Rita, forty-three, who was fifteen when her mother died, did her fact-finding through the mail. Frustrated by how little she knew about her

---

[1]Not one woman chose the answer "nothing." It seems that even a daughter who spent very little time with her mother manages to collect some information about her or identify with her experiences, and feels she knows something about her life.

mother, Rita created a thirty-six-page booklet titled "Questions I've Been Meaning to Ask" and sent copies to her parents' surviving relatives and friends. She typed the 108 inquiries in one sitting, a flood of pent-up questions rushing onto her computer screen: "How did Louise feel about herself physically?" "Why did she divorce her first husband?" "What was her pregnancy and labor with Rita like?" In an introductory note she wrote, "Please don't hesitate to tell the truth as you saw it. The whole purpose of this questionnaire is to gather facts and memories before they are forgotten. I appreciate your help."

"I almost felt like an orphan trying to find out about the mother who gave her up," Rita recalls. She mailed about a dozen questionnaires and waited for replies that she hoped would tell her about her mother's childhood, first marriage, and involvement in the Communist Party in the 1950s, but she was disappointed by the feedback. Although a few of her respondents were forthcoming with their memories, most either didn't remember or wouldn't share the kind of detail she craved. "With some of the questions, I already had bits and pieces of an answer," Rita says, "but it was important to me that I got it all. A lot of people wrote back asking, 'Why do you need to know this? Why do you want to know this?' They thought I was obsessed with the past, and that I had a problem. Including my brother. He had a hard time with me and my questions. I think he understands my need more now, because he and his wife just adopted a little boy and they're helping him develop a family history book, but that's definitely where he was at then."

Rita's critics raised a worthwhile question: Why would a daughter want to exhume her mother's past? Why do Rita, and I, and virtually every other motherless woman I've ever met have the urgent need to scour history like scavengers on a beach, waving our questionnaires and tape recorders like metal detectors, hoping to uncover valuable nuggets buried beneath the sand?

"Part of it is that I'm curious by nature," Rita says. "I like to know details about people. But I also feel like I missed out on getting to know my mother as a peer—an equal, as a human being, not just as my mother. And I wanted to know who she was. I felt like I had a vague notion of who she was, but the more I learned about who *I* was, the more I wanted to collect her stories and understand what kind of person she had been."

Storytelling serves a vital function in a daughter's development: It's one way that she makes sense of her past and develops a static identity for the future. For the motherless child, an attempt to fit individual life experiences together to form a meaningful whole often elicits the reminder of a missing piece. "These kids feel something is missing, and history is a part of it," Benjamin Garber explains. "It's not all that's missing, but at least if they can cognitively compose some kind of story for themselves, they have a sense of continuity and feel more complete."

To do this, a daughter needs to collect not only the details of her mother's life but also the facts about her own. The personal mythology a woman creates to define herself depends on her early memories and on the stories she's told, and mothers typically are the chroniclers of a family's narrative history. When she dies or leaves, many of the details are lost. My father awaited each of my "firsts" as anxiously as my mother, but she was the one who made the entries in my baby book, shared the news with friends, and later passed the details on to me. As the oldest child, I'm the only member of the family who remembers hearing my brother's and sister's first words, but no one can recall mine. I have no way of knowing how much of what I remember from my earliest childhood is real, how much is misperceived, how much could have been a dream. How can I be sure of my past if I have no living history, no one who remembers my first word, my first smile, my first step?

Without knowledge of her own experiences, and their relationship to her mothers', a daughter is snipped from the female cord that connects the generations of women in her family, the feminine line of descent that Naomi Lowinsky calls the "Motherline." A woman achieves her psychic connection to generations of feminine wisdom through hearing her mother's and grandmothers' narratives about women's physical, psychological, and historical changes—bleeding, birthing, suckling, aging, and dying, Dr. Lowinsky says.

When a woman today comes to understand her life story as a story from the Motherline, she gains female authority in a number of ways. First, her Motherline grounds her in her feminine nature as she struggles with the many options now open to women. Second, she reclaims carnal knowledge of her own body, its blood mysteries and their power. Third, as she makes the journey back to her female roots, she will encounter ancestors who struggled with similar difficulties in different historical times. This provides her with a life-cycle perspective that softens her immediate situation. It reminds her that all things change in time: Babies grow into school-age children; every recent generation has had different ideas about what's good for children; no child is raised in perfect circumstances. Fourth, she uncovers her connection to the archetypal mother and to the wisdom of the ancient worldview, which holds that body and soul are one and all life is interconnected. And, finally, she reclaims her female perspective, from which to consider how men are similar and how they are different.

Motherline stories ground a motherless daughter in a gender, a family, and a feminine history. They transform the experiences of her female ancestors into maps she can refer to for encouragement or warning. And to make these connections, she needs to know her mother's stories. "So many contemporary women will say, 'Find out about my mother? Forget it! She doesn't understand me. I'm mad at her. She's horrible. The last person I want to be like is my mother,'" Lowinsky says. "These are women who get blocked in their search. The woman who's lost her mother already knows she needs to find her in some way. But she can't hear the stories from her mother's lips, which makes getting them really hard. She has to go to other relatives. And she has to deal with her grief about this, too. If you've lost your mother and you start looking for your Motherline, you come right up against enormous amounts of grief and loss. You have to be ready to deal with those emotions."

A daughter knows about her mother only as much as both of them want her to learn, and for me at seventeen, that wasn't very much. Who knew we'd run out of time? When my mother told me stories of her childhood, I took only what I found immediately use-ful—*she almost drowned when she was seven, so I'd better learn how to swim*—and promptly ignored the rest. She, in turn, chose to relay stories as they coincided with comparable milestones in my life. I can tell you about her first menstruation, her first date, and her Sweet Sixteen in great detail, but her wedding, her first pregnancy, and her child-raising philosophy are almost complete mysteries to me.

Like Rita, I knew my mother as a mother, never as a woman or a friend. My memories of her are bracketed by the dawn of my cognition, when I was roughly three and she was twenty-eight, and her death when she was forty-two. Fourteen years—that's all I'm sure of, and even that is filtered through the perception of a child or a teen. I wasn't mature enough at seventeen to see my mother as an autonomous woman, with dreams and disappointments that didn't include me. I pushed away her attempts to coax me into adult confidences; they felt too premature. I didn't want to hear her opinions about her marriage or sex life when I was in my teens—I'm not even sure I'd want to hear them now—and I alternated between shifting my weight uncomfortably and bolting from the room.

I was twenty-five before I wanted to learn about my mother as a young adult and a wife, a desire that led me to my mother's longtime friends in Pennsylvania and Florida, and then around the neighborhood where I'd grown up, asking questions and gathering stories from women who'd known her well. Sandy told me about her as a sorority sister and young bride; another friend told me about the night she lost her virginity, a story that had elicited only an embarrassed, "On my wedding night, of course," when I'd asked her about it at fourteen.

Twenty-five wasn't an arbitrary year for my exploration—it coincided with two important thresholds in my life. First, I'd finally begun to mourn, and second, I was feeling almost uncontrollably jealous as I watched my female friends approach their mothers as quasi-equals for the first time. Their old parent-child power structures were still nominally in place, but my friends were beginning to assess their mothers' strengths and weaknesses, decide which characteristics they'd want to adopt as their own, and determine how far they'd be willing to stray from what they'd learned in their mothers' homes.

Whether she's a corporate vice-president or a homemaker, a single parent or a wife, the mother is the primary female image a daughter internalizes and refers to for comparison throughout her life, the mile marker against which the daughter measures her own travels. A twenty-year-old daughter with a forty-five-year-old mother mentally compares herself with two versions of her mother: the twenty-year-old she has pieced together in imagination from her mother's stories, and the forty-five-year-old she sees. When the daughter herself turns forty-five, she then compares herself to the forty-five-year-old mother she remembers, and also to the seventy-year-old one she knows.

But a mother who dies young is a woman interrupted, and her daughter's image of her freezes at that point. When I try to identify the similarities and differences between my mother and myself, I'm working with limited material. On the one hand, I'm comparing myself to a forty-one-year-old Marcia I knew only from a seventeen-year-old's point of view; on the other, I'm comparing myself to a woman who never ages. When I turned seventeen, she was forty-two. Now I'm forty-one and she's still forty-two. My mother will remain older and more experienced than me for only one more year. And I wonder, what then?

Twenty-nine-year-old Karen also is concerned about losing her mother as a psychological guide. Even though she won't reach her mother's age for more than thirty years, Karen is starting to pass her in other ways.

During Karen's childhood, her domineering mother frequently asserted her own superiority. After her mother's death nine years ago, Karen continued to perceive herself as the weak daughter of a powerful mother. But as she gets ready to complete her college degree, Karen is beginning to reconceive herself as intelligent and worthwhile, and now she wonders what place a mother who tried to convince her otherwise can occupy in her life.

Knowing that I will be more educated than she was is very difficult for me to accept. To excel somewhere beyond where my mother excelled ruins my mythic mother image. She won't always be older than me, she won't always be smarter than me, or better than me. Someday she's not going to be the great and powerful Oz. Someday she's going to be the little woman behind the curtain. I think she's getting there already. And that's very hard.

It's as if you're an athlete and you're competing to be the best. As long as you're not in the top spot, you always have somebody to strive against. But once you're the best in the world, you don't have anyone to compare yourself with anymore. I always compare myself to my mother to measure my progress. Well, once I've gone beyond what she achieved in areas she was concerned about—she very much wanted to finish her college degree and didn't because she had kids—I lose that protector image. What do you do once you're beyond those archetypal images in your head? Then who do you try to be like?

In a way, for me it's like the idea of existing without a God. If you don't have somebody who's monitoring your good deeds and your bad deeds, who'll praise you with heaven or punish you with hell, you grow up in a different way. You have to monitor your own ethics because then the universe is random. There isn't that arbiter of your behavior out there, and hey, then you're on your own.

Karen is right: Without a living mother to refer to for comparison, a daughter invents much of her identity alone. In theory, she's free to make her own decisions and learn from her own mistakes. In practice, however, she is frightened by the solitude this entails. Hoping to find a guide, she seeks out as much information as she can find about her mother's life. This generally happens during a woman's twenties, when the developmental urge to return to the mother seizes hold of her. A daughter's need for a woman-to-woman reunion doesn't disappear just because her mother is no longer alive. By collecting information to re-create the mother as she was—not only as a parent, but also as a woman—the daughter tries to mature her image of her mother by imagining what their relationship might have evolved into and giving herself the closest approximation to a reunion she can have. She also searches for similarities between her mother and herself in an effort to secure her place in the Motherline.

Until Margie, now twenty-five, began gathering information about her mother, she remembered her only as the solemn, depressed woman who committed suicide eighteen years ago. She hadn't wanted to identify with this mother in any way. But in her early twenties, Margie felt she needed to connect with a woman in her family, and she asked her maternal grandparents for the first time to tell her stories about her mother as a young woman.

> I had always thought my mother had been shy and withdrawn, kind of introverted and quiet, but then I found out from my grandparents she hadn't been like that at all. She was very open and extroverted, very loving and giving, a real life-of-the-party kind of person. That's why her depression was even more dramatic, because it changed her so much. I see myself more as an extrovert, like she really was, than as the kind of introvert I remember her being. My mother was also musical, articulate, and good in school. Those are other things I can identify with, and think, "Yeah, I'm like that, too." I didn't just grow out of a flower like Thumbelina. I do have some kind of biological connection to someone. It's not just that I look like her and might be prone to depression, but that I have these other, positive qualities that are related to her, too.

Instead of fearing a maternal connection because of its association with depression and death, Margie is reestablishing a bond with a mother she's still getting to know. But she's only completed half of her journey. Rediscovering the mother is a two-step process, first requiring the resurrection of her as a woman and then, through imagination, aging her to the point where she might be today. And that's the harder part. To have a sense of how my mother and I might have related now and to compare myself to both mothers—the forty-one-year-old I knew and the sixty-seven-year-old she would be today—I have to fast-forward her in my mind. I have to theorize how the cultural forces of the 1980s and 1990s might have shaped her, to imagine what she might have become if she hadn't been slowed down by cancer, to envision all the places she might have gone to, if she hadn't died.

I thought I knew what my mother wanted for me. I used to imagine the deathbed conversation we never had. She would hold my hand as she relayed her final wish. "I want you to grow up and be happy," she would have said. "Go to college and find a good husband. Preferably a Jewish doctor, who'll buy you a house on Long Island. But not Great Neck or the Five Towns. Go a little farther out, maybe Massapequa. Will you promise to do that for me?"

You think I'm joking, but I'm not. My mother grew up in the sector of suburban, Jewish New York in the 1950s and 1960s that sent daughters to college to marry professionals and measured a woman's success by the carat-count of her diamond ring. I'd like to think my mother would have developed more expansive dreams for her daughters if she had lived long enough to see us succeed in other areas—or at least as she watched the country's economy turn dual-career marriages into a necessity—but I remember her prepping me only for a future that included a white dress, a long aisle, and one of those good men who were so hard to find. This was her vision of female success, and she wanted it all for me. She was appalled by my first boyfriend, a reformed juvenile delinquent who wore his hair down to his chin. Of course, I chose him partly because I knew how strongly she'd object. We were at that stage of mother-daughter rebellion. And we were still in it nearly a decade later, because I got stuck there when she died.

Because certain elements of a daughter's personality can arrest when a mother dies, she may grow into adulthood retaining characteristics of the developmental phase she was in at that time. The child then grows into a woman still dependent on the lost mother. The adolescent may continue to reject and rebel against her as an adult.

That was how I operated for the first nine years after my mother's death, and it was a handy way of keeping the mother-daughter relationship alive. Death didn't silence my mother's demands. Inside the confines of my head, she still tried to give me advice I didn't want to hear, and I still refused to take it. I left New York at eighteen with no intention of living within a hundred miles of Long Island ever again, and I avoided pre-med students as if they were the eleventh plague. I remained determined not to live the life my mother had intended for me, and to assert my independence by creating one of my own design.

Perhaps I wouldn't have continued to rebel so forcefully if I hadn't felt a simultaneous, subterranean pull toward precisely the future I was rejecting so vehemently. That was the part of my little drama I never discussed with anyone: the deep guilt I felt for straying from my mother's preordained path, and a secret longing for the security that she had assured me such a future would supply. So at the same time that I was deliberately resisting my mother's wishes, I was also taking steps to accommodate us both. When I was twenty-three, I pledged my future to my college boyfriend. He wasn't Jewish and he wasn't from New York, but he was about to begin law school, and that seemed like an acceptable compromise to me. As I edged him toward marriage, I believed my mother would have been proud, knowing I was about to become a wife.

Only with my broken engagement and the hindsight of several years was I able to see that I wasn't just trying to live the life I thought my mother wanted for me. No, I was also trying to live the one she never had. She never lived outside New York. She taught music for a few years before I was born, but she never turned it into a career. And she never married that doctor (or dentist or lawyer or CEO) and bought that big house, all of which her mother had once wished for her, too.

I've yet to meet a daughter with a mother who would willingly sacrifice her own identity to satisfy her mother's vicarious urges, but motherless daughters do this all the time—out of guilt, out of obligation, out of grief, out of love. We try to honor our mothers' unfulfilled desires, as if we can somehow give them the years they never got to live. It's as if we believe that by becoming the daughters our mothers always wanted us to be, or by living the lives they always wanted to live—by, in effect, *becoming them*—we can keep our mothers with us and prevent them from leaving us again.

It's challenging enough to run one life. It can be utter confusion trying to fulfill the dreams of two. Gayle, now thirty-two, has been struggling with this identity conflict for the past fourteen years. She and her mother were closely bound during her childhood and adolescence, and since her mother's death from cancer when she was eighteen, Gayle has vacillated between the impulse to become her mother and the desire to remain her mother's daughter—both to the exclusion of claiming an identity for herself.

> If my mother had stayed alive, I might have learned I could have my own life. But when she died, it was like I couldn't. I wouldn't allow myself to do things that she would have said no to, and since she wasn't alive to ever say yes, the only guidelines I had to go on were what she'd allowed me to do or what she'd done herself in the past. It was perfectly fine for me to leave college, because my mother had dropped out, too. And I became involved with a man who wasn't at all good for me, but who I know my mother would have adored.
>
> I was trying to repeat her life and then finish it out, I guess. I started not taking care of myself physically or emotionally, and that's what she had done. That's how she got sick to the point she did, because she didn't feel she was important enough to tell people how she felt or what was wrong with her. I have to go for some tests next week to see if I have a precancerous condition, or cancerous condition, though I prefer to say precancerous. Which also feels like I'm living out her life, because the lymphoma she had is hereditary. It would be very ironic if I wind up taking care of my mother that way.

When her mother died, Gayle was just beginning a delayed and difficult psychological separation from her. Like every other adolescent girl, she had the confusing task of having to identify with the same person she was trying to separate from, and to somehow emerge from those years with an identity of her own. Her mother's death arrested this process at a critical point, leaving her half bound to her mother and half committed to herself. Like many other motherless women, Gayle then remained caught between the fear of repeating her mother's past (thus, the distance she put between herself and the word *cancer*) and her strong need to remain connected (which fueled her impulse to finish her mother's life). Kept in check by a psychological maternal police that still tailored its punishment and praise for an eighteen-year-old, Gayle had entered her thirties nearly powerless against the influence of a mother long dead.

Gayle is an example of a woman stuck between the competing forces of *matrophobia* and what I call *matridentity*. Matrophobia, as Adrienne Rich explains in *Of Woman Born,* is the daughter's fear of becoming her mother. A daughter sees her mother's weaknesses and feels helpless against the forces of heredity. At the same time that she chastises her mother for her mistakes, she prays she won't make the same ones. ("Oh, my God!" that anguished woman on the T-shirt cries. "I'm turning into my mother!") Matrophobia can be a source of intense psychological distress for the motherless daughter. To her, it often includes the additional fears of becoming the mother who lost control of her body or her mind, who abandoned her children too young, who lived an abbreviated life, who had too many dreams she never realized because she had too little time.

It would be easier to separate ourselves from these fears and suppress matrophobia for good if not for its twin sister, who snares us with equivalent guile. Matridentity—the inevitability that a daughter will identify with some of her mother's traits—makes it impossible for us to dissociate completely from someone when our bodies, mannerisms, and behaviors evoke memories of hers. Every time I catch myself saying, "That woman *sure is a piece of work,*" my little "Mom alert" sounds. It's a phrase my mother always used. I'm not even particularly fond of it, but sometimes the words just appear. With seventeen years of shared experience and 50 percent of her genes, it's bound to happen sometimes, I guess. And that makes me wonder how much of her I've internalized that I'm not aware of and, despite my conscious choices to differentiate, how similar to her I already am.

"I wonder whether in this struggle to become myself I have become what she was as a girl," writes Kim Chernin, in her memoir about mother-daughter identity, *In My Mother's House.* The idea that my life might parallel my mother's sounds like an impossibility to me. We are completely different people. She studied music; I work with words. She married a New Yorker and was the mother of three children at age thirty-two. I married an Israeli and gave birth to the first of two daughters at thirty-three. Yet the similarities are impossible to ignore. We're both first-born daughters. We both had two daughters. Both of us made teaching our secondary pursuits. And when I tilt the lens in this direction, I can't help but wonder: Aren't my mother and I really, underneath it all, very much the same?

In the spirit of narrative, here's a folktale I've heard:

A new bride is preparing her first meal, a roast. As her husband watches, she hacks off a chunk at one end before placing the meat in the pan.

"Why do you do that?" he asks.

Looking puzzled, she replies, "I don't know. That's how my mother always did it. Maybe it improves the flavor. I'll have to ask her."

The next day, she visits her mother's house. "Mother," she says, "last night when I was cooking a roast I cut off one end before placing the meat in the pan. I did it because you always did it. Can you tell me why?"

"I don't know," her mother says, looking puzzled. "That's how my mother always did it. Maybe it makes the meat more tender. I'll have to ask her."

The next day, she visits the grandmother's house. "Mother," she says, "last night when my daughter was cooking a roast, she cut off one end before placing the meat in the pan. She did it because I always did it. I did it because you always did it. Can you tell me why?"

The grandmother laughs. "I did it because my mother always did it," she says. "So one day I asked her why. She explained that when I was a child, we were so poor we had only one pan, and it was too small for a roast. She had to cut off the end to make it fit."

Three generations of women, using the mother's example as guide. It's a powerful subconscious model. Even if you don't graduate from the same college she did, or have three children like her, or cook a roast for dinner every Tuesday, or cook anything at all, the mother looms large in your conscience, goading you to make decisions similar to hers.

As mothers and daughters act as mirrors for one another, re-flecting images of the self, the mother projects a younger version of herself onto her daughter. To some degree, the daughter internalizes that image and co-opts it into her identity. This isn't always a con-scious process, as Donna recently learned. She was surprised when, at twenty-five, she recognized that she was living a life that closely resembled her mother's at the same age. Until then, her mother, an alcoholic who committed suicide when Donna was twenty-two, had provided her mostly with a model of how she *didn't* want to be. Donna had spent most of her teens and twenties creating distance be-tween the two of them, moving out of the family house at seventeen, putting herself through college, and starting a professional career—all experiences her mother never had. But when she discovered she'd been identifying with her mother all along, Donna became inspired to seek out her mother's stories and look for other similarities be-tween them.

My mother came to New York from Germany when she was twenty-five years old, got a job here, and met my father in a laundry room. They got married the next year. Here I am, just moved to New York to start my life and hoping to meet the right man. It's as if there are two overlays—the mother here and the daughter there, and if you lay one on top of the other, you see the steps she took are basically the same ones I've been tak-ing. Whatever molding is going to happen in my life now might happen to me here, as it did to her thirty years ago. It's really quite amazing.

If I could travel back in time, I'd love to meet my mother when she was younger, to travel around with her and see what she thought. When I was on the plane to New York, I met a woman from Germany. She had my mother's cheekbones and eyes and hair. Her accent and her mannerisms also reminded me so much of what my mother would have been like in her twenties. For the first time, I wondered what it would be like to get to know the person she was before she even moved to New York.

Our conversation was interrupted by a phone call from Paul, a man Donna had met the previous month. He was at a New York airport, about to leave the country for three weeks, and he wanted to let her know how much he'd miss her while he was gone. Six months later, Donna called me to share some good news. She and Paul had gotten engaged, she said—wasn't it an amazing analogy to her parents? She sounded less surprised than she had the last time we spoke. Despite Donna's initial antipathy toward her maternal model, she'd accepted that she could identify with some aspects of her mother's life while distancing herself from those she disliked or feared. She'd made choices that benefited her by using her mother's example as a guide, something she'd never expected would occur.

Every daughter's experience is one of identifying with and differentiating from the mother, and both processes are equally important. As Naomi Lowinsky points out, identifying connects us to our origins, while differing allows us to find our own destinies and not blindly repeat our mothers' lives. It's when the daughter feels the pull either to reject all aspects of the mother or to become an identical version of her—matrophobia and matridentity taken to their extremes—that her ability to sort out the "me" from the "her" and develop her own identity is impaired.

"I've seen one woman for a number of years who's patterned her life so she becomes the opposite of her mother," Therese Rando says. "Her mother was not a good mother. She alienated family members and taught her daughter to view herself negatively. So this woman is now trying not to alienate family members, to give her own children decent self-esteem, and to take care of herself and her body because her mother wound up dying of breast cancer that went undetected for too long. These are all positive choices, but my concern about this woman is that she's so determined to be the opposite of her mother, she's losing the freedom to do what she really wants. You can identify with your mother so much that it tells you everything you need to do, but you can also identify so much that it tells you everything you shouldn't do. I've seen it go both ways. In both situations, if a woman doesn't allow herself the freedom to make her own choices, I wouldn't consider that healthy."

Carol, thirty-six, described a similar conflict to me. Carol never had a close relationship with her mother, but since her mother's death nineteen years ago, she has felt compelled to adopt behaviors that have little to do with her own philosophy or desires. "I'm constantly finding things that I've embodied from my mother, ways to keep her with me," she says. "My frugality with money is really hers. When I tell myself I can't have seltzer and to just have water from the tap, it's her voice I hear. She was a very good example of how to be practical and make a dollar go a long way. I've taken some of her characteristics and multiplied their importance to an extreme to hold on to her. Now, I'm trying to shed those extra layers and get down to what's really right for me."

Detaching from a mother's posthumous control can be a long, arduous, and painful journey, but it's often a necessary step in a daughter's mourning process. When, like Carol, a woman adopts a mother's behavior as a substitute for her presence, letting go of that character trait means letting go of the mother a little bit more. But it also allows a daughter more opportunity to develop the characteristics that make her uniquely her.

Sheila's story illustrates this well. As we sit talking in her apartment, she shows me a few items that once belonged to her mother, who died when Sheila was fourteen. She gestures toward a rocking chair in the corner, shows me a sculpture on the wall, and displays some jewelry she wears. But the item Sheila values the most is her mother's green plastic recipe box, which she retrieves from an adjacent room to show me. The cards inside explain, in her mother's and grandmother's handwriting, how to cook the food Sheila remembers from her childhood. "This box is like a female history to me," she explains. "My mother continues to live through it, in a way."

As an early adolescent, Sheila was barely in the initial stages of individuation when her mother suddenly and unexpectedly died. Her identity formation process slowed to a crawl until her early twenties, when she discovered how to separate from her mother at a symbolic level and then return on her own terms. Sheila did it through her mother's possessions:

When I was in college, my apartment was like a shrine. I had all my mother's things. My home had nothing to do with me and everything to do with her. I'd felt so robbed of her and our life together that I wanted to re-create it. So I had all her stuff with me, to a ridiculous and scary, obsessive degree—things that didn't work, things I didn't even like, but that I kept because they'd been hers. She'd had green tin kitchen canisters from the seventies shaped like apples that were the ugliest things ever. When I moved away from that city, they were one of the things I threw away. It was a time when I'd started some of the separating, and I was beginning to see how my mother and I were similar in some ways, but not others. Once I recognized that she was within me, and started to gain some awareness of who I was as an individual, I didn't need to keep all of these external things around me. When I moved, I really went through the apartment and chose what I wanted to keep. The items I have now aren't indiscriminate anymore. I kept the rocking chair she rocked me in when I was a baby, and I repainted it after I moved. That was an important moment for me. I'd just moved to a new city and was starting a new life. I sat down alone one night in my new kitchen and repainted my mother's rocking chair a groovy shade of green.

We have no way of knowing what shape our lives might have taken if our mothers hadn't died. Might we, despite the loss, have arrived at the same place we occupy now? Some psychologists believe most of our individual identity forms within the first three years of life, and that personality structure remains basically intact from then on. Others see identity as more fluid and malleable, and self-concept as a process of continual evolution. Still others propose that identity is a life story that individuals begin constructing, consciously or unconsciously, during adolescence. A mother's death or absence occupies a central place in this story—often as the event on which the whole narrative pivots—and a daughter's identity thus becomes inextricably interwoven with the loss.

Just as I am one-half my mother's genes and one-half my father's, since my mother's death I have been one part my mother's daughter and one part motherless daughter. Both have become integral parts of my identity by now. From seventeen years with my mother, I learned how to be compassionate, charitable, and nurturing, and how to mother my own daughters. From the twenty-four years since her death, I learned how to be independent, competent, and strong. Sheila and I sit at her table, her mother's recipe box resting between us, and consider a question both of us have asked ourselves many times: Am I as I am—who I am, what I am, how I am—because my mother lived, or because my mother died? The answer, we agree, is both.

Chapter Ten

Mortal Lessons
Life, Death, Sickness, Health

FOR MORE THAN TEN YEARS NOW, I've kept my mother's medical records in a folder labeled "Documents." I can't manage more specificity than that. More precise words are just reflectors, cleverly disguised. If they weren't, I might be able to get through the twelfth page of her mastectomy records without having twenty-five years' worth of emotion bounced back at me. There's one sentence there that destabilizes me every time. A nurse scribbled it the day before the operation, in between my mother's age and a mention of her capped teeth: "Previous anaesthesia Caudal & Epidural, scared of her teeth chattering after the anaesthetic."

This was a woman entering a hospital to have her left breast removed, who knew that cancer had already invaded her lymph nodes, who had three children under the age of eighteen and no idea of what the surgeon might find, and she was frightened that her teeth might chatter in the recovery room. That kills me.

It kills me because it is so much like my mom. It is so much like her to worry in advance about scaring the patient in the next bed, or troubling my father, or losing her dignity in front of strangers. It is so much like her to remember every detail of her three childbirths, right down to the part where her jaw vibrated uncontrollably when she asked to hold a newborn daughter or son. I can imagine her telling that nurse about her last anesthetic trip, about how her body left her and how it first returned, of all places, inside her mouth. I can hear her use the word *scared.*

In fifty-six pages of medical notes, this was the only emotion recorded. It may have been the only one she expressed. Still, it makes me wonder: Was she angry? Did she feel grief? Easier, I suppose, to focus on the known quantities, on the medical tasks that could be regulated and controlled. "I'm scared my teeth will chatter," she told the nurse, perhaps a cryptic shorthand for, "I'm scared the cancer will be everywhere. I'm scared I won't wake up alive."

Whenever I read the words my mother spoke as she readied herself for a morning underneath a surgeon's knife, the safe distance between us collapses with startling speed. She is no longer the mythic mother of my imagination, or the tragic heroine of a plot gone horribly wrong. She is just a woman who found a lump in her breast and sat with it for too long. She is human and fallible and real. And when she shrinks to the level of a mortal, she becomes frighteningly similar to me.

I once read in a magazine that a woman feels the first pinch of mortality when she looks over her shoulder into a mirror and sees her mother's ass. What is the sensation then—a slap? a kick?—for the woman who turns around and sees much more than that? In the mirror, I find my mother's hips and hands and eyes. When I speak, I hear her voice, occasionally shaping itself around the same sentences I swore I'd never utter as an adult. And from there it seems only a short journey to the afternoon in an examining room when a doctor accidentally touches my armpit, feels a swollen lymph node, and asks, with sudden concern, "What's this?" Such things can happen. I know.

Genetic roulette awarded me my own face, but I inherited my mother's shape—small breasts, high waist, wide hips, slim ankles, big feet. She pointed out the similarities long before I understood that a body could feel like anything but my own. When I was five and sitting at the piano bench, she took my right hand and turned it over between both of hers. "You have piano hands, just like mine," she said, and she showed me how her long, thin fingers could span an octave on the ivory keys.

When I reached five feet, four inches in the sixth grade and my legs showed no sign of slowing their growth, my mother became determined to deliver me from the adolescent shame she'd once felt as the tallest girl in her class. In her walk-in closet she taught me the tricks of illusion she relied on to mask her body's perceived flaws:

cinch dresses at the waist to keep them from clinging at the hips. Use shoulder pads to offset small breasts. Avoid white shoes.

I wonder how it made her feel, to watch a first daughter's body unfold to produce a paper-doll image of her own. Was it a personal triumph for her, a chance to relive thirteen with a mother who knew modern fashion tips? Did it spawn a barely suppressed envy, reminding her of years spent in awkward adolescent solitude as she watched me flee the house each afternoon to join my small tribe of close-knit friends? Or, in the months after the diagnosis of cancer in her left breast, did she ever look at mine and wonder whether a lump could grow inside me, too—if an ability to cultivate malevolent cells would be her final gift to me?

Perhaps this thought plagued her, or perhaps she kept it forcefully at bay. I don't know. Although cancer runs like toxic sap up and down both sides of my family tree, we never discussed the possibility that it might show up in me. My mother didn't speculate about its future plans. Her father had survived colon cancer in his forties and had lived for another twenty years. This was our paradigm for serious illness; she may have trusted that the same sequence would repeat for her.

In the medical records from her mastectomy, I can see her trying to deny that cancer could interrupt her life. Or was she just replacing fear with the same blind hope she tried to encourage in me? Three days before the pathology report confirmed that all of her twenty-six extracted lymph nodes had tested positive for cancer, a female social worker visited my mother's hospital room. From the notes she left behind, this counselor apparently already knew how serious the pending diagnosis would be: "The patient is an emotionally resourceful woman who needs at this point to be very optimistic about her disease and its implications," she wrote. "Wishing to resume her previous functioning as soon as possible. Patient feels that the two weeks of preparations she had prior to surgery gave her time to think about her priorities—'getting back to life'—and to reduce some of the disorganizing effects of waking up to a mastectomy. Her hopefulness is what appears to be sustaining her at this time. Her sister, on the other hand, upset about MD's report that there was much more cancer than anticipated and patient will need chemotherapy. Talked with her at length so as to allow her then to support patient's defenses, i.e., a denial of its long-range implications."

I don't know whether my mother ever understood how far gone her cancer was, or that it would eventually win. But surely, the thought must have taunted her—how could it have not? From the pathologist's report, the likelihood of her survival was slim. Twenty-six positive lymph nodes is about the poorest diagnosis a woman can get. But I remember what she told me after her mastectomy, as I sat at the foot of her hospital bed: "The cancer was in some of my lymph nodes but not in others, which means the doctors removed it all." I believed her at the time—I had no reason not to—but twelve years later, I learned it wasn't true. Which means, as I see it, either that my mother never heard the pathologist's report or that, because she wanted to protect me from a truth too inconceivable for her to bear, she lied.

By the time this was revealed to me, however, I'd already spent more than a decade constructing lovely, complex metaphors about beautiful, brave women who died without dignity because their fate lay in the hands of manipulative men. On alternate days my mother was either a queen removed from her kingdom without warning or a soldier pushed into battle with neither sufficient training nor adequate arms. These fantasies sustained me, justifying and multiplying my anger toward her doctors and my father, and I'd organized most of my opinions about the medical profession, illness, and death around their romantic poles. Before I saw the severity of her medical condition spelled out in type, I'd never considered the idea that my mother, alone inside her body, might have known the truth all along.

And could she have suspected it even earlier? I remember the reason she gave me for avoiding the biopsy that would have diagnosed her cancer a year before the biopsy that finally did. "Operations are expensive," she said, "and money is tight this year." I accepted her explanation then, but I know better now. The whole family had major-medical coverage, which would have paid 80 percent or more of the bill. Lack of money wasn't a legitimate reason to put the surgery off.

After that conversation, we didn't speak about the lump again, until the evening of the mammogram that showed what she described as a "suspicious shadow," and we never discussed death. The only time I heard her mention her mortality was during a three-minute episode one afternoon about four months before she died. I was walking into the bathroom as she was walking out. Her eyes were red and her lips tight, the mask she wore between the toilet and her bed after a chemotherapy treatment earlier in the day. As she carefully lay down, I asked her, exasperated and confused, "Why, Mom? Why do you put yourself through this hell?"

She looked at me as if I'd said I'd just had a delightful tea with God. "Hope," she said. "I do it because I want to live."

Which, of course, is not what happened, not at all, because four months later she was dead at forty-two. And twenty-four years later, I am forty-one, the age she was when her cancer was found. The thirty minutes I spend sitting in the radiologist's waiting room every February while my mammogram screens are scrutinized for shadows or spots are the longest thirty minutes of my year. While I wait in a mauve armchair, I run through the mental list of differences between my mother and me. She was a stay-at-home mother; I work. She had her third and last child at thirty-two; that's about how old I was when I had my first. She spent her entire life in New York; I landed in California after fifteen years of jumping around. It's my personal form of prayer, as if the recitation will somehow convince God to grant me just one more difference, the big one, the one my family needs the most. And then the radiologist returns with a smile and good news for one more year. Blessed evidence, again, that my mother and I are not the same.

Then, as I exit the lobby onto Wilshire Boulevard, I catch a sideways glance of myself in the building's mirrored panels. It is my chin that juts out, my hair flapping against my back. But it is her chest pressing forward, her ass that protrudes. Her ass. And despite the morning's news, it is still so easy to imagine, with each thought gliding smoothly and silently into the next: Her ass, her breasts, her fate.

Breast cancer, heart attacks, aneurysms, depression—the specifics don't matter all that much. More than three-quarters of the motherless daughters interviewed said they're afraid they'll repeat their mothers' fates, even when the cause of death has no proven relationship to heredity or genes. Ninety-two percent of the women whose mothers died of cancer said they feared the same demise either "somewhat" or "a lot." The same was true for 90 percent of those whose mothers committed suicide, 87 percent whose mothers died of heart-related illnesses, 86 percent whose mothers died of cerebral hemorrhages, and 50 percent who lost mothers to accidental death.

Like many of these women, my alarm grows not only from watching a mother die but also from the shadow of an ominous family tree. Cancer afflicted both my parents, all four of my grandparents, and my maternal great-grandmother as well. One of my mother's younger sisters was diagnosed with breast cancer six years after my mother died, and despite what little certainty we have about the disease, we know it can hitch a ride on genes. I've lived for more than a decade now with the knowledge that I'm considered high-risk, that my lifetime chance of developing breast cancer, according to the medical geneticist who reviewed my family's history, is as high as one in three. My challenge is to find a way to live that allows me a realistic amount of concern yet frees me from the certainty that, any day now, I will find the lump that is already programming me to die. It's a delicate balance, and I haven't quite achieved it yet. On good days, I figure my chance of getting breast cancer is so slim that I need not think about it at all. On bad days, I reassess my risk as inevitable. One hundred and one percent: That's me.

Here's what's available to the high-risk daughter: Statistics. Odds. And, for heart disease and some cancers, early detection tests—which may or may not improve long-term survival, depending on which article you read. But statistics and test results don't completely calm a woman's fears. They appeal to her rational side, which isn't necessarily averse to optimism but can't squash her panic alone. My mother's death from breast cancer left an emotional imprint on me, and that's the part that can't quite believe the same won't happen to me.

When a daughter watches a mother die, especially from an illness, she becomes aware of her own physical vulnerability as a female. At some level, she already understands that the female experience is one of relinquishing complete control over the body.

Menstruation, gestation, and menopause progress at paces of their own unless deliberate medical intervention changes their course. But to see her mother's system taken over by disease confirms one fear and encourages another: Her mother's body failed too young, and the same can happen to hers.

This cognitive leap from the horror of a mother's death to the fear of self-demise is a broad one, but easy for a daughter to make. The psycho-physiological connection between daughters and mothers begins the moment the physical tie is cut. With the severing of the umbilical cord, two female bodies face each other, separate, yet the same. A mother looks at a daughter's body and sees her younger self; a daughter looks to a mother's body for clues about her physical future. Bound by this symbiotic identification, daughters and mothers act as mirrors for each other, reflecting anachronistic versions of the self.

Alison Milburn, Ph.D., a psychologist in Iowa City, Iowa, who has counseled many motherless daughters, has observed that women with the most extreme fears of contracting their mothers' diseases typically over-identified with their mothers during childhood. "As adults, they still see themselves as being very, very much like their mothers," she explains, "and their mothers, most often, really reinforced that. As their daughters were growing up they said things like, 'You look exactly like me,' or 'You're exactly like me,' or they responded strongly to events that happened to their daughters as if the events were happening to them." When boundaries between mother and daughter are so fluid and ill defined, a daughter also can't properly distinguish between her mother's experience and her own. If cancer or heart failure or suicide took her mother's life, she reacts to the illness as if it were a threat to her system, too.

Working in tandem with the hospital's obstetrics and gynecology clinic, Dr. Milburn has seen this fear taken to its extreme. She's counseled a college student who demanded a hysterectomy at twenty-five because her mother died of uterine cancer; a corporate executive who showed up for a breast exam with a chest full of pen marks, indicating the lumps she'd been monitoring daily for several months; and several mothers who requested prophylactic mastectomies in their thirties because they believed it would reduce their cancer risk.[1] Through relaxation and thought-stopping strategies, occasional medication management, and discussions of risk factors and family histories, Dr. Milburn tries to disentangle these women from the belief that a mother's and a daughter's destiny must be the same. "The best way these women can emerge intact from a difficult health situation with their mothers," she says, "is to begin to become less psychologically identified with them."

That's not an easy task, especially when a daughter has inherited her mother's appearance or physical shape. Because this daughter can easily imagine her body overcome by the same disease, she's the one who identifies most strongly with a mother's experience when the mother falls ill. "Of course, having your mother's shape doesn't mean anything about the reality of what's going to happen to you, but that embodied sense of connection runs very, very deep," Naomi Lowinsky says. "The problem for the motherless daughter is, she winds up in a horrendous catch–22. In order to fully identify with her femaleness, she's got to be in her body. But that also means identifying with her mother's body, and if she associates her mother's body with a terrible illness and an early death, it feels like the last place in the world she wants to go."

Yet it can seem, at the same time, like the only possible place for her to end up. This is the secret that motherless daughters share: We fear we will die young. And not at some unspecified point in the future—no, we fear it will happen when we reach the ages our mothers were when they died.

"The magic number," one motherless woman called it. "Oh, the invisible line in the sand," another daughter said. "I don't know if any other women have said this," about eight dozen women have confided in me over the years, "but I'm afraid I won't live longer than thirty-nine (or forty-five or fifty-three)."

The last math class I took was in high school, and I have to use my fingers to add any single digit to a nine. But I have always been able to tell you, without pause for calculation, how many years have stood between my current age and forty-two. Now, as I fast ap-

[1]These were women who had not tested positive for a BRCA gene. Motherless daughters who do test positive often opt for prophylactic mastectomies and reconstructive surgeries, with full support from their doctors.

proach that deadline I've started to include months as well. And it gives me a small amount of comfort to know my mother was forty-two years and ten months when she died, which is practically the same thing as being forty-three.

This is Mortality Math 101, in which a mother's age at death is a fixed value, and the only distance worth measuring is the one between here and there. We fixate on mental additions and subtractions, anxious about approaching the dreaded age—because what if we, too, die?—joyful, yet still fearful, about leaving it behind.

Living beyond a mother's final year is a daughter's exquisite reminder of her separateness. She did not—and now cannot—repeat her mother's exact fate. This realization, says Therese Rando, can evoke a reaction similar to survivor guilt. "For some women, it's very uncomfortable to survive past the age of a mother," she explains. "They feel like they got extra time, and got something their mothers didn't. They feel almost as if they were bad for getting away with it, and that if the mother didn't have those extra years, they shouldn't have them, either." She believes this is why some people die when they predict they will, especially when they're convinced they'll die at the same age a parent did.

Two-thirds of the motherless women aged fifty-five and younger surveyed for this book admitted that they fear reaching the ages their mothers were when they died either "somewhat" or "a lot." Some are so certain they'll die that same year, they've designed their lives in preparation. Take Janine, for example. She was not quite two when her thirty-three-year-old mother died in a car accident, and although she was sitting in the back seat when it happened, Janine says she has no conscious memories of the crash. Nevertheless, she spent the next thirty-one years subconsciously waiting for the same accident to happen again, this time with her in the driver's seat. "I never thought I'd live past thirty-three, which I didn't even realize until I turned thirty-four," she says. "All that time, I just never planned for the future. I sort of lived thinking in the back of my mind somewhere that I'd be in a car accident at thirty-three and die, so why plan beyond that? I had no future orientation whatsoever. I dropped out of college. I got a job, but I'd work only thirty hours a week so I had time to be an activist instead of working forty hours and saving money to go back to school or to open an IRA."

So what happened, I asked, when she turned thirty-four?

"Well," she says, "one thing was that I really started thinking about my mother. For years I could talk about her without crying. I'd just sort of tick off the facts very rationally. But when I kept living at thirty-four, I started getting very emotional about her death." Passing her mother's age shifted Janine's focus away from her own mortality and allowed her to mourn her mother for the first time. She also found herself moving forward, without plans, into years she hadn't expected to see. She recalls, almost wryly, "When I turned thirty-four, the future suddenly was here. Figuring out what to do with it, however, has been another story. It took me five years to come up with a plan. At thirty-nine, I'm just getting ready to implement it. But I worry about all those lost years. I sort of think that at sixty I'm going to be a bag lady unless I get my act together quickly."

Janine's fear of a foreshortened future is common among motherless women. Because a same-sex parent acts as a natural buffer zone between a child and her own mortality, as long as the mother is present, life—and not death—is the daughter's image of her future. When that barrier is removed, death feels more imminent to her, and decidedly more real. A girl who at a young age loses a mother, also loses the ability to perceive herself growing into old age. If a mother dies or leaves at forty-six, she can represent a physical model for her daughter only until that age. Instead of envisioning herself as a matron of seventy-three, the daughter then sees early demise as a potential—or even inevitable—physical future for herself.

The psychologists Veronika Denes-Raj and Howard Ehrlichman tested this theory in 1991, when they compared a group of New York City college students who'd lost parents prematurely to a group whose parents were still alive. When they asked the students in both groups to predict how long they'd live, based on objective criteria such as their genetic backgrounds, medical history, and past and present health behavior, those with parents still alive estimated that they'd live an average of seventy-nine years. Those who'd lost parents predicted that they'd live for only seventy-two.

Even more telling was the discrepancy between the groups when participants were asked to predict again, based on their "gut feelings," that is, their hopes, fears, and dreams. This time, the group with parents estimated lifespans of an optimistic eighty-three years. Subjects who'd experienced early parent loss predicted that they'd live an average of fifteen years less—to sixty-eight. Once again, emotion prevailed over rationality. Even those whose parents were victims of random accidents with no potential for genetic inheritance expected to die young. That's how powerful the parental model can be.

Most of us didn't spend our childhoods obsessed with conscious thoughts about our mothers dying. Occasionally, we might have wondered about our own demise—Who'll come to my funeral? Will anybody cry?—but chances are that we didn't think about that very often either. To live in a world constantly aware and afraid of impending death would mean living in a state of perpetual fear and anxiety, a situation so intense it would ultimately consume us. From a very early age our protective mental faculties begin shielding us from the ongoing realization that life comes stamped with an expiration date. Because the concept of self-demise is too enormous, too incomprehensible for anyone to grasp fully at the conscious level, we exist instead in an ongoing tug-of-war between the fear of death, which we must have for purposes of self-preservation, and the illusion of immortality, which allows us to enjoy life.

The loss of a parent—especially a same-sex one—can drastically tip this balance. A mother's death is as close as a daughter can get to experiencing her own, leaving her with the sudden realization of vulnerability and exposure. When my mother died, I remember feeling as if a tornado had blown through town and carried my roof away. Although I'd turned away from religion a few years before, I'd been raised in the Judeo-Christian tradition that houses its almighty God in a kingdom in the sky, and those early images never completely evaporate. The week after my mother died, I developed a bizarre, painful (and probably psychosomatic) stomach ailment, and I went to sleep each night for a week half-expecting a divine hand to reach down from the heavens and snatch me before I woke. This sounds ridiculously dramatic to me now, but I can remember how it felt then—that I was the next woman in line, that the next one to go would be me.

This wasn't exactly what I'd expected to be thinking about at seventeen. When I tell this story to twenty-eight-year-old Sheila, who was fourteen when her mother died, she says her adolescence and young adulthood were filled with similar fears. For her first five years, her mother was an alcoholic with little time or energy for her children. After she stopped drinking, she and Sheila became so close that when Sheila found her mother dead of heart failure, she became convinced that the same could happen to her at any moment—and probably would.

> When my mother died, my safety net was removed. From then on, I felt that if something bad was going to happen, it was going to happen to me. I work with adolescents now, and I see their feelings of invulnerability all the time. I never felt that. I always took precautions, because I never felt safe. I was religious about birth control, because I was sure if someone was going to get pregnant, it was going to be me. At the same time, I definitely did some stupid things. I got into cars I shouldn't have, with people who shouldn't have been driving. I drank a lot in high school, and I took a lot of drugs in college. But I was always aware that I was taking a risk, and that there was a very good chance I wasn't going to get through. It felt like the beginning of the end for a long time.

Sheila spent those years courting death like an ambivalent lover, daring it to find her at the same time she took deliberate steps to keep it away. In my twenties and early thirties, before I had children and the stakes became too high, I also tested the limits many times. I would take the subway alone at midnight, go rock climbing in a remote gorge with someone of questionable skill, and accept rides from people I'd never met before. Internally, I knew, I was vulnerable to cancer, but I would delude myself into thinking nothing external could take me down. "Nothing bad will happen to *me*" was my insistence that I was immune to harm, that bad luck no longer had an interest in me, that I was one who could take risks and win. It was my urgent self-reminder that *I am not my mother,* when, of course, underneath it lay the very visceral fear that I was.

Confronting feelings of vulnerability with the actions of the invulnerable is a behavior so common that clinicians have a name for it: "counterphobic mechanisms." Like the acrophobe who takes flying lessons to overcome her fear of heights, motherless daughters will try to master their fears of dying by taking risks that give them the illusion of having control over their destinies. To gain the exhilaration and validation that come from tempting fate and winning, they'll often engage in precisely the behaviors—for example, smoking after a mother dies of lung cancer—that put them at highest risk for getting a mother's disease.

"Some women really walk the line, and not only with health behaviors," Dr. Milburn says. "Women are less likely than men to drive recklessly or jump out of airplanes. Their risk taking usually is interpersonal, like doing things to screw up their relationships. I see a lot of women who respond to their fears of illness or death by making crummy choices with regard to sexual partners, or having a lot of affairs."

As Denes-Raj and Ehrlichman discovered, the college students in their study who feared dying early and from the same cause as their parents were also the ones most likely to engage in harmful health habits such as smoking or eating poorly. This may be because children model their parents' health behaviors, the authors suggest, or because poor health is a consequence of bereavement. But Dr. Denes-Raj believes it more likely that parent loss leads children to develop a sense of fatalism, which in turn leads to the belief, "If my destiny is to die young, or if the disease is already in my genes, why should I bother taking care of myself now?"

As researchers have found, many high-risk women don't. When Kathryn Kash, Ph.D., was the head psychologist at the Strang Cancer Prevention Center in New York City studying women at high risk for breast cancer, she initially expected to find that women who perceived themselves to be most vulnerable to the disease would be the ones most likely to engage in regular screening. Instead, she found the opposite to be true. Women with the most anxiety about developing breast cancer rarely did breast self-exams and often canceled or missed their appointments for clinical checkups. "These women say if they feel okay, then they're not going to come in or do self-exams," Dr. Kash says. "It's easy to think that if you don't do any screening, you won't find anything, because if you don't do any screening, you can't."

Brenda, thirty-two, who was sixteen when her mother died of breast cancer, says because her maternal grandmother also had the disease, she perceives herself as especially high-risk. The memory of her mother's two-year illness, however, prevents Brenda from taking the suggested precautionary measures for herself.

> You think I'd be careful about my own health, but I'm not. I physically can't bring myself to do breast exams. I have the instructions hanging in my bathroom, but I just can't do it. My older sister has had a mammogram already. I'm still a little young for it, but I know early detection is the thing. It's something I've got to come to terms with and start taking to heart, because with three girls in the family the odds are, one of us is going to have to deal with this. Every New Year's, I say this is the year I'm going to start, but then the fear kicks in. I'm not ready to find something. I can't cope, so I don't.

Avoidance becomes a high-risk behavior when it prevents a woman from obtaining adequate care. When the mother evaded or eluded medical care, a daughter's avoidance also can be an attempt to identify with her mother. I won't say motherless women consciously want to die; I don't know one who truly hopes for a life-threatening disease. But I have met daughters who long for a connection, any connection, with the mothers they lost during childhood or their teens. For example, a woman whose obese mother died of heart failure may, years later, gain enough weight to put a dangerous strain on her own heart. Or a woman whose mother committed suicide may refuse to get therapeutic help for her bouts of depression.

Twenty-two-year-old Stacey, who lost her mother to AIDS three years ago, says she's terrified of dying from the disease yet took few steps to protect herself from it after her mother died. She's been tested for the virus several times and has always received negative results. "But the scary part about it is that losing a mother to AIDS didn't make me a self-proclaimed, rejuvenated virgin, or even make me more discriminate about men," she says. "In fact, after she died, I even went through a very promiscuous period. I still had that part of me that needed to feel loved, and I needed to escape, so I did it through men. I didn't even feel present during those sexual encounters, but for some reason it felt necessary for me to do it as a way to hurt myself. It was weird, because I would almost wish the disease upon myself so that I could feel the pain my mother felt. At the time I felt, and sometimes I still do, that I deserve to feel the same pain, because it's not fair that she had to go through it alone."

Stacey's mother contracted the AIDS virus through heterosexual sex, and her daughter felt compelled to take the same chance, over and over. In a similar interplay of identification and risk, Sheila says her drug and alcohol use during high school and college kept her feeling close to her mother, who drank heavily when she was the same age. "I had my first drink at fifteen, which is how old my mother was when she had hers," she recalls. "I was using her same coping skills for escape. My aunt even pointed out to me that I was drinking gin, just as my mother had." Only when she began differentiating from her mother in her midtwenties and mourned her loss for the first time could Sheila leave her self-destructive behaviors—and her expectation of premature death—behind.

> After I'd finished college, worked for a while, and started to get some recognition for it, my ego started to get strengthened. I really started dealing with grief for my mother and anger toward my dad. When I started to face up to the emotions I'd spent so much energy on keeping at bay, when I stopped having to hold them back, I was eventually able to start looking at who *I* was as an individual, and not just as my mother's daughter.
>
> I don't take excessive precautions anymore, or take the same kind of chances I used to. I've kind of pulled it in at both ends. I don't necessarily always bring an umbrella, but I'm more tuned in to what would be painful, what might be difficult for me, and so I look out for that. Because I'm not afraid of every-

thing, I can see where there might be actual danger points. I'm learning to trust my feelings about what's safe for me, emotionally and physically. I just moved into a new building where I don't have to kick crack vials away from my door anymore. I can listen to being scared but also live in a city and not be afraid that everything bad I see on the news is going to happen to me.

By separating from her mother while still honoring her importance, Sheila actively engaged in what Naomi Lowinsky calls "attending to the ghost." "When we don't have enough of a relationship with the ghosts, they come get us," Dr. Lowinsky explains. "Once you can develop and maintain some kind of relationship with the lost mother, your fears can become more realistic. You can sort out what was your mother's fate and what's your own, and realize that we all have fates that are out of our control. In this culture, we often act as though if we jog every day, go to the doctor, and eat right, we're not going to have a fate. Well, terrible things happen all the time in everybody's life, and it's not because you didn't eat right.

"I think a lot of motherless daughters tend to place all the responsibility for their fates on their mothers," she continues. "It almost clears them of the burden. All a daughter has to do is worry about not getting cancer when she turns the age her mother was, or not commit suicide at the age her mother did. It's important to understand that your mother had her fate and you have yours, that yours is going to have all kinds of things in it, and a lot of them aren't going to be things you signed up for." Until a woman separates what's fear from what's fact, she remains captive to the belief that her mother's destiny will double as hers.

The first time I met Rochelle, I was immediately attracted to her energy. Her leather pumps clicked quickly across the wooden floor as she approached me with her arms raised, rushing to kiss me hello the first time I walked through her front door. Petite and slender, she darted from room to room, tossing deep laughs toward the ceilings, her long, curly hair framing her face in a chic halo of disarray. At fifty-three, she was just about the age my mother would have been. But she was younger, much younger, than I imagined my mother would be. If she hadn't told me, I never—and I mean never—would have guessed that Rochelle survived two separate cancers, one in her colon and the other in her breast.

You see, I never imagine cancer as a disease you can survive. (Never mind that my maternal aunt is alive and thriving eighteen years after her diagnosis. Never mind that one of my friends underwent a double mastectomy and reconstruction in her early forties, and three years later is doing fine. My mother's death skewed my illness paradigm so dramatically that I automatically equate the threat of cancer with the inevitability of death. I realize this when I speak with female friends whose mothers had mastectomies ten or twenty years ago and today still join their husbands for weekend rounds of golf. Their daughters have some concern about breast cancer, but fear doesn't dictate their days. They view illness through the eyes of survivors. "Sure, I take precautions," my friend Cindy says. "But if I get it, I get it. And if it happens, what would I do? Probably the same thing as my mother—have the surgery, do a few months of preventative chemotherapy, and get on with my life."

Mothers teach us how to cope with illness, both through modeling and suggestion. "One of the things we learn from mothers when they're sick is how to be sick," Dr. Milburn explains. "They teach us how to think about our bodies and about physical symptoms. A lot of women come from families that focus on physical symptoms as a sort of style. And lots of daughters whose mothers died young become highly attuned to any physical changes in their bodies. Whereas somebody who didn't already have a set of beliefs about her potential for illness or early death might ignore a particular physical symptom, a motherless daughter may not be able to ignore it. I try to give women insight into their health behaviors, which gives them a chance to make choices about changing them. We begin with, 'What did you learn about illness from your mother? How did she think about it?' and try to interpret a daughter's beliefs from there."

"If it happens," Cindy said, "what'll I do? Probably the same thing as my mother." For me to affirm the same would mean to say I would, among other things, die at forty-two. Which I most emphatically don't want to do. So I've been looking for other models now, women who, unlike my mother, caught their cancer in time.

Rochelle, whose pragmatic outlook seems the perfect antithesis to my hypochondriachal fears, says that before her diagnosis she viewed cancer very much as I do. She was twenty-three when her mother died of lung cancer that had spread to her brain and bones, and after seeing her mother undergo four years of grueling chemotherapy in the 1960s, Rochelle left the funeral convinced she was already heading down her mother's path. "I always knew I'd get cancer, but it was 'later on,'" she says. "That's why I had a catastrophic health-care policy. My mother was sixty, and I thought it would be like that. Later. All of my mother's relatives also had cancer, so I assumed it was going to come along for me. But I didn't assume it would come when I was forty-nine." Twenty-six years after her mother's death, that first cancer diagnosis inspired Rochelle to separate from her mother by making choices of her own.

> I can't tell you to this day how I got home from the doctor's office when I found out I had colon cancer. I don't know if I walked, took a bus, or a cab, or a bus and a cab. To me, my life was over. I was certain I would end up like my mother, which I always said I would never do. So the first thing I did was sign a living will. I made about twelve copies, and not only did I tape it to my bed, but I also taped it to the door of my hospital room. I handed it to everyone who walked in there. Every resident and intern got a copy. I told my doctor, "If you open me up and see the cancer is all over, I want you to just close me up." If it was all over, no one was going to make me a guinea pig like they made my mother. My fourteen-year-old daughter was not going to see me suffer and turn into a vegetable like my mother did. No how, no way.
>
> After the surgery, the doctor was so confident he made me very confident. The final biopsies were all negative, so I left very upbeat, counting my blessings, never thinking cancer could be somewhere else in my body. Then, the next year a tumor showed up inside a cyst that was removed from my breast.
>
> There is no question in my mind right now that there's cancer somewhere else in my body. The point is, they can't find it yet. My oncologist said I'll probably be one of his classic,

chronic cancer patients. My husband talks about his retirement and I look at him and think, "Mmm-hmm. I'm glad you think so, dear." I don't make plans like that. My daughter is what keeps me from crawling under the covers. I'll be good god-damned if my husband's third wife is going to raise my child. That's one thing. The second thing is that life is so interesting. Why would I want to give it up?

I tell Rochelle I can't imagine how I'd cope with cancer twice, submit myself to the monthly tests she does, and still tell the story in a tone as upbeat as hers. I've never had a model for this type of approach, and I'm not convinced such optimism is part of my natural constitution. "Where does your courage come from?" I ask her. "How do you find your strength?"

She leans forward at her desk and rests her chin on her right hand. She is serious now. Her eyes search out mine. "I don't know if it's denial or not, but I can sit here and talk about my cancer and it doesn't feel like it's me," she says. "Or at least it's not all I am today. I guess if I gave you a complete story of those fourteen months, you'd wonder how I was still walking. But I honestly do not dwell on it. The only time I think about it is when I find a breast lump, which I periodically do, and they're basically cysts. But that's it. Depression is just not in my makeup. Right now, as long as I'm feeling well and I'm healthy, I'm going to go on with the rest of my life."

I went alone into the hospital room ten minutes after my mother died. I thought I should say a proper goodbye. I was afraid to press my lips against her forehead, so I kissed my fingers and brushed them against her cheek. It was still warm. My mother believed in heaven, but not hell; she told me once that no sin on earth could be so unforgivable to separate a person from God. If there is such a thing as a soul, I have to believe hers had already taken off for that other place. Her body no longer contained any trace of life. It just looked like a shell to me.

Death loses its romanticism when you're introduced to it so young. It's no longer the portentous visitor who rides in on the dark to carry loved ones away. It becomes hard and factual, an event instead of an abstraction. Margie, now twenty-five, learned this at the age of seven when her mother committed suicide. "When someone you love dies, death loses its unreality," she says. "To me, it's real. It's just as real as taking a shit. I never attempted suicide, but death never felt like an extreme I wouldn't contemplate. It didn't seem that bizarre to me. It was just another option, an alternative to life. I figured that if my mother could do it, I could, too."

Children who've been traumatized by death are robbed of its beauty and mystery, Andrea Campbell explains. Death is more an abrupt disruption than a cycle of completion and rebirth to the daughter who sees it happen to her mother during childhood or her teens, and she loses her psychic connection to the natural feminine cycle that gives structure to a woman's life. "The female experience is one of being a cocreator and partaking in the mystery of life," Dr. Campbell says. "That also means partaking in the mystery of death, and seeing it as a transition and a birth into another place. The young woman is the cocreator who brings forth life, and the crone is her initiator into death. And that passing of the wisdom should take place when a mother is in her cronehood, not her thirties or forties."

The real tragedy of my mother's life is not that it ended, but that it ended so soon. Most of us who've lost our mothers are less afraid of dying than we are of dying *young*. This is the fear of the maiden, not the crone. It's the reason why the motherless daughters who were most likely to report that they think about their mortality either all of the time or most of the time are the ones currently between the ages of eighteen and thirty-nine.

As I sit here writing, I am forty-one years old. I am the daughter of a woman whose cancer started growing when she was in her thirties, a mother of three who died absurdly young. I am also the mother of two daughters who are far too young to lose me. It does not escape me that I am the same age my mother was when her cancer was discovered. I think about it almost every day. I'm on a rigorous six-month screening schedule now, a mammogram every February and an ultrasound in the fall. The radiologist doesn't need to send me little postcard reminders in the mail. I never forget. The gynecologist also checks me by hand every spring. It's overkill, some physicians have told me. It doesn't hurt to be cautious when you're at high risk, others have said. I don't listen to anything but my own intuition any more. As long as screening doesn't hurt me, I say, bring it on. I can never be too sure.

The high-risk label is an identification with my mother that I'd rather not have. But it's been my front for differentiation, too. My mother had her first mammogram when she was forty-one, the one that found her lump. The only mammograms I've missed in fifteen years were when I was pregnant or breastfeeding. I eat an extremely low-fat diet. I practice yoga. I take fifteen supplements a day. Preventive medicine and early detection aren't guarantees of anything, I know, but they're the best I've got.

"Everyone who is born holds dual citizenship, in the kingdom of the well and in the kingdom of the sick," the author Susan Sontag writes in *Illness as Metaphor*. "Although we all prefer to use only the good passport, sooner or later each of us is obliged, at least for a spell, to identify ourselves as citizens of that other place." My mother's illness gave me a temporary visa to that second kingdom, and I've spent as much time there as I wish. But should a lump ever appear that confirms my worst fear, or should I wake up one morning with any other disease that requires me to visit that place again, I would like to believe the choices that guide me through will be mine, and not ones dictated by my mother's past. Like my mother and so many other women in her position, I hope I too would commit myself to "getting back to life." But I also hope that—in sickness or in health—I can make the decisions my mother never made, the ones that might have saved her life. The best way I can separate my fate from my mother's is to survive.

Chapter Eleven

The Daughter Becomes a Mother
Extending the Line

I WAS CERTAIN during my first pregnancy that I was carrying a boy. There was no logical reason for me to think this. I just knew I was having a son.

A son. It was a strange yet wonderful idea. He would wear those cute little denim overalls and grow up to play shortstop in Little League. I would be one of those mothers who sat on the sidelines in blue folding lawn chairs, coolers of orange Gatorade handy, jumping up to cheer uninhibitedly every time he got a hit.

I loved the way it sounded, the measured balance of both words. *My son.*

My certainty about his gender was so unshakable that when, during my twenty-second week of pregnancy, the ultrasound radiologist announced that the image on the screen was female, I couldn't find a way to make the news fit.

"It's not a *boy*?" I asked, incredulous, lifting myself up onto my elbows for a better look. "But I'm *sure* it's a boy." I looked over at my husband, who—ever trusting in my powers of prophecy—looked equally as confused as I. "It's a *girl*?" I said. "That's not possible."

The doctor swung the screen toward us and pointed at two small, parallel white lines hovering near the bottom. "Those look like labia to me," she said.

"You're *sure* it's not a boy?" I asked.

She tried to contain her smile as she typed into the ultrasound keyboard. "You'd better hope it's not a boy," she said, "or he's going to have some real problems."

A daughter. The image of that blue lawn chair dissolved into the fluorescent lights above me. It was replaced by the sound of a wooden bat cracking against a softball, then dully hitting the ground as a pair of flowered high-tops dug into the packed dirt and headed toward first base.

That's when I started to cry. Because only then did I understand how much I'd wanted a daughter, and how the fantasy son I'd created had been a protection for myself against the disappointment of not getting a girl.

Over the next four months, I waged an endless battle between exhilaration and self-doubt. *How will I know how to mother a daughter if I haven't been mothered in so long?* I wondered. *Relax,* I would tell myself. *How hard can it be?* And then I'd start worrying, *Who will help me after the baby comes?* My cousin volunteered to come from Australia for two weeks; that helped me stay calm. But I was still left with the big concern: What if I die young and have to leave a child, as my mother left me? From the moment I first learned I was pregnant that thought has surrounded me like a constant background hum.

My daughter arrived in 1997, followed four years later by her sister. Now my weeks are ripe with the details and items of little-girl life: fairy princess costumes, Rapunzel puzzles, pink body glitter and butterfly barrettes, and every form of Hello Kitty paraphernalia imaginable. Five hours per day, five days per week I'm a writer and a teacher. The rest of the time I'm a confidante, cheerleader, referee, cook, personal shopper, and chauffeur to two very short, noisy people who bear a not-so-coincidental resemblance to my sister and myself more than thirty years ago.

I once read somewhere that having a child is akin to having your blood circulate outside your own body. Sometimes I feel that it's more than my blood they have: It's fragments of my being, my essence, my very soul. And because of this, I have to keep reminding myself that my daughters are separate entities from me, that they're individuals in their own rights, and not merely younger versions of myself. The temptation to mother them as I wish I'd been mothered, and to heal the child within me by doing so, is ever present. Parenting often doubles as self-parenting when a mother still longs to be mothered. Every day, I have to work hard to keep the distinctions clear.

This phenomenon isn't as problematic as it might sound. Every new mother naturally identifies with her child to some degree. While remaining adult and in the present, she simultaneously regresses psychologically to an earlier infant state which, according to the psychoanalyst Nancy Chodorow, activates her earliest memories with a mother or mother-figure. When her baby smiles or cries, she then has an intuitive idea why and senses the appropriate response.

At the same time, a new mother also identifies with her mother—or the mother she wishes she'd had—as she holds, feeds, and nurtures her baby. Our earliest memories of nursery care remain imprinted on our psyches, and we refer to them as models for our own maternal actions. In this manner, a woman unconsciously repeats the caregiving behaviors she received as a child, unless she has previously recognized them as harmful and taken conscious steps to change them in some way.

Every daughter splits her identifications between her mother and her child-self to form a third image of herself as a parent. The motherless daughter's challenge is to resist *overidentifying* in either direction. As the psychiatrists Sol Altschul and Helen Beiser observed in their clients at the Barr-Harris Center in Chicago, women who suffer the early loss of a mother often become mothers who have confused identifications with their lost parent and their child, particularly with their daughters. A motherless woman who looks at her child and sees only herself projects an unnatural identity onto that child and may overprotect or smother in an attempt to repair herself. At the other extreme, the motherless woman who identifies strongly with her mother will fear dying young and may either emotionally detach from her children or avoid having them at all.

Therese Rando counsels women to help them find a comfortable balance. "Identification can be healthy, as long as it's appropriate to other things you're doing and congruent with other roles you need to maintain," says Dr. Rando. When a motherless daughter becomes a mother, she may need to build a new relationship with the mother she lost. "Her mother can still be seen as somebody who protected her as a child," Dr. Rando explains, "but not as someone who's protecting her now. These distinctions might not sound like much, but they're profound. As a therapist, I have to say, 'Your mother was like that once, but she's not anymore.' I don't try to take the previous identification away, or say, 'You have to let it go,' but I try to find a way to work it in to a woman's adult life and find a new, internal relationship with her mother that's appropriate for her now. When my baby was born, and the nurse first brought her to me a few hours later, the very first thing I did was sing her a song my mother always sang to me. It was a beautiful connection to my mother. I feel even closer to my mother now, being a mother myself."

Fear and Desire

A motherless daughter's concern that she might leave a child motherless is often matched by an equally powerful drive to give a son or daughter the childhood—with the mother—she never had. Fear and desire are silent partners in the mother dance. It's no surprise that the most common sentiment among the sixty-five motherless women ages eighteen to forty-five in my survey who don't have children is, "I want to have a child one day, but I'm afraid." Afraid of contracting a mother's disease, afraid of knowing too little about childbirth or child rearing, afraid of never being as good a mother—or of being just as bad—as the one who died.

Half of all motherless women surveyed said they either fear or once feared having children. These are women like twenty-seven-year-old Paula, who was fifteen when her mother died of a rare blood disease. When Paula, who's African American, first met her husband, who's Caucasian, the couple spent long afternoons naming future children. After marrying, however, they decided against raising an interracial child in the current social climate. Making this intellectual choice secretly relieved Paula, who says her real reason for avoiding pregnancy is much more emotionally charged:

I've always had two fears. One is that I'll fall down the stairs backwards and break my back. I don't know why, but I've just always been afraid of that. The other is of dying during child-birth or soon after and leaving my husband to raise a baby. I go through this every now and then, thinking that I don't want to leave him, and he's not a U.S. citizen, and how could I do that? I keep having thoughts of having a child and then not being there, or of dying before my husband does and leaving a child mother-less, and repeating the cycle all over again. When I sit down and think about it, I think, "What an irrational fear." But who's to know? Who's to know what will happen?

Paula's anxiety about dying young comes from both her per-ceived vulnerability as a motherless daughter and from an overiden-tification with her mother. Her fear that an event as random as her mother's disease could take her from her own child monopolizes her vision of motherhood. She's put childbearing on hold, even though she admits she still longs for the type of mother-child connection she lost.

Forty-three-year-old Darlene, on the other hand, endured three unsuccessful surgeries for endometriosis in her determined quest to have a baby. She was heartbroken each time she thought about re-maining childless. "I had such a feeling of hopelessness and empti-ness," recalls Darlene, who was ten when her mother died. "I hadn't had my mother in so long, and then I couldn't be one. I so badly wanted to give something back to someone else." When she and her husband adopted a baby boy, "the emptiness went away that very day," she says. "I didn't think I'd ever have a child, but with the adoption, all my dreams fell into place."

Watching one life end can inspire the powerful urge to nurture another—especially when a birth or adoption can create a bond similar to the one lost. As the psychotherapist Selma Fraiberg has observed, "The largest number of men and women who have known suffering find renewal and the healing of childhood pain in the experience of bringing a child into the world. In the simplest terms—we have heard it often from parents—the parent says, 'I want something better for my child than I have had.' And [she] brings something better to [her] child." For the motherless daughter, this means giving a child a stable, loving home with a mother who lives long into that child's adulthood.

Motherless daughters often say they feel whole again when they have a child of their own. They say the type of intimacy they lost when their first mother-child bond broke returns when they reenter the relationship from the other side. And they say becoming a mother allows them to reconnect with their mothers, and in doing so regain a small part of the original mother-daughter relationship.

Motherhood provided Mitzi, now fifty-seven, with the satisfaction of giving her daughters some very specific elements of the mother-daughter relationship that she lost at the age of twenty when her mother died.

> I don't know much about my parents' relationship, or my mother's opinions about this or that. So I've always encouraged my daughters to feel free to ask me questions. If they want to understand why their father and I broke up or how I feel about anything, I believe it's important for them to have that resource. And I want to be that resource, because it's been very frustrating for me not to have that access. I also miss knowing how my mother felt about me, because I know how strongly I feel about my daughters. I mean, they're human and they have their faults and their weaknesses, but I'm very proud of them and I would like to have known if my mother was proud of me. That information, I think, would have helped me understand more about myself and to know what influenced me.

Motherhood allowed Mitzi to reenter the mother-daughter dyad as a mature, experienced participant with the insight to raise daughters who knew more about their mother than she knew about hers. Because Mitzi believes her identity formation suffered from her mother's absence, she consciously took steps to aid her daughters' processes.

Ideally, a motherless mother remains in the position of parent—and, as Mitzi did, allows her child to be the child. But if the mother suffered a deprivation of parental love during childhood or adolescence that left her with an exaggerated need for love as an adult, she may expect her child to provide it, especially if her husband or partner is emotionally unavailable to her.

When a woman bears a child to fill the empty space within herself, this "fulfillment baby" never has a shot at an identity of his or her own. The mother reads each of the child's attempts to individuate as a betrayal, and each act of resistance as a threat to the secure base she spent nine months creating for herself. Fearing that the child will abandon her as her mother once did, she may try to exercise excessive control to suppress the child's emerging autonomy. The child then grows up anxious, guilty, and phobic or, at very best, resentful toward the mother.

"If a woman loses her mother very young and never mourns the loss, she often unconsciously tries to regain the closeness to her mother through the baby," explains Phyllis Klaus. "When she has this extreme, nonaware aspect to her mothering, she can become an over-enmeshed mother, trying to get all the love and nurturing from the baby that she never got. And that's not a good use of the baby. You don't have a baby in order to give it what you didn't get; you have a baby so you can fully give to it what it needs to grow."

The key phrase here is "never mourns the loss." Women who lose a loved one prematurely and never reconcile their feelings of loneliness or abandonment may go on to form problematic attachments with their children. When Mary Ainsworth and her associates at the University of Virginia studied infant-mother attachment behaviors among thirty mothers who'd lost an attachment figure during childhood or adolescence, they found that *100 percent* of the mothers whose mourning was judged as "unresolved"[1] had children who seemed anxious and disorganized. Instead of seeking comfort from their mothers, these children acted as if the mothers were a source of stress. In comparison, only 10 percent of mothers whose mourning was judged "resolved" and 20 percent of mothers in a control group that had experienced no loss had children with similar attachment problems. From these findings, the researchers concluded

---

[1] The researchers defined *resolved*, a term I prefer to avoid, by the subjects' scores on the Lack of Resolution of Mourning Scale, which is based on John Bowlby's discussion of normal and pathological grief. Researchers also took into account a mother's behavioral response at the time of loss, as well as her adult preoccupation with thoughts of early attachments.

that it is a mother's *unresolved* early loss—and not early loss per se—that leads to troubled attachments with her own child.

Andrea Campbell, who was ten when her mother died and twelve when her father committed suicide, never felt safe or secure enough as an adolescent to mourn. She married and gave birth while in her teens. "I had a daughter, and that daughter was so precious to me," she explains. "Somehow I had my mother back by being a mother, and by giving my daughter that love. But I was really trying to heal myself, and when we unconsciously try to heal ourselves through another person, we instead inflict our wounds on that person. So even though I was a loving mother and I could give love because I'd been well nurtured for my first ten years, my deprivation still wounded my daughter." After she mourned her mother as an adult, Dr. Campbell was better able to see how she'd viewed her daughter as a replacement figure, and the two have worked together since to change and heal their relationship.

Gender Matters

"I don't care what sex my baby is, as long as it's healthy," nearly every pregnant woman says. It's the maternally correct response, and it's also usually true. But as Dr. Campbell acknowledges, a same-sex child offers a parent an additional vicarious potential that an opposite-sex child can't, and in confidence, many motherless women will reveal their secret desires to give birth to girls. Three-quarters of the women interviewed for the book *Motherless Mothers* admitted they'd hoped for a daughter during their first pregnancies, usually because they saw this as a way to resurrect the mother-daughter relationship they'd lost. Others wanted to name a daughter for their mothers, or were hopeful a girl would physically resemble her and, in some small way, bring the mother back to life.

"I'll be honest with you," says thirty-four-year-old Cecilia, who was twenty when her mother died and is now trying to get pregnant for the first time. "I want to have a daughter for that reason. I mean, I want to have any baby, a boy or a girl, but I told my husband, 'We'll keep trying for a daughter.' Like if we had two boys, I would still want to keep trying for a girl. When you're trying to get pregnant there's this taboo that you shouldn't say such things, but it's how I truly feel."

A small, yet notable, minority of motherless daughters say they want a son, often because they're worried they don't have the emotional tools or the mother-daughter experience they need to raise a girl. "I was filled with dread by the thought of having a daughter," admits fifty-one-year-old Adele, whose mother was institutionalized for Adele's entire childhood and died when Adele was twenty. "I can't relate to girls. I relate more to men. And we wanted a son anyway, but when we found out we were having a boy I was very relieved. If I'd had a daughter, I don't know what I would have done."

Shari Lusskin, M.D., the director of reproductive psychiatry at New York University School of Medicine, advises that women who have a strong preference for either gender do prenatal testing to find out their baby's gender in advance. "I saw a woman in my office the other day who's four months pregnant and said to me, 'You know, I really want a girl. So I don't want to find out the sex, because if it's a boy I'm just going to be disappointed,'" Lusskin recalls. "I said to her, 'Find out the sex. Please. Because then we have five months to get over any disappointment.' It doesn't get better in the delivery room."

To the woman who feels deprived of mother love, a daughter offers the most direct route to maternal reconnection. If, as Carl Jung proposed, every woman extends backward into her mother and forward into her daughter, then giving birth to a daughter ensures the immortality of her female line. A baby girl in the nursery also brings a woman's lost mother back into the room. And because daughters are typically socialized as society's nurturers, a mother sees in her daughter the potential to enjoy a close, empathetic female relationship again.

As close as the mother-son bond may be, a son is less likely than a daughter to become the object of his mother's self-projections. Mothers tend to view daughters as continuous with themselves and their sons as male opposites. Physiologically, a son is an imperfect mirror. He reflects back body parts his mother doesn't possess, and can never represent a complete, gendered extension of her self. Socially, he moves through lands in which his mother has traditionally lacked power—street games, fraternities, war. "The amazement of sons is that they are of us, such intimates, and yet so other," explains Naomi Lowinsky, who has one son and two daughters. For exactly this reason, a son can offer his motherless mother the opportunity for unexpected and extraordinary personal growth.

Annie: Moving Beyond the Mother

Annie leans back in her eleventh-floor office, her feet propped on a nearby chair. Her hands rest gently on her abdomen, poised to feel her first child's impatient kicks. At thirty-seven, she has all she always hoped for: a successful career, a happy marriage, and a baby on the way. The baby part is important. Ever since she lost her mother to cancer when she was eight, Annie has been waiting to re-experience the mother-daughter bond.

There's only one small hitch: Annie is going to have a son.

A *son*? That's what she thought when she first heard the news. "It had never occurred to me that having a child was not synonymous with having a daughter," she says. "I was so shocked at this little person being a boy. It was like a punch in the stomach. It really was. When I got the amnio results, I wanted to say, 'What do you mean it's a boy? There must be some mistake.' Over the next few days, I really felt cheated. I felt robbed. My huge, sustaining fantasy had been taken away from me."

You see, for twenty-nine years Annie had been planning to re-create her childhood and give it the happy ending it deserved. As an only child, she had endured terrible loneliness after her mother's death and had comforted herself with the fierce resolution to one day share with a daughter all that her mother had once shared with her—going to art classes, listening to music, reading, watching thunderstorms from the terrace—and then continue their relationship forward. When Annie and her husband decided to have only one child, she grew doubly determined to become the idealized mother she imagined her mother would have been. The script was already written, and Annie knew her part. All she needed was the little girl who would play her as a child.

The amniocentesis results, Annie says, quickly destroyed her fantasy of a perfect reunion. But knowing the child inside her is a boy has guided her toward a more realistic vision of motherhood, she says. "The first thing that happened was that I got terrified, because I realized the responsibility of motherhood," she recalls. "It was no longer a fairy tale. It became very present tense. I thought, 'Oh, my God. This person is going to be Other.' I don't know that I would have let a daughter become separate from me. Because that girl was me. She was supposed to react exactly the way I reacted to everything. If she had come out a tomboy hating to read, I would have been so lost. I would have felt so betrayed."

Instead of rewriting her childhood, Annie decided to rewrite her script for motherhood. She began by listing her prejudices about boys—*they're aggressive, they're uncommunicative, they're little things with sticks who hit people*—and worked to overcome them. She spoke with mothers of boys who told her how much sons love their mothers. And she reconsidered the activities she'd once imagined sharing with a daughter—going to art classes, listening to music, reading, watching thunderstorms from the terrace—and realized she could just as easily share them with a son.

"The real reason I wanted a daughter was to create the insulated cocoon I still crave, that place where you belong uniquely," she says. "What I didn't realize was that a son could occupy that place, too." She and her husband recently chose a name for the child, who she says is becoming more real to her every day. "I feel like there's such a fresh start with this baby boy," she explains. "Instead of looking at what I'm losing, which is the fallacious opportunity to complete my life, I can look at what I've got, which is an opportunity to be a mother."

At the same time that Annie identifies with her mother by becoming a mother, she is separating from her, too. Annie is an only child because her mother found a malignant breast lump during pregnancy and had to postpone treatment until after the birth. When Annie was born, her mother was told she had only six months to live. Even though she survived for another eight years, she died at the age of thirty-four, and the message Annie internalized was that pregnancy equals early death.

The joy of completing her first trimester inevitably intermingled with that fear. "But at a certain point," Annie says, "I made a very conscious choice not to be afraid. I'm going to be pregnant once, and I want to enjoy it. To do that meant having to give up that negative association and attachment to my mother. I've passed the point in pregnancy when my mother was diagnosed, and I was okay with it.

"My husband was shocked last weekend when I told him I wanted to go to my mother's grave," she continues. "I want to go there pregnant with this child and say, 'I'm not doomed to what happened to you.' Because her death was synonymous with my birth, this is even more powerful than passing her age. This is passing her death sentence."

Her healthy pregnancy and her revised vision of motherhood have helped Annie mourn another piece of her loss. By letting go of both the fantasy and the fear of repeating her mother's history, she is coming closer to accepting the finality of her mother's death. "For the first time, my past is really different from my mother's," Annie explains. "She had a daughter. I am having a son. It's such a huge difference. This is the first time in my life I really feel like I'm moving beyond my mother. And I feel a tremendous sense of freedom."

Pregnancy and Birth

"In the middle of my first pregnancy, I panicked because I felt that I didn't have a support system," says Bridget, thirty-six, who had her first child three years ago. "I didn't like the doctor I was going to, so I found a midwife. She was in her sixties and very maternal. She was wonderful. But then when my son was born, it was as if my mother had died the year before. The loss felt fresh again. And it blew me away. It totally blew me away."

During pregnancy and childbirth, as the generational cycle prepares to begin again, the biological mother looms large in the consciousness of the mother-to-be. A husband can offer emotional support and a father a sense of family, but birthing is the business of women. How many men know the specific irregularities of a mother's menstrual cycle, the duration of her labor, or the kind of painkillers she received? This is the verbal legacy that passes from mother to daughter, and which daughters rely on for comparison and guidance. When the mother-daughter relationship is going well, the daughter depends on her mother to help her build self-confidence, asking for stories about her birth and early childhood and seeking encouragement that she can handle motherhood's demands.

Mothers-in-law, older sisters, aunts, and close friends can help fill this void in a motherless woman's life. But a pregnant woman without a strong maternal substitute, and especially one who hasn't mourned her mother, often feels isolated and adrift. Pregnancy ranks high among the worst times in a woman's life for her to feel alone. It's a natural time of dependency—even the most independent woman can't always manage the emotional and physical demands by herself—and an expectant mother has a strong need for security and support.

"Even women who have terribly difficult relationships with their mothers and have mixed feelings about their mothers being present still want them around when the baby is born," Naomi Lowinsky says. "You're so opened up by pregnancy and birth. It's a transformative experience, and it leaves you in pieces. A woman really needs to have a sense of mother at that time."

Pregnancy and the postpartum period can be bittersweet times for the motherless daughter, who feels closer to her mother as she becomes one but also feels an intense sadness as she confronts her loss again. As a milestone event in a woman's life, childbirth—particularly with a first child—commonly triggers a new cycle of mourning for the lost mother, involving intense feelings of grief, sadness, anger, or despair. The woman mourns not only the loss of her mother's advice and support but also the loss of a grandmother for her child. As a mother-to-be, she also looks at her mother through the eyes of a prospective mother. When she sees her as a woman with children, a woman *very much like the woman she will soon be,* she can understand more fully what her mother lost. Instead of mourning exclusively as a daughter, she mourns as a mother as well.

For some motherless mothers, the birth of a first child unlocks blocked mourning and eases a woman toward a fuller acceptance of her loss. When Nancy Maguire, Ph.D., studied forty first-time mothers, twenty of whom had lost their mothers between the ages of six and twelve, she found that many of them experienced grief, depression, and parenting stress during the transition to motherhood. "A lot of women felt this was a good time for them to go into therapy," she says, "because they were confronted with issues about loss and mourning. And it was an opportunity for them to overcome some of the issues around loss that might interfere with their relationship with their child, and to feel that they could become a better parent because of it."

When a woman hasn't grieved her loss before pregnancy, she needs the safety to release any feelings that surface during that time without being made to feel overly needy or weak. An emotionally available spouse or partner can often give her the support she needs. But because husbands and lovers also feel anxious about parenthood both partners need to communicate their fears to avoid feeling over-burdened by each other's needs.

A pregnant woman typically splits her dependency needs between her mother and her partner, whose importance as a member of her new family unit increases. A woman without an available mother or mother-figure, however, often shifts most of her needs onto her partner. Nearly every pregnant woman feels some anxiety about losing her partner and being left to parent a child alone, but this fear can become especially pronounced in a motherless woman. She knows all too well that people she loves can leave, and she remembers what happened to the last person she depended on to such a degree.

At the same time, the lack of control a pregnant woman feels over her body and the gestation process can be disorienting and difficult—especially for those who became accustomed to taking charge of their own destinies at an early age. As the sociologist Susan Maushart describes pregnancy in *The Mask of Motherhood,* "Physically, it's like taking the backseat in what used to be your own car. Someone—or is it something?—else is doing the driving. And what's more, the route, at times stunningly beautiful, at times terrifying and precipitous, is at all times unfamiliar. . . . Some women make marvelous passengers in the journey of pregnancy: They sit back and wonder and delight at the passing strangeness. For others, the anxiety of having surrendered the wheel makes joy-riding impossible."

An expectant mother's need to feel nurtured and supported peaks around the time of birth when, in the span of only minutes, she transforms from a laboring woman in need of assistance to a primary caretaker of a fully dependent infant. Even though few grand-mothers actually assist in the births of their grandchildren and many are too physically or emotionally distant to share in the postpartum period, these are nevertheless times when motherless daughters deeply miss their mothers. They mourn the loss of advice and assis-tance, and often glamorize their mothers' birthing experiences, for-getting that women of the previous generation frequently bore their children in a drug-induced "twilight sleep" while their partners paced outside in the hall.

As birthing embraces more natural techniques, researchers have begun to notice that laboring women and new mothers benefit from the presence and assistance of a nurturing, experienced woman. In their studies of 1,500 pregnant women, Phyllis Klaus and Marshall Klaus, M.D., discovered that women who were aided during child-birth by trained, female labor companions required fewer cesarean births, needed less anesthesia, had more interest in their newborns, and interacted more with their babies than women who delivered without this assistance.

The Klauses call these birthing companions *doulas,* the Greek term for an experienced woman who helps other women. A doula optimally meets with the prospective parents a few times during the third trimester of pregnancy, returns when the woman begins her la-bor, and remains with her throughout the labor and delivery. She holds the mother close when she needs physical reassurance, mas-sages her back, and helps her breathe. "She never leaves the mother alone, and that is an essential aspect of this," explains Phyllis Klaus. "She tells her, 'I will never leave your side.' Just that assurance is in-credibly powerful for the pregnant woman. If she has lost her mother, or if her own mother is unable to be involved in the birth, the doula becomes a mothering figure to her. She helps the laboring woman allow her body to work for her, so the woman can become dependent and independent at the same time. She feels both nurtured and empowered. Women have told me afterward, 'I never realized how much nurturing I needed until I had that experience. I'd put all my nurturing needs aside.' Other women have told their doulas, 'Your trust in me and your support at that time have made me realize I can do anything I want to in my life.'

"We've noticed that the mother seems to internalize the doula's nurturing behaviors," she continues. "The labor period is a time when the mother is especially sensitive to environmental factors and open to learning and growth. When she's held close in such an emotional way at this time, and feels nurtured, she becomes more able to give the same care to her child." According to the Klauses, the women who received doula support had higher self-esteem and decreased incidence of postpartum depression six weeks after delivery than mothers who delivered without this support. The mothers who had doulas felt more confident and competent when caring for their newborns and also benefited from continued visits and advice from their doulas for as long as a year and a half after the birth.

What does this mean for the motherless woman? Support, advice, and the assurance that she's not alone. Unlike the woman who feels her support system is guaranteed, the motherless woman has to create her own, and she fears its failure—and, by extension, hers as a mother—more intensely than most new mothers do. Her childhood fears of being left alone and unprovided for are reactivated at precisely the time when she needs to calm those fears in her child. And often, they're not unfounded. When asked, "Who helped you, other than a husband or spouse, after the birth of your first child?" 52 percent of motherless mothers surveyed answered, "No one." When the same question was presented to a comparison group of women with mothers still alive, only 15 percent said they'd had to manage alone. More than half of the women in that second group cited their mothers as the person who helped them with newborn care.

Is the disparity because motherless mothers truly have no one to turn to for help? Or because they've become so practiced at not asking for or expecting it? Because their needs often went unmet after their mothers died, many of these women grew up believing that "no one noticed," which may have become internalized as "no one cares."

"Women who have experienced early mother loss are more likely to be caretakers to other people in their lives," Nancy Maguire explains. "And that part of their personality style would prohibit them from being able to ask for the support they need, and to feel justified in getting their own needs met."

All new parents have periods of self-doubt, but a motherless mother often has the additional worry that if a real problem develops, she won't have anyone to call. She flips through Dr. Spock books with the frenzy of a dozen hummingbirds. She puts 911 on her speed-dial—twice.

"The bottom drops out when you bring that first baby home from the hospital and you just don't know what to do," says Alice, who has two daughters and a grandson. The presence of a supportive, experienced woman during her first postpartum period helped her find the self-confidence she needed as a new mother.

Alice: Extending the Maternal Line

In 1957, Alice was somewhat of a double anomaly: She was giving birth to her first child at the age of thirty-six, and she knew virtually nothing about babies. She hadn't worried much about the delivery, having grown up with a mother who frequently told her what a joyful experience it had been. Birthing was the easy part. Infant care was her challenge.

Dr. Spock's advice had seemed straightforward enough when she was still pregnant. But as soon as she was alone with a screaming baby in the nursery, Alice was terrified by her lack of experience. She found herself longing for advice, guidance, and reassurance from her mother, who died just before Alice turned twenty-four.

"I'd never been around a baby before, and I worried about everything," she recalls. "Should I let her cry? Pick her up? Why did she want orange juice for breakfast and milk for a snack instead of the other way around, as the book said it should be? Every book and pamphlet I had began with a description of bathing the baby, but she cried every time I tried to bathe her, and I didn't know why."

When her mother's first cousin announced she'd be paying a visit, Alice began to worry. She looked forward to seeing the woman she'd grown up calling "Aunt" Elaine, but she was afraid an experienced mother would label her clumsy and inept. Necessity quickly overtook Alice's pride, however, and when Elaine arrived, Alice shared her self-doubt and fears. Instead of affirming her incompetence, the older woman provided her with a much-needed infusion of relief.

"Elaine was wonderful," Alice recalls. "She'd go and get the baby when she cried and sit holding her, gently rocking her and murmuring, 'You win!' When I confessed my problems with the bath she said, 'Well, she's not really very dirty. Why don't you just use oil for now?'

"I told her how grateful I was, and she told me about her experience with her first baby. 'Everyone criticized me,' she said. 'I was so busy that the house was a mess. Every time I sat down I saw the clutter and the dust balls under the furniture. And then your grandmother came over one day. She was not in the least critical. She said I was doing fine. Instead of standing there asking how she could help, she just went and got a mop. I'll always remember that.'"

Just three days with a practical, nurturing, and experienced model for infant care helped calm Alice's fears. Equally as important, Elaine's visit helped her reconnect with her maternal line. Elaine and Alice's mothers had raised their children side by side, and Alice's grandmother had been their resource for advice and reassurance. "Having Elaine in my house reestablished the feeling of continuity in my life," Alice explains. "I had that feeling of being back in the family, and that everything would be all right."

In 1962, Alice gave birth again. She felt confident with the rudiments of childcare this time, yet she found herself missing her mother again. "My second daughter was a difficult child to bring up," she explains. "And so was I. I really would have appreciated hearing my mother tell me I was doing okay, and assure me that my daughter would turn out all right." Today, Alice smiles when she tells this part of her story. Not only did her second daughter grow up without major incident, but she also became a mother herself four years ago, and Alice was right there coaching in the birthing room as her grandson entered the world.

Just as Alice's mother had told her daughter about the joy of childbirth, Alice told her daughter the same. Of all the women in her Lamaze class, Alice's daughter was the only one who said she didn't fear the pain. Her primary fear—just like her mother's—was of bringing the baby home and not knowing how to care for it alone. This time Alice knew exactly what to do. "I kept telling my daughter, 'You'll be okay,'" she says. "I assured her she'd have help." And she did—from her mother. Alice took great pride in giving her daughter the immediate maternal encouragement, assistance, and advice that had once taken several anxious months to reach her.

Raising Children

"I read every book there was on how to raise children," remembers Sarah, who lost her mother at the age of one and went on to have two children. "I searched high and wide, because my daughter and I were having problems when she was young, and I couldn't find anything on first daughters or firstborns. I had no model at all. But there were things I figured out based on common sense. I believed that we had to take responsibility for ourselves, and that there was such a thing as consequences, good and bad. And I didn't believe in punishing, because I was never punished. My kids used to say, 'Please shut up already and hit us,' because I talked them to death, rationalizing everything. I think that was the way I finally accepted my mother's death, by figuring out how to raise my children by myself."

Although many motherless women spent childhood and adolescence watching their mothers raise their younger siblings, or even raising those siblings after her death, they still feel the loss of a living mother-model. Many of them say they learned how to parent on their own. Yet as individual as their approaches have been, studies with motherless mothers reveal they share common challenges, triumphs, and fears.

In the early 1990s, Donald Zall, D.S.W., a psychotherapist in Concord, Massachussetts, studied twenty-eight middle-class mothers whose own mothers had died when they were children or adolescents, and who now had at least one child between the ages of six months and fifteen years. Zall identified six distinct parenting traits the women shared. These were an overprotective parenting style; an increased determination to be a good mother; an emphasis on cherishing time with their children; a belief in the fragility of life; a fixation on the possibility that they, too, could die; and the impulse to prepare their children for a premature separation.

"The bereaved women saw the impact of their mother's death burdening them with anxieties with which other mothers did not have to deal but which also provided them with an impetus to 'be the best that they could be,'" he explains.

Zall, as well as other researchers, found that motherless mothers report higher levels of stress, sadness, and depression than other mothers do. They also think of themselves as less competent in the mothering role than other women, are more preoccupied with their roles as mothers, are more focused on how well they're doing, and, not surprisingly, frequently report they "feel different" from other mothers.

Nonetheless, many of these studies found that the process of parenting—despite the deficits, real or perceived, in these women's backgrounds—deepened and enriched their mourning processes. Raising children, and giving them emotionally engaged, involved, and loving mothers went far to undo much of the pain of the past. And this focus and determination on good parenting seems to have a positive effect on children, as well. Despite motherless mothers' self-doubt and uncertainty about filling the maternal role, their children appear just as well-adjusted as children raised by women whose mothers did not die. As Gina Mireault, Ph.D., the author of a 2002 study on this subject explains, the women she interviewed "were kind of hard on themselves [as mothers], but they seemed to be doing the good job they were afraid they *weren't* doing."

Interviews with motherless mothers also revealed the following shared parenting experiences:

The Mother on the Pedestal

When a daughter believes she was well mothered, she often tries to replicate specific parenting behaviors she remembers from her past. This allows her to identify positively with her mother, as well as to relive and perpetuate happy moments of her childhood. For many women, particularly those who've mourned their mothers, this approach can be both successful and fulfilling.

Daughters who have idealized the lost mother, however, create a standard for parenting that is difficult, and occasionally impossible, for them to achieve. When comparing themselves to the idealized Good Mother, these daughters often interpret their own "shortcomings" as evidence that they're Bad Mothers. But mothers are perfect only in our minds. Trying to replicate their approaches exactly, without acknowledging their deficits, is often a daughter's attempt to honor her mother after death, and she frequently overlooks the circumstances that make her experience as a mother unique.

When Bridget set out to choose a nursery school for her son, she imagined how her mother would have approached the task: methodically, carefully, and with the knowledge gained from a graduate degree in preschool education. What Bridget didn't take into account was that her mother was a homemaker, whereas she was a mom with a full-time job who also needed daily physical therapy appointments to correct a problem with her wrists. Nevertheless, she explains, "It really freaked me out that I was struggling to do something that my mother would have done so well. I felt I somehow wasn't living up to her standards."

To please her mother, Bridget chose an expensive private school for her son, but she made the decision hastily and without calculating the financial strain that the tuition would place on her marriage. Six months later, she and her husband reviewed their budget and realized they had to choose a less expensive school with more flexible hours for working parents. Now her son attends a well-respected program at a daycare center that Bridget had originally shunned because she believed her mother wouldn't have approved. The truth is, her son is quite content at his school, and she and her husband are happier with its hours. As she now prepares to select her son's elementary school—and to have her second child—Bridget says she plans to rely on her instincts and her own experience, rather than on the idealized memory of her mother.

Another Magic Number

Just as women fear reaching the age their mothers were when they died, they also view their children's maturation with a certain apprehension. Watching a child go through various phases reactivates the same developmental struggles in a mother. She doesn't simply project her past experiences onto her child; to some degree, she relives them.

As a motherless daughter sees her child, and especially her daughter, approach the age she was when her mother died, she reconnects with the fears and anxieties she felt at that time. With the memory of loss as her guide, she does a double identification with her child and her mother. *Will I die now?* she wonders. *How will my child cope without me?*

"Many motherless women develop a depression when their child gets close to the age they were when their mothers died," Phyllis Klaus says. "I'll see clients who talk about their child's fifth year, and how that was a terrible time for them. They totally blocked it out. They became ill, or they became depressed. When I research their histories, it turns out that they were five when their mothers died. Their fear of 'Will I repeat that history?' gets replayed through their children."

When children know the details of their mothers' early loss, they often identify with the child she once was. Alice, who was twenty-four when her mother died, says both her daughters approached her when they reached their twenty-fourth years. They wanted to discuss her mortality and made a point of telling her how hard it would be for them to lose her at that age. A more dramatic example comes from thirty-eight-year-old Emily, who was fourteen when her mother committed suicide. She panicked as her daughter approached adolescence, aware she had no personal experience to refer to as the mother of a child older than fourteen. Her oldest daughter panicked at the same time. "The year she turned fourteen was horrendous," Emily says. "She made a suicidal gesture, she acted out in every possible way, and she insisted that I let her go live with her father. As she left, I felt again that a part of me was dying, and in some ways I had to let our relationship die in my heart." Although fourteen may have been a coincidental age, it seems possible that Emily's daughter identified with her mother's experience and insisted on leaving before her mother could leave her. As Emily watched her daughter's struggle, she revisited her own fourteenth year, a time of confusion and lack of power. She felt helpless to stop her daughter, and once again, a mother-daughter separation occurred at the fourteen-year mark.

The Independence Factor

As discussed in a previous chapter, one of the most common out-comes that motherless women identify with their early loss is inde-pendence. Not surprisingly, this is one of the most common qualities they hope to instill in their children, especially in their daughters. Because they needed to develop self-reliance to survive, these women hope to save their children the pain of that adjustment. As fifty-three-year-old Gloria, the mother of two daughters who are now in their twenties, explains, "I tended to do relatively little of the 'moth-erly chores' such as making beds or packing lunches for our children when they were growing up. I wanted them to be independent both in lifestyle and thinking, so that if anything ever happened to me, they would get along well by themselves. Emotionally, I didn't feel I had much 'mothering' to give out because I was so starved for it my-self. When they were teenagers, I sometimes felt I was acting more like a father than a mother. But they seemed to turn out fine, in spite of all this. Sometimes, to my surprise, my daughters mother me, which I love dearly."

Even though Gloria is married, she still raised her daughters to "get along well by themselves" if something should happen to her. Gloria felt alone at the age of thirteen when her mother died of can-cer, despite the presence of her father and two older sisters. When she became a mother, she did a double identification with her mother and her children, and took what she thought were necessary steps to protect her daughters if she, like her mother, should die young.

Yvonne, thirty-seven, who was twelve when her mother died, says her identifications with both her mother and her daughter in-spired her to raise her son and daughter quite differently, even though they're less than two years apart in age. "I have been, in my opinion, an excellent mother. But I have done one strange thing with my daughter that I haven't done with my son," she explains. "Every year that passes, I consider a victory. There! She is one year older in case I die. When she passed the age I was when my mother died, I was very relieved. Now that she's sixteen and super independent, I feel that I'm almost out of the woods. I know that this outlook of mine is probably having an effect on my daughter, but I truly see the world this way. One day I'll explain it to her, but my mortality isn't something I can discuss with her now."

Self-reliance is often a positive trait to instill in children, but as Yvonne suspects, the mother's intent and approach can have long-lasting effects on them. When a mother guides her children toward premature independence based more on her past experience *without* a mother rather than her present experience as one, she overlooks the dynamics of the current relationship. As she minimizes her importance in a son's or daughter's life because she loves them, because she wants to spare them from the pain of her childhood, she is, in effect, preparing them for an event that's not likely to occur, and they grow up unconsciously expecting a trauma that never arrives. By deliberately retreating into the emotional background of their lives, she does exactly what she's trying to avoid: she deprives her children of a fully engaged mother.

(Re)Discovering Maternal Love

When the early mother-daughter relationship ends prematurely, the daughter's evolving sense of herself suffers a devastating blow. This is especially true when a child loses a mother to suicide or physical abandonment, although it also occurs when the child knows the mother died of an illness she couldn't prevent or cure. Daughters who were so young when their mothers died that they have no conscious memories of mother love, who were raised by women who never showed affection, or who were abused by the very person who was supposed to love them most suffer the deepest self-esteem injuries of all. Having never felt valued, accepted, or loved by their mothers, they may grow into women who have a hard time valuing themselves.

Women in this position may choose not to have children. They may doubt their ability to love and raise a child, or fear they'll repeat the same parenting behaviors they received, with similar results. But many who do become parents find that when they feel that first rush of maternal love toward a child, the past breaks open in unexpected ways.

Shelly, a forty-year-old mother of two young daughters, was raised by a mother she describes as "not nurturing at all, very overbearing, a woman who showed her love by trying to make me be what she wanted me to be instead of giving me room to express myself" and a father who parented from the sidelines. As a long-awaited daughter in a family with two older sons, Shelly grew up feeling she was meant to mirror her mother's image, and that she was never valued for being herself. She and her mother remained at odds until her mother's death from cancer when Shelly was twenty-three. Shelly devoted the next ten years to building a career and dating several different men, none of whom gave her the emotional warmth or honest communication she craved.

When she was in her mid-thirties, she started seeing a therapist, and soon afterward she met the man who became her husband. At the age of thirty-seven, Shelly gave birth to their first daughter. One week into motherhood she had an experience that still makes her tear up when she talks about it.

"My daughter was colicky," she recalls. "All she did was cry. And for the first couple of weeks I was depressed. I was like, 'What have I done? This is the worst thing I've ever done. It's horrible.' I will never forget—she must have been a week old, and she was screaming. I'd finally talked to enough people about colic to know there wasn't anything I could do. She was comfortable, she wasn't hungry. I just needed to hold her. So I sat, and I was holding her, and obviously I didn't know her yet, she was just a week old. I didn't know anything about her, but I was feeling how much love I had for her, and how much I wanted to hold her and make her feel better. And all of a sudden, *boom,* I realized that my mother was this person once, with a week-old baby, and that she was a human being. She wasn't mentally ill, or anything like that. And I realized she *must* have loved me, because this feeling wasn't a feeling I chose to have. It was just there. And I just sobbed. I sat there rocking Sofie and crying, and thinking for the first time in my life, at the age of thirty-seven, *oh, I guess my mother must have loved me.* She couldn't not have. It's not really a choice."

Her mother, Shelly realized, wasn't just the controlling criticizer of her childhood. She'd been a woman, just a woman, who'd expressed her love in damaging ways. And Shelly understood at that moment that she hadn't been an unlovable child who'd gotten everything wrong. She'd been a child, like her own daughter, who'd gotten deserving of a mother's love. As she cried in the rocking chair, Shelly was grieving for the child who'd never felt her mother's love, for the mother who didn't know how to express it, and for the relationship they'd both missed.

The Generational Effect

Thousands of children in America develop characteristics of motherless children, even though their mothers are still alive. Why? Because they've been raised by motherless daughters. When early loss is co-opted into a child's emerging personality, the survival skills she develops at that time become the ones she applies to later tasks—including parenting. Because motherless daughters, like all other daughters, often reproduce the parenting behaviors they received, their children can end up profiting or suffering from the loss of a grandmother they never knew. And these children, in turn, are likely to parent *their* children in similar fashion. Forty-six-year-old Emma knows how this can happen. Four generations of women in her family, she says, are still feeling the effects of her maternal grandmother's death more than seventy years ago.

Emma: Breaking the Chain

Emma's mother was only three when her mother died in childbirth. Or was she four? Emma can't say for sure. Her mother doesn't talk much about the loss, and Emma is uncertain about the details. She knows her mother bounced from home to home throughout her childhood, raised by relatives and friends, but that's about all the information she has. When Emma recalls her childhood, discussion isn't what comes to mind. Activity is.

"We were always encouraged to constantly do things, go places, and achieve," she says. "It looked from the outside as if my siblings and I were superachievers. We were always very busy. My mother, too. She was a teacher, and she has volunteered everywhere. Everyone thinks she's wonderful. But I've since realized that being busy all the time was just her way to avoid her feelings."

Emma's mother lost her younger brother the year before her mother, and her father disappeared soon after his wife's death. "She was three years old, and nobody was left," Emma says. "I've always thought that was why she was so strong. She had to be." The coping skills that insulated Emma's mother during her teenage and young-adult years became the same ones she encouraged in her children: Don't get sick. Don't cry. Be strong.

When Emma was nine and the family's house burned to the ground, her mother reacted without visible grief or loss. "It was the week before Christmas, and we lost everything, including our cats and dogs," Emma remembers. "But it didn't stop anything. We just went on. We treated it like it wasn't a big deal, which I suppose is good, in a way. To my mother it probably wasn't a big deal, if no-body died. But having to act like that as a child doesn't prepare you to understand anything about yourself. It doesn't allow you to be human. You have to act like a robot. And then you get to be an adult and you wonder, 'Well, then, what *is* a big deal?'"

Throughout her childhood and adolescence, Emma didn't need to ask. Her mother always made that decision—and most other deci-sions—for her. As a motherless daughter who knew the cold neces-sity of independence, she encouraged it in her daughters, but as a mother who so badly wanted to give her children what she hadn't re-ceived, she became overzealous and controlling in their daily lives. "You understand the contradiction," Emma says. "She said one thing and did another. It was so important to her that my sister and I be able to take care of ourselves. That became the theme of our lives. But I also remember thinking that I wouldn't know what to do or how to respond if my mother died, because she took care of every-thing for me. She chose what was important and what wasn't. And I know I've done the same thing with my children, telling them, 'That's not worth being upset about' before they have a chance to de-cide for themselves."

When Emma was a young mother with a daughter and son, she reproduced her mother's parenting behaviors almost perfectly. She kept her children home with her and had few outside friends. She designed and implemented all their daily activities. She took for granted that her son would become independent but gave her daughter an extra push. And she maintained a cool emotional distance, trusting them to handle matters of the heart alone.

She thought it had all gone just fine, until one day a few years ago when she was visiting her daughter at home. As she watched her young granddaughter acting out, Emma recognized something was terribly wrong.

"I realized that the three of us just have an awful time together," she explains. "Two of us are fine. My granddaughter and I are fine. My daughter and I are fine. But the minute the three of us get together, something triggers that little girl. She just turns into a brat. It's horrible to watch. My daughter and I obviously do something that sets off this kid. I'm still not sure what it is, except that none of us seem to know how we're supposed to be. There are pieces missing. And I can't help but believe it comes from my mother not having anybody teach her first how to be a person, then a wife, and then a mother."

Not long after that afternoon in her daughter's home, Emma entered therapy to examine her relationships with both her mother and her daughter. It took almost three years for her to break through her idealized image of her mother. "One of the first things I said in therapy was that my mother was perfect," she says. "Over time, I realized you could probably find fault with everything she did. And I became very angry with her. How could she have been the way she was? Why didn't she know we needed more than just a rock that was never able to be anything but strong? That doesn't allow a child to be the least bit weak." With the help of her counselor, Emma is moving beyond blame and anger as she reevaluates her mother as a motherless child to understand some of her behaviors. "I'm at the point now where I can see my mother's strength as something wonderful again," she explains. "And I can also see that what went on wasn't her fault. She couldn't give me what she didn't have. But that hasn't made it any less painful for me, my daughter, or my granddaughter."

Emma's daughter recently joined her in therapy, where they're working together to revise their mother-daughter relationship and model new parenting behaviors for her granddaughter. Emma has also been encouraging her mother, who's now seventy-six, to join them. She doesn't expect a turnaround, but she's hopeful. As multiple generations of women in her family are learning, it's never too late for a daughter to reconsider the past, and to heal.

Chapter Twelve

The Female Phoenix
Creativity, Achievement, and Success

FROM THE AGE OF THIRTEEN until her forty-fourth year, Virginia Woolf was obsessed by the memory of her mother. Julia Stephen, who died of rheumatic fever when her youngest daughter was thirteen, lived on as an "invisible presence" in Woolf's life as she emerged first as a literary critic and then as a novelist. "Then one day walking round Tavistock Square I made up, as I sometimes make up my books, *To the Lighthouse;* in a great, apparently involuntary rush," she explained in the essay "A Sketch of the Past."

> One thing burst into another. . . . I wrote the book very quickly; and when it was written, I ceased to be obsessed by my mother. I no longer hear her voice; I do not see her.
>
> I suppose that I did for myself what psycho-analysts do for their patients. I expressed some very long felt and deeply felt emotion. And in expressing it I explained it and then laid it to rest. But what is the meaning of "explained" it? Why, because I described her and my feeling for her in that book, should my vision of her and my feeling for her become so much dimmer and weaker? Perhaps one of these days I shall hit on the reason.

Ever since Freud described creativity as an attempt to compensate for childhood dissatisfaction and lack of fulfillment, psychologists and artists have been theorizing about connections between early loss, creativity, and achievement. "When we talk about parent loss, we usually talk about the pathology and the pain," Phyllis Klaus says. "But any kind of tragedy in life can be a springboard for creativity and growth, and for working that tragedy out in very healthy ways. What's interesting is to look at what helps these people get to that point. Sometimes it's their own ability to look inside and develop who they really want to be, to make life count and not waste it."

Throughout history, early mother loss has acted as an impetus for a daughter's later success. Just as tuberculosis was the artist's disease, mother loss was her early tragedy. Dozens of eminent women throughout history lost their mothers during childhood or adolescence, including Dorothy Wordsworth (at birth); Harriet Beecher Stowe (age five); Charlotte, Emily, and Anne Brontë (five, three, and one); George Eliot (sixteen); Jane Addams (two); Marie Curie (eleven); Gertrude Stein (fourteen); Eleanor Roosevelt (eight); Dorothy Parker (five); Margaret Mitchell (nineteen); and Marilyn Monroe, who spent her entire childhood in foster care and orphanages.

History books are also filled with men who lost their mothers young, including statesmen (Thomas Jefferson, Abraham Lincoln), artists (Michelangelo, Ludwig van Beethoven), thinkers (Charles Darwin, Georg Hegel, Immanuel Kant), and writers (Joseph Conrad, John Keats, Edgar Allan Poe). When the psychologist Marvin Eisenstadt conducted a historical study of 573 famous individuals from Homer to John F. Kennedy, he found that the rate of mother loss among "eminent" or "historical geniuses" in the arts, the humanities, the sciences, and the military is as much as three times that of the general population, even after the mortality rates of earlier centuries are taken into account.

But other studies have revealed equally high rates of mother loss among juvenile delinquents and prisoners. It appears that children who lose parents generally respond in one of two ways: they develop a sense of fatalism, expecting and even encouraging future unfortunate events to occur, or they pick themselves up, brush themselves off, and find the determination and motivation to continue.

What guides one girl who loses her mother into brushes with the law and another into personal or creative success? With any motherless daughter, the age at the time of loss, the cause of a mother's death, and the support systems available afterward all affect how she will cope. Two additional conditions also appear necessary:

the drive to accomplish goals early and evidence of an already existing artistic or intellectual talent.

Veronika Denes-Raj, who has studied the relationship between
early parent loss and perceptions of life expectancy, believes that an
early confrontation with death inspires some children to adopt a
more existential philosophy toward life, which in turn motivates
them to succeed. "Freud said we can't look at our own deaths," Dr.
Denes-Raj explains, "but existentialists believe you must be aware
of your own limits to succeed. Only if you feel that life exists between two anchors—birth and death—can you accomplish what
you want. Existentialists understand that life is not infinite. After a
parent dies, they'll look around and ask, 'What's left to do?' and
then try to do it."

Because a mother's death is as close as a daughter can get to experiencing her own, the loss teaches her that all life—and especially
hers—has limits and can end quickly, without warning. Even though
she typically sees the world as less controllable than other women
do, she sets explicit goals for herself and becomes determined to
achieve them before her time runs out. Explains Dr. Denes-Raj,
"These people will say, 'Okay, I may only live until the age of fifty-
five or sixty, but I want to do X or Y. Therefore, I have to do it faster.
And then if I live longer, I'll do other things, too.'" Her mother may
have died with dreams she never fulfilled, but this daughter is insistent that the same won't happen to her. Death she can't control, but
personal action she can.

Anna Quindlen, the *Newsweek* columnist and best-selling author, was already planning to write for a living before her mother
died of ovarian cancer when Quindlen was nineteen, but the experience, she says, made her determined to achieve even more in less
time. "When I was a young reporter—because I got to be a reporter
when I was nineteen, and I went to the *New York Times* when I was
twenty-four—people would say to me, 'Why are you in such a
hurry? You've got the rest of your life,'" she recalls. "And there was
a part of me that just thought, 'Tell it to the Marines, buster. The
whole rest of my life could be five years, ten years.' I felt like everything was sort of speeded up."

Like Quindlen, most other successful motherless daughters had a predisposition toward intellectual or artistic ability before their mothers died. Loss doesn't give a daughter skills she didn't possess. Instead, it acts as a trigger event that inspires a latent talent to emerge, or it provokes the spirit and will she needs to push her abilities beyond safe and predictable limits.

When early loss becomes a defining element of a daughter's identity, it can consciously or unconsciously steer her specific career choices. A forty-one-year-old fiction writer who was eight when her mother died, for example, says she writes stories about mother-daughter relationships because stories allow her to mourn from a safe distance. A forty-nine-year-old attorney who was sixteen when her mother died now fights for women's rights because she remembers how her mother strained against traditional gender limits during the 1950s. And a fifty-four-year-old professor of tumor biology, who watched her mother die of breast cancer in 1953 decided, at the age of thirteen, to devote her professional life to researching the disease:

> I remember on one of those days gawking around my mother's bed as a skinny, awkward, barely pubertal girl, watching her lying peacefully unconscious after a morphine injection. I made myself the definitive promise: "Someday, when I grow up, I'm going to do something about this." As subsequent years passed, this promise periodically resurfaced to influence which fork in a path I'd take. I chose biology over music in high school and college, because music would not help solve the problem of my mother's death. I chose graduate school in genetics and microbiology rather than medical school, because physicians had not been effective in saving my mother's life. More research needed to be done to give them the proper tools to work with. Today, I'm a university professor with a research program in breast cancer. I'm working on finding the cause, so the disease can be prevented and women will never have to die from it, as my mother did.

Today, we need only turn on the television, open the newspaper, or walk into a bookstore to find motherless women who've earned acclaim in spite of their early losses. Jane Fonda was fifteen and Roma Downey ten when their mothers died; country singer Shania Twain was twenty-two; the actress Mariska Hargitay three; and the author Jacqueline Mitchard nineteen. Carol Burnett was raised by her grandmother, while her alcoholic mother lived in a separate apartment down the hall. Liza Minelli was twenty-three when Judy Garland overdosed. From the age of three onward, Maya Angelou lived mostly with her grandmother in Stamps, Arkansas. And two of the most influential women in the American entertainment industry—Oprah Winfrey and Madonna—grew up without their mothers. Oprah was raised by her maternal grandmother for her first six years and her father for most of her teens, and Madonna was five when her mother died.

Ruth Simmons, president of Brown University and the first African-American president of an Ivy League institution, was 15 when she lost her mother. Olympic track-and-field star Jackie Joyner Kersee was eighteen. Sarah Ferguson, the former Duchess of York, grew up with an absentee mother. The actress Meg Ryan was fourteen when her parents divorced; she remained with her father. Doris Kearns Goodwin, author and presidential historian, was thirteen when she lost her mother; actress and comedian Janeane Garafolo was twenty; and Olympic gold-medal figure skater Oksana Baiul was orphaned at thirteen. Rosie O'Donnell, the comedian and former talk-show host whose acting career began with the 1992 movie *A League of Their Own*, was ten when her mother died. The first day she met Madonna on the movie set, she shared this bit of personal background with her and the two became fast friends.

The Roots of a
Motherless Woman's Success

It's no coincidence that motherless women rise to the top of their respective fields. Many of the conditions that are advantageous to achievement—conditions other women typically have to strive to attain—already exist in a motherless daughter's life, making her a natural candidate for superior creativity, accomplishment, and success.

Autonomy and Personal Power

Throughout childhood and adolescence, girls are typically more obedient and compliant with parental attitudes than boys are. This is particularly true when a daughter is deeply under her mother's influence. But when the mother or mother-figure is removed from the family, a girl with a role-reversed, distant, or nonexistent father-daughter relationship suddenly can choose and decide for herself. Although this absence of social control nearly overwhelms some daughters, for others it offers an environment without limits and provides the freedom necessary for individual growth.

The author and activist Letty Cottin Pogrebin says she was well on her way to becoming "a kind of '50s kid, very much a demure, self-effacing, male-oriented, marriage-directed, I-need-a-man-to-take-care-of-me sort of person" before her mother died when she was fifteen. Her mother had been the parent who offered her consistent care and warmth, and after her father's quick remarriage and withdrawal from her life, Pogrebin clearly understood that she had to take care of herself. To defend against her feelings of abandonment and anger, she says, she reconceived herself as a brave, independent soul. Instead of marrying or moving in with relatives, as most women in her college graduating class did when they finished school, at the age of twenty she found a publishing job in New York City and took her own apartment in Greenwich Village.

> This was in 1959, when women didn't live alone. They lived in residence hotels that had people downstairs to clear your visitors. Women who lived alone were still a little suspect. Until my apartment became ready, I lived in a hotel in Times Square for a few months. My father saw where I was living and just didn't seem to care. There was every possible type you could imagine hanging around in that hotel. Although things weren't as unsavory as they are there today, they were, according to the standards of that period, pretty gamey. I know that if my mother had been alive, I never would have been there. I would lay in bed at night and say, "I would never be here, for half a millisecond, if she were alive."

By that time, I was really starting to enjoy the forbidden life. The idea that I was an iconoclast, a rebel. I lived a Village life, which I'm sure I never would have done if my mother were alive, not for a minute. When *Breakfast at Tiffany's* came out, I identified with it in such a powerful way that when Audrey Hepburn died it really upset me. She had been sort of my Hollywood alter ego in that movie. I had a motor scooter, I had a dog, I had a duck, I had a rabbit. I did all kinds of bananas things. I just indulged my whims. I did some drugs, I went out with every possible man that interested me. It wasn't a destructive way of life, but it certainly was unbridled in every way, and for the late 50s and early 60s, it was not what good Jewish girls did.

I don't think I would have become the sort of fighter I became, the sort of go-against-the-grain and damn the torpedos kind of person, and I don't think I would have led a nonconventional single life for that period if my mother hadn't died. Although after I married and became politically active and became a feminist I have led a very conventional life. So it is ironic, in a way, that I've repeated my mother's life. I'm monogamous, I'm happily married, I have three children. The only difference is my mother was unhappily married, but she was very much a marriage and family person, and so have I become. But my need to be very politically involved and very public in my struggles in supporting the values that I care about . . . I don't think I would have had the *chutzpah* if I hadn't had those years by myself.

Relaxation of Gender Barriers

Fathers, who typically feel less competent tending to their daughters' emotional needs, may concentrate on their intellectual pursuits instead. Both Marie Curie (motherless at age eleven) and Dorothy Parker (motherless at five) had close relationships with their widowed fathers, who nurtured their early interests. Curie's father, left with four children to raise, guided his daughters toward academics, encouraging them to learn chemistry and physics and to speak five languages. Parker and her father exchanged playful verses through the mail when she was a child on summer vacations, exercises that served as prototypes for her later literary wit. Girls who grow up free of the traditional social and cultural roles that often exist in a two-parent family may become women who refuse to acknowledge or accept gender barriers, which the psychologist Barbara Kerr, the author of *Smart Girls, Gifted Women,* has identified as a characteristic many eminent women share.

Mariska Hargitay, the award-winning star of NBC's *Law and Order: Special Victims Unit,* says she owes much of her success to her father, Mickey Hargitay. Mariska was three years old when her mother, the actress Jayne Mansfield, died in a car accident, and her father helped boost her confidence and self-esteem in later years. "He went to every one of my swim meets, told me I could be president or do anything I wanted, and said I'd be great at whatever I did," she recalls. "I'd have to eat it, drink it, sleep it, he said, but if I wanted to be the best I could do it. He was a champion—an Olympic speed skater, Mr. Universe. I really feel I shaped my career after his."

The Need to Work Through Grief

Grief needs an outlet; creativity offers one. Some psychiatrists see mourning and creativity as the perfect marriage, the thought processes of one neatly complementing the other. A child's contradictory impulses to both acknowledge and deny a parent's death represent precisely the type of rich ambiguity that inspires artistic expression. The art that a motherless daughter creates may be strongly influenced by her mourning and may show evidence of it in style, content, or purpose. Margaret Mitchell, who was nineteen when her mother died, knew how Scarlett O'Hara would feel about mother loss. Susan Minot could make the seven siblings in her first novel, *Monkeys,* respond so realistically to the aftermath of their mother's death in an automobile accident because Minot was twenty-one and one of seven siblings when her mother died the same way. The same is true for her younger sister Eliza, who was eight when their mother died. Eliza Minot's debut novel, *The Tiny One,* follows a day in the life of eight-year-old Via Revere, who has just lost her mother in a car accident.

As Virginia Woolf discovered after writing *To the Lighthouse*, the completion of a mourning cycle can result in an outpouring of creative energy. Other daughters rely on creative activity to help them work through their mourning. Young children often use creative play to express their emotional pain. Older daughters may turn to writing, art, music, acting, or other forms of self-expression. Even in daughters who show little talent for the arts, psychologists have seen creative responses to mother loss—in the beginnings of a new relationship, in the ability to feel joy, or in the first sense of satisfaction a daughter feels with herself.

Mary Swander, a poet, playwright, memoirist, and professor of English at Iowa State University, says that her graduate writing workshops kept her sane during her early twenties as her mother slowly died of cancer. Estranged from her father and geographically separated from her two older brothers, Swander cared for her mother alone while completing her undergraduate and graduate degrees. "When I look back at those years, I think, 'What was I *doing*? Why was I trying to go to school?'" she recalls. "On the other hand, if I weren't writing I would have gone nuts. It gave me some other focus, and I was working through my grief in the stories I was writing." After her mother's death, she continued to mourn through her poetry. Her first book, *Succession,* was based on her mother's family history, and her second, *Driving the Body Back,* immortalized her five-hour ride across Iowa with a funeral director and her great-aunt as they transported her mother's body to the family cemetery for burial.

Patricia Heaton, who co-starred in the CBS sitcom *Everybody Loves Raymond* from 1996 to 2005, remembers having a serendipitous opportunity to act out her grief—literally. She was twelve when her mother died suddenly from a brain aneurysm, and nineteen years later she landed the lead role in a stage production about a woman whose mother died during her childhood.

> The character is pregnant and wants to have an abortion, and what comes down, as her sister and her boyfriend try to talk her out of it, is the death of her mother. She doesn't want to do that same thing to her child. She actually wants the child, but she blames herself for her mother's death, and she's a bag of

mixed and confused emotions. She has a big speech in the end that talks about her mother dying, and how angry she was at the doctors, and the way the whole thing went. She breaks down and starts crying, and remembers the wonderful things about her mother, and how much she loves and misses her. Another actress was supposed to play the part and dropped out at the last minute because she was having such a hard time with it. I thought to myself, "Boy. I can see how every night the actor doing this part would loathe coming up to this point, because you have to do all this emotional work." But for me, all I had to do was say the words and they expressed every-thing I'd ever felt.

I did that part for six weeks, five times a week, and I felt it was a real gift. Because I went into the play with only four days to rehearse, and it was the lead role. I read the play and immedi-ately wept at the end, and just flew with it. It really helped me act out and work through a lot of my feelings about my mother's death. I think actors are so fortunate that way. If they're smart, they can really work through their stuff, and get applause at the end. And it was so easy to do. All I had to do was say the words, and the tears would just flow. It helped alle-viate some of the demons of the whole situation for me, al-though they've still come up a few times since then.

The Need for a Distraction

Introspection and focused activity become welcome escapes from the family chaos that typically occurs after a death, and some daughters depend on them, to great personal gain. Linda Shostak, one of the first female partners at Morrison and Foerster law firm in San Francisco and a well-respected trial attorney in California, remem-bers immersing herself in activity the summer her mother died of cancer when she was thirteen:

My father's mechanism for dealing with it was not to deal with it, and not to talk about it. I remember being very unhappy that summer, but I don't remember having a lot of trouble adapting.

Right after my mother died, my father said to me, "Why don't you finish whatever merit badges you have to finish to get your curve bar?" which was the highest thing you could get as a Girl Scout. I also read *Gone with the Wind* that summer, and I painted. I just wanted to be busy. If it was really hot, we'd go to a movie because the movie would be air-conditioned. When I came home and my mother wasn't there to talk about the movie with, I'd get very upset. To avoid having any down time where I hadn't planned anything, I tried to stay busy. So I learned how to throw myself into projects so I wouldn't have to think about it. If I thought about my mother, I'd get very, very upset, and I just learned to turn it all off.

After I finished high school, I went to Vassar for undergraduate work and then to Harvard Law School. I worked in New York for about a year and a half and moved out here to work for MoFo in 1974 and have lived here since. In a way, it's a very unfashionable biography. I was in a deposition on Monday defending a very successful insurance salesman, and when he gave his bio he'd done all these things, supported himself by playing music and driving a bus. But I just went straight through till law school. I never veered.

Maintaining a high level of activity helped Shostak manage her grief, and she sustained her previously high level of academic success for more than a decade after her mother's death. As she learned, however, consistent achievement and activity often keep a daughter from mourning at all. Twenty years after her mother's death, she found she had to relive parts of that summer, sort out her feelings, and create a place for the image of her mother within the new life she'd created for herself.

The Courage to Journey Alone

Success often involves a departure from family and home, a risk other women may not be willing to take. But the motherless daughter frequently isn't leaving a place where she feels safe and secure; she's looking for one where she can belong. When the death of her mother also means the dissolution of her family, a daughter loses whatever secure foundation she had. Her search for safety and security requires that she keep moving forward. Once she starts, there's no going back—because there's often nowhere to go back *to*.

As Roma Downey, a star of the CBS drama *Touched By an Angel* from 1994 to 2003, explains, "You've heard of the expression that you need something to fall back on? When there's nobody there to catch you, that's not really an option. But the positive outcome is that it's a tremendous motivator." Downey was ten years old, living in Derry in the north of Ireland when her mother died of heart failure. "In the community where I grew up, kids didn't leave, really. Everybody is still pretty much within the community. They have children, and their children live there and so on and so forth. So for me to have left—first I hopped over to England, and then I made the great leap across the pond—was a wee bit shocking. And of course, for me that was compounded once my father died. I had been returning home with regularity out of duty and love for him, but once he died, there was no reason to go back. I also think I wouldn't have felt the ease of immigration, the freedom, if I'd had aging, elderly parents. I have moved with great ease, all my life. I very much feel that home is a state of mind, and that it goes with you. I nest with great enthusiasm when I land somewhere, but it's just as easy for me to pack up and move on."

The Quest for Immortality

Just as artists give their objects eternal life, motherless daughters hope to do the same for their mothers and for themselves. Art, writing, and music offer a daughter the promise of an immortality she believes her mother was denied and also provide her with a means to bring the image of her mother—the one she had or the one she believes she would have had—back to life.

Charlotte Brontë's earliest surviving work indicates that she may, at the age of eight, have been trying to do just this. In a brief story she wrote three years after her mother died, she told of a little girl named Ann whose mother fell ill. "Once Ane [sic] and her papa and her Mama went to sea in a ship and they had very fine weather all the way," she wrote, "but Anns Mama was very sick and Ann attended her with so much care. she gave her her meddcine." Charlotte dedicated the story to her younger sister Anne, whose birth had begun their mother's painful decline.[1] By allowing the Ann of the story to save her sick mother, Charlotte rewrote her sister's history for her and, as author and creator, gave herself equivalent power to cure her mother and prevent her death. By becoming her mother's savior, she also gave herself a mother again.

The comedian Diane Ford aims for a similar effect in the comedy routines she writes. Both her parents died in a car accident when she was thirteen. Today, she often incorporates her mother and father into her jokes as if they were still alive. "I project what my mother would have said in certain instances," she explains. "She never really said it, but it's what I think she might have said, so I stick it in there. It's a way of making me more normal. After I lost my parents, I hated that I was so different. I wanted two parents like everyone else. I don't know that I've ever gotten over that. Also, putting my parents in my jokes is a way to connect me to a past that I didn't really have. Some parts of my made-up past are much better than anything I could have possibly ever lived."

The Desire to Honor the Mother

When a mother offered inspiration and encouragement to a daughter when alive, what better way is there to honor her after death but to fulfill her wishes—and to achieve what she never had a chance to achieve herself?

Supreme Court Justice Ruth Bader Ginsburg, who was seventeen when her mother died, remembers her mother as a "very strong, extremely intelligent individual" who encouraged her daughter to work hard and strive for self-sufficiency from a very early age.

---

[1]When Charlotte wrote this story, Anne was five—the same age Charlotte was when their mother died. According to Branwen Bailey Pratt, the author of the article "Charlotte Brontë's 'There was once a little girl': The Creative Process," observing Anne at age five may have reactivated Charlotte's emotional response to her mother's death, which caused her to choose this topic for her story.

She wanted so much to get across to me the importance of being independent. The way she put it in her day was, "Be a lady." By that, she meant don't get yourself in trouble and get your life ruined by it.

From the time I was thirteen until she died, she was in and out of the hospital. I would go from my high school classes, take the subway to the hospital, meet my father there, have dinner someplace in the hospital neighborhood, come back home, get up and go to school the next morning. The routine carried me along. Plus, she was so determined that I make something of myself. She thought that being independent and being able to fend for myself was important. I think my father came to realize that he didn't do her any favor by supporting her so that she wouldn't work. In those days, it was considered improper for a man to have a wife who worked. She would work only if it was essential to the family's economic well-being. I think he came to realize that she would have been more fulfilled, happier, if she had worked outside the home.

One thing my mother taught me was to do everything the best way I possibly could. Of course, she didn't have very much of a chance to do that herself, but she certainly got that message across to me, that everything I did, whether it was my piano lessons or whatever I wanted to take, I should spend the time it took to do it as well as I could.

I chose to go to law school, thinking it was something I could do well, to the encouragement of one of my teachers at Cornell. So I took the LSAT before my husband did, even though he was a year ahead of me at Cornell. And then my mother's sister and my father's brother, who were the ones I visited on school vacations, decided it was acceptable for me to go to law school because I wouldn't have to support myself, so I could do this crazy thing. In fact, my aunt recently died and my daughter found a letter I had written in college saying something about just taking the Law School Aptitude Test, and saying I did fine on the English but I don't think I did well on the math, and maybe if I get a low grade that will end this crazy idea of mine about going to law school. Sometimes I'll reflect on what my mother might have counseled me if she had lived longer and seen the way my interests developed, and I think that she would have been with me.

My view is that I am what she would have wanted me to be, in fact far beyond any of her wildest dreams of what I could be, not because of my limitations but because of the limitations of society. I have her picture on the wall in my chambers, and it's where I can see her every day when I leave. I kind of smile when I look at it and say, "She would have been proud of me."

Resilience and Determination

Surviving a disruptive family can inspire the type of personal strength that insulates a daughter against professional despair. As Victoria Rowell, who plays Drucilla Winters on CBS's daytime drama *The Young and the Restless,* explains, the years she spent living as a foster child in five different homes helped her withstand the rejections she experienced first as an aspiring ballet dancer and later as an actress, long after other performers might have given up:

> Overall, my foster experience was very successful. But because of the rejection aspect of the situation, you're definitely more prepared for a situation later when you hear, "No thank you. Don't call us. We'll call you." You're accustomed to it. You've learned how to accept "No." There's a toughness that occurs as a result, and that plate of armor makes you more prepared, and protects you in a variety of situations that may arise in the business. I'm not saying that rejection feels good, but I'm saying that I've found I've been able to take it and let it roll off my back. It's interesting, because rejection in the business is completely different than rejection in personal life experiences. Personal rejection hurts worse. You never get used to that.

Because a motherless daughter usually interprets personal rejections as a narcissistic injury similar to the loss of a mother, she often has trouble coping with breakups, divorce, and death as an adult. However, having already survived one profound loss, she also may develop what psychologists call a "diminished sense of crisis." Smaller losses, such as waiting for a call-back that never comes or being passed over for a job, then feel minor in comparison to losing a loved one, and she can manage them without severe distress.

Access to Deep Emotions

Self-expression allows a daughter to transform her emotion and experience into positive action, and to turn misfortune into useful material. Mariska Hargitay says her ability to connect to loss so deeply in her personal life has helped her access those emotions in her acting as well.

> I remember being in an acting class where people couldn't be emotional. We had to do an exercise where you came through a door with a circumstance. That was easy for me to do—to pretend there had been an accident, to pretend I'd just lost someone. But I remember sitting in the class, thinking that the other people weren't emotionally available [in their scenes]. My boyfriend at the time still had his parents, and he could never imagine what it would be like if someone told him there had been an accident and someone died. But I'd already experienced so many of these deep, profound emotions that I didn't have to learn them. I could imagine anything. And I think that's one of the reasons I can be so emotionally available as an actor. I understand pain and drama. I understand that it only takes one second for a life to change. I think children who experience that have a different understanding than children who don't.

Anna Quindlen says the subject matter she chooses to write about and the way she conveys her ideas both have been deeply influenced by her mother's death from ovarian cancer when she was nineteen.

> I really feel my mother's death is the dividing line between the self I am and the self I became. That was probably the time in my life when that dividing line would have existed anyhow,

but it's difficult for me to adequately communicate the difference in the person I feel like I became after she died. I was quite immature, very self-centered, and kind of frivolous in many ways before this happened, and it just changed me radically in ways that only became clear to me later on. When I was doing [the syndicated column] "Life in the 30s," people would always say to me, "I don't understand how somebody your age has these kinds of insights into everyday life." What became clear to me after a while was that one of the reasons I did was because the unexamined life became impossible for me to have after that year.

My mother's death made me a much happier and more optimistic person. People are always a little incredulous when I say that. I really felt that from this experience, you could take away one of two things. One is you could just think, "What's the point? It's all over so quickly." But the other is that you can look at life and think, "My god. Every day that you have is so precious and so important." When somebody dies you realize that if they had it to do all over again they wouldn't want to win the Pulitzer Prize or make the bestseller list. If they had to do it all over again, they'd just want one more day at the beach, or to sit with their kids quietly on a blanket somewhere and talk about something one more time. I think the experience of my mother's death made me treasure those little things in a way I never would have before, and I think that's a real element of my writing that comes out. I'm not interested in writing about the inauguration or the hostage releases. I'm interested in looking at the little moments in people's lives. I think those are the most illuminating, and the most dear.

Overcoming Survivor Guilt

Writing, acting, dancing, academic achievement: all of these accomplishments are realized most easily within optimal social and financial environments. Even the most prodigious talent will have trouble reaching its full potential in a severely troubled family or under crushing socioeconomic conditions.

In some families, a mother's death will free a daughter from these constraints. A daughter whose single mother raised her on welfare, for example, goes to live with her brother and sister-in-law in a middle-class community after her mother dies. A daughter whose mother prohibited her from attending college away from home is free to accept an offer from a prestigious university in another state. Or a daughter who spent her childhood caring for an alcoholic mother suddenly has time to devote to her own interests.

The daughter who believes opportunity arrived because of—rather than in spite of—her mother's death may have an even stronger will to succeed. By creating a productive and satisfying life for herself, she can attach meaning to her mother's death—she did not die for naught. But this daughter also may carry a heavy burden of guilt for enjoying a success that exists only, she believes, because her mother died.

Twenty-eight-year-old Sheila struggled for more than a decade with her competing feelings of entitlement and regret. She believed the world owed her a satisfying adult life after an adolescence of loss and disruption, yet at the same time she felt certain that if not for her mother's death when she was fourteen, she never would have left the working-class urban neighborhood where she grew up. Instead, Sheila spent her adolescence living with her father and stepmother in an affluent suburb where 80 percent of her high-school classmates were college bound. She went on to earn both bachelor's and master's degrees, but she always felt uncomfortable, believing she had used her mother's death for her own personal gain.

> In graduate school, I found my niche. I thought, "This is it. This is what I do, and I do it well." Then I had sort of an attack of feeling like if my mother were alive, I wouldn't be getting such praise from respected members of my field or starting this career. It dawned on me at a certain point that although the thing I wanted most was to have my mother back, I wasn't willing to give up what I'd gotten since she died. A few years ago, I finally admitted to my dad, "I think if Mommy had lived, I wouldn't have achieved the things I've achieved." It took me eleven years to say that because I'd been so overcome by the guilt of enjoy-

ing the life I had. He told me, "You'd still be doing what you're doing, because you are who you are. You've always been a person who was going to get what she wanted to get." It took me a long time to realize my father is probably right. My life would have been different if my mother were here, but I think I'd still be somewhere I wanted to be, doing something I wanted to do.

Like Sheila, some motherless daughters believe they're dishonoring their mothers by leading a happy, productive life after the death. Success represents an individuation they may not yet be ready to make. As thirty-two-year-old Roberta explains, "After my mother died when I was sixteen, I almost felt, out of love for her, a need not to have my life work. It was as if I were saying, 'If I love my mother, I have to prove it to myself by screwing up. By not going to school. By not being happy.'" This is another way to honor the mother, but it's not a daughter's destiny. It's her choice. And it's a sacrifice that few mothers would truly want their daughters to make.

If a mother's death offers a daughter the chance for a more fulfilling, more challenging, or more productive life than she believes she would have had otherwise, the daughter has every right to that future. There is no disgrace in using whatever raw materials are available to succeed. There is no shame in turning loss into life. Like the phoenix, the mythological bird that ascends from the ashes of its own destruction, every motherless daughter has the potential within herself to rise from tragedy, and take flight.

Epilogue

THE REDWOODS, my mother said, were taller than our house, their trunks so wide that cars could drive right through. "That's right," she said, "a little tunnel, right through the base." We lived on what was once an apple orchard, and all our trees bore fruit. I couldn't imagine that one could ever grow that high or that thick. But the postcards and pictures she brought back from her trip to northern California with my father offered proof that what she said about the redwoods was true. In one photograph she stood alongside a massive russet sequoia, her hand raised in a playful wave. The first branches were so high they didn't even appear in the frame.

I wish I had those photographs now. I don't know where they wound up. Time and mobility and lack of organization have scattered our family photos so that most have landed in a glossy paper shopping bag I keep in the bottom drawer of a filing cabinet in my Los Angeles home. I keep thinking I'll find the time to lay them all out on the carpet and organize them into chronological albums, but the task feels too daunting every time I begin. There are hundreds, literally hundreds, of photos. Maybe even a thousand. They span the period between my parents' engagement in 1959 and my mother's final months of illness in 1981, her entire adult life. When I shuffle through the images I can't help thinking of the ones that should be there but aren't, the pictures of her smiling at college graduations, holding her grandchildren, laughing from beneath a halo of grey hair. My mother would be sixty-seven if she were alive today. Sixty-seven. It's impossible to project the last image I have of her, at forty-two, that far into the future. To me, my mother is forever young.

I've tried to find her over the years, in the various places I've lived, but she's remained elusive. In Tennessee, a therapist put an empty chair in front of me and had me pretend to talk to her, but the conversation was one-sided and strained. An astrologer in Iowa couldn't find her anywhere in my chart. A shaman with a crystal pendulum in Malibu smiled and nodded and said she's "in the light." If I had to pinpoint my mother's location myself, I'd say she's nowhere and everywhere, at the same time. She's a foggy memory I can't quite bring into focus and a gentle spirit that infuses all my days. She exists in the background of my life now, hovering, suspended, shapeless, like familiar air.

To be a motherless daughter is to live with the awareness of a presence, but not its physicality. Something is missing, yes. But we must not forget that something has been given to us, too.

To be a motherless daughter is to be riddled with paradoxes and contradictions, to live with an eternally unresolved longing, but it is also to know the grit of survival, to hold an insight and maturity others did not obtain so young, and to understand the power of renewal and rebirth. "We gain so much, whether we like it or not at the time," says Colleen Russell, who was fifteen when her mother died. "The strength comes from the adversity and the challenges. I wouldn't have had the sensitivities I have if I hadn't lost my mother. I know I would have taken more for granted. And I have different ideas about life and death than I think I'd otherwise have."

In my late teens and twenties, I used to play a mental game with myself. I'd look around and weigh all the good things in my life against the possibility of having my mother back. During college, the choice was easy. Would I trade my education for the chance to have my mother back? Of course. My boyfriend? Yes, even him. In my twenties, the answers weren't quite so clear. Would I give up my career as a journalist? Okay. My graduate degree in writing and the years I spent in Iowa? Well, all right. My apartment in New York, my first book contract, my core of faithful friends? Probably. Maybe. I didn't know. And then I reached my early thirties, and I had to stop playing the game. It ended the day I looked around at my husband and my daughters, at the life we'd created together in California, and knew I would no longer be willing to make the trade.

Does this make me a selfish person, or one who has finally found a life that she loves, despite her early loss? I believe it's the latter. Thirty-one-year-old Debby agrees. When Debby was a teenager, her younger sister and her mother were her two closest friends. But when Debby was twenty-two, her sister died in an accident, and one year later she lost her mother to cancer. "I've had people ask me, 'If some things could have happened differently in your life, what would they be?'" she says. "And I'd have to say there isn't anything I'd change. I'm sorry for different things that have happened, but I wouldn't have done it any other way. The losses are so entwined in my life and so much a part of my personality and my maturing, and so much a part of the person I am today. And I like who I am today. It stinks that these things had to happen to me, but I can make the decision to let them be a plus or a minus."

Adds forty-four-year-old Wendy, who was fifteen when her mother died and is now the married mother of a sixteen-year-old daughter, "It amazes me sometimes, how things have reframed themselves over time, and how if you work on your grief, you eventually do heal. So many things that used to be so painful to me because of my mother's death have now become so rich and rewarding because of her death, if that makes sense."

We have all learned something from mother loss—lessons that perhaps no child or adolescent should have to learn, but valuable lessons nonetheless. We have learned, if nothing else, how to take responsibility for ourselves. The next, and even more important, step is to move into the place where we can take consistently good emotional care of ourselves, too—not by excluding others from our lives, but by learning how to trust, respect, and value the children we were and the women we are. As twenty-five-year-old Margie, who was seven when her mother died, explains, "I think I'm a very strong person, and I know it's because of my mother's death and everything that happened afterward. Somehow, I managed to grow to love and respect myself and take pride in who I was, as that child who managed to take care of herself and survive. If my mother had lived, could I have had self-confidence and self-love? Well, I don't know. I think it came from me having to be competent and realizing no one was going to take care of me but me. Sure, other people might come

and go and aid me, but I can take care of myself. That's really important to me as a woman. We're taught to be other-directed and to get
affirmation externally, so I feel pretty powerful in that sense, because
I feel that I get a lot of nurturing and love from myself."

Forty-four-year-old Carla, who was twelve when her mother
died and fifteen when she lost her father, adds, "Sometimes when life
doesn't go exactly as I wish, or when I meet with disappointments, I
think, 'Would someone else who's gone through what you've gone
through be able to do what you've been able to do as an adult?' It's
my way of saying, 'Carla, you've had to deal with a lot. And you've
still done all right.' That's served as my barrier against great feelings
of defeat. When life hasn't gone exactly the way I would have
wished, I think, 'You've made a good life for yourself in spite of all
you've been through, and that's something to recognize and be
proud of.'"

Margie and Carla have discovered how to give themselves the
kind of comfort and praise they believe they lost when their mothers
died. Over the years, they developed the kind of inner guidance and
emotional security that motherless daughters so often say they lack.
They did this by learning to encourage, praise, and comfort themselves. And this is the best kind of substitute mothering a woman can
hope to receive.

I visited northern California for the first time in November 1992,
when I was researching the first edition of this book. On an unsea-
sonably warm Saturday afternoon, Phyllis and Marshall Klaus offered to take me sightseeing. We had time for only one major attraction: They suggested either Sonoma Valley or Muir Woods. I
remembered the postcards and photographs of the redwood forests,
where branches grew higher than houses, and cars could drive
through trees. I chose the woods.

I knew nothing about redwoods, except what my mother had
told me about their size—which was pretty accurate in Muir Woods.
I'd never seen trees so tall. As the Klauses and I shuffled through the
ferns and sorrel, we reached a small, odd group of redwoods growing
in a circle around a charred stump. The burned trunk stood maybe
six feet high, but the trees surrounding it were young and healthy.

Park rangers call these clusters "the family circle." The less botanically inclined call them the mother tree and her daughters.

This is why: In the redwood ecosystem, buds for future trees are contained in pods called burls, tough brown knobs that cling to the bark of the mother tree. When the mother tree is logged, blown over, or destroyed by fire—when, in other words, she dies—the trauma stimulates the burls' growth hormones. The seeds release, and trees sprout around her, creating the circle of daughters. The daughter trees grow by absorbing the sunlight their mother cedes them when she dies. They receive the moisture and nutrients they need from their mother's root system, which remains intact underground even after her leaves die. Although the daughters exist independently of their mother above ground, they continue to draw sustenance from her underneath.

For years, I searched for my mother in the air or the cosmos around me. I kept forgetting to look under my feet. The foundation she gave me in my first seventeen years was a solid one. If it hadn't been, I don't think I could have managed on my own after she died.

I've now been without a mother for much longer than I had one. Before long, my time as a mother of daughters will exceed the amount of time I spent as my mother's daughter. This is how healing works. Years pass. Pain dulls. Lived experience begins to supplant memory. Details blur. But we never forget.

Three years ago, my husband and I took our daughters on a four-day road trip from Los Angeles to southern Oregon. In Humboldt County, California, we took a short detour off Highway 101 to drive the Avenue of the Giants through 51,000 acres of redwood groves. As my husband maneuvered us along the narrow ribbon of shady road, I sat in the back seat between my daughters and told them about the postcards my mother had brought home to New York, and how I hadn't believed her when she said a car could drive through a tree. My older daughter, Maya, said she didn't believe it, either. A few miles up the road, we came upon the Shrine Tree, and saw that my mother's story had been true.

The photograph I have now shows our big white car emerging from a huge slit in a massive redwood trunk, my husband and Maya waving crazily from the front seats. As I took the photo from the side of the road, I tried to imagine my mother standing alongside the same tree, her hand raised in the same playful wave she gave the camera in 1974. She could have been saying hello. She could have been saying goodbye. Or she could have just been saying, "Hey, you. Remember me?"

Always.

Time alters some things. It beautifully preserves others. The words that closed the first edition of *Motherless Daughters* are just as relevant today as they were in 1994:

> I am fooling only myself when I say that my mother exists now only in the photograph on my bulletin board or in the outline of my hand or in the armful of memories I still hold tight. She lives on beneath everything I do. Her presence influenced who I was, and her absence influences who I am. Our lives are shaped as much by those who leave us as they are by those who stay. Loss is our legacy. Insight is our gift. Memory is our guide.

Motherless Daughters Survey

Between September 1992 and October 1993, 154 motherless women participated in a mail questionnaire. These are the results of that survey:

1. How old are you now?
   18 to 29—19%
   30 to 39—30%
   40 to 49—29%
   50 to 59—12%
   60 to 69—3%
   70 and older—7%

2. What is your profession?
   Results indicated:
   78% employed outside the home
   10% homemakers
   7% retired
   5% students

   marital status?
   49% married
   32% single[1]
   16% divorced or separated
   3% widowed

   educational level?
   3% less than high school

[1]May include women cohabiting with partners

29% high school
68% college and postcollege

state of residence?
34 states and the District of Columbia

race? (optional)
89% Caucasian
 8% African American
 2% Latina
 1% Native American and Asian American

religion? (optional)
22% Protestant
16% Jewish
13% Catholic
 6% atheist and agnostic
 4% Unitarian
 1% Muslim
16% other
22% none

3. Do you have children?
   55% yes
   45% no
   grandchildren?
   18% yes
   82% no

4. How old were you when your mother died or left?
   32% 12 or younger
   42% 13 to 19
   26% 20 or older

5. If your mother died, what was the cause of death?
   44% cancer
   10% heart failure
   10% accident
    7% suicide

3% pneumonia
3% infectious diseases
3% childbirth, abortion, miscarriage
3% kidney failure
3% cerebral hemorrhage
2% alcoholism
2% overdose
2% aneurysm
1% stroke
7% other or unknown

6. If your mother left or disappeared, what were the circumstances?
No respondents in this survey reported abandonment as a cause of loss.

7. Did you have any siblings at the time?
85% yes
15% no

What sex and ages were they then?
Results indicated:
28% of respondents were oldest children
25% middle children
31% youngest children
15% only children
 1% twins

8. Were your parents married, divorced, or separated at the time?
80% married
11% divorced
 2% separated
 1% never married
 6% of the mothers had been widows

9. Did your father remarry?
59% yes
41% no
If yes, how soon after your mother's death?
58% 0–2 years later

25% 2–5 years
12% 5–10 years
 5% 10 years or more

The following questions are multiple-choice format. Please circle the letter(s) that best describes your feelings.

10. The loss of my mother was:
    a. the single most determining event of my life—34%
    b. one of the most determining events of my life—56%
    c. a determining event of my life—9%
    d. not a determining event of my life—1%

11. If you answered a, b, or c to question 10, when did you begin to realize the loss of your mother was influencing your development?
    a. immediately—47%
    b. less than 5 years after the loss—14%
    c. 5 to 10 years after the loss—14%
    d. 10 to 20 years after the loss—12%
    e. more than 20 years after the loss—12%
    f. it has not influenced my development—1%

12. How often do you think about your own mortality?
    a. all of the time—9%
    b. most of the time—20%
    c. some of the time—69%
    d. never—2%

13. Please write in the number that best describes the degree to which you fear or have feared the following, with 1 = a lot, 2 = somewhat, and 3 = not at all.
    a. routine check-ups or annual exams
       17% a lot
       40% somewhat
       43% not at all

    b. getting the same disease or mental impairment as your mother
       36% a lot
       40% somewhat
       24% not at all

c. the yearly anniversary of your mother's death
20% a lot
34% somewhat
46% not at all

d. reaching the age your mother was when she died
29% a lot
35% somewhat
36% not at all

e. the death of your remaining parent, if still alive
29% a lot
36% somewhat
35% not at all

f. having children
27% a lot
24% somewhat
49% not at all

g. other (please specify)
1. Death of loved ones
2. Leaving children motherless
3. Dying young

14. How would you describe your current relationship with your father, if he is still alive?
a. excellent—13%
b. good—33%
c. fair—23%
d. poor—31%

15. Did you find a mother substitute after your mother died or left?
63% yes
37% no

If yes, who?
33% aunt
30% grandmother
13% sister
13% teacher
13% friend

9% neighbor
7% stepmother

16. Would you say your mourning period for your mother is:
    a. fully completed—16%
    b. partially completed—53%
    c. not at all complete—27%
    d. never begun—4%

17. How much do you know about your mother's life?
    a. a great deal—30%
    b. some—44%
    c. very little—26%
    d. nothing—0%

    From where did you get this information?
    a. members of the immediate family—63%
    b. members of the extended family—40%
    c. friends—21%
    d. mother herself—30%

18. Can you identify any positive results of your early loss?
    75% yes
    25% no

These next questions require short answers. Please keep your responses to one or two paragraphs.

19. How would you describe your current attitude toward separation and/or loss?

20. Which do you feel affected you more: the actual loss of your mother or the subsequent changes in your family? Please explain.

21. How, if at all, has your loss affected your romantic relationships?

22. If you are a parent, do you think the loss of your mother affected your parenting? How?

   If you are not a parent, what are or were your thoughts about having children?

23. What are some of the coping mechanisms you have used over the years to manage without a mother?

24. When do you miss your mother the most?

25. Please tell us about a specific experience you've had that illustrates what it meant for you to be a motherless daughter. We will try to include some of these anecdotes in the book.

Resources

The following organizations offer support, social events, or both for motherless daughters. Additional resources and news about upcoming groups and events are added and updated frequently at www.motherlessdaughters.net and www.motherlessmothers.com.

Motherless Daughters of Los Angeles
P.O. Box 64373
Los Angeles, CA 90064
310-474-2208
www.motherlessdaughtersbiz.com
Contact: Irene Rubaum-Keller, MFT

Motherless Daughters of Orange County (MDOC)
9053 Suva St.
Downey, CA 90242
562-862-6653
MDofOC@hotmail.com
www.motherlessdaughtersoc.com
Contact: Mary Felix

Metro Detroit Motherless Daughters (MDMD)
45333 Kensington
Utica, MI 48317
586-337-3110
metrodetroitmd@yahoo.com
www.metrodetroitmotherlessdaughters.net
Contact: Vicki Waldron

Motherless Daughters of Chicago
Chicago, IL
773-233-5460 (Chicago)
630-424-8081 (western suburbs)
mdofchicago@hotmail.com
Contacts: Ruta Grigola (Chicago); Dawn Klancic (western suburbs)

Motherless Daughters of New England
Boston, MA
mdonema@yahoo.com
http://motherlessdaughtersofnewengland.intranets.com
Contact: Linda Mills

Circle of Daughters
4637 Ironwood Dr.
Hamburg, NY 14075 (Buffalo area)
716-627-4934
MomsSpirit@aol.com
www.circleofdaughters.com
Contact: Day Cummings, CSW, RN

Mommy's Light Lives On
P.O. Box 494
Lionville, PA 19353
www.mommyslight.org
(for girls ages 3 to 18)

Motherless Daughters of Switzerland
(Toechter ohne Muetter)
Winterthur, Switzerland
41 (0)52 243 18 40
toechterohnemuetter@hotmail.com
www.geocities.com/prettyswiss/Toechter_ohne_Muetter.html
(in German)
Contact: Andrea Allen

The Motherless Mothers Foundation—Israel
(Imahot L'lo Imahot)
C/o Rahav
Grizim 7, Apt. 2
Tel Aviv, Israel
972 54 471-4044
972 54 442-5856
motherlessmothers@mail.com
www.motherlessmother.org.il
(Hebrew and English)
Contacts: Julie Rahav; Shoshanit Lupo Feigenberg

To find a bereavement group near you for children, teens, or family members, contact:

The Dougy Center for Grieving Children & Families
3909 SE 52nd Ave.
Portland, OR 97206
866-775-5683
help@dougy.org

Or use the "Center Locator" option at www.dougy.org, which lists more than three hundred bereavement centers in the United States, Canada, and seven other countries.

Appendix C

Motherless Daughters
in Literature

Over the years, many readers have asked me to write more about the circumstances surrounding their specific types of loss. Although an in-depth discussion of every type of mother loss is beyond the scope of a single book, many excellent memoirs and novels feature female protagonists who for many different reasons are motherless at various ages. These include such classics as *To Kill a Mockingbird, I Know Why the Caged Bird Sings, Their Eyes Were Watching God, Anne of Green Gables, Pippi Longstocking, Emma, Persuasion,* and the entire Nancy Drew series. (For nineteenth-century motherless protagonists, pick up virtually anything by George Eliot or the Brontë sisters.)

What follows is a list—by no means comprehensive—of books published in the last twenty-five years that feature real-life and fictional motherless daughters. If one of your favorites isn't listed here, please send the title, author, and a brief synopsis of the book to info@motherlessdaughters.net for inclusion in an online list.

Memoirs

Cournos, Francine. *City of One* (2000). Fatherless at three, then motherless at eleven, the author grows up in foster homes, always looking for a place to belong. Now a psychoanalyst and happily married mother, she looks back at the feelings of abandonment and depression that she managed to overcome.

Di Mari, Christina. *Ocean Star* (2006). The daughter of a neglectful, depressed mother and a violent fater with a checkered past, Christina grows up in 1960s and 1970s San Francisco with help from her Italian-American extended family and a strong connection to God. Close sibling relationships, lifelong friendships, and a stable, loving husband also help her find her way.

Epstein, Helen. *Where She Came From* (1997). After the death of her mother, a Holocaust survivor, the journalist Helen Epstein travels to the Czech Republic to uncover details of her family's past. She weaves together a history of three generations of Jewish women, including the story of her grandmother Pepi, who, at age eight, lost her mother to suicide.

Hammer, Signe. *By Her Own Hand: Memoirs of a Suicide's Daughter* (1991). Hammer was nine when her mother committed suicide in the kitchen of the family home. Now an adult battling chronic depression, she plumbs family memory for the roots of her mother's ailment as well as her own.

Felman, Jil Lynn. *Cravings* (1997). The author, the third daughter in a Jewish Midwestern family, writes of mother loss as an adult, and the cravings for food, love, and women that have shaped her life.

Fox, Paula. *Borrowed Finery* (reprinted 2002). Abandoned as a baby by her biological parents, Fox is raised by a constantly changing cast of eccentric relatives and strangers, including a kindly Congregational minister. At twenty-one, she surrenders her own daughter for adoption, to be reunited many years later.

Goodwin, Doris Kearns. *Wait Till Next Year* (1998). A young female Dodgers fan grows up in 1940s and 1950s Brooklyn. Her childhood is idyllic until her mother dies and her father—an early orphan himself—sinks into despair.

Harrison, Kathryn. *The Kiss* (1997). A few years after losing her mother, the author meets, and becomes sexually involved with, the biological father she never knew.

_____. *The Mother Knot* (2004). The author, now a mother of three, comes to terms with her mother's death and legacy in this slim, elegant memoir.

Karbo, Karen. *The Stuff of Life* (2003). Karbo was a teenager when her mother died of cancer. When her stoic, uncommunicative father is diagnosed with lung cancer, Karbo, now a mother of two, shuttles back and forth between her home in Oregon and his trailer in Nevada. He's a terrible patient and she's a self-doubting nursemaid, but they find their own common ground.

Kraus, Caroline. *Borderlines* (2004). The narrator loses her mother to cancer and moves to San Francisco, where she falls under the influence of an unstable female coworker. A story of losing and finding oneself after grief.

Lauck, Jennifer. *Blackbird* (2000). Seven-year-old Jennifer loses her mother, then her father, and endures additional hardships in the custody of a stepmother who leaves her at a church commune in 1970s Los Angeles.

_____. *Still Waters* (2001). As a teenager and young adult Jennifer investigates her brother's suicide.

_____. *Show Me the Way* (2004). A collection of essays about parenting as a motherless mother.

Lord, M. G. *Astroturf* (2005). The author, an eighth-grader when her mother dies of cancer, is raised through adolescence by an engineer father—one of the country's first rocket scientists. The book is part memoir, part history of the male-dominated Jet Propulsion Laboratory in Pasadena and the characters who sent missions to Mars.

Lyden, Jacki. *Daughter of the Queen of Sheba* (1997). A National Public Radio journalist tells about her unpredictable childhood with a manic-depressive mother who had episodes of delusional grandeur.

Marin, Pamela. *Motherland* (2005). The author was fourteen when her mother died of cancer at a Christian Science retreat, 2,000 miles away from the family's Illinois home. At age twenty-nine, Marin starts dreaming of her mother and embarks on a journalist's odyssey to piece together the true story of her mother's life and death.

O'Fallon, Ann, and Margaret Vaillancourt, eds. *Kiss Me Goodnight* (2005). A collection of stories, poems, and essays by fifty-one women, all of whom were young when their mothers died of various causes, including cancer, suicide, alcoholism, accidents, and the Holocaust.

Pogrebin, Letty. *Deborah, Golda, and Me.* (1991) An exploration of female Jewish identity, written by an author left motherless at age fifteen.

Saffian, Sarah. *Ithaka* (1998). Sarah's adoptive mother dies when Sarah is six. Eighteen years later, she receives a phone call from a woman claiming to be her birth mother.

Schreiber Le Anne. *Midstream: The Story of a Mother's Death and a Daughter's Renewal* (1991). A forty-year-old Manhattan newspaper editor is about to leave New York to move to the country when her beloved mother is diagnosed with pancreatic cancer, and she decides to move in with her instead.

Scofield, Sandra. *Occasions of Sin* (2004). Raised Catholic in West Texas in the 1950s and 1960s, the author finds her adolescence is disrupted by her mother's death from kidney disease when she is sixteen.

Steiker, Valerie. *The Leopard Hat* (2003). The author, who at age twenty loses her mother to cancer, recounts her childhood as the daughter of a beautiful, cultured, and elegant woman, and the special relationship they shared. Set in Manhattan in the 1970s and 1980s.

Swander, Mary. *Out of This World: A Journey of Healing* (1995). The author, motherless since her early twenties, recovers from a near-fatal illness while living among the Amish of Kalona, Iowa.

_____. *Desert Pilgrim: En Route to Mysticism and Miracles* (2003). While a visiting professor at the University of New Mexico, the author learns about alternative forms of healing, reflects on her Catholic childhood, and remembers the mother who died of cancer many years ago.

Yen Mah, Adeline. *Falling Leaves* (1997). Yen Mah's mother died during her birth, and the child is considered an ill omen in the family. Raised by her wealthy, indifferent father and his beautiful, cruel second wife in 1950s Shanghai, she endures crushing emotional abuse yet finds solace from a loving aunt. Eventually she immigrates to the United States, where she finds love and becomes a successful doctor.

Novels

Allende, Isabel. *Portrait in Sepia.* (2001). Aurora del Valle, motherless since birth, tells the story of her remarkable life in a wealthy, powerful Chilean family. A narrative that spans fifty years, picking up where 1999's *Daughter of Fortune,* the story of Aurora's grandmother Eliza, left off.

Berg, Elizabeth. *Durable Goods* (1993). Eleven-year-old Katie, recently motherless, comes of age with a violent father and older, rebellious sister in early 1960s Texas.

_____. *Joy School* (1998). Katie, now on the cusp of thirteen and recently relocated to Missouri, struggles to make friends; falls in love for the first time; and learns about what holds people together.

Fitch, Janet. *White Oleander* (1999). Fifteen-year-old Astrid Magnussen endures a succession of Los Angeles foster homes after her single mother, a poet, is imprisoned for poisoning an ex-boyfriend. Made into a 2002 film with Michelle Pfeiffer and Alison Lohman.

Fletcher, Susan. *Eve Green* (2004). Eve Green was eight when her single mother overdosed in their apartment in Birmingham, England, leaving Eve to live with her grandparents in a remote Welsh town. Now twenty-nine and pregnant, Eve looks back at those years and the characters who helped her emotionally survive.

Gibbons, Kaye. *Ellen Foster* (1987). Eleven-year-old Ellen tragically loses her mother, survives an abusive father, and relies on her wits and courage to find herself a nurturing home. Set in the American South.

Godwin, Gail. *Father Melancholy's Daughter* (1991). Margaret was six when her free-spirited mother took off with a girlhood friend for a vacation from which she never returned. One year later she died. Fifteen years later, Margaret is emotionally attached to her depressed, Episcopalian minister father and struggling to understand her mother's choice.

Golden, Arthur. *Memoirs of a Geisha* (1997). An orphaned nine-year-old girl from a small fishing village in Japan, sold into slavery after her mother's death, becomes a leading geisha of the 1930s and 1940s.

Gordimer, Nadine. *Burger's Daughter* (1979). The orphaned daughter of two white South African activists searches for her own identity, while the government keeps her under watch.

Gordon, Mary. *Pearl* (2005). Maria Meyers was raised as a Catholic by her single, converted-Jewish father after her mother dies. She's now a single mother trying to save her adult daughter, Pearl, a political activist in the midst of a hunger strike in Dublin.

Hobhouse, Janet. *The Furies* (reprinted 2004). Helen is born into a family of idiosyncratic women, all widowed or abandoned by their men. Her mother—lovely, unstable, girlish—sends her to boarding school and later commits suicide in Helen's home. Believed to be an autobiographical story, in novel form.

Kidd, Sue Monk. *The Secret Life of Bees* (2004). Motherless since age four, fourteen-year-old Lily Owen runs away from her abusive father to search for clues about her mother's past. Taking her beloved nanny Rosaleen along on her quest, she lands in the home of the Boatwright sisters, three elderly beekeepers, who take her in. Set in 1960s South Carolina against a backdrop of racism and social tension.

Kincaid, Jamaica. *The Autobiography of My Mother* (1995). Seventy-year-old Xuela Richardson, whose mother died giving birth to her, narrates the story of her life on the island of Dominica in the West Indies, including the abuse she suffered as a child, her marriage to a European doctor, and her deliberate decision to remain childless.

Kingsolver, Barbara. *Animal Dreams* (1990). Codi Noline returns to her Arizona hometown after her sister's death to care for their ailing father. Once there, she must face his reticence, a devastating secret from her motherless adolescence, and the cloudy memory of her mother's death.

Livesey, Margot. *Eva Moves the Furniture* (2001). Young Eva McEwen, raised by a father and aunt in a small Scottish town after her mother dies, is periodically visited by two ghostly "companions," a woman and girl that only she can see. The story follows Eva through nursing school and into adulthood, in the postwar years, until the significance of her visitors becomes clear.

McAll, Alexander. *The No. 1 Ladies Detective Agency* series. (1998–2005). Precious Rambotswe, who lost her mother in a fatal train accident as a baby, opens Botswana's first private detective agency, specializing in domestic dramas, while encountering a few of her own.

McGowan, Heather. *Schooling* (2002). Thirteen-year-old Catrine Evans moves with her father from Maine to England to attend boarding school after her mother dies. Scapegoated by her class-conscious schoolmates, she develops a relationship with her chemistry teacher, Mr. Gilbert. Written in an experimental style.

Minot, Eliza. *The Tiny One* (2000). Eight-year-old Via Revere, the youngest child in a large Catholic family, narrates the aftermath of her mother's sudden death, from a sensitive child's point of view.

Minot, Susan. *Monkeys* (1986). Seven siblings in an established New England family mourn the death of their mother in an auto accident in this slender, semiautobiographical first novel.

Morris, Mary. *The Night Sky* (1997). Ivy Slovak, the single mother of a newborn son, is haunted by memories of her own mother, who abandoned seven-year-old Ivy but took her younger sister.

Nahai, Gina. *Moonlight on the Avenue of Faith* (1999). Lili's father sends her from Iran to a boarding school in Los Angeles after her beautiful, mysterious mother—"Roxana the Angel"—sprouts wings and flies off their Teheran balcony one night, disappearing for the next thirteen years. This is also a story, tinged with magical realism, of the Persian diaspora to the United States.

Oates, Joyce Carol. *I'll Take You There* (2002). Blamed for her mother's death, raised by stern grandparents, Anellia enrolls in an upstate New York university in the 1960s, where she joins in a sorority, has an interracial relationship, and eventually leaves to become a writer. An intellectual coming-of-age story.

Pera, Pia. *Lo's Diary.* (1999) This controversial book offers an alternative point of view to Vladimir Nabokov's *Lolita*. In this version, the motherless Lolita is precocious, manipulative, and self-serving. Translated from the Italian.

Picoult, Jodi. *Harvesting the Heart* (1995). Paige was only five when her mother left. Now a young mother with a newborn son, she doubts her maternal capacity and sets out to find the mother who abandoned her long ago.

Pietrzyk, Leslie. *A Year and a Day.* (1994). Fifteen-year-old Alice, living with an eccentric great-aunt and a secretive older brother, comes to terms with her single mother's unexpected suicide. Set in 1975 small-town Iowa.

Quindlen, Anna. *One True Thing* (1994). Ellen Gulden leaves her fast-track career in Manhattan to return home and care for her cancer-stricken mother. Then she's accused of helping her mother die. Made into a 1998 film with Meryl Streep and Renee Zellweger.

Resnick, Rachel. *Go West Young F*cked Up Chick* (2000). Twenty-something Brown University graduate Rebecca Roth moves to the glitz and chaos of Los Angeles to escape the memory of her mother's suicide.

Robinson, Marilynne. *Housekeeping* (1981). Sisters Ruthie and Lucille are raised by a series of eccentric female relatives, including the unconventional Aunt Sylvie, in 1950s Idaho, after their mother dies by suicide. Made into a 1987 movie starring Christine Lahti.

Rossi, Agnes. *The Houseguest* (2000). Six-year-old Maura learns that her mother has died of tuberculosis and her father, soon to leave Ireland for New Jersey, doesn't want to raise her. He starts a new life in America, while Maura grows up first with two stern aunts, and then in an Irish boarding school. Loosely based on events from the author's mother's life.

Schumacher, Julie. *The Body is Water* (1999). Twenty-eight-year-old Jane Haus, pregnant and unmarried, returns to her family's beach house to confront truths about her mother's life and death, and make peace with her father and sister.

Schwarz, Christina. *Drowning Ruth.* (2000). Ruth is raised from age three by an aunt and war-wounded father after her mother drowns under mysterious circumstances. A tale of psychological suspense set in Wisconsin against the backdrop of post–World War I America and the flu epidemic that followed.

Shields, Carol. *The Stone Diaries* (1993). The life story of Daisy Stone Goodwill, motherless since birth, and her descendents spans almost the entire twentieth century. An epic narrative of an ordinary yet inspiring life.

Smiley, Jane. *A Thousand Acres* (1991). Winner of the 1992 Pulitzer Prize for fiction. Three sisters, now adults, encounter the long-term effects of early mother loss and childhood abuse in this modern version of King Lear, set on the Iowa prairie. Made into a 1997 film starring Jessica Lange, Michelle Pfeiffer, and Jennifer Jason Leigh.

Straight, Susan. *I Been in Sorrow's Kitchen and Licked Out All the Pots* (1992). Fourteen-year-old, pregnant Marietta Cook leaves tiny Pine Gardens, South Carolina, to seek her fortune in Charleston after her mother dies. The story traces her life from 1959 to 1983.

Tan, Amy. *The Joy Luck Club* (1989). After her mother dies, Jing-Mei ("June") succumbs to her father's pressure to take her mother's seat in a weekly Mah jongg game, dubbed "The Joy Luck Club" by its members. From the three other Chinese women, her mother's best friends, she learns the secrets of her mother's—and everyone else's—life in China and the

United States. Made into a 1993 film starring Ming-Na Wen and Tamlyn Tomita.

Walker, Alice. *The Color Purple* (1982). Winner of the 1983 Pulitzer Prize for fiction. Celie, motherless since fourteen, is raped by her father, separated from her beloved sister, and married off to the abusive Mister, who needs her to care for his motherless children. But when the flamboyant Shug Avery arrives in town, Celie's options expand. Written in the African-American vernacular of the turn-of-the-century American South. Made into a 1985 film starring Whoopi Goldberg and Oprah Winfrey.

Weiner, Jennifer. *In Her Shoes* (2002). Older sister Rose is a successful, though frumpy, attorney. Younger sister Maggie is a gorgeous, self-centered underachiever. Their manic-depressive mother committed suicide when they were children. After a major falling out, the sisters are brought back together when their maternal grandmother reappears in their lives after a twenty-year absence. Made into a 2005 film starring Cameron Diaz, Toni Collette, and Shirley MacLaine.

Williams, Joy. *The Quick and the Dead* (2002). Three high school girls, motherless for various reasons, meet and pass an idle summer in Arizona in this quirky, insightful book.

Winspear, Jacqueline. The *Maisie Dobbs* series (2003–2005). Thirteen-year-old Maisie loses her mother and is sent to work as a maid for a wealthy London family in the 1920s. Ten years later, after attending Cambridge and working as a nurse during World War I, she opens a detective agency, through which she encounters mysteries in the present and ghosts from her past.

Young Adult Novels

Baskin, Nora Raleigh. *What Every Girl (Except Me) Knows* (2002). A sensitive and insightful motherless twelve-year-old grows up with her father and brother in upstate New York, and tries to piece together facts about her mother's mysterious death when she was a child. Ages 11 and up.

Berry, Liz. *Mel* (1993). Seventeen-year-old Melody is the daughter of a mentally ill mother in England. Driven almost to the brink of suicide herself, Melody gets a chance to reinvent her life when her mother is institutionalized. Ages 14 and up.

Birdsall, Jeanne. *The Penderwicks* (2005). Four lively motherless sisters, ages four through twelve, and their widowed, botanist father rent a summer cottage on the grounds of a New England estate. They soon meet the adventurous boy and his cold, distant, status-obsessed mother who live there. Ages 9 and up.

Brisson, Pat. *Sky Memories* (1991). Emily is ten when her single mother is diagnosed with cancer. The child poignantly narrates the story of the next ten months, leading up to her mother's death. Ages 8 and up.

Cook, Karin. *What Girls Learn* (1997). Twelve-year-old Tilden, eleven-year-old Elizabeth, and their mother relocate to Atlanta to live with the mother's boyfriend. Soon after the move, the girls' mother is diagnosed with breast cancer and dies. Ages 12 and up.

Creech, Sharon. *Walk Two Moons* (1994). Winner of the 1995 Newbery Medal. Salamanca Tree Hiddle is thirteen when she takes a road trip with her grandparents to Lewiston, Idaho, to look for the mother who disappeared. On the way, she draws from her Native American ancestry to weave a story that helps her cope with what she learns. Ages 11 and up.

DiCamillo, Kate. *Because of Winn-Dixie* (2000). Ten-year-old Opal was only three when her mother left. Now, with her newly adopted dog Winn-Dixie by her side, Opal finds the courage to ask her father about what happened. Made into a 2005 movie with Jeff Daniels and Cicely Tyson. Ages 8 and up.

Farmer, Nancy. *A Girl Named Disaster* (1996). Winner of the 1997 Newbery Medal. Nhamo, an eleven-year-old motherless girl in Mozambique, flees her Shona village to find her father in Zimbabwe, a perilous journey that takes her a year to complete and forces her to rely on survival skills she didn't know she had. Ages 10 and up.

Hermes, Patricia. *You Shouldn't Have to Say Goodbye* (1982). Thirteen-year-old Sarah, a gymnast, is having an uneventful year at school until her mother is diagnosed with cancer. In the remaining months they have together, Sarah's mother tries to prepare her daughter for her death. Ages 9 and up.

Johnston, Julie. *In Spite of Killer Bees* (2002). Aggie, Jeannie, and Helen Quade, ages fourteen to twenty-two, are orphans who receive an inheritance from a grandfather they never knew. To receive it, however, they have to live in his dilapidated house with an eccentric great-aunt and learn how to work through their conflicts. Ages 12 and up.

Kimmel, Elizabeth Cody. *In the Stone Circle* (2001). A motherless girl and her widowed father move into a 16th-century Welsh house for the summer. They're joined by a family struggling to cope with a divorce, and a mysterious young female ghost who needs their help. Ages 9 and up.

Kline, Christina Baker. *Sweet Water* (1993). Cassie, a twenty-five-year-old artist who was only three when she lost her mother under mysterious circumstances, inherits a house in rural Tennessee near her mother's family. The story is told in alternating chapters by Cassie and her maternal grandmother, who knows the details of the mother's tragic death. Ages 13 and up.

Leonard, Alison. *Tina's Chance* (1988). Tina sets out to discover the truth about the mother who died when she was two. From her Aunt Louise, a lesbian, she discovers that her mother died of a disease she has a 50 percent chance of inheriting. Ages 13 and up.

MacLachlan, Patricia. *Sarah, Plain and Tall* (reprinted 1987). Jacob and Anna, two motherless children on the Midwestern prairie, meet a potential new stepmother when their father places an advertisement in a New England newspaper, looking for a bride. Made into a 1991 TV movie with Glenn Close as Sarah. Ages 8 and up.

Marvin, Isabel. *A Bride for Anna's Papa* (1994). Twelve-year-old Anna and her nine-year-old brother Matti try to arrange for a mail-order bride for their father in 1907 Minnesota. Ages 9 and up.

Mazer, Norma Fox. *Girlhearts* (2002). Fourteen-year-old Sarabeth loses her young, widowed mother to a heart attack and moves in with family friends. Soon after she embarks on a journey to her mother's hometown to uncover secrets about her past. Ages 12 and up.

_____. *When She Was Good* (reprinted 2000). Teenaged Em loses her mother and runs away with her emotionally troubled older sister. After her sister dies, Em must face her family's legacy of abuse. Ages 12 and up.

Maynard, Joyce. *The Usual Rules* (2003). Thirteen-year-old Wendy moves to California to live with her father after her mother dies in the Twin Tower attacks of September 11, 2001. But she must leave a beloved stepfather and half-brother behind. Ages 13 and up.

Penson, Mary E. *You're An Orphan, Mollie Brown* (1993). After their mother dies, Mollie and her twin brother live with relatives while their father goes off in search of work. Set in 1870s Texas. Ages 8 and up.

Radley, Gail. *Nothing Stays the Same Forever* (1988). Twelve-year-old Carrie has a widowed father who plans to remarry, an older sister who just started dating, and an elderly friend in poor health. Ages 9 and up.

Snicket, Lemony. *A Series of Unfortunate Events* series (1999–2004). Violet, Klaus, and Sunny Baudelaire lose their parents in a fire, inherit a fortune, and try to elude the evil Count Olaf while searching for a stable home in this eleven-book series. Made into a 2004 film with Jim Carrey and Meryl Streep. Ages 9 and up.

Sones, Sonya. *One of Those Hideous Books Where the Mother Dies* (2004). Fifteen-year-old Ruby loses her mother and is sent to live with her father, a famous actor in Los Angeles whom she has never met. Written as a series of prose poems.

Whelan, Gloria. *A Time to Keep Silent* (1993). Thirteen-year-old Clair stops speaking after her mother dies. Then she befriends Dorrie, also thirteen and motherless, who lives alone because her father is in jail. Ages 11 and up.

Woodson, Jacqueline. *I Hadn't Meant to Tell You This* (1994). Marie, an African-American eighth-grader whose mother left two years ago, befriends a white girl at school who confides that she's being molested by her father. Ages 12 and up.

Wyman, Andrea. *Red Sky at Morning* (1991). Callie Common and her older sister Katherine go to live with their aging grandfather after their father leaves for Oregon and their mother dies in childbirth. Set on a hardscrabble Indiana farm in 1909. Ages 9 and up.

Children's Picture Books

Holmes, Margaret M. *Molly's Mom Died* (1999). School-aged Molly talks about the emotional aftermath of her mother's death from illness. Includes a special note for caregivers at the end. Ages 5 to 9.

Madonna. *The English Roses* (2003). Four little English girls are envious of their "perfect" classmate—until they learn she's motherless and in need of a friend. Ages 4 to 8.

Moore Campbell, Bebe. *Sometimes My Mommy Gets Angry* (2003). School-aged Annie lives with a mother who suffers from bipolar disorder that can make her 'angry on the outside.' A supportive grandmother and a pair of silly friends provide Annie with consistent acceptance and love. Ages 4 to 8.

Ruben Greenfield, Nancy. *When Mommy Had a Mastectomy* (2005). Coping with a mother's breast cancer, from a young child's point of view. Ages 4 to 8.

Bibliography

Altschul, Sol, ed. *Childhood Bereavement and Its Aftermath.* Madison, Conn.: International Universities Press, 1988.

Bassoff, Evelyn. *Mothering Ourselves.* New York: NAL-Dutton, 1992.

_____. *Mothers and Daughters.* New York: Plume, 1988.

Becker, Ernest. *The Denial of Death.* New York: Free Press, 1973.

Bowlby, John. *A Secure Base.* New York: Basic Books, 1988.

_____. *Attachment and Loss,* Volume III: Loss. New York: Basic Books, 1980.

Cahill, Susan, ed. *Mothers.* New York: Mentor-Penguin, 1988.

Carlson, Kathie. *In Her Image.* Boston: Shambhala, 1990.

Carter, Betty, and Monica McGoldrick, eds. *The Changing Family Life Cycle.* Needham Heights, Mass.: Allyn & Bacon, 1989.

Chernin, Kim. *In My Mother's House.* New York: HarperCollins, 1984.

Chodorow, Nancy. *The Reproduction of Mothering.* Berkeley, Calif.: University of California Press, 1978.

Commins, Patricia. *Remembering Mother, Finding Myself.* Deerfield Beach, Fla.: Health Communications, Inc., 1999.

Cowan, Carolyn Pape, and Philip A. Cowan. *When Partners Become Parents.* New York: Basic Books, 1992.

De Beauvoir, Simone. *A Very Easy Death.* New York: Pantheon, 1985.

_____. *The Second Sex.* Middlesex, England: Penguin Books, 1972.

DeSpelder, Lynne Ann, and Albert Lee Strickland. *The Last Dance.* Mountain View, Calif.: Mayfield, 1992.

Dunne, Edward J., John L. McIntosh, and Karen Dunne-Maxim, eds. *Suicide and Its Aftermath.* New York: Norton, 1987.

Eisenstadt, Marvin, Andre Haynal, Pierre Rentchnick, and Pierre de Senarclens. *Parental Loss and Achievement.* Madison, Conn.: International Universities Press, 1989.

Emswiler, Mary Ann, and James Emswiler. *Guiding Your Child Through Grief.* New York: Bantam Books, 2000.

Ernaux, Annie. *A Woman's Story.* New York: Ballantine, 1992.

Estés, Clarissa Pinkola. "Warming the Stone Child." Boulder, Colo.: Sounds True Recordings. Tape no. A104, 1990.

Friday, Nancy. *My Mother/My Self.* New York: Dell, 1987.

Furman, Erna. *A Child's Parent Dies.* New Haven, Conn.: Yale University Press, 1974.

Granot, Tamar. *Without You.* Philadelphia: Jessica Kingsley Publishers, 2005.

Grollman, Earl A. *Explaining Death to Children.* Boston: Beacon, 1967.

Gundlach, Julie Kettle. *My Mother Before Me.* Secaucus, N.J.: Lyle Stuart, 1986.

Hammer, Signe. *By Her Own Hand.* New York: Vintage, 1992.

Harris, Maxine. *The Loss That Is Forever.* New York: Plume, 1995.

Kennedy, Alexandra. *Losing a Parent.* New York: HarperCollins, 1991.

Klaus, Marshall H., John H. Kennell, and Phyllis H. Klaus. *Mothering the Mother.* Reading, Mass.: Addison-Wesley, 1993.

Kübler-Ross, Elisabeth. *On Death and Dying.* New York: Macmillan, 1970.

Lauck, Jennifer. *Blackbird.* New York: Pocket, 2000.

Lowinsky, Naomi Ruth. *The Motherline.* Los Angeles: Tarcher, 1993.

Miller, Alice. *The Untouched Key.* New York: Anchor-Doubleday, 1990.

_____. *The Drama of the Gifted Child.* New York: Basic Books, 1981.

Minot, Susan. *Monkeys.* New York: Washington Square Press, 1987.

Moffat, Mary Jane, ed. *In the Midst of Winter.* New York: Vintage, 1992.

Myers, Edward. *When Parents Die.* New York: Penguin, 1986.

O'Fallon, Margaret, and Margaret Vaillancourt, eds. *Kiss Me Goodnight.* St. Paul, Minn.: Syren, 2005.

Pogrebin, Letty Cottin. *Deborah, Golda, and Me.* New York: Crown, 1991.

Quindlen, Anna. *Living Out Loud.* New York: Ivy Books, 1988.

Rando, Therese A. *Treatment of Complicated Mourning.* Champaign, Ill.: Research Press, 1993.

_____. *How to Go on Living When Someone You Love Dies.* New York: Bantam, 1991.

_____. *Grief, Dying, and Death.* Champaign, Ill.: Research Press, 1984.

Rich, Adrienne. *Of Woman Born.* New York: Norton, 1986.

_____. *On Lies, Secrets, and Silence.* New York: Norton, 1979.

Secunda, Victoria. *Women and Their Fathers.* New York: Delacorte, 1992.

_____. *When You and Your Mother Can't Be Friends.* New York: Delta, 1991.

Sheehy, Gail. *Passages.* New York: Bantam, 1977.

Silverman, Phyllis Rolfe. *Never Too Young to Know.* New York: Oxford University Press, 2000.

Smiley, Jane. *A Thousand Acres.* New York: Fawcett Columbine, 1992.

Viorst, Judith. *Necessary Losses.* New York: Fawcett Gold Medal, 1987.

Vozenilek, Helen, ed. *Loss of the Ground-Note.* Los Angeles: Clothespin Fever Press, 1992.

Walsh, Froma, and Monica McGoldrick, eds. *Living Beyond Loss.* New York: Norton, 1991.

Worden, J. William. *Children and Grief.* New York: The Guilford Press, 1996.

"It is the image in the mind . . . ": Colette, *My Mother's House* (New York: Farrar, Straus & Young, 1953), cited in Mary Jane Moffatt, ed., *In the Midst of Winter* (New York: Vintage, 1992 edition), 193.

Introduction

xx   "My mother died when I was nineteen . . . ": Anna Quindlen, "Mothers," *Living Out Loud* (New York: Ivy Books, 1988), 210.

xxii   The Dougy Center Web site . . . : http://www.dougy.org

xxiii   As Phyllis Silverman, Ph.D. . . . : Phyllis Rolfe Silverman, *Never Too Young to Know* (New York: Oxford University Press, 2000), 15–16.

xxiii   At least 2,990 children and teenagers . . . : Andrea Elliot, "Growing Up Grieving, With Constant Reminders of 9/11," *New York Times,* September 11, 2004.

xxiii   Six years earlier, more than 200 . . . : Personal correspondence, Jane Thomas, Collections Manager, Oklahoma City National Memorial, January 25, 2005; backed up by personal correspondence with Betty Pfefferbaum, Director, Terrorism and Disaster Branch of the National Center for Child Traumatic Stress, University of Oklahoma Health Sciences Center, February 11, 2005.

xxiii   Accidents and cancer are . . . : Table 1, "Deaths, percent of total deaths, and death rates for the 10 leading causes of death in selected age groups, by race and sex: United States, 2002," *National Vital Statistics Reports* 53, no. 17 (March 7, 2005): 18.

xxiii   But the U.S. cancer rate among women . . . : Table No. 109, "Death Rates from Malignant Neoplasms, by Race, Sex and Age: 1950 to

2000," U.S. Census Bureau, *Statistical Abstract of the United States 2004–2005*, www.census.gov/prod/2004pubs/04statab/vitstat.pdf.

xxiii The AIDS epidemic in the United States . . . : Hope Edelman, *Motherless Daughters* (New York: Delta, 1995), xxii; "Estimates of the Number of Motherless Youth Orphaned by AIDS in the United States," *Journal of the American Medical Association* 268 (December 23–30 1992): 3456–3461.

xxiv As of March 2005, seven American . . . : Jerry Adler, "Children of the Fallen." *Newsweek*, March 21, 2005, 27–32; Lisa Hoffman, "Six Moms Have Been Killed in Iraq," Scripps Howard News Service, December 15, 2004, www.shns.com/shns/warkids/warkids-moms.cfm.

xxiv Among some of its findings are . . . : J. William Worden, *Children and Grief* (New York: Guilford Press, 1996), 95–96.

xxvi In every racial group in America . . . : D. L. Hoyert, H. C. Kung, and B. L. Smith, "Deaths: Preliminary Data for 2003," *National Vital Statistics Reports*, 53, no. 15 (Hyattsville, Md.: National Center for Health Statistics, 2005), Table A, 3.

xxvi Today, the average twenty-year-old Caucasian male . . . : Table No. 93, "Selected Life Table Values: 1979 to 2001," U.S. Census Bureau, *Statistical Abstract of the United States 2004–2005*, 71, www.census. gov/prod/2004pubs/04statab/vitstat.pdf.

xxvi Among African Americans . . . : Ibid.

xxvi American men of all races . . . : Hoyert, Kung, and Smith, "Deaths," 7.

xxvi In 2003 alone: Ibid.; Table 1, "Deaths and death rates by age, sex, and race and Hispanic origin and age-adjusted death rates, by sex and race and Hispanic origin: United States, final 2002 and preliminary 2003," 7; and Table 2, "Deaths, death rates, and age-adjusted death rates for 113 selected causes, injury by firearms, drug-induced deaths, alcohol-induced deaths, and injury at work: United States, final 2002 and preliminary 2003," 15.

xxvi More than 676,000 American children . . . : Calculated from statistics printed in Neil Kalter, et al., "The Adjustment of Parentally Bereaved Children, *Omega* 46 (2002–2003), 15–34; Katherine Porterfield et al., "The Impact of Early Loss History on Parenting of Bereaved Children: A Qualitative Study," *Omega* 47 (2003), 203–220; U.S. Census Bureau, Table No. 11, "Resident Population by Age and Sex:

1980 to 2003," www.census.gov/prod/2004pubs/04statab/pop.pdf; U.S. Census Bureau, Table No. 12, "Resident Population Projections by Sex and Age: 2005 to 2050," www.census.gov/prod/2004pubs/04statab/pop.pdf.

xxvi Nearly 25,000 girls have . . . : Ibid.

xxvi I calculate that there are . . . : Ibid.

xxvi Fn: More than 532,000 children . . . : The AFCARS Report: Preliminary FY 2002 Estimates as of August 2004, U.S. Department of Health and Human Services, Administration for Children and Families, www.acf.hhs.gov/programs/cb.

xxvi Fn: Approximately 126,000 children have mothers . . . : Christopoher J. Mumola, "Incarcerated Parents and Their Children," U.S. Department of Justice, Bureau of Justice Statistics, August 2000, NCJ 182335, 2; J. Poehlmann, "Incarcerated Mothers' Contact with Children, Perceived Family Relationships, and Depressive Symptoms," *Journal of Family Psychology* 19 (Sept. 2005), 350–357.

xxvii When a parent dies young . . . : Maxine Harris, *The Loss That Is Forever* (New York: Plume, 1996), 48.

xxvii "Some events are so big . . . ": Ibid., xvii.

xxvii As Maxine Harris points out . . . : Ibid., 10–11.

Part I: Loss

1   "The loss of the daughter to the mother . . . ": Adrienne Rich, *Of Woman Born* (New York: Norton, 1986), 237.

Chapter One: The Seasons of Grieving

7   "Some individuals become . . . ": Tamar Granot, *Without You* (London: Jessica Kingsley Publishers, 2005), 11.

7   Vacillation over a career . . . : Ibid.

7   (One grief counseling Web site . . .): TLC Group, Dallas, Texas, "Beware the Five Stages of Grief," www.counselingforloss.com/article8.htm.

8   I prefer J. William Worden's Four Tasks of Mourning . . . : Worden, *Children and Grief,* 12.

8   Unlike adults . . . : Erna Furman, *A Child's Parent Dies* (New Haven, Conn.: Yale University Press, 1974), 12.

9   They do it in the midst . . . : Mary Ann Emswiler and James P. Emswiler, *Guiding Your Child Through Grief* (New York: Bantam Books, 2000), 18.

10   "They know how much pain . . . ": Ibid., 19.

11   It's difficult for children . . . : Harry Hardin and Daniel Hardin, "On the Vicissitudes of Early Primary Surrogate Mothering II: Loss of the Surrogate Mother and Arrest of Mourning," *Journal of the American Psychoanalytic Association* 48 (2000), 1246.

11   Researchers have found . . . : National Public Radio, "Morning Edition," August 30, 1988; Furman, A Child's Parent Dies, 16–17, 22–23, 112–113; Nan Birnbaum, personal communication, October 25, 1991; Russell Hurd, "Adults View Their Childhood Bereavement Experiences," *Death Studies* 23 (1999), 17.

11   Some therapists have viewed adolescence . . . : Martha Wolfenstein, "How Is Mourning Possible?" *Psychoanalytic Study of the Child* 21 (1966): 93–123; Anna Freud, "Adolescence," *Psychoanalytic Study of the Child* 13 (1958): 255–278; Moses Laufer, "Object Loss and Mourning during Adolescence," *Psychoanalytic Study of the Child* 21 (1966): 269–293; Max Sugar, "Normal Adolescent Mourning," *American Journal of Psychotherapy* 22 (1968): 258–269.

12   In response to a major loss . . . : Wolfenstein, "How Is Mourning Possible?" 111.

12   Because she equates crying . . . : Ibid., 110–111.

13   Fathers may feel grief . . . : Therese Rando, *How to Go on Living When Someone You Love Has Died* (New York: Lexington, 1988), 65–67.

16   Rage, rather than grief . . . : Judith Mishne, "Parental Abandonment: A Unique Form of Loss and Narcissistic Injury," *Clinical Social Work Journal* 7 (Fall 1979): 17.

19   As Virginia Woolf . . . : Virginia Woolf, "A Sketch of the Past," *Moments of Being* (New York: Harvest/Harcourt Brace Jovanovich, 1985), 89.

20 But negative emotion . . . : Therese Rando, *Treatment of Complicated Mourning* (Champaign, Ill.: Research Press, 1993), 476.

22 A mother who inflicted . . . : Ibid., 473–474.

22 It doesn't invalidate . . . : Ibid., 476.

24 Certain days or times . . . : Ibid., 64–77; Rando, *How to Go on Living*, 77.

24 Holidays, crises, and sensory reminders . . . : Ibid.

24 Therese Rando calls these . . . : Rando, *Treatment of Complicated Mourning*, 64.

27 Full resolution of mourning . . . : Camille B. Wortman and Roxane Cohen Silver, "The Myths of Coping with Loss," *Journal of Consulting and Clinical Psychology* 57 (1989): 353.

28 Sigmund Freud believed . . . : Sigmund Freud, "Mourning and Melancholia," *Sigmund Freud: Collected Papers*, vol. 4, ed. Ernest Jones, M.D. (New York: Basic Books, 1959), 152–170.

28 But more recent scholars . . . : Phyllis Silverman, "The Impact of Parental Death on College-Age Women," *Psychiatric Clinics of North America* 10 (1987): 387–403; Furman, *A Child's Parent Dies*, 52.

28 When Phyllis Silverman . . . : Silverman, "The Impact of Parental Death on College-Age Women," 402.

28 Many of the 125 children . . . difficulty over time: "Phyllis R. Silverman: An Omega Interview," 259; Worden, *Children and Grief*, 5.

28 It seems that a child's memory . . . : Granot, *Without You*, 46–47.

28 We're finally moving . . . : Silverman, *Never Too Young to Know*, 21.

Chapter Two: Times of Change

36 This usually occurs between . . . : Furman, *A Child's Parent Dies*, 41–42; John Bowlby, *Attachment and Loss*, vol. 3, *Loss: Sadness and Depression* (New York: Basic Books, 1980), 429.

37 Daughters whose mothers died . . . a parent they never knew: Harris, *The Loss That Is Forever*, 17–19.

37 Although young children's capacity . . . : Bowlby, *Attachment and Loss*, 424.

37   He observed that children . . . : Ibid., 435.

38   Although toddlers don't yet fully . . . : Sandra E. Candy-Gibbs, Kay
      Colby Sharp, and Craig J. Petrun, "The Effects of Age, Object, and
      Cultural/Religious Background on Children's Concepts of Death,"
      Omega 15 (1984–1985): 329–345; Richard A. Jenkins and John C.
      Cavanaugh, "Examining the Relationship between the Development of
      the Concept of Death and Overall Cognitive Development," *Omega*
      16 (1985–1986): 193–194.

38–   A child's first and most profound . . . : Nancy Chodorow, The
39   *Reproduction of Mothering* (Berkeley, Calif.: University of California
      Press, 1978), 86.

39   As Bowlby and other attachment theorists have observed . . . : Bowlby,
      Loss, 428, as well as the comprehensive research and writings of Mary
      Salter Ainsworth and Mary Main, especially Russel L. Tracy and Mary
      D. Salter Ainsworth, "Maternal Affectionate Behavior and Infant-
      Mother Attachment Patterns," *Child Development* 52 (1981),
      1341–1343; Mary Main and Donna Weston, "The Quality of the
      Toddler's Relationship to Mother and to Father: Related to Conflict
      Behavior and the Readiness to Establish New Relationships," *Child
      Development* 52 (1981), 932–940; Mary Main and Jude Cassidy,
      "Categories of Response to Reunion with the Parent at Age 6:
      Predictable From Infant Attachment Classifications and Stable Over a
      1-Month Period," *Developmental Psychology* 24 (1988), 415–416; and
      Robert Karen, *Becoming Attached: Unfolding the Mystery of the
      Infant-Mother Bond and Its Impact on Later Life* (New York: Warner
      Books: 1994), 131–226.

39   Among children of all ages . . . : Michael Rutter, "Resilience in the Face
      of Adversity," *British Journal of Psychiatry* 147 (1985): 603; Elliot M.
      Kranzler, David Shaffer, Gail Wasserman, and Mark Davies, "Early
      Childhood Bereavement," *Journal of the American Academy of Child
      and Adolescent Psychiatry* 29 (July 1990): 513–520.

39   Although she often makes it clear . . . : Bowlby, *Attachment and Loss*,
      419.

39   Elizabeth Fleming's case study . . . : Furman, *A Child's Parent Dies*,
      219–232.

40   "She had never been . . . ": Ibid., 223.

41 Some therapists believe that children . . . : Sol Altschul and Helen Beiser, "The Effect of Early Parent Loss on Future Parenthood," in *Parenthood: A Psychodynamic Perspective,* ed. Rebecca S. Cohen (New York: Guilford Press, 1984), 175.

42 "[They] will skirt the mention": Mishne, "Parental Abandonment," 17.

42 SigmundFreud called this phenomenon . . . : Sigmund Freud, "Splitting of the Ego in the Defensive Process," *Sigmund Freud: Collected Papers,* vol. 5, ed. Ernest Jones, M.D. (New York: Basic Books, 1959), 372–375.

45 While an adult brings . . . : David M. Moriarty, ed., *The Loss of Loved Ones: The Effects of Death in the Family on Personality Development* (Springfield, Ill.: Thomas, 1967), 96.

45 When Anna Freud observed . . . : In Mishne, "Parental Abandonment," 22.

45-
46 "I have to telephone . . . ": Ibid.

46 She'd be left in what Anna Freud called . . . : Anna Freud, *Infants without Families* (Madison, Conn.: International Universities Press, 1973), cited in Christina Sekaer, "Toward a Definition of Childhood Mourning," *American Journal of Psychotherapy* 16 (April 1987): 209.

46 The loss of a mother creates . . . : Mishne, "Parental Abandonment," 77. See also Joan Fleming, Sol Altschul, Victor Zielinski, and Max Forman, "The Influence of Parent Loss in Childhood on Personality Development and Ego Structure" (paper presented at the annual meeting of the American Psychoanalytic Association, San Francisco, Calif., May 1958); and George Krupp, "Maladaptive Reactions to the Death of a Family Member," *Social Casework* (July 1972): 430.

47 When researchers at . . . have exited the scene: J. William Worden and Phyllis Silverman, "Parental Death and the Adjustement of School-Age Children," *Omega* 33 (1996), 91–101.

47 Adolescence, a period of intense . . . : Anna Freud, "Adolescence," 255–278.

48 In addition, sleep disturbances . . . : Heather Servaty and Bert Hayslip, "Adjustment to Loss Among Adolescents," *Omega* 43 (2001), 313–314.

48 Two years after the loss . . . : Ibid., 314.

49 This is not a time of . . . : Sumru Ekrut, "Daughters Talking about Their Mothers: A View from the Campus," working paper no. 127, Wellesley College Center for Research on Women, 1984, 1.

49 As a study of a hundred autobiographical . . . : Ibid., 4.

54 A 1950s study of orphaned children . . . : Anna Freud, "Adolescence," 266.

54 "It was marked by feeling . . . ": Furman, A Child's Parent Dies, 194.

56 In fact, a teen is more likely . . . : Ross Gray, "Adolescents' Perceptions of Social Support After the Death of a Parent," *Journal of Psychosocial Oncology* 7 (1989), 127.

57 Adolescents, as they undergo symbolic . . . : Rose-Emily Rothenberg, "The Orphan Archetype," *Psychological Perspectives* 14 (Fall 1983): 181–194.

57 The teenaged girl who thinks . . . : Benjamin Garber, "Mourning in Adolescents: Normal and Pathological," *Adolescent Psychiatry* 12 (1985): 378.

57 This is in part to conform . . . : Ann Marie Lenhardt and Bernadette McCourt, "Adolescent Unresolved Grief in Response to the Death of a Mother," *Professional School Counseling* 3 (February 2000), 190.

57 The more composed a teen . . . : Ibid., 189–190.

57 At the same time the teenager . . . : Ibid.

60 And some research suggests . . . : Rutter, "Resilience," 605; Mary D. Salter Ainsworth and Carolyn Eichberg, "Effects on Infant-Mother Attachment of Mother's Unresolved Loss of an Attachment Figure, or Other Traumatic Experience," in *Attachment Across the Life Cycle,* ed. Colin Murray Parkes, Joan Stevenson-Hinde, and Peter Marris (London: Tavistock/Routledge, 1991), 165.

60 It also forces her into maturity . . . : Garber, "Mourning in Adolescents," 379.

62 Many of us have had access . . . : Rosalind C. Barnett, "Adult Daughters and Their Mothers: Harmony or Hostility?" working paper no. 209, Wellesley College Center for Research on Women, 1990, 1.

67 Elizabeth Nager and Brian De Vries . . . : Elizabeth Nager and Brian De Vries, "Memorializing on the World Wide Web: Patterns of Grief

and Attachment in Adult Daughters of Deceased Mothers," *Omega* 49 (2004), 45.

67   Between the ages of forty and sixty . . . : Andrew Scharlach and Karen Fredriksen, "Reactions to the Death of a Parent During Midlife," *Omega* 27 (1993), 307.

67   Still, Nager, and De Vries say . . . : Nager and De Vries, "Memorializing on the World Wide Web," 45.

67   Three months after the loss . . . : Miriam Moss, et. al. "Impact of Elderly Mother's Death on Middle-Age Daughters," International Journal of *Aging and Human Development* 37 (1993), 1.

67   74 percent said . . . : Ibid., 8.

67   67 percent continued . . . : Scharlach and Fredriksen, "Reactions to the Death of a Parent During Midlife," 309—310.

67   86 percent reported . . . : Ibid., 312.

67   40 percent reported . . . : Ibid., 313.

68   36 percent developed . . . : Ibid.

68   75 percent saw it . . . : Moss, et. al., 8.

68   72 percent did not feel . . . : Ibid.

68   80 percent believe . . . : Ibid.

68   Women who were younger . . . : Ibid., 10.

68   Because an adult daughter . . . : Moss, et al., 10.

68   Research from the Wellesley College Center . . . : Barnett, "Adult Daughters and Their Mothers," 10.

69   In the healthiest scenario . . . : Evelyn Bassoff, *Mothers and Daughters: Loving and Letting Go* (New York: Plume-NAL, 1988), 224.

69   "Although the primal bond . . . ": Martha A. Robbins, *Midlife Women and Death of Mother* (New York: Lang, 1990), 246.

Chapter Three: Cause and Effect

76   Of 149 motherless women . . . : Motherless Daughters survey, question 5 (see Appendix A).

79 "When a child witnesses . . . ": Harris, *The Loss That Is Forever*, 26.

79 A mother is a daughter's natural . . . : Jacqueline May Parris Lamb, "Adolescent Girls' Responses to Mothers' Breast Cancer" (Ph.D. diss., University of Pittsburgh, 1984), 61.

86 Mothers who are institutionalized . . . usually unpredictable: Therese A. Rando, *Clinical Dimensions of Anticipatory Mourning* (Champaign, Ill.: Research Press, 2000), 481.

86 Death always feels sudden . . . : Silverman, *Never Too Young to Know*, 84.

86 "It is one of the mysteries . . . ": From the *Autobiography of Mark Twain*, quoted in Moffat, *In the Midst of Winter*, 6.

86 When a daughter's assumptions . . . : Rando, *Treatment of Complicated Mourning*, 542.

88 Losing a parent to . . . : Ibid., 523.

88 A mother's suicide leaves . . . : Ibid., 524.

88 Therapists have observed . . . : Karen Dunne-Maxim, Edward J. Dunne, and Marilyn J. Hauser, "When Children Are Suicide Survivors," in *Suicide and Its Aftermath,* ed. Edward J. Dunne, John L. McIntosh, and Karen Dunne-Maxim (New York: Norton, 1987), 243.

88 Child survivors also may . . . : Ibid., 234–240.

89 When the psychologists Albert Cain and Irene Fast . . . : Albert C. Cain and Irene Fast, "Children's Disturbed Reactions to Parent Suicide: Distortions of Guilt, Communication, and Identification," in *Survivors of Suicide,* ed. Albert C. Cain (Springfield, Ill.: Thomas, 1972), 93–111.

89 Other daughters develop . . . : Ibid., 106–107.

89 The violence or mutilation often involved . . . : Rando, *Treatment of Complicated Mourning*, 512.

90 Lenore Terr, M.D., a specialist . . . : Lenore Terr, *Too Scared to Cry* (New York: Basic Books, 1990), 44–45.

90 The psychologist Lula Redmond . . . : Lula Redmond, *Surviving: When Someone You Love Was Murdered* (Clearwater, Fla.: Psychological Consultation and Education Services, 1989), cited in Rando, *Treatment of Complicated Mourning*, 536–537.

91   In 43 percent of all homicides . . . : Federal Bureau of Investigation, *Crime in the United States 2003: Uniform Crime Reports,* Table 2.11, Murder Circumstances, by Relationship, 2003, http://www.fbi.gov/ filelink.html?file=/ucr/ cius_03/xl/03tbl2–11.xls.

91   One need look no farther . . . : Marilyn Johnson, "A Place to Heal," *Life,* June 1995, 44.

91   Because homicides are sometimes . . . : Rando, *Treatment of Complicated Mourning,* 541.

92   Counselors at the Dougy Center . . . : *After a Murder* (Portland, Ore.: The Dougy Center for Grieving Children, 2002), 17.

92   Perhaps nowhere has this been . . . : Elliot, "Growing Up Grieving, With Constant Reminders of 9/11, B6.

92   For the "9/11 kids" . . . : Ibid., B6.

92   Children who lost parents in Oklahoma City and on September 11 have the difficult task . . . sum of its parts . . . : Rando, *Clinical Dimensions of Anticipatory Mourning,* 171–173.

93   "Why hadn't I heard her . . . ": Leslie Pietrzyk, *A Year and a Day* (New York: William Morrow, 2004), 166.

95   Death has a finality to it . . . : Mishne, "Parental Abandonment," 15.

96   Judith Mishne, in her article . . . : Ibid., 15–32.

99   Victoria Secunda, the author . . . : Victoria Secunda, *When You and Your Mother Can't Be Friends* (New York: Delta, 1991), 145.

99– "Because acknowledging that one . . . ": Bassoff, *Mothers and*
100 *Daughters,* 240.

101 "Feeling and talking through . . . ": Ibid., 241–242.

Chapter Four: Later Loss

105 Nobody knows for sure . . . : Rutter, "Resilience," 600; Therese Rando, personal communication, January 29, 1993.

105 Most therapists agree . . . : Sidney Moss and Miriam Moss, "Separation as a Death Experience," *Child Psychiatry and Human Development* 3

(1972–1973); Furman, *A Child's Parent Dies,* 182; Therese Rando, personal communication, January 29, 1993.

105 In her audiotape . . . : Clarissa Pinkola Estés, *Warming the Stone Child: Myths and Stories About Abandonment and the Unmothered Child,* Sounds True Catalog, A104, 1990.

105 The British psychiatrist . . . : John Bowlby, *A Secure Base* (New York: Basic Books, 1988), 172–173.

106 A daughter who perceives herself . . . : Rutter, "Resilience," 606–608.

106 When she believes she has acted . . . : Ibid.

107 Erna Furman, who studied . . . : Furman, *A Child's Parent Dies,* 178–183.

107 Later loss reactivates . . . : Ibid.

108 Six percent of . . . : Motherless Daughters survey, question 8 (see Appendix A).

109 It's part of what . . . : Harris, *The Loss That Is Forever,* 6.

109 "For these individuals . . . ": Ibid., 260.

109 People don't usually . . . : Gina Mireault and Lynne Bond, "Parental Death in Childhood: Perceived Vulnerability and Adult Depression and Anxiety," *American Journal of Orthopsychiatry* 62 (October 1992), 522.

109 A sense of inner fragility . . . : Granot, *Without You,* 103.

110 "Often, adults do not understand . . . ": Ibid., 133

110 As the child matures . . . : Jennie Long Dilworth, and Gladys J. Hildreth, "Long-term Unresolved Grief: Applying Bowlby's Variants to Adult Survivors of Early Parental Death," *Omega* 36 (1997–1998), 153.

113 "They're highly intuitive . . . ": Estés, *Warming the Stone Child.*

114 Although *orphan* is defined as . . . : UNAIDS 2004 Report on the Global AIDS Epidemic, July 2004, www.unaids.org/bangkok2004/GAR2004_html/GAR2004_05_en.htm#P599_122278.

114 In 2003, 29,140 U.S. children . . . : personal communication, Felicitie Bell, actuary, U.S. Social Security Administration, Baltimore, Md., August 2, 2005.

114 "double orphans . . . ": UNAIDS 2004 Report.

114 And about another 32,000 were between the ages of nineteen and thirty-six . . . : U.S. Bureau of the Census, *Statistical Abstract of the United States: 1990*, chart 613 (Washington, D.C.: GPO, 1990), 370.

114 For such a child . . . : Granot, *Without You,* 135.

115 Outsiders intrude on . . . : Ibid.

115 Multiple losses within . . . : Kenneth Kaufman and Nathaniel Kaufman, "Childhood Mourning: Prospective Case Analysis of Multiple Losses," *Death Studies* 29 (2005): 238.

115 Instead of mourning for . . . to process it: Granot, *Without You,* 136.

116 The alchemists originally . . . : Rothenberg, "The Orphan Archetype," 182.

116 They compared the orphan . . . : Ibid.

117 In her essay . . . : Lila J. Kalinich, "The Normal Losses of Being Female," in *Women and Loss,* ed. William F. Finn (New York: Praeger, 1985), 3–7.

118 "After the first death . . . ": Dylan Thomas, "A Refusal to Mourn the Death, by Fire, of a Child in London," *The Collected Poems of Dylan Thomas 1934–1952* (New York: New Directions, 1971), 112.

Part II: Change

119 "Sophie stared at the pans . . . ": Susan Minot, *Monkeys* (New York: Washington Square Press, 1987), 130–131.

Chapter Five: Daddy's Little Girl

124 When the author Victoria Secunda . . . : Victoria Secunda, *Women and Their Fathers* (New York: Delacorte, 1992), 4.

124 "One man, two fathers . . . ": Letty Cottin Pogrebin, *Deborah, Golda, and Me* (New York: Crown, 1991), 38.

125 I've heard that . . . : Bassoff, *Mothers and Daughters*, 148.

126 Only 13 percent . . . : Motherless Daughters survey, question 14 (see Appendix A).

126 A good deal of research . . . after the loss: Granot, *Without You*, 12; Worden, *Children and Grief*, 78; Dilworth and Hildreth, "Long-Term Unresolved Grief," 149; Linda Leucken, "Parental Caring and Loss During Childhood and Adult Cortisol Reponses to Stress," *Psychology and Health* 15 (2000), 841–851.

126 "Without a doubt . . . ": Granot, *Without You*, 12.

127 When they compared . . . : Kathrin Boerner and Phyllis Silverman, "Gender Specific Coping Patterns in Widowed Parents With Dependent Children," *Omega* 43 (2001), 201–202; J. William Worden and Phyllis Silverman, "Grief and Depression in Newly Widowed Parents With School-Age Children," *Omega* 27 (1993), 252–258.

127 In 2002, approximately 840,000 American girls . . . : U.S. Bureau of the Census, Current Population Report, P20–547, Children's Living Arrangements and Characteristics: March 2002, Table C3: Living Arrangements of Children Under 18 Years and Marital Status of Parents, by Age, Gender, Race, and Hispanic Origin of the Child for All Children: March 2002, www.census.gov/population/socdemo/ hh-fam/cps2002/tabC3-all.pdf.

127 Fn: According to U.S. Census data, about 63,000 . . . : Ibid.

127 According to Richard A. Warshak . . . : Richard A. Warshak, *The Custody Revolution* (New York: Poseidon/Simon & Schuster, 1992), 142.

127 This is partly . . . : Ibid., 157–160, 168.

129 In a 1993 University of Detroit–Mercy study . . . : Bette Diane Glickfield, "Adult Attachment and Utilization of Social Provisions as a Function of Perceived Mourning Behavior and Perceived Parental Bonding after Early Parent Loss" Ph.D. diss., University of Detroit Mercy, 1993, 49.

129 "Being able to talk . . . ": Ibid., 50.

130 Though it may sound . . . : Alfred B. Heilbrun, Jr., "Identification with the Father and Sex-Role Development of the Daughter," *Family Coordinator* 25 (October 1976): 411–416.

130 Fathers also tend to reinforce . . . : Miriam Johnson, "Fathers and 'Femininity' in Daughters: A Review of the Research," *Sociology and Social Research* 67 (October 1982–July 1983): 1–17.

130 Husbands don't expect . . . : Scott Campbell and Phyllis Silverman, *Widower.* (Amityville, N.Y.: Baywood Publishing Company, 1996), 18.

131 Right when children . . . : Ibid., 64.

132 He rarely speaks about . . . : Lenhardt and McCourt, "Adolescent Unresolved Grief in Response to the Death of a Mother," 192.

132 (Fifty-two percent of all widowers . . .): Ibid., 20.

132 Because children often mimic . . . : George Krupp, "Maladaptive Reactions to the Death of a Family Member," *Social Casework* (July 1972): 431.

134 When Oedipus discovered . . . : Sophocles, *The Complete Plays of Sophocles,* ed. Moses Hadas (New York: Bantam, 1982).

137 Whereas mothers tend to think . . . : Boerner and Silverman, "Gender Specific Coping Patterns in Widowed Parents With Dependent Children," 203.

137 Adolescence is such a tricky time . . . : Helen A. Mendes, "Single Fathers," *Family Coordinator* 25 (October 1976): 443; Nan Birnbaum, personal communication, October 25, 1991.

139 A 1983 study of seventy-two . . . : John M. Musser and J. Roland Fleck, "The Relationship of Paternal Acceptance and Control to College Females' Personality Adjustment," *Adolescence* 18 (Winter 1983): 907–916.

144 Seventy-six percent of the women . . . : Motherless Daughters survey, questions 9 and 14 (see Appendix A).

147 Although some degree of . . . : Secunda, *Women and Their Fathers,* 16–17.

147 These sexual feelings . . . : Ibid.

148 "surrogate goddess ... ": Signe Hammer, *By Her Own Hand* (New York: Vintage, 1992), 175.

149 Ginny Smith, the narrator ... : Jane Smiley, *A Thousand Acres* (New York: Fawcett Columbine, 1992).

150 As Therese Rando explains ... : Therese Rando, *How to Go on Living*, 65–69.

150 "As the only parent ... ": Harris, *The Loss that Is Forever*, 49.

Chapter Six:
Sister and Brother, Sister and Sister

155 Eighty-five percent of the ... : Motherless Daughters survey, question 7 (see Appendix).

155 But those of us who have siblings ... : Esme Fuller-Thompson, "Loss of the Kin-Keeper?: Sibling Conflict Following Parental Death," *Omega* 40 (1999–2000): 548.

155 Instead, as in my family ... : Margaret M. Hoopes and James M. Harper, *Birth Order Roles and Sibling Patterns in Individual and Family Therapy* (Rockville, Md.: Aspen, 1987), 144; Esme Fuller-Thomson, "Loss of the Kin-Keeper?" 549.

156 Children as young as three ... : Robert B. Stewart and Robert S. Marvin, "Sibling Relations: The Role of Conceptual Perspective-Taking in the Ontogeny of Sibling Caregiving," Child Development 55 (1984): 1322–1332; Robert B. Stewart, "Sibling Attachment Relationships: Child-Infant Interactions in the Strange Situation," *Developmental Psychology* 19 (1983): 192–199.

156 About half of all preschool age ... : Elizabeth M. O'Laughlin, Elizabeth C. Meeker, and Lisa G. Bischoff, "Predictors of Children's Emotional Distress in a Mother-Absent Situation: Implications for Caregiving Research," *Journal of Genetic Psychology* 161 (2000): 235.

156 In a 2002 study ... later in life: Russell C. Hurd, "Sibling Support Systems in Childhood After a Parent Dies," *Omega* 45 (2002): 299–320.

158 "Just go away ... : Jennifer Lauck, *Blackbird* (New York: Pocket Books, 2000), 165–166.

161 After a death in the family . . . : Froma Walsh and Monica McGoldrick, eds., *Living beyond Loss* (New York: Norton, 1991), 34.

161 Sons are usually expected . . . : Ibid.

161 Daughters typically are . . . : Ibid.

162 Although taking on the role . . . : Rutter, "Resilience in the Face of Adversity," 605; James H. S. Bossard, *The Large Family System* (Philadelphia: University of Pennsylvania Press, 1956), 155.

162 When the psychologist Mary Ainsworth . . . : Ainsworth and Eichberg, "Effects on Infant-Mother Attachment of Mother's Unresolved Loss of an Attachment Figure, or Other Traumatic Experience," 165.

163 Approximately 140,000 children . . . : Heather von Tesoriero, "Siblings Raising Siblings," *Time*, May 14, 2001.

164 As Russell Hurd has pointed out . . . : Hurd, "Sibling Support Systems," 301.

164 Of all the women who said . . . : Motherless Daughters survey, question 15 (see Appendix A).

165 "a bond that's often gratefully acknowledged . . . ": Hurd, "Sibling Support Systems," 307.

165 A 1983 study of seven . . . : Benjamin Garber, "Some Thoughts on Normal Adolescents Who Lost a Parent by Death," *Journal of Youth and Adolescence* 12 (1983): 175–183.

169 We're not usually aware . . . : Betty Carter and Monica McGoldrick, eds., *The Changing Family Life Cycle* (Needham Heights, Mass.: Allyn & Bacon, 1989), 229.

169 According to the psychologists . . . : Hoopes and Harper, *Birth Order Roles*, 31.

169 When sibling positions duplicate . . . : Ibid., 129.

170 In a 1989 Amherst College study of . . . : Rose R. Olver, Elizabeth Aries, and Joanna Batgos, "Self-Other Differentiation and the Mother-Child Relationship: The Effects of Sex and Birth Order," *Journal of Genetic Psychology* 150 (1989): 311–321.

170 Only one out of ten oldest ...: Motherless Daughters survey, questions 7 and 14 (see Appendix A).

170 May feel overlooked or excluded ...: Walter Toman, *Family Constellation*, 3rd ed. (New York: Springer, 1976), 22.

170 Is least likely to find ...: Motherless Daughters survey, questions 7 and 15 (see Appendix A).

171 Of all the women surveyed who said they feared ...: Ibid., questions 7 and 13e.

171 Forty-eight percent of the youngest ...: Ibid., questions 7 and 10.

171 In addition, half of the adult ...: Ibid., questions 7 and 18.

171 Is typically more adept ...: Toman, *Family Constellation*, 27.

172 May have been cared for by ...: Bossard, *The Large Family System*, 156.

172 May see a natural leader/teacher emerge ...: Hurd, "Sibling Support Systems," 307.

172 May depend on a sibling cluster ...: Toman, *Family Constellation*, 24.

172 Because a sibling usually has ...: Ibid., 20.

173 Can draw her sense of emotional ...: Bossard, *The Large Family System*, 223–228.

173 On the other hand, large families ...: Ibid., 230–231.

Chapter Seven: Looking for Love

178 "Surely whoever speaks ...": Walt Whitman, "Vocalism," *Complete Poetry and Selected Prose* (Boston: Riverside/Houghton Mifflin, 1959), 271.

179 As Clarissa Pinkola Estés points out ...: Estés, *Warming the Stone Child*.

180 As John Bowlby observed ...: John Bowlby, *A Secure Base* (New York: Basic-Books, 1988), 177.

181 Attachment theorists generally divide ...: Phillip R. Shaver and Cindy Hazan, "A Biased Overview of the Study of Love," *Journal of Social and Personal Relationships* 5 (1988): 473–501.

181 Secure adults typically divide . . . : Ibid., 487.

181 Anxious-ambivalent adults usually . . . : Ibid.

181 Avoidant adults rely almost . . . : Ibid.

181 Most psychologists now agree . . . : Jane L. Pearson, et al., "Earned-and Continuous-Security in Adult Attachment: Relation to Depressive Symptomatology and Parenting Style," *Development and Psychopathology* 6 (1994), 359; Gina Mireault, Kimberly Bearor, and Toni Thomas, "Adult Romantic Attachment Among Women Who Experienced Childhood Maternal Loss," *Omega* 44 (2001–2001), 98.

181 Even when an infant . . . on a child: Leila Beckwith, Sarale E. Cohen, and Claire E. Hamilton, "Maternal Sensitivity During Infancy and Subsequent Life Events Relate to Attachment Representation at Early Adulthood," *Developmental Psychology* 35 (1999), 693–700.

181 In a population of nonbereaved . . . : Phillip R. Shaver and Cindy Hazan, "Adult Romantic Attachment: Theory and Evidence," in *Advances in Personal Relationships,* ed. D. Perlman and W. Jones, cited in Bette Diane Glickfield, "Adult Attachment and Utilization of Social Provisions as a Function of Perceived Mourning Behavior and Perceived Parental Bonding after Early Parent Loss" (Ph.D. diss., University of Detroit Mercy, 1993), 52.

182 When the psychologist Bette Glickfield . . . : Glickfield, "Adult Attachment," 53.

182 The significantly higher percentage . . . : Ibid.

182 A 2001 study at . . . : Gina Mireault, Kimberly Bearor, and Toni Thomas, "Adult Romantic Attachment Among Women Who Experienced Childhood Maternal Loss," 97–104.

182 Taken together, these findings . . . : Ibid., 102.

183 A 1990 study of 118 undergraduates . . . : Nancy L. Collins and Stephen J. Read, "Adult Attachment Working Models and Relationship Quality in Dating Couples," *Journal of Personality and Social Psychology* 58 (1990): 651–655.

184 As Maxine Harris found . . . : Harris, *The Loss That Is Forever,* 152–155.

184 As the psychologist Martha Wolfenstein pointed out ...: Martha Wolfenstein, "Loss, Rage, and Repetition," *Psychoanalytic Study of the Child* 24 (1969): 434–435.

185 A daughter who can't evoke ...: Phil Mollon, "Narcissistic Vulnerability and the Fragile Self: A Failure of Mirroring," *British Journal of Medical Psychology* 59 (1986): 317–324.

186 But this kind of loyalty can go ...: Emswiler and Emswiler, *Guiding Your Child Through Grief*, 194.

188 "Self reliance is perhaps ... ": Harris, *The Loss That Is Forever*, 159.

190 Forty-six percent of the adults ...: Glickfield, "Adult Attachment," 53.

190 Of the 154 motherless women surveyed ...: Motherless Daughters survey, question 2 (see Appendix A).

190 Bette Glickfield found the presence ...: Glickfield, "Adult Attachment," 49–50.

190 Other research indicates that ...: Michael Rutter, "Resilience in the Face of Adversity," *British Journal of Psychiatry* 147 (1985): 604.

191 Carolyn Pape Cowan, Ph.D. ...: Carolyn Pape Cowan and Philip A. Cowan, *When Partners Become Parents* (New York: Basic Books, 1992), 140–144.

192 As they prepared to ...: Gary Jacobson and Robert G. Ryder, "Parental Loss and Some Characteristics of the Early Marriage Relationship," *American Journal of Orthopsychiatry* 39 (October 1969): 780.

192 Instead, they found that ...: Ibid.

192 These couples exhibited a ...: Ibid.

194 "If women are the earliest sources ...: Adrienne Rich, "Compulsory Heterosexuality and Lesbian Existence," in *Powers of Desire*, eds. Ann Snitow, Christine Stansell, and Sharon Thompson (New York: Monthly Review Press, 1983), 177–205.

195 "The unmothered child often wants to ...: Estés, *Warming the Stone Child.*

195 But without a mother-figure or caretaker ...: Joyce McDougall, "Parent Loss," in *The Reconstruction of Trauma*, ed. Arnold Rothstein (Madison, Conn.: International Universities Press, 1986), 151.

196 "Compulsion is despair . . . : Geneen Roth, *When Food Is Love* (New York: Plume/Penguin, 1992), 15.

199 There are two common relationship strategies . . . : Harris, *The Loss That Is Forever,* 144.

Chapter Eight:
When a Woman Needs a Woman

202 The French author Simone de Beauvoir asked . . . : Simone de Beauvoir, *The Second Sex* (1949) (Middlesex, England: Penguin, 1972), 13.

205 The "deep feminine" . . . : Naomi Lowinsky, personal communication, November 21, 1992.

205 Adrienne Rich has described . . . : Adrienne Rich, *Of Woman Born* (New York: Norton, 1986), 220.

205 The sociologist Miriam Johnson, in a review . . . : Miriam M. Johnson, "Fathers and 'Femininity' in *Daughters: A Review of the Research,*" *Sociology and Social Research* 67 (October 1982–July 1983): 2.

205 Fathers, she says, influence the . . . : Ibid., 1–17.

205 Mothers provide the . . . : Ibid.

206 Nancy Drew in business . . . : "GNotes," *Glamour,* August 1993, 185.

206 One out of three motherless women . . . : Motherless Daughters survey, question 18 (see Appendix A).

211 The most important factor . . . : Phyllis Klaus, personal communication, November 25, 1992; Nan Birnbaum, personal communication, July 9, 1992. See also Bryan E. Robinson and Neil H. Fields, "Casework with Invulnerable Children," *Social Work* (January–February 1983): 65; Michael Rutter, "Resilience in the Face of Adversity," *British Journal of Psychiatry* 147 (1985): 605.

212 Of the ninety-seven women . . . : Motherless Daughters survey, question 15 (see Appendix A).

212 "Such 'most similar' persons . . . ": Toman, *Family Constellation,* 47–48.

213 In more than half of the eighty-three stepfamilies surveyed . . . : Motherless Daughters survey, question 9.

213 Because the actual mother . . . : Rose-Emily Rothenberg, "The Orphan Archetype," 190.

215 The British psychiatrist John Birtchnell . . . : John Birtchnell, "Women Whose Mothers Died in Childhood: An Outcome Study," *Psychological Medicine* 10 (1980): 699–713. See also Rutter, "Resilience," 603.

218 Although fathers do pass on . . . : Eileen Hepburn, "The Father's Role in Sexual Socialization of Adolescent Females in an Upper and Upper-Middle Class Population," *Journal of Early Adolescence* 1 (1981): 53–59.

218 A Widener University . . . : Ibid., 55.

218 In this study, conducted . . . : Ibid., 56.

218 For two thousand years . . . : Rich, *Of Woman Born*, 237–240; Naomi Ruth Lowinsky, *The Motherline* (Los Angeles: Tarcher, 1993), 6–9.

220 An adult woman dissatisfied . . . : De Beauvoir, *The Second Sex,* 309, 533.

220 Menstruation is hardly . . . : Ibid., 536.

Part III: Growth

221 "They remember what she gave . . . ": Susan Griffin, *Woman and Nature* (New York: Perennial/Harper & Row, 1978), 210–211.

Chapter Nine:
Who She Was, Who I Am

224 Of the 154 motherless women . . . : Motherless Daughters survey, question 17 (see Appendix A).

224 Grandmothers, aunts, sisters . . . : Ibid.

224 More than half . . . : Ibid., questions 4 and 17.

224 Likewise, only 13 percent . . . : Ibid.

224 Daughters who were adolescents . . . : Ibid.

226 Storytelling serves a vital function . . . : George S. Howard, "Culture Tales: A Narrative Approach to Thinking, Cross-Cultural Psychology, and Psychotherapy," *American Psychologist* 46 (March 1991): 187–197.

226 "When a woman today comes . . . ": Lowinsky, *The Motherline*, 13.

235 Matrophobia, as Adrienne Rich explains . . . : Rich, *Of Woman Born*, 235.

235 "I wonder whether . . . ": Kim Chernin, *In My Mother's House* (New Haven, Conn.: Ticknor & Fields, 1983), 306.

238 As Naomi Lowinsky points out . . . : Lowinsky, *The Motherline*, 53.

240 Some psychologists believe . . . : Judith Kegan Gardiner, "On Female Identity and Writing by Women," *Critical Inquiry* 8 (1981): 353.

240 Others see identity as more . . . : Ibid., 352.

240 Still others propose . . . : Don P. McAdams, Power, *Intimacy, and the Life Story* (Homewood, Ill.: Dorsey Press, 1985), 57–58, cited in Howard, "Culture Tales," 193.

Chapter Ten:
Mortal Lessons

246 More than three-quarters . . . : Motherless Daughters survey, question 13b (see Appendix A).

247 Ninety-two percent . . . : Ibid., questions 5 and 13b.

247 The same was true . . . : Ibid.

247 . . . according to the medical geneticist . . . : Matthew B. Lubin, M.D., personal interview, August 17, 1993.

250 Two-thirds of the motherless women . . . : Motherless Daughters survey, question 13d (see Appendix A).

251 The psychologists Veronika Denes-Raj . . . : Veronika Denes-Raj and Howard Ehrlichman, "Effects of Premature Parental Death on Subjective Life Expectancy, Death Anxiety, and Health Behavior," *Omega* 23 (1991): 309–321.

252 Because the concept . . . : Ernest Becker, *The Denial of Death* (New York: Free Press, 1973), 16–17.

252 A mother's death is as close ...: Denes-Raj and Ehrlichman, "Premature Parental Death," 317.

254 As Denes-Raj and Ehrlichman discovered ...: Ibid., 316–319.

254 But Dr. Denes-Raj ...: Veronika Denes-Raj, personal communication, October 15, 1993.

261 It's the reason why the ...: Motherless Daughters survey, questions 1 and 12 (see Appendix A).

262 "Everyone who is born ... ": Susan Sontag, *Illness as Metaphor and AIDS and Its Metaphors* (New York: Anchor-Doubleday, 1990), 3.

Chapter Eleven:
The Daughter Becomes a Mother

265 While remaining adult and ...: Nancy Chodorow, *The Reproduction of Mothering* (Berkeley, Calif.: University of California Press, 1978), 89–90.

265 At the same time, a new mother ...: Ibid., 90.

265 As the psychiatrists Sol Altschul ...: Sol Altschul and Helen Beiser, "The Effect of Early Parent Loss on Future Parenthood," in *Parenthood: A Psychodynamic Perspective*, eds. Rebecca S. Cohen, Bertram J. Cohler, and Sidney H. Weissman (New York: Guilford Press, 1984), 181.

266 It's no surprise ...: Motherless Daughters survey, questions 1 and 22 (see Appendix A).

266 Half of all ...: Ibid., question 13f.

267 Watching one life end ...: Naomi Lowinsky, personal communication, November 21, 1992; Carolyn Cowan, personal communication, November 24, 1992.

267 As the psychotherapist Selma Fraiberg ...: Selma Fraiberg, "Ghosts in the Nursery: A Psychoanalytic Approach to the Problems of Impaired Infant-Mother Relationships," in *Clinical Studies in Infant Mental Health* (New York: Basic Books, 1980), 166.

268 But if the mother suffered . . . : Gordon Parker, *Parental Over-protection: A Risk Factor in Psychosocial Development* (New York: Grune & Stratton, 1983), 22.

269 Fearing that the child . . . : Deborah B. Jacobvitz, "The Transmission of Mother-Child Boundary Disturbances across Three Generations," *Development and Psychopathology* 3 (1991): 515.

269 The child then grows up anxious, guilty, and phobic . . . : Bowlby, *A Secure Base*, 37.

269 When Mary Ainsworth . . . : Mary D. Salter Ainsworth and Carolyn Eichberg, "Effects on Infant-Mother Attachment of Mother's Unresolved Loss of an Attachment Figure, or Other Traumatic Experience," 160–183.

271 If, as Carl Jung proposed . . . : C. G. Jung, *The Archetypes and the Collective Unconscious*, 2nd ed. (Princeton: Princeton University Press, 1968), 188.

271 Socially, he moves through lands . . . : Lowinsky, *The Motherline*, 42.

271 "The amazement of sons . . . ": Ibid., 41.

274 When the mother-daughter relationship . . . : Phyllis Klaus, personal communication, November 25, 1992.

275 When Nancy Maguire, Ph.D. . . . : Nancy B. Maguire, "The Impact of Childhod Maternal Loss on the Transition to Motherhood" (Ph.D. diss., The California School of Professional Psychology, 1–2).

276 As the sociologist Susan Maushart . . . : Susan Maushart, *The Mask of Motherhood* (New York: Penguin Books, 1999), 49.

277 . . . these are nevertheless times . . . : Motherless Daughters survey, question 24 (see Appendix A).

277 . . . . forgetting that women of the . . . : Marshall H. Klaus, John H. Kennell, and Phyllis H. Klaus, *Mothering the Mother* (Reading, Mass.: Addison-Wesley, 1993), 34.

277 In their studies of 1,500 . . . : Ibid.

278 When asked, 'Who helped you ... ': Hope Edelman, *Motherless Mothers* (New York: Harper Collins, 2006), Appendix 1, Motherless Mothers Survey, question 31.

278 When the same question ... : Ibid., Appendix 2, Control Group Survey, question 26.

278 Because their needs often went unmet ... : Cynthia J. Pill and Judith L. Zabin, "Lifelong Legacy of Early Maternal Loss: A Women's Group," *Clinical Social Work Journal* 25 (Summer 1997), 189.

281 In the early 1990s ... : Donald S. Zall, "The Long-Term Effects of Childhood Bereavement: Impact on Roles as Mothers," *Omega* 29 (1994), 219–230.

282 "The bereaved women saw the impact ... ": Ibid., 227.

282 Zall, as well as other researchers ... : Ibid.; Maguire, "The Impact of Childhood Maternal Loss on the Transition to Motherhood."

282 They also think of themselves ... : Gina C. Mireault, Toni Thomas, and Kimberly Bearor, "Maternal Identity Among Motherless Mothers and Psychological Symptoms in Their Firstborn Children," *Journal of Child and Family Studies* 11 (September 2002), 287–297.

282 Nonetheless, many of these studies ... : Zall, "The Long-Term Effects of Childhood Bereavement: Impact on Roles as Mothers"; Edelman, *Motherless Mothers.*

283 Watching a child go through ... : Altschul and Beiser, "Early Parent Loss," 176.

285 Not surprisingly, this is ... : Motherless Daughters survey, question 22 (see Appendix A).

Chapter 12:
The Female Phoenix

292 "Then one day walking round ... ": Virginia Woolf, "A Sketch of the Past," 81.

292 Ever since Freud ... : Sigmund Freud, "The Relation of the Poet to Daydreaming," *Sigmund Freud: Collected Papers,* vol. 4,173–183.

293 Including statesmen . . . : Marvin Eisenstadt, André Haynal, Pierre Rentchnick, and Pierre de Senarclens, *Parental Loss and Achievement* (Madison, Conn.: International Universities Press, 1989), 201–225.

293 When the psychologist Marvin Eisenstadt . . . : J. Marvin Eisenstadt, "Parental Loss and Genius," *American Psychologist* 33 (March 1978): 217.

293 But other studies . . . : Ibid., 218.

294 Because a mother's death is . . . : Denes-Raj and Ehrlichman, "Effects of Premature Parental Death on Subjective Life Expectancy, Death Anxiety, and Health Behavior," 317.

295 Loss doesn't give a . . . : George Pollock, "On Siblings, Childhood Sibling Loss, and Creativity," *Annual of Psychoanalysis* 6 (1978): 481.

297 Throughout childhood and adolescence . . . : Barbara Kerr, *Smart Girls, Gifted Women* (Dayton, Ohio: Ohio Psychology Press, 1985), 23.

298 Curie's father . . . : Ibid., 36.

298 Parker and her father exchanged . . . : Marion Meade, *Dorothy Parker: What Fresh Hell Is This?* (New York: Penguin, 1987), 23–27.

299 . . . which the psychologist Barbara Kerr . . . : Kerr, *Smart Girls, Gifted Women*, 63.

299 A child's contradictory impulses . . . : Martha Wolfenstein, "The Image of the Lost Parent," *Psychoanalytic Study of the Child* 28 (1973): 455.

299 The art that a motherless daughter creates . . . : George Pollock, "Process and Affect: Mourning and Grief," *International Journal of Psychoanalysis* 59 (1978): 267.

300 . . . the completion of a mourning cycle . . . : Ibid.

300 Other daughters rely on . . . : Ibid.

300 Young children often use . . . : Christine Sekaer, M.D., personal communication, February 8, 1993.

300 Even in daughters who show . . . : Pollock, "Process and Affect," 267.

303 "Once Ane and her papa ... ": Branwen Bailey Pratt, "Charlotte Brontë's There Was Once a Little Girl': The Creative Process," *American Imago* 39 (Spring 1982): 31–39.

307 "diminished sense of crisis ... ": Harris Finkelstein, "The Long-Term Effects of Early Parent Death: A Review," *Journal of Clinical Psychology* 44 (1988): 3.

Epilogue

315 In the redwood ecosystem ... : Mia Monroe, park naturalist, Muir Valley National Monument, personal communication, October 14, 1993.

PHOTO CREDIT: DEBORAH VANCELETTE
(WWW.PHOTOGRAPHYCHICK.COM)

HOPE EDELMAN has a bachelor's degree in journalism from Northwestern University and a master's degree in creative nonfiction writing from the University of Iowa. Her articles and essays have appeared in numerous publications, including the *New York Times*, the *Chicago Tribune*, the *San Francisco Chronicle*, the *Washington Post*, the *Dallas Morning News*, *Glamour*, *Child*, *Parenting*, *Seventeen*, *Real Simple*, *Self*, and *The Iowa Review*. She is the recipient of a *New York Times* Notable Book of the Year designation and a Pushcart Prize for creative nonfiction. Currently an associate faculty member in the MFA program at Antioch University-LA, she lives with her husband and their two daughters in Topanga Canyon, California.

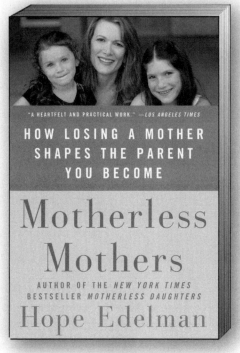